Dora Russell's autobiography is a fascin[ating portrait of one of the] most remarkable women of our times, a[nd a vivid account of] the century through which she has lived.

She visited Russia immediately after the 1917 revolution, lived with Bertrand Russell in China in the 20s, married him, bore two of his children and shared his public and private life until their painful divorce twelve years later.

At a time when the vote had been won, Dora Russell fought for a still more positive approach to women's values and strengths. One of the first women to stand for Parliament, she campaigned for birth control, maternity leave, sexual reform and progressive education. She worked with such notable figures as Wells, Shaw, Strachey, Marie Stopes, the Laskis, and of course Russell himself, concerned always to connect her political ideas with her personal life.

Inevitably her book is invaluable for the new light it sheds on Russell, but even more remarkable is the extraordinary spirit of Dora Russell herself: a woman of integrity, great intelligence, endless courage and compassion.

Dora Russell settled in Cornwall many years ago: now in her eighties, she lives there still.

VIRAGO

is a feminist publishing company:

'It is only when women start to organize
in large numbers that we become a
political force, and begin to move towards
the possibility of a truly democratic society
in which every human being can be brave,
responsible, thinking and diligent in the struggle
to live at once freely and unselfishly'

SHEILA ROWBOTHAM
Women, Resistance and Revolution

VIRAGO
Advisory Group

THE
TAMARISK
TREE

My Quest for Liberty and Love

DORA RUSSELL

Virago
London

Published by VIRAGO Limited 1977
Ely House, 37 Dover Street,
London W1X 4HS

First Reprint 1978
Second Reprint 1980

First published in Great Britain 1975 by Elek Books Limited

ISBN 0 86068 001 0

Printed in Great Britain by litho at
The Anchor Press Ltd, Tiptree, Essex

By the same author:

PROSPECTS OF INDUSTRIAL CIVILIZATION
(with Bertrand Russell)

HYPATIA, OR WOMAN AND KNOWLEDGE

THE RIGHT TO BE HAPPY

IN DEFENCE OF CHILDREN

*The photograph of Bertrand Russell on the cover
is reproduced by kind permission of
George Allen and Unwin*

Contents

Acknowledgements

There are three women whom I want to thank, but for whose encouragement and insistence this book would not have been written. One, whose friendship went back to 1919 and to whose love and loyalty over the years I owe so much, was Thérèse Nicod, widow of Bertie's pupil Jean Nicod. For her, more than for anyone, this book was written. Tragically, she died suddenly in Geneva in 1973.

The second is Irina Stickland, a woman of Russian origin and of remarkable knowledge, literary taste and gifts. For years she had been associated with our family and we owe much to her friendship and wisdom. In the last few years she and I were in close friendship and consultation over this book and literature and research. She was the author of *The Voices of Children 1700–1914*, published by Blackwell, and had begun work on her own interesting life. She died only recently, on 17 March 1974, at the age of fifty-six, in Penzance; had she lived on there was so much that she would have accomplished.

The third is Dolly Farrelly, of Bristol, who constantly nagged at me to get on with the work, who has come to give me a hand with my many daily tasks, that I might have some hours of freedom, but who, above all, herself created and decorated for me, out of a dingy room, a colourful study where work and papers are undisturbed and from whose window as I write I can look out to the expanse of the Cornish hills and sky. But for this room of my own I doubt whether my typewriter and I would ever have gone into action.

I wish also to thank Robert Graves for permission to reprint his letter to me, Messrs Allen and Unwin for permission to quote from my contribution to Russell's *Practice and Theory of Bolshevism*, and Denys Val Baker, Editor of the *Cornish Review*, in which my poem 'Sea Magic' appeared; also the Bertrand Russell Archives, McMaster University, Hamilton, Ontario, Canada for permission to quote the letter from Bertrand Russell that appears on page 222 (copyright © Res.-Lib. Ltd 1975). My further thanks are due to Christopher Macy, formerly of the Rationalist Press Association and Editor of the *New Humanist*, for encouragement and understanding editing, as also to Jane Heller and Antony Wood of Elek for their great patience and skill in the final editing and preparation of this book.

Preface

For many years I turned over in my mind whether or not to write my autobiography. Several friends urged me to do so. To a literary agent I once said that I was still too busy living to have time for writing a book.

It was perfectly true that, until very recently, I was an extremely busy extrovert, preoccupied with public affairs and 'causes' and often still called upon for activity by my fairly numerous family. There is vanity, too, in thinking that oneself and one's doings are of interest to the general public. Not that I lack vanity, quite the contrary. But there are not very many still living, whose memories span the period from before the First World War to the present day. So great have been the changes during those sixty-odd years, and so tragic some of the events, that it still seems worthwhile to add another personal record to those of my generation already published.

This, then, is the story of a girl growing up from an Edwardian childhood through the period of women's emancipation, changing sex relations, the expansion of industrialism, revolution and the rising of the working class. In all of these my personal life and thought were involved. To some, such as the cause of women and the consequences of industrialism, I made some small contribution which will perhaps be better understood today.

I had the fortune, through the circumstances of my life, to have a brief inside view, at their critical and formative period, 1917–20, of three widely differing civilizations, the United States, the Soviet Union and China.

Another reason for this book is that I was for twelve years married to Bertrand Russell and took part with him in political and public affairs. We parted more than forty years ago. He became increasingly a national and world figure and, as inevitably happens to famous people, his work, mind, activities, and personal relationships have become of interest to many enquiring researchers. He has written his own life and there exist vast quantities of documents and letters concerning him. No one intimately associated with him, therefore, is likely to escape attention and comment. In such circumstances, legends arise, inspired guesses are made. Since there are others besides myself involved in the story of our relations to one another, it seems to me necessary to set down the facts as I know them and what I believe to

9

be the truth. Inevitably, this is the story of my own life and the way I see it, but it should be understood that, so far, my voice has not been heard. I have endeavoured, throughout the book, to bring to life fairly and honestly the other figures that appear. I have tried, also, to place them in the political setting of each period, to show how personal and public life were interwoven and, moreover, the mood of those concerned, not viewed with hindsight.

The tamarisk tree of the title of my book was, as I indicate, by chance a sight that delighted me as a young child, and became an enchanted fairytale object, belonging with the fairytale world in which I grew up. It symbolized for me my youthful idealistic aspirations, and I use it in the book as the symbol of the dreams and ideals for which we were striving. It so happens that the tamarisk is also reputed to be the tree from which, in the desert, manna to feed the Israelites was obtained. It is thus endowed with a heavenly quality.

This story tells how far we fell short of our ideals. But its thesis is also that, contrary to the basic assumptions of the times, it is not material circumstances that shape our ends, but human consciousness. The vision that we may have of our past, present and future life is relevant both for the individual and for society. The extent to which we are able to realize, or fail to realize, our ideals can be of supreme importance. This may matter very greatly to each of us, living his or her individual life. What we hope to do, what we in fact achieve, makes the pattern of our lives. But inevitably this pattern is interwoven with the lives of others and with the social structure and culture of our times. We are not alone, but live within this structure and on one small planet, and thus cannot escape responsibility for what we may contribute, either by conformity or by efforts to reform and to change. To study the patterns of human lives in this context, and what we may learn from them, is, I suppose, the reason for our interest in biography.

Some poems, quoted or original, are included in this book. Emotions do not always find full expression in narrative prose; in life they surge forth in music, song, painting, or other arts. In a book the only vehicle for them is the poem which, at the time, they may have recalled or inspired. I think, therefore, that they rightly find a place in a biography.

Other biographical sources of much value are personal contemporary letters. Some of those written by me to family and friends were preserved; it has been a benefit to me to make use of them. With respect to my relations with Russell the position is different. The unpublished private papers and letters to and from Russell are, for the most part, not yet available for use. Since there may be many who are interested, and because I think it a matter that should be known to the public, I give here a brief explanation. In his last years, as stated in his autobiography, Russell established two foundations to carry on his work. One, the Atlantic Foundation, is a charity; the other, the Russell Foundation, is a limited liability company. Ralph Schoenman was the chief trustee in both. Russell gave a considerable amount of his archives to the Foundation; these were sold, under Schoenman's auspices, to the McMaster University, Hamilton, Ontario, Canada, for a very considerable sum, accruing to the Foundation. Russell himself later sold other papers to McMaster's. Many have regretted the departure of these archives, like so many others that have left our country, but the integrity of McMaster's and the great care they have given them are fully recognized.

Russell's original intention was that after his death his literary trustees were to be his widow, the present Countess Russell, and Ralph Schoenman. In the event of Lady Russell's early death, Ralph Schoenman would have been in virtual control of everything. However, in the last year of his life, Russell wrote a full memorandum repudiating Schoenman, whom, for reasons given, he had come to distrust. Schoenman was excluded from provisions under the will and removed from his position on the Russell Foundation. Thus, the literary trustees are now Countess Russell and Anton Felton, in whom are vested the copyright of many of Russell's published works and the right to dispose of them as they think fit. Russell's two sons and daughter have no say and no rights in respect of his archives, nor in all but one of his published works. His library will also, eventually, go to Mc-Master's. When disposing of his papers, Russell himself placed some embargoes on them as to dates when they might be allowed to appear. This applies also to some letters addressed to him. The copyright law is such that although the right to publish letters written by me is mine, the recipient, in possession of the actual paper, can prevent publication. Russell placed on my letters to him an embargo until five years after my death.

The memorandum on Schoenman, as is known, was published (as I understand, contrary to the wishes of the Foundation) after Russell died. This brought great relief to those of us who loved Russell and cared about his personal reputation. It did, however, cast a shadow over the endeavours of the Foundation to continue its work. I feel that I must say that I consider it unfortunate that the Foundation has never made any public statement about these events, nor about the disposal of the large sum received originally for the archives. (Two articles which appeared in the *Sunday Telegraph* of 8 and 21 December 1974, four years after Russell's death, querying the Russell Peace Foundation's use of its finances, elicited conflicting statements from Ralph Schoenman and the present Director of the Foundation, Ken Coates, which still leave the position obscure.) A body which caters for, and seeks to influence, public opinion has more to gain than to lose by taking the public into its confidence. But no Foundation can, in effect, truly carry on the work of Bertrand Russell, which will stand as a permanent inspiration.

Dora Russell, January, 1975

way and a pair of snowy-white, frilly knickers became thick with mud. Sensible dark blue bloomers were as yet unknown for four- and five-year-olds.

Our gangs had great contests, though we did not attack one another with fists or hard weapons. There was the game in which one side was besieged, behind the side gate, while the others tried to scale it. We inside got hold of the bottom half of a cucumber frame, set it on end and looked down from it on the enemy, mocking them in true medieval style, hurling rotten apples or some such harmless ammunition. Suddenly the rectangle of the frame became a rhombus; the defenders collapsed in disarray as the attacking force came over the top in style.

I had no grand toys: dolls and dolls' houses, wooden tops that I whipped with a leather thong on a stick, wooden hoops, until I managed to prevail on Mum and Dad that I was old enough for an iron one—this was glorious fun, guiding it with the iron hook you went at a fantastic pace downhill. The roads were safe, there were no motor cars. Teddy bears had not been invented, but I had a lovely, furry monkey with a long tail; he was hugged and cherished till the tail and half the fur were off. I screamed with passion once when an aunt teased me by throwing my shabby pet about. It was not yet understood how the young can breathe life into things of rag and straw.

Once a week came the delight of going to Croydon for the dancing class. Besides waltzes, polkas and the lancers, costume dances fed the imagination—to be a flower fairy, a jockey, an Eastern dancing girl. Our devoted and accomplished mother made all our garments and the varied fancy dresses for the dancing displays.

A terrifying experience stands out from the kindergarten days—a great fire in some premises near our house. This planted in me a fear of fire that has never been completely overcome. I hated and feared, too, the winter cold. In unheated bedrooms not even bedsocks gave one the courage to stretch out to the icy bottom of the bed.

As children we delighted in picture books that opened out into cut-outs that stood up. Once I had a birthday card that revealed just such a very red rose. Inside my father had written: 'To Dodor on her fourth birthday.'

> Happy and bright
> Like the sunlight
> And sweet as the rose
> My Dodor grows.

I record this as one of the clearest and tenderest of those very early memories, because it serves as an introduction to my father and mother and my relation to them and their families.

My father and I were very close to one another. My elder sister, Mary, was very intelligent, but diffident and shy; as the second child I had the usual determination to catch up and thus perhaps became more sure of myself. My father talked to me often and was ambitious about my education. He was himself in process of working his way up, from a childhood on the Isle of Wight, where he went to the County School for Boys, and from there passed into the clerical division of the Civil Service, his first appointment being in the Colonial Office. He married my mother, as I always understood, when he was earning no more than thirty shillings a week. Her father was a Civil Servant employed in some capacity in dockyards. Later my father was at the Admiralty; there was a connection with the Navy on both sides of the family.

My paternal grandfather, whom I never knew, was at one time agent to the Liberal candidate on the Isle of Wight. His family, the Blacks, consisted of five sons and two daughters. Of one uncle, Arthur, I also have no memory, since he died of enteric fever in the Boer War, but Uncle Jim, solicitor on the island, Uncle 'Troopy', bank clerk, Uncle Albert, chemist at Crouch End, and Aunts Emmy and Fanny, who stayed on the island, all played their part in our lives. Westminster House, the family home in Newport, was for me a romantic place: it housed also my typically perfect grandmother Black. She wore a grey alpaca dress with an apron and a lace cap; she was small and bent and walked with a stick, and her sharp nose and chin nearly met. Mostly she would be sitting in a high-backed chair by the fire, and would tell us the story of the 'Three Silly People', among others; she used to have a tin full of delicious chocolate biscuits by her side. She was Cinderella's Fairy Godmother to the life and prototype of all the magical old ladies whom I encountered in the fairytales to which I was addicted. As the Andrew Lang fairy books came out with their richly coloured illustrations, I would get one for Christmas or for my birthday.

Westminster House stood, sideways on, beside a millstream which ran between two mills. It had big back kitchens and a wash-house, and, between two of the walls, access to the stream. When the millrace was running we played a marvellous game: we dropped tins into the stream, dashed madly through the house and down the garden, and fished them out at the other end before they drifted away across the second millpond. To reach our argosies one sometimes had to hold on to a tree which leant perilously over the water. Many years later I visited Uncle Jim and Aunt Fanny there with my husband, Bertrand Russell. The tree had fallen across the stream and the two old people remarked that 'that tomboy' Dora would have been the first to scramble along it. Nearing middle age, a bit stiff from sciatica following a pregnancy, I honoured my obligation to them by doing just that.

Mother's family, the Davissons, were also numerous; there had, I believe, been nine children. Those whom I knew were two uncles in the Church, Jas and Pearse, one in the brewery business, Uncle Bill, and two aunts, Edith and Maud, who both married Naval officers, and, of course, my mother Sarah Isabella, who married Frederick Black.

Grandmother Davisson was a lively old lady, tiny and plump, with frizzy ginger hair correctly drawn back into a neat bun. I remember how her hands, which were chubby and freckled, but also delicate, with many rings, hovered over the tea things, which of course consisted of silver teapot, milk jug, sugar basin—with tongs—and slop basin. There was the small kettle, too, over the spirit lamp. Grandma had a ready laugh and her eyes would twinkle. She liked to sing:

> O rootity toot, she played on the flute,
> In a very surprising manner
> And pinkety pong, she rattled along
> The keys of the grand pianner.

If she thought we were talking nonsense she would exclaim 'aler-mackerdoosh', which convulsed us with laughter, but which was never explained however much we pestered her.

Grandmother Davisson said she was married very young to a dominating husband. Was he so? Then he must have mellowed with age, for the Grandpa we knew, though nearly twice her size, was mild and genial, with a broad, red, mastiff-like face, and a huge expanse in front, draped with his gold watch-chain.

We often went to stay with our relations because my father would be posted abroad in Hong Kong, Ceylon, or Malta, where there were Naval stations, sometimes taking my mother with him. Then I was a bit lonely, and scared of the Davisson aunts, who were at that time still single and would teach me manners by offering me a plate for my elbows every time I put them on the table. Once I nearly missed a delirious treat—a children's party on a battleship—because of some misdeed. But they did relent. Are there still parties like that, with obstacle races over and under sailcloths and rope nets, aerial flights in a canvas bag slung on a wire, ending in a bump on a mattress, a real sailor painted up to play Aunt Sally, who was so quick at dodging and laughing at us as we utterly failed to hit him with our missiles?

Visiting the Davissons was most fun when I was older and Grandpa, who could not endure to live away from the sea, had retired to Folkestone. Of all the Davisson aunts and uncles only Uncle Pearse, unmarried, was still likely to be at home. As we all sat at table he would look out of the window and suddenly exclaim: 'I say kids, see the elephant going by with the brown man on his head and the monkey with the red cap sitting on the elephant's ear?!' We would rush to the window and swear we saw all this, or some other invented nonsense, while Grandma's bosom shook as she wiped away her laughter tears, and from Grandpa came a deep, rebuking rumble: 'Pearse, Pearse.'

Uncle Pearse ought never to have been in the Church. He was dazzlingly handsome in the Greek style. As a curate he was pursued by the young ladies of his Parish, and he would often take me walking with him as a bodyguard. He much enjoyed the typical Anglican jokes. He would take me by the arm most confidentially and then suddenly bellow: 'Dora, WHY do the heathen so furiously rage together?' Uncle Pearse was a sincere Churchman none the less, and he was for me an important example of an admirable male, as was Uncle Phil, a sailor uncle, who went down in the *Aboukir* in 1914 at the outbreak of war.

All the Davisson aunts and aunts-in-law were lively, pretty and rather smart. They wore their hair in fringes and not too severe buns, their skirts flowed and rustled; sleeves were leg-of-mutton, bodices tight fitting, from which rose, to high in the neck, elaborate yokes with faggot-stitch joins and sewn-in supports that must have dug uncomfortably into the skin.

Uncle Bill and his wife were a gay couple who took part in amateur dramatic shows—*Floradora*, the *Cloches de Corneville*. At the local theatre in Rochester I saw with them tear-jerking melodramas such as the *Two Little Vagabonds*. But emotion was a trifle inhibited at sight of the baby being thrown out of the lighthouse into a sea of lengths of billowing art muslin. Over the proscenium was written: 'Let the Evening's Entertainment bear the Morning's Reflection.' Somehow we rather doubted whether it did.

Perhaps the best times were when staying in the Isle of Wight with Aunt Emily, my father's sister, whom I found more homely. She had the strong family face, like my father, with aquiline nose, rounded, broad forehead, warm, dark brown eyes. Her roomy home with its large garden was at Shide, on the outskirts of Newport. Nearby were fields and a stream where we caught tadpoles and sticklebacks, and hung from the little railway bridge to dangle toes in the clear water rippling over the pebbles. Not far away rose the lovely blue-grey downs; to go up these was one of the great joys. Aunt Emmie's milk came from a farm kept by farmer Rose. This little old man was the image of one of the dwarfs in *Snow White*, ample silver-grey beard and all. He would let me ride with him in a high, open cart, up the never-ending lanes to the cow pastures, and he gave me a stick, painted pale blue, to help him drive his herd. One morning our breakfast milk had a vile taste; those cows had managed to eat garlic.

When I was about six years old I was on the Island because of a winter cough. My Aunt Fanny kept a Dame school where we still wrote on slates. Day by day I made up instalments of a fairytale about a Wednesday's child, 'born to woe', to read to my fellow pupils.

Many family holidays were spent on the much-loved 'Island'. At Easter we often went to Sandown, to wake with joy in attics in the early morning to the magic sound of the sea. There would be picnics at Yaverland where there were lots of primroses to pick, and church on Sundays in lovely Yaverland Church. Carisbrooke Castle fed my romantic imagination, but even the patient donkey treading the wheel to wind up the bucket could never entirely allay my dread of the deep castle well.

One of my delights at Sandown was to balance-walk along the iron bars of the esplanade to see how far I could get, from one small iron post to the next, without overbalancing. At times I was infuriated by elderly gentlemen who would distract me by exclaiming: 'Take care, little girl, you'll fall', when I was about to beat my record.

I have to admire the forbearance of my parents who must have suffered considerable anxiety when my friends and I climbed trees or up the outside of the banisters, or demonstrated our daring jumps from a nine- or ten-foot-high summerhouse roof. I often felt very scared, but I never came to any harm. I do recall sheer terror on one or two occasions when my bicycle ran away with me on steep hills. Once, too, on one of our picnics on Boxhill, when we lived at Sutton, I began to run down its steep side and could not stop. Some sensible man, seeing my plight, put out an arm and knocked me on to my back, which I had not the sense to do for myself. Such moments of great excitement, of fear or of achievement, stand out like beacons in one's memory.

Holidays at Sandown had many delights: the pier, the Pierrot troupe, and the donkey rides. There was also the Children's Special Service Mission—a group of young men in blazers and flannels who would conduct a service on the sands and talk to us about Jesus. They also organized sports and Bible competitions; we found this type of religion very attractive.

When we moved from Thornton Heath to Sutton I must have been about six or seven. My brother and younger sister had by then been born, and I have vague recollections of Davisson aunts arriving because the monthly nurse had got drunk, or had otherwise proved unsatisfactory. Perhaps it is to such times that the memory belongs of looking out wistfully at twilight to see the lamplighter kindle the gas lamps one by one with his torch. On winter evenings we watched, too, for the muffin man with his tray covered with green baize, and we would chant:

> O do you know the muffin man?
> O yes, I know him well,
> He comes along at four o'clock
> And rings a little bell.

While at Thornton Heath my father had taken to the dangerous practice of riding a bicycle; whether it was the risk or expense that worried my mother his jingle does not explain:

> Up and down the Foulsham road,
> Father used to bike it,

That's the way the money goes,
'Mary Ann' don't like it.

The Boer War loomed in the background with murmurs about
Ladysmith and Mafeking and gloom at the death of Uncle Arthur.
My mother was distressed one day at a march of the unemployed she
had seen just after the war. By now my father had obtained his external
London degree, the stepping-stone to rising further in the Civil Service.

My father and mother were much of a height, about five feet nine I
should say, though my father looked shorter when he was fatter in
middle age. Both had dark brown hair and dark brown eyes; my
mother's were the larger and softer, indeed the tender expression of
those eyes was one of the loveliest things about her. She could not be
called beautiful, except in her colouring and complexion, for she had
an odd-shaped nose about which my father used to tease her. He was
proud of his, which was Roman. He was, in fact, quite handsome. He
had the sort of medium moustache which many men of his generation
wore, but he never shaved it, as some of them did in later life.

I cannot fault them in any way, as a married pair or as parents; they
were devoted, and, I am convinced, absolutely faithful. Their marriage
was a partnership in the sense that they did share responsibilities and
take decisions together. My father spent what time he could with us
and helped with us in the holidays. There was no question, however,
but that he was the boss. Every week my mother used to bring him
the tradesmen's bills, which he would pay by cheque. I could see that
my mother was at times embarrassed, in case she was overspending.
This stirred in me some indignation on her behalf and perhaps it was
the beginning of my feminism.

But my father was not an ungenerous man, on the contrary; other
members of his family looked up to him as a success, and he helped
them financially as well as with advice. The latter was not always
welcome: my father was an extremely upright man and deprecated his
brother Albert's addiction to betting and excessive theatre-going, of
which he did not disapprove if indulged in in moderation. His other
brother, 'Troopy', did follow my father's advice—though not his
example—by not marrying on a bank clerk's salary. Thus I knew him
as a gay bachelor in straw boater and blazer, who had me to stay with
him once at Ware when I was a very small girl, and took me on the
river with his bachelor friends. I owe a lot of mental stimulus to this
uncle; he read a great deal, and we talked much over the years, discussing Bergson's philosophy when I was still very young. By contrast,
Uncle Albie, in pinstripe frockcoat, topper, spats, and opera-glasses,
endures for me as a real Edwardian 'masher' of his day.

Fortunately for me, Daddy's disapproval of Uncle Albie did not go
so far as to prevent me from staying with him, his wife, Aunt Hattie,
and my Cousin Dolly, their only daughter and my best friend. We

were of an age and similar tastes. I spent part of many Christmas holidays in the flat over the chemist's shop at Crouch End.

The shop had the huge globular bottles filled with different coloured water which then were indispensable to the apothecary's display; it exuded fascinating antiseptic odours and perfumes. Often there were samples in miniature from which we made chemist's shops of our own. Aunt Hattie never scolded or punished, not even when, in the storeroom, we turned a huge roll of corrugated cardboard into a maze by wriggling our way into its centre.

Just up the road was a shop with all sorts of gadgets and penny toys. We would save up our farthings, aided and abetted by Aunt Hattie, then go to this shop, which was kept by an old lady called Mrs Bunce. Entering as the door bell tingled, we would advance very demurely to the counter and say: 'Do you take farthings, Mrs Bunce?' 'Yes, my little dears' would be the answer, until about the hundredth time, when we got an acid: 'Shouldn't do any business if I didn't.'

Best of all in the Crouch End holidays were the pantomimes, not only one, several; Uncle Albie would never stint us. Party-dresses, a box of chocolates, the gilt and red plush of the circles and boxes filled with chattering pleasure-seekers. Then the silence, the music, the darkened auditorium as the curtain went up on the marvellous transformation scenes, the flying fairies. I saw Dan Leno, George Robey, Vesta Tilley, Marie Lloyd, in fact most of the famous stars of Edwardian days, and I acquired a love for the old variety world that went very deep. This was when I formed my ambition to go on the stage, never, alas, to be fulfilled.

> Every little girl would like to be
> A fairy on a Christmas tree. . .

So sang Gracie Fields many years later, and too often revived the pang of that blighted ambition.

The pantomime which we almost invariably attended on Boxing Day was a less opulent affair. It was at the Old Vic, then under the redoubtable Miss Baylis. My father and mother made a point of taking us there; they were closely associated with Morley College for Working Men and Women where both did some teaching before family responsibilities supervened. For many years my father continued as President of their Cycling Club. We went to show days and watched young women swinging clubs, men leaping over vaulting horses; opportunities for physical exercises which most working people in towns then lacked. There were labs; once I stood amazed when the scraping of a violin bow on a metal sheet produced fascinating patterns in the sand that lay upon it. They had odd competitions; my mother once won one for the very best boiled potato. After these evening excursions our way home lay through the New Cut—a street-market with flaring gas-jets on the stalls, reputed to be a tough neighbourhood, through which my father piloted us with care. How many people now remember the dress of working-class women of those days—long bedraggled skirts, a blouse, and a man's cap, peak at the back, crammed on to their heads?

Our new home in Sutton was called the 'Chestnuts', a semi-detached on the Brighton Road, almost at Belmont, a few doors from the entrance gate of the huge place that was once a workhouse and now, I believe, is partly used for mental patients. Our garden ran right down to the railway branch-line from Sutton to Epsom Downs. By nipping across this line we children could get into the grounds of the Belmont Institution, quite empty for years. We used to swing on the marvellous giant strides that were in its playgrounds; no one ever caught us there. Another entertainment at the bottom of the garden was, on Derby Day, the passing of the Royal Train. I don't know quite why this amused us. One train would go by with a notice at the rear, 'royal train to follow'; then it would come, with whitewashed coals and the bald head of King Edward just visible at the window.

But our front gate offered the best show on Derby Day. From quite early the race-goers would pass in their thousands, in pony traps, waggonettes, coaches and four-in-hands—no motor traffic of course. They wore comic paper hats and false noses, blew paper squeakers and waved paper 'teasers', things like African fly whisks; they sang 'I'll be your sweetheart, if you will be mine' and 'You are the honeysuckle, I am the bee', 'Daisy, Daisy'—all the tunes familiar to us from our pantomime orgies. By dinnertime they would be gone; but in the evening they came back, louder and more raucous than ever. If we had any flowers worth picking in our front garden on Derby Day they would disappear in the small hours.

The Chestnuts really did have a chestnut tree by the front gate, which afforded an ample supply of 'conkers' in season. The long garden, a world in itself, was the scene of my play, my activities and my dreams until adolescence. Every corner of that garden I can still describe in detail. I peopled it with the creatures of my imagination, I was myself some other mortal or immortal person. Most of all I enjoyed playing the spirit of the wind, especially at the top of a slender young sycamore where I caught the thrill of danger as I made it sway. At Sandown I often went down to the edge of the sea, and, with considerable awe, addressed the sea god. I had an imaginary refugee friend called—unromantically—Mrs White, no doubt because I was 'Black'. She lived in a dark cupboard in the house, where I talked with her and pretended to bring her food.

Then there were the sunsets. What child has not become utterly lost in contemplation of those islands of scarlet and gold, afloat in pale green seas, on which the spirit in flight sets sail, until the colour passes and the magic fades. I used to set down the time and date of a specially wonderful sunset; whether in the belief that it would come again, or in the hope that by recording it it would not be lost forever, I am not sure.

More down to earth were my efforts at bicycling—pedalling madly on a peculiar small bike with wooden wheel rims to keep up with my father and sister to be allowed to join a Morley Cycling Club Outing, and choking with dust on those unasphalted roads.

Across the road from our house was a real farm with a yard, barns and fields. We were allowed to play there freely. Early on summer mornings I would slip across into a field full of the scent of hay and the song of birds, pick flowers in the hedges and note the dewdrops on the spiders' webs. We were into all sorts of muck over there and were scarcely welcome when we came home with stinking boots. Insatiable curiosity led me and my companions to climb into half-built houses and to trespass at will. Many of our exploits would land the child of today in the juvenile court, or result in him or her being taken 'into care'. We were indeed fortunate in that we lived on the edge of open country. Banstead was then a small village with a marvellous deep well into which one dropped stones to enjoy that terrifying booming as they went down.

At a small private co-educational school a few doors from our house I learned all my tables by recitation, and spelling by standing in a line for practice, moving up if the person ahead of you made a mistake. I learned many poems by heart and began French before I was seven.

The time we younger ones had scarlet fever is imprinted on my memory because I, as the eldest patient, though barely eight years old, had to go away to the isolation hospital out on Banstead Downs. Scarlet fever in those days was a terrible business; you were not pronounced free of infection for six weeks, or until every scrap of skin had been scraped off your body. My splendid parents trekked out to the hospital —on foot of course—every Sunday to encourage me by waving through the window.

Soon after this I won a junior scholarship to Sutton High School in Cheam Road, a long way away, involving a journey through Sutton High Street and beyond. This was one of the Girls' Public Day School Trust schools, to which many women owe a good education. Once I was at school, its world in term time absorbed me. Day after day every minute was taken up with work, duties, homework and extra school activities.

Class teaching was from 9 a.m. to 1 p.m. But there would be science practicals in the afternoons, language orals, gymnastics, hockey practice, and, in summer, swimming. This meant journeying to school on foot or bicycle twice a day; there were no school bus services, and few pupils, until older and undertaking more, stayed to school dinners. Our time-tables were quite rigid, and, though most intelligent children learned eagerly and well, they never had time to consider what they were most interested in, and what they would like, later, to pursue. It was possible to pass all through school life without becoming truly aware of what kind of person you were, or even in what subjects you were most able and likely to do well in future. The notes in school reports were scanty, though our teachers probably had a fair estimate of what we were worth in ability, or to what extent we were a credit to them or the school, but no one talked with us about our own feelings on the matter.

This was an academic, intellectual and literary education, with, as was rare in girls' curricula, quite good science. As such, it was excellent. I have never regretted all that I learned in this sphere at school and later at university. What was lacking was stimulation of interest in the arts. There were no handicraft rooms such as modern schools provide, nor in kindergarten or primary school did I mess about with sand and water, poster paints and clay. Immense emphasis was placed by traditional education on the intellectual and rational, in line with the spiritual, which in turn was instilled by religious teaching. For sensuous appreciation of beauty and flights of imagination there was little space or time once you were in the school system. That section of the brain which deals with such impressions must have been, and still is to a large extent, undeveloped in our people. This is now, perhaps, beginning to be understood.

At school, like many of my generation, I was not conscious of this lack. I, at any rate, lived from day to day instinctively and unconsciously in those early years. But one fact was ever-present to my mind. This was the pressure of competition. Each form had, term by term, its class order. If you reached the top of your form the struggle to keep your place was unrelenting and one in which pupils would be encouraged, both by teachers and by parents. My school life was a long process of holding my place against one girl, who was very able and also my friend, who came second. Sometimes there would only be about three marks between us. I am convinced that this was very harmful to her and damaging to my own character. I consider the whole system based on such competition to be disastrous. Not only does it set one child against another at school, where, if anywhere, habits of co-operation and tolerance can and should be acquired, but it lays the foundation for fierce competition in later life. Some means of testing ability may certainly be necessary; thus our modern system of having to pass the requisite number of 'A' levels to obtain a grant for university may be an improvement. Yet students of today object to this system, and I am often told that competition in education in these times is an intolerable strain. None the less, I think that in my day it was worse; there was no such general scheme of grants, and the chances of winning a scholarship to university, especially for a woman, were very slender.

Very many adults, looking back and writing of their childhood, recount one long saga of misery and frustration. Despite the pressure of school work, I must confess that, apart from some of the usual upsets and griefs of the young, I was very happy in my childhood. There was always so much to do, to think, to see, and there was little of all this that I did not find interesting. I had many opportunities for mental and physical fulfilment. This was, too, the Edwardian age, when people in England looked forward to an ever-prosperous future; what is more, they had begun to indulge and enjoy themselves in many ways, now that the straitlaced Victorian reign was over. None the less, we lived in a closed and sheltered world.

Our family was not rich, but neither were we very poor: we learned to think of the poor as people we ought to be sorry for; we joined the Children's League of Pity; we took bunches of flowers every Friday to school for the hospitals; our old and not too broken toys went to the same destination at Christmas; it was usual to give up something in Lent and use the sacrifice to benefit someone or some cause. I also knew, from my father's interest in Morley College, that working people did not live by bread alone. This was, I think, one of the best of the lessons my father taught me.

I was told nothing whatever about sex, not even where babies come from. The books on anatomy and physiology, which did exist in the school library, had certain dangerous pages stuck fast together. I really did not know the full facts about sex and reproduction until I was in my twenties; four-letter words I learned much later. My Cousin Dolly and I did speculate a bit: once she told me that 'there was something that men had to get rid of from time to time, and they gave this to the Piccadilly women'. Needless to say, the image that I formed of this transaction bore no resemblance whatever to the reality. The notion that children who are told nothing find out about these mysteries from other boys and girls was totally false in my case. For instance, I always enjoyed the company of boys and was hardly ever without such companions and even admirers. We flirted, kissed shyly at party games, but we neither explored nor knew about sex. Once only the physical reality intruded: I was crossing the school playground, deserted in the lunch hour, when a man attracted my attention over the side fence, exposing himself. I was alarmed, because I thought that he had some horrible disease. But I decided not to show fear by running. The incident left no emotional disturbance.

Life, even in a day school, did not consist entirely of academic instruction. Something should be said about the staff and ourselves in what was an important, pioneering enterprise in women's education.

Our teachers were, I believe, very different from the highly-trained ones of today. In a school of no more than two hundred girls, we knew most of them as personal friends and certainly never as enemies. We were very well taught and cared for both in work and in play. A Fräulein taught us German, a Mademoiselle French, already by the direct method, and in person. Language is human communication, it is poetry, it is literature; I would hate to learn a language from a machine. Our science mistress would have her fun: one day she got an elaborate experiment going and, turning to us, said: 'Look now, see that pink gas being given off, girls?' 'O yes, Miss Hunt,' we answered in chorus. 'Silly little idiots, there's no such thing.' I stood rather in awe of the games mistress, but her vitality and quick temper spurred me to a long-lasting enthusiasm for hockey, then thought a bit unlady-like for women.

Opposite our school was another, described on its front gate as a 'School for the Daughters of Gentlemen'. So we at Sutton High rather prided ourselves on not being ladylike, got rebuked by our Head for racketing around the roller-skating rink and all over the town without hats or gloves. Not to wear gloves became for me almost a matter of principle that has lasted all my life. It began when, if I could be ready in time, I would walk down the road with my father, on his way to catch his train, he with his briefcase, I with satchel on shoulder. Sometimes, especially on very cold days, we would go hand in hand. And I noticed that, even carrying his briefcase, his ungloved hand was always warm. I took pride in following his example.

Like the schools in the story books, we had a head girl in the sixth form who was adored by all. She was tall and fair and willowy, her flaxen plaits wreathed about her head. To crown all, her name was Elaine: to us, it goes without saying, the Lily Maid of Astolat. We would lie in wait for her on the way to school, hoping to carry her satchel and enjoy a few words of conversation. There would be rivalries and misunderstandings, skilfully contrived to bring abut those little private reconciliations that meant so much.

Came the day, however, when some of us reached the conclusion that all this sentimentality might not be good for the morale of the school. Mollie, the hockey captain, grey-eyed, broad of face, with a generous laughing mouth, was one of my friends. She was not prim or censorious, just matter-of-fact and jolly. Together we concocted a plan for a secret society—the League of the Torn Rubber Band—whose members wore a piece of a wide rubber band fastened by safety pin to blouse or dress. This badge signified that the member was pledged to break the bonds of sentimental attachments and treat everyone in a normal, friendly way. Gradually more and more girls became aware that something was afoot, and in time it reached the head girl that it had to do with her. We kept our counsel and quietly went about our business. One afternoon, after a class, Elaine stopped me, demanding to know what it was all about. There followed a long and very painful interview, but I had to go through with it. Finally I came home in one of those states of agony, known perhaps only to adolescents, to face a very angry mother; I had not arrived for my violin lesson, the teacher had gone. It was impossible to explain my absence, or that this emotional crisis was for me a matter of far greater importance.

Another occasion, when I faced my father's anger in considerable trepidation, was merely the result of an absurd prank. I was coming up the Brighton Road, with a friend, close behind a very dignified old gentleman. My friend dared me to poke him in the back with my umbrella. I poised the umbrella, merely pretending to do the deed. Unluckily, my hand slipped. We took to our heels down a side road, chased by the offended gentleman who proved to be by no means so old as to our extreme youth he appeared. He caught my friend and found out who I was. Later in the day my father solemnly sent for me; he sat beside my mother with a letter in his hand.

'What is this about my daughter assaulting a gentleman on the public highway?' Did he say that? Intensely embarrassed, I told my story, was severely reprimanded, given a letter and ordered to take it at once to the gentleman's house. As I left the room hastily, relieved at no worse penalty, I heard my father mutter, 'Pompous ass.'

In my childhood both cinema and gramophones were in their infancy, no radio existed, motor cars had only just been created, telephones were scarce, electric light—and rather dim at that—was only beginning to replace gas. We did have those funny cylinders that played scratchy music and ended with the nasal 'Edison Bell Record'. We had to make our own amusements at home or in our friends' houses: parlour and card games abounded; Christmas and birthday parties were a great joy. Parties are a joy for every generation of children, but my impression is that nowadays you need only provide some sumptuous food and a radiogram; the guests eat and drink and then spend their time wriggling about, calling this dancing. We took time and pleasure in preparing entertainments for our friends and there were very many party games, which I suppose are now out of fashion. We did also dance at parties, but someone had to play the piano for us. To break the ice you usually began with Nuts in May; then there was Puss in the Corner, Postman's Knock, Blindman's Buff, Dance Dance the Cushion Dance—so many opportunities for choosing, or being chosen by, the one who for the time being was your sweetheart. To exercise the mind there were Clumps, Subject and Object, Charades, Hunt the Thimble; then also Up Jenkins, Musical Chairs, My Friend's Chair—and a final romp of Hide and Seek all over the house. As we grew older we prepared guessing games of all sorts. We made up and performed plays, for which our drawing and dining-room, which had large folding doors between them, were well adapted.

One unusual and special party took place in the late summer. This was the Morley College Cycling Club special Saturday run to our house. Weather permitting, the first part of the party was in the garden. In the morning we children went up to my little school to borrow trestle tables and benches. Then we would lay the cloths and set the places. The day before my mother did a vast cooking: a huge joint of cold beef and a ham, marvellous thick beefsteak or veal and ham pies, as well as all the sweets, tarts and trifles to follow. There were great bowls of mixed salads, crates of beer and an urn of tea. Father and Mother carved and served and we helped to carry round the plates. Fifty or more would arrive, men and women. Bikes would be stowed; the visitors washed, then feasted. After this they played various games outside until dark, when all came indoors to make a concert with solos, recitations and choruses. A few speeches, compliments, thanks, then tea and small tartlets and sandwiches. About midnight the party would assemble at the gate, with bikes, in good order. A leader went first, then the main body, last of all the Captain. As he mounted we would watch all the winking red tail-lights of the Club vanishing into the distance—another of what we looked on as our very special treats over till next year.

The semi-basement at the Chestnuts was our playroom, with a huge deal table, a rocking horse, and a tall cupboard for our toys. Books were my chief delight; we had some pink paperbacks, 'books for the Bairns', an innovation unlike the more moralizing Victorian children's books. But I read everything I could lay my hands on, including *The War Cry*, brought in by one of our maids who belonged to the Salvation Army, *Home Notes* and *Home Chat*, which informed me that 'the hand that rocks the cradle rules the world', a most misleading statement, as I was presently to discover. The strange thing about the stories in these journals and books, even those for children, was their lugubrious nature. Children died of fatal illnesses with amazing fortitude and resignation, their motto *Laetus Sorte Mea*; love affairs ended in tragic renunciations for admirable moral reasons. Once I was found sobbing and repeating, 'O poor man', for a hero whose fate was not to marry the damsel of his desire. Songs were mournful too, like 'The Lost Chord'.

Incurably romantic, I still cherish the novels of Sir Walter Scott, in which I steeped myself, as in his narrative poems. While growing up I had not much use for Dickens, though *A Tale of Two Cities* had its appeal; after all, it, too, dealt with romantic sacrifice. My father also had a romantic turn of mind; he liked to pretend to me that, because our name was Black and we came from Scotland, we might be descended from Roderick Dhu (the Black) in the *Lady of the Lake*. To name a rebel chieftain as my ancestor was my pride; I never ceased urging my father to take us to Scotland. I longed to see the sunset in the Trossachs, to 'press up' the hillsides as the Highlanders did with the Fiery Cross, to chant the Coronach among the heather. When finally we did get that promised holiday, it fulfilled all my longings; the Island of Arran still haunts my dreams.

Poetry was a constant guide and inspiration in my father's life, as it has always been in mine. He read me Milton's 'Lycidas', Tennyson, Swinburne: 'The hounds of spring are on winter's traces . . .' We happened to be in the Isle of Wight when Swinburne was buried at Bonchurch. My father and I filed past his grave, which was lined all down the sides with primroses.

My parents did not take much part in social life in Sutton, except when their children were involved. There was a Dramatic Society and a literary and discussion club of sorts. In the local amateur dramatic shows I immensely admired the acting of Gladys Young, who became one of the most famous of the early radio players on the BBC.

I went with my father to some literary meetings: what must have been my début as a speaker or lecturer was when I read a paper there just after the outbreak of war in 1914, on Norman Angell's *The Great Illusion*. That book, by now barely remembered, had been the stock argument of that optimistic and prospering age, when people believed that economic ties and interests would render war in our modern world impossible. This, and not war itself, has proved to be the great illusion.

As a fledgling undergraduate at that time, I was not then a pacifist, even in Norman Angell's sense: I was merely considering these problems. My entire education had been, as is clear, in the conventional patriotic mould. With uncles in the Church and Navy, daughter and grand-daughter of the Civil Service, I lived well within the aura of the Estab-lishment. I watched the Trooping of the Colour from my father's Admiralty windows, from similar official windows I saw two Royal funerals; the marching and the pageantry meant little to me, it was the strains of the funeral march that registered.

At school I was fed upon martial and patriotic poems: Sir Richard Grenville and *The Revenge*, 'Toll for the brave', the Armada and *Lays of Ancient Rome*. My generation kept that bridge with Horatius against 'fearful odds'; for me the moment when he 'saw on Palatinus the white porch of his home' was emotionally even more significant. I kept company, too, with the Argonauts and Greek heroes, with the Norse-men and their savage sagas.

Neither was my religious education neglected; on the contrary, it was most varied. My parents were not pious, they were good Church of England. Our church in Sutton was modern red brick and a bit on the smart side; the Vicar was tall, plump and jolly, with a round, red face and a deep, resonant voice admirably suited to the reading of Browning's poems and to singing Somersetshire folk songs at socials.

There came to our church a curate called Shepherd Walwyn, pale, thin, ascetic. 'Always stop eating, dear children, just BEFORE you have had enough.' He would arrive on his bicycle and embarrass my sister Mary and myself by inviting us to go for rides with him: we did not know how to talk to such a saintly man. Needless to say, he did not last long in our worldly parish. After he left we received a pamphlet, *On Christ Church the Light hath shined*, with a portrait of him in a pulpit as 'the stone which the builders rejected'. In spite of my recoil from his sanctimonious ways, I felt for him. A purple crocus growing alone in the desert of a gravel path was manifestly his symbol. Pressed and mounted on a card, it was dedicated to his memory. His successor was a jovial Irishman who saluted me with a kiss on my way to communion. This also was not to my taste.

Another brand of religion was the Salvation Army meetings, to which I went sometimes with the maid who belonged to the Army, enjoying the stirring music, the hymns and the public confessions of the converts. The notion of giving oneself to Jesus was very prevalent; people were always asking me if I was 'saved'. In the end I began to believe that I really was.

Whether with intent or not, my father would drop a salty comment on religious fervour, telling of the old man who rose up in a Salvation Army meeting crying: 'O Lord forgive me, for I was a wit in my youth.' And once, during the war, my father did tell me that, for the time being, he could no longer read any of the Bible except the Old Testament.

Determined that as soon as we were old enough the family should see something of other countries, my father, when my younger sister was only a year old and I about eight, took us all for a holiday to Knokke in Belgium, then a quiet and unfashionable town. This release into the Continental way of enjoying life had a lasting influence on my own attitude.

One summer we were on the Normandy coast, where, throwing quoits at the fair, I learned of the alliance between France and Russia as the woman stall-keeper's screechy voice reiterated: '*La France et la Russie gagnent DEUX barres de nougat.*' Another holiday was by steamer on the Rhine, to cafés roofed with climbing vines, past Bishop Hatto's castle and the Lorelei rock. My Rhine was not a polluted stream fringed with factories and chimneys. Not until 1958, driving beside it, did I renew my acquaintance with the great river: it was a bitter experience.

A very important highlight of my school days was my first real experience of politics. I was too young to understand much about the Boer War; votes for women was something that I talked about but as yet had little real meaning for me. But in 1906, when I was twelve, the General Election in which the Liberals had such a sweeping victory took place. My father who, as he explained to me, could not take part in politics because he was a Civil Servant, was at heart a keen Liberal. So, taking only me with him, he went to London to stand in Trafalgar Square and watch the election results. We stood there, packed tight among thousands of excited people who were waving 'teasers', blowing paper squeakers, and agitating rattles, just as on Derby Day. On a high screen above St Martin's Church the results were flashed one by one, to be cheered or booed as the case might be. For the first time I was carried away by mass emotion, utterly intoxicated with it all. It was, indeed, a famous victory and my father and I came home exhausted and content.

By the time I was about sixteen I had passed most of the exams necessary if I were to qualify for university, except for Latin and Greek for the Little Go at Cambridge. Those who were, unknown to me, planning my future, took the view that, given a year, I could 'mug up' enough of these languages to get a Third, all that was needed to enter. So it was arranged that I should spend a year in Germany at a modest finishing school for young ladies, after which I would do Latin and Greek back at school and then try for a scholarship at Girton in modern languages.

In 1911 my father escorted me and May, a school friend, to Halberstadt, where he left us in a small *Pensionat*, run by Fräulein Stuhr, intellectual and masculine, and Fräulein Feuchter, pale and nondescript, immensely kind, who did the cooking and domestic chores and was, as we soon guessed, bullied by her dominant partner.

We also were somewhat intimidated by Fräulein Stuhr, who seemed to demand an affection that we did not find it easy to give. But to read and discuss German literature with her was a pleasure. On Fräulein Feuchter's cooking and the rye bread—*belegtes Brot*—I soon got very fat. With her we did chip carving and *Lochstickerei*, a horrid process of digging holes in linen articles and stitching round them. The German girls were making their trousseaux with this type of embroidery, garments solid enough to last a lifetime. These girls were intensely domesticated and very warm-hearted. I enjoyed their company and their nonsense: '*Du bist verrückt mein Kind, du musst nach Berlin . . .*'; '*Ach du lieber Augustin, alles ist hin . . .*'.

There was much more '*Schwärmerei*' in our *Pensionat* than in my school; when the photos of the new repertory company went up at the local theatre, there would be a rush to choose a '*junger Held*' (juvenile male lead) to rave about. To avoid competition I fixed my preference on Pastor Knopf who, with his narrow face and pointed fair beard, white stock over his black gown, was in the pulpit on Sundays at the cathedral-type church which we attended. I liked to watch him deliver his good Lutheran sermons, a figure straight out of the Renaissance. '*Nun danket*', the Old Hundredth, proceeded from the throats of the congregation at an extraordinarily slow and heavy pace, but with a volume that filled the ample church.

We were taken to the theatre, where, in the foyer, duly chaperoned, we met local people. Needless to say, it was the theatre that mattered most to me. German provincial repertory theatres are a model that should be followed everywhere. State-financed, each season the company brought a varied programme of classical and lighter plays, supplemented by visiting singers and opera companies. And I was entranced by the dark blue vault of the theatre ceiling, in which lights were placed like golden stars. Here I lived in plays by Goethe and Schiller, here heard the lovely German *Lieder*—Mendelssohn, Schubert —here I first heard *Carmen* in German and have never since been able to think of it in any other language.

Auf in den Kampf Torero
Stolz in der Brust
Siegesbewusst.

We were steeped in the life and works of Goethe whom, in those days, Germans seemed to cherish as if he were a near relation, discussing his love affairs, weeping with young Werther, exalted, and at times bewildered, over Faust. The later history of Germany has cast so dark a shadow that I want above all to recall the Germany that took me to its heart in 1911, warm, domestic, sentimental, feeding richly, yet with a Protestant discipline of work and duty and an iron military framework, expressed however, at that date, rather by the *Wacht am Rhein* and *Ich hatt' einen Kameraden* (then uncontaminated by Nazi use) than in any thirst for conquest; a Germany withal passionate about music, poetry and culture. This was a deeper life of insight than I had so far known in my own country. Oddly enough, I was hardly homesick at all; my school German sufficed for conversation, but at first I caused some amusement by speaking a literary language, as if someone were to talk Shakespearian English.

The time in Germany would not have been complete without a love-affair. Hardly that, perhaps, since it was all on the level of perfectly correct courtship. Kurt was a law student, fair and blue-eyed, of course, with peaked cap and duelling scars on his face, fortunately not very disfiguring. On a social occasion we met and danced. We did somehow manage some clandestine meetings, with long talks, but no more than a kiss on the hand. Such restraint is said to be rare nowadays among adolescents, yet it may well be that many first affairs still have this enchanting atmosphere of delicacy and wonder. Kurt and I wrote to one another till the war intervened. Then (in 1921!) came a letter, evidence of his survival and previous honourable intentions, for he informed me that he was about to get married and would I like the return of my letters? To my regret now I said no: I would much like to recall what I wrote then. I still have the soft leather-bound *Faust* and Goethe's *Tasso* which he gave me.

Halberstadt is close to the Harz mountains, made famous by Heine's journey. After seeing something of Berlin and the Goethehaus in Frankfurt with my father and Uncle Troopy, I stayed on with my mother that summer at Wernigerode. We met and talked much there with an American Professor and his wife, who were closely concerned with friendly relations between their country and Germany. The Professor discussed politics with me; something that he said remained fixed in my mind and was to bear fruit years later. It was that England was likely to decline and that the United States and Germany would then be the dominant powers. His wife was very affectionate to me, and said that if ever I came to America she hoped that I would marry one of her three sons.

In December I was homeward bound and reached England in time for Christmas. I came ashore at Folkestone in the dark of an early morning and sheets of driving rain to find my father and mother on the quay. By this time I could speak German well enough to be taken for a native, and I spoke English, for a time, with a German accent. Now I had to tackle my Greek and Latin. At home there was a little back room, a sort of study for my father, with his bookcases, a large old-fashioned desk and a horrid little inadequate gas fire. My father and I rose at about 6 a.m. on many mornings to study the *Medea* to the sound of that popping gas in the chill of dark winter days. The horrors in the play embarrassed my father somewhat, so we worked with a crib. Yet the power and poetry of that play came over to me so intensely that it partly inspired my very first book, *Hypatia, or Woman and Knowledge*, thirteen years later.

Then to Cambridge to take the Little Go and to try for a modern languages scholarship at Girton, where I was bidden to coffee with the dons and asked by whom and how I had been taught. Finally the results: to the intense amusement of my father and myself, I had, though only needing a Third, got a First in the Little Go, and Girton had awarded me the scholarship, so that my path to university was now wide open. And I sat down, with seven telegrams of congratulation in my hands, and burst into tears.

2

Life at Cambridge

Nowadays we hear a lot about young people in their teens agonizing in search of their identities, and, in so doing, behaving outrageously and causing much anxiety to their parents. Trying now to recreate myself as a child and young woman as truthfully as I know how, I have asked myself why was my adolescence (and that, I feel sure, of so many of my contemporaries) so different?

As I have indicated, our lives were very much directed by our parents and, by the school, regimented. This does, however, still obtain to a considerable extent today, except that parental control is much weaker and receives less acceptance. Nor could I maintain that I, at any time, did not have very full opportunities for expressing my individuality. Introspection was not encouraged, to that extent I was not self-conscious; I lived and worked, enjoyed and sorrowed from day to day, on the whole in harmony with my surroundings and my parents. Self-questioning was prompted only by religious teachers and thus confined itself to taking account of your actions, good or bad, stirring a sense of guilt and doubts as to whether your life was being lived in accordance with the example of Jesus Christ. All those whose influence surrounded us believed, or professed belief, in Christianity; there seemed little reason to doubt it, or to speculate on the mysteries of the universe. Parallel with security in faith was the security of the social and economic system. True, we knew about the poor, but they were the recipients of Christian charity, and, what is more, increasing prosperity and growing compassion for their welfare would presently make things better for them also. There was the Empire and trade and little sign of unrest at home and abroad, except for the Boer War and a few other trouble-spots which hardly affected the home population. Unquestionably there were many signs of what was to come in political and intellectual life, but the significance of socialist advocacy and the growing number of Labour Members of Parliament disturbed the complacency of the general public but little.

Freud, whose work was to be of such immense importance to the next generations, had not been heard of. As individuals we therefore saw ourselves as entirely responsible for our own actions, we had no grounds for blaming our home background for anything that we did wrong (or even for praising it for what we did right), nor could we fall back on 'complexes' involving our parents, or their treatment of us, as determining our conduct. As citizens of the British Empire we had been indoctrinated in a rather smug dignity, which offered us certain privileges, but, at the same time, certain responsibilities. Maybe we had little need to search for our identity, it was only too well established for us.

By contrast, the adolescent of the past few decades looks back on two devastating wars, the invention of ghastly war weapons in which some of the most eminent men of science are involved; the decay of religious faith and of confidence in the social order; the loosening of family ties and consequent loss of support; awareness of false teaching on sex and the probing into human relations and the non-rational depths of our nature, first begun by psychoanalysis. How can we wonder that the present-day adolescent asks himself, 'Who am I, where do I belong, where do I come from, whither shall I go?', and, in his dilemma, blames his failures and inadequacies on all those persons and forces that shaped his past.

The tears which I shed at the news of my scholarship award were the sign of a growing, but half-conscious, desire to direct my own life. Many times over I had said to relatives and friends that my true ambition was to go and train for the theatre; this was regarded at that time and in that milieu, quite naturally, as a passing notion of one stage-struck. I could do a number of things well and was a good scholar—the decision as to which probable talent to cultivate had to be made. In spite of my fortunate circumstances, which might seem to have been favourable to a full discussion, there was really no one to whom I felt I could speak freely and from whom I might get impartial advice. I did not, in fact perhaps could not, then know how to measure the standard of my ability or my chances of success in the outside world; I knew that I had done well in relation to my fellow pupils at school and now came the scholarship to indicate that I stood well in wider competition. This pre-empted my choice. I was not in control of my own destiny. I had said to myself that I would go in for the scholarship, as I would very likely not get it anyway. And now in the back of my mind lurked a suspicion that my teachers had known all along that my success was almost certain. I am not arguing that able children should be constantly reminded of their talents and thus be elevated into an élite, on the contrary, for we soon become conceited enough. My contention is that any young person, with whatever type of ability, should get enough free time and encouragement to find out what he or she is really like and what best adapted to do. In other words, even in my day, we had need to search for our identity.

Accepting what appeared to be the decision of fate, I accordingly went up to Girton College, Cambridge. Architecturally rather hideous, Girton was commodious and also, in its way, homely. A study of your own and an adjoining bedroom, separated either by doors or a curtain, gave you a feeling of privacy and the dignity of being grown-up. Apart from some lectures and private coachings, there was great pleasure in disposing of your own time, in immersing yourself, if you wished, for hours in one subject or one writer. There was hockey, or tennis, the swimming bath, the grounds to walk in with your friends, the lawns to laze on in the summer sun. Released from the discipline of a rigid timetable, many students found it difficult to organize their own work, but this was never a problem to any who found their imagination or intellect caught by some aspect of their subject. With no one to interrupt, it was possible to wrestle all day with Pascal or my old friend Goethe and forget to descend to the hall for a meal. To get to Cambridge to attend the University lectures we had to go in the old horse cabs or on our bicycles, but there were tutors who came out from Cambridge to give individual coachings.

Girton, even more than Newnham, was like a large girls' boarding school. Intellectually we were reckoned to be adult, but as young inexperienced women we had to be guarded with care. You could not receive a young man in your room; you might be permitted to have him to tea in one of the public reception rooms, but you could accept no invitation from young men to tea or other entertainment without a chaperone from the College. There was, naturally, competition to enlist the younger dons for this duty, sometimes with the sad result that the young men found the dons' conversation more amusing than that of the shy young ladies.

When I was at Girton there was still a marked difference between the older and younger generation of dons. The older ones belonged to the days of the pioneers, Victorian in dress and hairstyle, indeed almost nun-like. The Mistress, Miss Jones—commonly known as Jonah—who retired quite early while I was there, was fragile and exceedingly lady-like. She was so susceptible to draughts that in chapel and her own room she would be surrounded on three sides by a glass screen. She was succeeded by Miss Jex Blake, 'Kits', a classics don, who was thoroughly robust and rather like a horse; this is not unkindly meant, for I liked and respected her, there was much more to her than she allowed to appear. At coffee with her we would maliciously solicit her opinion about some book or play, which was held to be improper, and she would continue placidly knitting and then say in her slow, deliberate way: 'I think it is very—dull.' She had a great sense of humour; I imagine that this was the very opposite of what she really thought. I was myself back at Girton as a Fellow on the lively occasion when, just after the First World War ended, a horde of undergraduates stormed out from Cambridge, up the drive and under the archway and lit a bonfire in the quad, yelling, 'Where are the women we have been fighting for?' Hanging out of every window and preparing to descend were, needless to say, the women in question. Miss Jex Blake, like an Abbess, in her plain alpaca bodice and full long skirt, followed by a retinue of senior dons, received the invaders at the doorway under the arch, stood with clasped hands before her and, with great dignity, enquired: 'Gentlemen, to what do we owe the honour of this visit?' Then she invited them to a dance at the College on the following Saturday. Such a function would not have been thought of only a few years previously; though already there was much restlessness at the rigid rules, it was scarcely what one might call a revolt.

Of the younger dons with whom I was personally concerned one was Miss Beard, for German language and literature, a tall, elegant Irishwoman with a slight stoop and a lorgnette and a very agreeable brogue. Often in her company was Eileen Power, whom I saw but little then, as she dealt with history. She became distinguished for her fine scholarship and her utter charm, which captivated many of both sexes. We always found it a pleasure to watch her, tall and placid and very much a personality, as she came in to take her place for dinner at high table. She had very beautiful, candid blue-grey eyes.

The don to whom I came closest was Clara Kirchberger. Her subject was French; but she, who came of a Jewish family and had become converted to Christianity, was passionately concerned with religion to the exclusion of almost everything else. High Church was very much in vogue; Father Waggett was preaching very effectively in Cambridge, it was said, to all those atheists hiding behind the pillars of his church although there were plenty of the hearty 'muscular Christians', as the Low Church and Nonconformists were disparagingly called; if you really meant religion seriously you had to keep the Church fasts and festivals, examine your conscience rigorously, spend much time on your knees in prayer, and begin to think of going to confession and to retreats. Several of my friends at that time were of this way of thinking, especially Vera Mendel, who, like Clara Kirchberger, came from a Jewish family. At this time Vera also took religious observance seriously and wielded considerable influence among her contemporaries; she had beauty, poise and dignity and a withdrawn lost look in her grey eyes that made her, when we performed Yeats' *Countess Cathleen*, the ideal choice for the title role. My own part in that show was as a sea spirit who chanted repeatedly and with doubtful veracity that 'Sorrow hath made me dumb'.

The *Countess Cathleen* was well adapted to our mood at that moment, with its tale of the Countess bartering her soul to the devil merchants of death in return for food for her people. We discussed endlessly the claims of religion as related to the teaching of the Churches, but so far taking no account of politics, or of social and economic questions. I did not belong to any political club or party during my university years. What I personally felt and believed about the purpose of the universe was the first and most important consideration in my mind; following on this came the riddle of the destiny of all mankind in this world, and after, if there were such a thing as immortality. My mind was so exercised and troubled by these deep matters that my academic work began to suffer. My writing of essays, once easy and flowing, now became so uncertain and confused that I would cross out sentence after sentence as they were written in search of what I was trying to say. My tutor in German, Miss Beard, with real insight, suggested a rest from written work and attendance at some lectures on philosophy in Cambridge. This crisis was in part due, I believe, to the long strain of striving and concentration that had gone on throughout my school days. No doubt, too, the Girton authorities feared that I might not do them, or myself, justice in the final Tripos examinations.

In any case, forth I went to sit under Professor Dawes Hicks and imbibe the wisdom of Immanuel Kant, while Clara and I continued to agonize and wrestle over Pascal and the Jansenists of Port Royal. Kant was very difficult, but fascinating, and the more enjoyable in that he would not be 'set' in my Tripos; my interest in philosophy grew, though I knew nothing then of the philosophers of the new school, George Moore and Bertrand Russell. But here, as Dawes Hicks expounded his subject at a snail's pace, new vistas of speculation and argument opened before me. The Professor went slowly. He would sigh deeply as with boredom, and he had a habit of repeating a phrase about three times before going on to finish the sentence. As a student of literature, I was critical of his style. 'This,' he would begin, 'this I say, this was, this I say, was the thread, this was the guiding thread that paved the way to Kant's later discoveries.' I have an endearing memory of the Professor, small, delicate, with three white curls standing up from the top of his head, which I used to refer to as the 'curls transcendental'.

The richness and depth of German thought, which I found not only in their philosophy but also in the literary essays of Schiller and Heine, the marvellous simplicity of rhythm, the lovely rounded vowel sounds of their poetry, were contrasted, for me, by the greater clarity and austerity of French prose and verse. The earlier French lyric poets, Ronsard and Du Bellay, were easy to appreciate, but it had taken me longer to enjoy the rolling, unaccented syllables of the classical Alexandrines. Racine's *Athalie*, a set book when I was at school, was the cause of what may have been my first revolt against religious authority and cost me a severe reprimand when I expressed my unorthodox views in an essay. What outraged me, who had been taught that, all through history, churches were sacred sanctuaries, was that the High Priest in the play lured Athalie into the temple, there to have her murdered. I can't help thinking that the young ladies of St Cyr, for whom the play was written, may well have been as bored with it as I was.

At Girton, Port Royal, with its powerful influence on Pascal and its hold on Racine, came back on to the scene; the moral and theological disputes of the period are no mere detail of my literary studies, but part of the central dilemma of my life. Should one, with Pascal, decide that it was the part of prudence to bet on the truth of Christianity since there was nothing to lose if this were to prove mistaken? This seemed a poor argument from a man of Pascal's distinction, hardly to be commended to a young seeker, any more than Paley's *Evidences of Christianity*, whose arguments we found absurd, but which you had to do for the Little Go unless you took logic. The Jansenists revealed themselves as gloomy people, Puritan, almost Calvinist. Did this religion of suffering involve the denial of all pleasures, of spontaneous joy in life? From early years I had lived my life close to plants, trees, animals and flowers; I had cradled tiny kittens, or white mice, in my hands, coaxed my pigeons to my shoulder and my doves to take hempseed from my lips. I talked with them all with the instinctive pantheism of primitive peoples, and I responded to a like pantheism which I had found in Goethe. It had never occurred to me that these impulses were in conflict with my accepted religion, nor had I, in spite of the repeated exhortations of the 'elect' to get saved, ever—as it seemed I should have done—allowed the sense of my awful sinfulness to enter like iron into my soul. 'If there is a God,' wrote Pascal, 'we must love Him and not His creatures.' This was a very hard doctrine and a stony path to tread.

I can recall the very moment when, at my prayers, it occurred to me that the extreme of Christian renunciation amounted to the virtual annihilation of oneself. Following on and opposing Pascal came Voltaire with his declaration that he 'would take the part of humanity against this sublime misanthrope'. And had not God, said Voltaire, endowed man with natural instincts which even compelled him to love wife and family and his country and not hold them in contempt? Later I came to study with increasing delight the French eighteenth-century hedonists who campaigned against very severe strictures on the smallest pleasures. In 1700 a light-hearted dialogue on pleasure in which a gentleman debated whether he would be damned for eating partridges and pears, the gift of one of his apparently misguided friends, was suppressed and publicly burnt. It may be argued that this intensely ascetic, Manichean version of Christianity, which was presented to me at this time, both in my studies and in the personal encounter with my friend and tutor Clara, was not the whole story. None the less, it did not differ greatly from what I had been taught in my childhood.

Acceptance of the religion of suffering was Clara's choice, which ultimately took her into an Anglican convent. The agony of this faith was expressed in the poetry of Francis Thompson—*The Hound of Heaven*—a powerful inspiration of those days. He was indeed a not inconsiderable poet, who, but for his association with the religious mood of his period, might well be more read and appreciated today. Long before I emancipated myself I, like Clara, was deeply immersed in these emotions; yet it was she who gave me one key to my deliverance—two small leather-bound volumes of Meredith's poems. I read them avidly and have returned to them again and again. Anyone who has ever had the mystic experience of feeling oneself to be an integral part of the very structure of our planet, will find its echoes in his *Reading of Earth*.

> She, the white wild cherry, a tree
> Earth-rooted, tangibly wood,
> Yet a presence, throbbing, alive,
> Because earth-rooted, alive.

His sonnet sequence, *Modern Love*, has never been sufficiently valued. I went on to read all the novels, and found that he had ideas as to what women were really like.

Thus it was, gradually, that I came to reject the religion in which I had been brought up and to form by degrees a view of life by which to determine my actions.

Serious, and at times morbid contemplation was only a small part of my life at the University. I had many other friends besides those who were concerned with religion, and even they were not occupied with it all of the time. I played hockey for my College and later very nearly for the Cambridge women's team, there was swimming and diving too in inter-university rivalries, and debates in the College, though women were not yet admitted to the University Union. We did join the University Choral Society: singing Bach's 'Jesu Priceless Treasure' at a concert was a great experience. One of my friends was the calm and warm-hearted Hebe Bentwich, through whom I experienced a stay in an orthodox Jewish family; with another, Marjorie Lockwood, from Sheffield, I experienced the marvellous sight of a Bessemer blow at the steelworks. There was lovely Nancy Barlow, actually studying Russian, a rare pursuit in 1912.

Contrary to the current opinion, we Girton girls did not wear severe shirt blouses with formal ties, nor did we drag back our hair; we were most fashion-conscious, much given to saucy hats, designed to impress male colleagues at lectures, who would stamp their approval when any one of us entered looking especially glamorous. Appreciation was occasionally expressed in more definite terms, as when I found in my satchel, after a German lecture, verses designed for my friend Nancy and myself:

> They are those ladies of Girton
> The twins of the purest gold,
> This theme I can glibly dissert on
> Although they appear rather cold.
> Never the signs they advert on
> We give them, so shamelessly clear,
> They are those ladies of Girton
> The prettiest couple up here.

Severity of rules notwithstanding, the sexes did make acquaintance; at a social evening of the University German Society, the identity of the poet was revealed.

All the same, social contacts were few; it was a different non-academic woman whom undergraduates invited to the May Week balls. But in vacation we too went to dances, in our modest evening dresses, and our long white kid gloves, with pretty dance programmes and their dangling little pencils. There was the moment when we 'put up our hair' and were supposed to become modest, shy young ladies, forsaking our schoolgirl tomboy habits. Bryher, the novelist, relates that her parents did not permit her even to go and post a letter without putting on hat, coat and gloves. At Girton I still wore boned corsets with back lacings which, still proud of small waists, we would pull in tightly. Dresses were long, there were some draped fashions and hobble skirts, though when I went up to College I do recall that we were wearing circular skirts that were not very long and swung neatly as one took a good long stride. The suffragettes were not ugly old harridans, but elegant, often beautiful women, whose long skirts and large hats must have been a fantastic hindrance in fighting with the police.

But girls and young women were doing gymnastics and playing hockey; we were conscious of our ability in education and of our physical health and strength. My girlfriends and I disliked our swelling breasts; somehow we sensed the approach of the restrictions of womanhood. We used to mock our elder sisters when they began to get 'spooney' about men, and vow that we would never do the same. My sister Bindy and I for years called each other 'boys', and the habit persisted. Freud would call this penis envy, no doubt. But we knew nothing about penises, barely even saw each other in the nude. It was, and is, simply the prestige of male power and dominance which leads women to imitate the opposite sex. Like young men, we demonstrated our physical endurance on long bicycle rides; fifty miles on a machine without a freewheel was no joke. We took, like men, to walking tours. On one occasion my brother, sister and I, with a friend, walked back to Sutton, in Surrey, from Bournemouth, where we had spent part of the summer holiday. No hitch-hiking or cheating with lifts.

Gradually the emancipation of women was becoming part of the general atmosphere—the *Zeitgeist*. My father believed that his daughters should have as good an education as his son, and he joked sometimes about the query of an old-fashioned friend of his: 'Does it improve their chances?' (of marriage). He read H. G. Wells's *Kipps* with great enjoyment and often quoted from it. I expect that it expressed for him some of the feelings of every young man struggling out of a cramped environment into a position of greater power, influence and financial security. The book for us young women was Wells's *Ann Veronica*, which came out in 1909, followed by *The New Machiavelli* in 1911. At College, from 1912 onwards, we naturally read these books. I was quite unaware at the time of the difficulty that Wells had in getting them published. Indeed, I only learned lately that it was Stanley Unwin, then a young man starting out with his uncle Fisher Unwin, who finally, after it had been rejected all over the place, got *Ann Veronica* into print.* Later, Stanley Unwin was to make his own and Bertrand Russell's reputation in the literary world by backing his hunch to publish Russell's books.

As I attended more lectures in Cambridge I entered more into University life, and began to absorb the atmosphere of the Cambridge mind. As is well known, this was a great period in Cambridge: there were the scientists at the Cavendish Lab, the philosophers and mathematicians, Moore, M'Taggart, Russell, Littlewood, Ramsey, Hardy, Eric Neville; Maynard Keynes the economist at King's, E. M. Forster, Leonard Woolf, Goldsworthy Lowes Dickinson.

My main concern at first was literature: German drama, the functions of tragedy, Schiller and Goethe on moral purpose and art. On English literature 'Q' (Quiller-Couch) was lecturing; I got in as and when I could. It was fun to watch his great mastiff's face and hear the roar of stamping when the audience appreciated one of his sallies. Once Brandes came from Denmark to lecture on Nietzsche to a packed amphitheatre. His accent gave great delight as he spoke of 'Nietzsche ze great zinker of ze epoch'—a verdict with which we heartily stamped our agreement. When he went on to say how Nietzsche had looked around at 'ze miserable specimens of humanity zat zurround us', the outburst of stamping and cheering from the concourse of very healthy and rather handsome undergraduates was stupendous.

Looking back I have wondered how women ever managed to free themselves from their corsets, frills and furbelows and the iron strait-jacket imposed on them by religion, morality and social sanctions. One might wonder also at the emancipation of men's minds from dogma and the abstruse and obscurantist flights of traditional idealistic philosophy which took place during the first quarter of the twentieth century. I find in my notebook an undocumented French quotation, the gist of which is that idealism in philosophy is analogous with mysticism in religion, the one seeing the reality of the things of this world in thought, the other the reality of the things of heaven in feeling. Thought and feeling, during those very years when I was in Cambridge, were to be turned by Cambridge minds in very different directions.

In the year that I was born, Bertrand Russell had taken his degree in moral sciences at Cambridge. A few years later he was listening to Moore's criticism and rejection of Kant and Hegel. Before I went up to Cambridge, Russell had already faced hostility in a by-election when he stood for Women's Suffrage.

* see Lovat Dickson, *H. G. Wells: His Turbulent Life and Times* (Macmillan, 1969). Women's emancipation had the support of many writers of genius: not forgetting Ibsen's *A Doll's House*, there were Barrie's *Twelve Pound Look*, Shaw's *Fanny's First Play*, and Arnold Bennett's *Lion's Share*

Moore disliked high-falutin' humbug, such as 'seeing all things in God', or supposing, with the solipsists, that we create for ourselves the external world. He stressed common sense and the analysis of thoughts and motives; moral judgments were no longer to be the Kantian categorical imperative, but a matter of individual states of mind, personal intuitions, similar to aesthetic appreciation. Critical analysis and rejection of authority were the core of this teaching and became very much the characteristic of the Cambridge mind and its subsequent influence on Bloomsbury. A whole trend in conduct, art and interior decoration, such as the Omega workshops, can ultimately be traced to these new theories, by which my friends and I were to be greatly affected. Russell consistently held the view, to be found in his own succint words, as late as August 1953, in the *Report on the Science and Freedom Congress* of Hamburg, that 'the belief that metaphysics has any bearing on practical affairs is a proof of logical incapacity'. Logical incapacity or not, I have always disagreed with this view, about which we came to argue later. I believe that the metaphysical discussions that went on in Cambridge from 1900 onwards had very great political and social repercussions, not the least of these the emancipation of women.

However that may be, we women at Girton had, before long, discovered the Heretics Society. Not very many of us, I regret to say. Instead of favouring holy retreats at occasional weekends, or going to College chapel on Sunday evenings, we would ask for an exeat permit and be off to Heretics. This was not much favoured at the top level in Girton, but it was not forbidden. C. K. Ogden, who was the prime mover in the Heretics, was to become one of my real friends and a considerable influence in my life. He had a flat high up in Petty Cury, which he called Top Hole. It was here that the Heretics used to meet. I used to bicycle off there of a Sunday evening with a most agreeable feeling of defiance and liberation. If you joined the Society you were called upon to reject authority in matters of religion and belief, and to accept only conviction by reasonable argument. You could, if not certain of your position, become an associate, who merely believed in open discussion but had not entirely rejected authority.

It seems to me significant that the core of the Heretics' protest, even before the First World War, was against authority. At that time what mattered was opposition to authority in religion and the dogmatic precepts of idealistic philosophy; analysis, discussion and individual views on ethics, belief, and taste were to become the basis for a growing democracy also in political life. Today authority is once more challenged, but now the object of the attack is the authoritarian State itself, which, in some countries, has been the outcome of a move towards democracy, while in others it forms the autocratic power of large-scale industrialism based on technology, which has grown up behind a screen of democracy now felt to be a fake.

Mass demonstrations and protests were on their way, but their time had not yet come. At the Heretics our weapons were ideas and talk and the knowledge that heresy is contagious. Throughout history the target of reaction has always been not only freedom of speech, but freedom of thought; thought is considered the dangerous innovator and forerunner of revolution. On the other hand economic causes have been regarded by a very great many as the driving force for change. I have always held the contrary view. Economic man is an invention of the statistician; I do not believe in him. But I do not define 'thought' as pure reason in the academic sense, rather as the creative impulse that springs from a combination of the reasoning faculty, intuitions, imagination, instincts of the organism that is man. This is the unique gift of human beings; by this alone, for good or ill, they shape their future.

Many distinguished people came to speak to the Heretics, or were associated with the society. Philip Sargent Florence and Brian W. Downs were active members. The Sitwells came to speak, as did Harold Monro the poet, Ogden presiding with his usual impish provocation of argument. We were a trifle cramped for space at these meetings, for Ogden had a great many books which lay in piles, and there were besides piles and piles of papers and letters through which one waded or sat on. This was Ogden's method of filing, one which I am sure would commend itself to anyone who knows that, once a thing has got into a folder or a filing cabinet, it will never be found again. Ogden never threw anything away, not even a telegram inviting him to dinner, and always knew where everything could be found.

C.K., as his friends called him, was a small man with a round head thinly covered with fair hair, the forehead of an intellectual, gold-rimmed glasses over grey eyes, a round pink face with the complexion of a baby. There was something gnomish about him; I used to say that he was either a changeling, or had been born just like that, neither a baby nor a mature man. His chuckle was gnome-like too. He disliked fresh air and healthy pursuits; at least this was the impression that he chose to give. He would live in a stuffy room and then acquire a thing called an ozone machine, the artificial substitute being immensely preferable, as he would tell us, to the real article. C.K. had a flair for knowing what was the latest thing, and its latest exponent, in a vast number of subjects, which made him invaluable to colleagues in work and to the Heretics Society. What is more, he could, by some subtle stimulus, prevail on people to speak or produce articles or books, a great gift for an editor, which he did become. At one time he pressed upon his visitors a booklet about the population explosion and the necessity for birth control, apparently by a lady called Adeline More. This was Ogden's own pioneer contribution to a serious and then neglected question.

My best friend at College, who went with me to the Heretics, was Dot Wrinch. She was a mathematician of high ability and consequently consumed with admiration for Bertrand Russell. Dot had lovely dark red hair, a broad, agreeably freckled face and a great deal of charm. She was a quite passionate and persistent intellectual, a quality rare in women, who, by reason of the terms on which they must live in our society, are too easily diverted. Dot was, to her credit, more concentrated on her purpose than I, who probably spread myself then, and in later life, over too many kinds of activity. This may have been because of my original thwarted ambition to become an actress. However that may be, Ogden at times would tell me that he wished I would break my leg or become otherwise incapacitated, in which case I might do the good writing for which he knew I had both the imagination and the brains.

At Girton we pursued our undergraduate life with happy enthusiasm: we went on talking about the universe, giving cocoa-parties to our friends in the evenings, worrying about the second year Mays exams which loomed for some of us and in which we had to do ourselves credit. As I recall, we never spoke of politics, except votes for women, and were quite oblivious of any shadow hanging over our future. In the vacation I went with my family to Newquay, where we had been before and where some enthusiasts organized exciting, fast, mixed hockey on the huge smooth sands. My father, I believe, had remained at the Admiralty. Here, at Newquay, we learned of the outbreak of war on 4 August 1914.

3

The Years of War

So far as I remember, we did not cut short our holiday at the outbreak of war. There was nothing, at that stage, that any one of us, except my father, could do. He slept at the Admiralty and was only rarely home at Sutton in the early days of the fighting. Once or twice I was on the point of going into a hospital to train as a V.A.D. Belgium had been overrun, the flood of war refugees into England had begun. I saw in the press that a Women's Voluntary Corps was being started to help them. I went up to London and did voluntary work until term began. The leaders of this group, whose names I have completely forgotten, accepted me, but laughed at me because I was small and seemed very young; I got nicknamed the Squirrel. One night I went to Tilbury to help with reception, comforting the people and seeing them into trains to go on to London to the Alexandra Palace. Young and un-political as I was, this was my first experience of the meaning of war to ordinary, innocent people. I have never forgotten the tired, tear-stained faces of the children, the weary, haggard old women, the pathetic bundles of possessions tied up in big check tablecloths and bedcovers.

Much has been written by those who knew our world before 1914, and who inevitably felt, with Leonard Woolf, that since that date it has been 'downhill all the way'. For me, certainly, as I did what I could to help at the 'Ally Pally', went round to listen to any complaints from people who had been placed in lodgings, ran messages, and made reports, my fairytale world of the tamarisk tree began to fade into the past as I looked into the now terrible reality of the present. This war, thought by so many to be the great illusion, which would never come to pass, was now upon us.

Back at Girton, though, things were still much the same at first. Like several of my friends, I had no immediate personal anxieties. My brother was still too young to be called up. I could, of course, have no news from Germany. The elder of two young men I had met on holiday at Besançon was killed in the early days of the war; this distressed but did not touch me closely, since he was no more than an acquaintance. I did grieve greatly for Barbara Wootton at the time her husband was killed, so soon after their marriage; though I did not know her person-ally, I remember vividly seeing her blank, shut-in face, which told me what such a loss meant to her and would mean for so many others as the slaughter went on. The disappearance of a whole generation of young men, sound in mind and body and many of them brilliant, was felt very much in Cambridge by those who knew and taught them. We were a community of women, and, oddly enough, the war concentrated at least some of us more upon our studies, in that it removed some social distractions and, in great measure, speculation about the future.

I soon became aware that there were young men in Cambridge who were opposed to the war and would plead conscientious objection. C. K. Ogden viewed the whole war as a lot of nonsense, something he could not have imagined would be embarked upon by intelligent people. He was running the *Cambridge Magazine*, devoting a section, with the help of the Noel Buxtons, to extracts from the foreign press. He defiantly opened bookshops as if to tell the public that here was something more important than their fall into barbarism. (Ogden was unfit for military service.) Later he had to cease from publishing the foreign news, and was even attacked physically by some patriots. I went in to help him from time to time with reviewing books for the magazine, over which we would sit chuckling and thinking of spiky things to say.

Girton had taken in two or three refugee students from Belgium. It seemed natural that I would fraternize with them and try to make them welcome. One of them, Maria Winska, was Polish by birth; we much enjoyed each other's company. Maria had a round baby face, with pouting lips, rosy cheeks and brown, curly hair. She was lively and uninhibited, a relief from the reserve that so often acted as a barrier to intimate friendship with the English. Unfortunately, these Continental students could not make head nor tail of the odd regulations governing the lives of women students in England, so they were packed off to study in London, where they might have more freedom to live as they were accustomed to, and also so that they would no longer be in a position to disturb the morals of Girtonians.

In 1914 Bertrand Russell was away lecturing in the United States, where he already began speaking out against the war, and continued to do so in London and Cambridge the following year.

By June came my finals in the Tripos, in which I succeeded in obtaining my First Class Honours, gaining a special distinction in Orals.

To decide what to do next was not simple. In my former mood I would probably have gone into some form of war work. But by now I was in a state of indecision; all my earlier beliefs and loyalties were being called in question, and I found it hard to determine just where I stood. The man with whom I was in love was a conscientious objector, as were several of his friends. My father was in a very important position in the Admiralty and soon to become head of the Department of Munitions. The Naval officer uncle whom I had most admired, although I had not seen much of him for years, had gone down in the *Aboukir*. I learned later from my mother that my father had been appointed to go with Lord Kitchener on his fatal voyage, but at the last moment another man had been sent in his stead. In April of my last year at Girton, Rupert Brooke, who had been a Fellow of King's College, and the adored poet of many, died in Greece. His poems were passionately read; for some they became a symbol of a patriot's sacrifice, for others one more indication of the appalling waste of war. Siegfried Sassoon began to produce his satirical poems, repeated with delight by those who had begun to detest the old men's attitude to the war and the 'nobility' of parents 'giving' their sons as cannon-fodder.

I no longer had any heart for helping in the holocaust, but I still could not convince myself that I ought to oppose it. By now my interest in literary research had intensified and was at times completely absorbing. Accordingly, I wanted to go on working in this field at least for the present. Girton would have awarded me a postgraduate grant, but they were doubtful on two counts: whether academic life was really my métier, and whether the near breakdown I had had might not be an indication against my continuing in it.

My father was not entirely in favour of continued study; he spoke of a time spent exercising one's brain, sharpening a tool as it were, which must now be put to use in the outside world. However, I had begun to take the bit between my teeth and strike out on my own. Looking back, I am often well able to appreciate the dilemma of some of our modern students, who find themselves unable to support the assumptions of the social system under which they live and thus remain in a state of suspension. This was my own state of mind in 1915, and for a time I felt very much alone with my dilemma.

I had a small amount of money saved in a post office account. I said that I would go up to London and live and study. I do not now remember how it came about that I got entry to University College, to work under Professor Prior in French. My father gave me an allowance, and Girton, later, a small grant. As I took a typical small, cold room in Torrington Square behind the British Museum, I swelled with pride at the thought that this was just what Ann Veronica would have done. I owe to Professor Prior the suggestion that I pursue my interest in the eighteenth century and look at the *Treatise on Pleasant Sensations* by Louis Jean Levesque de Pouilly and his relation to Lord Bolingbroke.

My attachment to the B.M. Reading Room is something that I find hard to describe, it resembles that of a lover. The silence, the smell of old leather, the circle of massive catalogues in the centre; your shiny black desk, where you could be utterly alone with your thoughts or commune with the thoughts of men and women long dead, yet speaking to you, individually, with perhaps a new meaning and a new voice— how can I tell what that great library meant to me, as other great libraries must have meant to other scholars? The lofty dome, the roundness, contributed to the magic. You could walk to a shelf and find that you were not where you expected to be, as if in a maze; at times it symbolized the round world itself, and seemed to contain the whole of its wisdom, assembled for your pleasure. I began to visualize the book that I meant to write on the movement of thought in eighteenth-century France. It was a time to take stock of things; a momentary refuge in time of war.

Playing Ann Veronica was not very comfortable in winter in the bitter cold of my Bloomsbury room; a scuttle of coal was not cheap, and the fire was apt to be cheerless. Only female visitors could be received, or my landlady would have turned me out. I would eat my breakfast quickly and then hurry to the warmth and fug of the B.M. library. Sometimes I made my way through the vast Egyptian and Assyrian effigies to lunch at the small inexpensive restaurant, where I first made the acquaintance of Stanley Unwin, who came in from his nearby office. As I remember him then, he was tall and gangly, red-haired and red-bearded, rather like Shaw. When I saw him briefly in his office in 1958, both hair and beard were white, and he seemed to have shrunk. But he had lost none of his shrewdness as a publisher.

Those who experienced only the Second World War may find it odd that life went on so normally in London in 1915–16. The difference, of course, was that there was virtually no bombing, and all the horrors took place in Belgium and France. I did personally experience two minor scares; I saw the first daylight raid in London as I was crossing Trafalgar Square, and one night heard what was unmistakably a Zeppelin overhead when I was at Sutton. On the first occasion I went to see my father in his office, finding, to my amazement, that all and sundry were being ushered in to take cover, without regard to filling in the usual forms required.

University College was a lively place and did not entirely lack men students, in spite of the war. There were the medicals from University College Hospital over the way, some theological students, and some not physically fit. I got involved in the Dramatic Society; in the short space of time that I was there we produced the medieval morality *Noah's Fludde*, the *Countess Cathleen* and *Prunella, or Love in a Dutch Garden*. Lack of men gave me the joyful opportunity of playing the minstrel Alleel in the *Countess*. Jane Joseph, a Girton friend, who was studying with Gustav Holst, wrote some eerie haunting music for the songs I had to sing:

> Impetuous heart be still, be still,
> Your sorrowful love may never be told . . .

'Gussie', as Jane called him, himself came to the performance and thrilled me with his comment that I ought to take up acting professionally.

My mother, who was now lodging with me in a more comfortable house in Torrington Square—my father was on war business in India—

performed a remarkable feat of patience and endurance by lengthening our proscenium curtains there where they hung, which involved crawling along the stage floor.

Maria Winska, studying in London at some of Professor Karl Pearson's lectures at University College, had a room in the same house as myself, but, for a time, she seemed to have disappeared. Suddenly she arrived in the University College Refectory where I was having lunch, exclaiming 'O Dora, Dora, what shall I do? I am arrested!'

'You don't look very arrested to me, wandering around like this,' I said. It seemed that at an au pair job in the country, police had swooped on her, taking all her possessions and not letting her for a moment out of their sight. When they arrived in London, they simply told her to report to Scotland Yard at 4 o'clock. I could not desert her: after a trek to Chelsea seeking help from Josiah Wedgwood M.P. who, unluckily, was not at home, we turned into Scotland Yard, when I realized that we had been shadowed.

Summoning all the dignity I could, I explained my identity and protested on my friend's behalf. But I had to wait anxiously while they took her away, until presently I was invited inside. In a large office Maria was seated on a chair in their midst, looking very small indeed. Behind a very large desk sat an impressive, high-ranking police officer; standing each side of him were a Red Tab from Army Intelligence and someone from the Navy. Sundry policemen stood about, one taking notes, another on guard by the door. Maria, they told us, had met at some party a man posing as a modern Scandinavian artist, who was in fact a spy. They were now satisfied of Maria's innocence, she was free to go. 'But what,' said poor Maria with some courage, 'shall I do if I meet him again?'

'We do not think that that is at all likely.'

On this sinister note we thanked them and took our leave. Recovering from the shock, we had a good laugh. Indeed Maria confessed that she had nearly laughed at my absurdly dramatic entry on the scene: 'O Dora, you came in like a Queen!' She had been cross-examined about formulae in her Karl Pearson lecture notes, which—with what we two impudent young women considered lamentable ignorance—the trained experts had taken for a code. My mother was convinced that, in our absence, a man had watched the house all afternoon. To me this incident was an early and salutary lesson in how easily secret agents put two and two together to make five, thus reaching stupid and dangerous conclusions; as also of the propensity of those in authority to take sledge-hammers to crack nuts.

After years, I heard from Maria again. From South America she sent me her photo, looking very Spanish in a shawl, and press cuttings describing her as an 'escritora' of talent. Bless her.

Other friends of mine from Cambridge, pacifists who refused military service, were in more serious trouble. The tribunals mostly failed to exempt them; they were called up and then perhaps refused to put on military uniform. One of these, George, had numerous adventures, though I was not personally involved. My father, who was not unsympathetic, would at times ask me humorously, in the phrase from *Three Men in a Boat*, 'Tell me the worst, what has happened to George?' One day I found a policeman at the door of the house in Torrington Square, talking to the landlady.

'Ah, here is the young lady,' they said. The policeman asked me if I knew where George was.

'Good Lord, no,' I said, 'he is in prison'—which was the last I had heard about him.

'Is he?' said the Law in a menacing tone.

'You don't mean to tell me that you have let him escape?' said I. Since this was just what had happened, it took me some time to persuade the copper that I knew nothing about the affair (his severity perhaps due to the levity with which I had laughed at the law). Soon after, I received a note to lunch with George at some obscure restaurant, to which I repaired to warn him to keep away from me for his own good. With the help of his girlfriend he was on the run for a time, but in the end himself decided to go back to gaol.

At Cambridge my friend Dot Wrinch had another year to go. Through her I had news of what was going on in the University. Russell, who had now declared himself no longer a Liberal but a Socialist, and whose activity with the No Conscription Fellowship had earned him an admiration amounting almost to worship among many of the young, and a corresponding contempt and hatred from the old, was prosecuted for a leaflet he had written on behalf of the pacifists, and fined £100, which he refused to pay. Young men of military age were especially grateful to him since he was over the age at which he could be called up. In default of the fine, his goods at Trinity were seized, but his friends bought them up and put them in store. The War Office now took the comical step of restricting his movements, thus forbidding him to go anywhere near the coast; Trinity College took away his lectureship.

Russell shook the dust of Cambridge from his feet and went to stay part of the time with his brother, Earl Russell, who was then in Gordon Square, Bloomsbury, and also with the group at Garsington, in the lovely old manor house of Lady Ottoline Morrell and her husband Philip, who was an M.P. and had, almost alone in the House, spoken against the war. In Lady Ottoline's memoirs* are passages describing Russell's desperate emotional state on 4 August, how he had walked up and down with Ottoline behind the British Museum, quarrelled all along the Strand with George Trevelyan, found to his horror that A. N. Whitehead, with whom he had written *Principia Mathematica*, and Mrs Whitehead were now war-like, as were Gilbert Murray and

* *Ottoline*, ed. Robert Gathorne-Hardy (Faber, London 1963), pp. 265 ff.

H. J. Massingham (Editor of *The Nation*). These were all Liberals, hence perhaps the dramatic change in Russell's political allegiance. He was to find new friends in Fenner Brockway and Clifford Allen, and, at this time, in Miles Malleson and his wife Lady Constance. Miles's first play, *Black 'Ell*, was anti-war; his pacifism and that of his wife earned them lack of opportunity in the theatre. But we pacifist sympathizers flocked to a superb performance of *Trojan Women* at the Old Vic, in which Lady Constance (Colette O'Neill) played Helen of Troy, and Sybil Thorndike, as Hecuba, shook me to the core.

By contrast, H. G. Wells had published *Mr Britling Sees It Through*, and was writing pro-war articles, in one of which he was contemptuous of conscientious objectors, and referred to them as feeble, bloodless, and lacking in vitality. I was angry that a man whose ideas and imagination I had admired so much, should write what seemed to me arrant drivel on this subject. At my desk in the British Museum I wrote to explain to him that such pacifists as I knew were not at all feeble, but quite as vigorous and red-blooded as those who went to war, that to be a pacifist required a high degree of courage, and such men should not be derided as cowards. Much to my surprise, H.G. replied to me in his own small, neat handwriting, said that he was interested in what I had to say, and invited me, if I should be in the neighbourhood, to come and visit him at Easton Glebe, Dunmow. I pondered a great deal about this and wondered if the invitation was really meant. Then, one very cold Sunday, when it was particularly dismal in my Bloomsbury room, my mother being then back at Sutton, I decided to make the pilgrimage and took a train, as I thought, for Dunmow. Unfortunately there were no Sunday trains on the branch line from Bishop's Stortford. Having embarked on this enterprise, I knew that I would never have the nerve to start again if I gave up now. So I set out to walk to Dunmow.

It began to snow, but the going was not bad and I finally arrived in the afternoon at the door of Easton Glebe. My idea had been to make just an afternoon call and then withdraw. The whole expedition was, of course, quite crazy, but the chance to meet a writer whom one admires is too tempting to resist. I had no idea what I would do to get back, since there were no trains, but supposed I might find somewhere to stay the night. Naturally, H.G. and Jane were dumbfounded, but for this very reason made me genuinely welcome. My embarrassment was so great that I doubt whether I made my points about conscientious objection with any coherence, or indeed, whether we discussed this question at all. First impressions of Jane and H.G. are vivid: Jane, with her freckles and soft brown eyes, her gentle manner, which none the less conveyed that she was the pivot and background of the running of the household, an efficient and gracious hostess. And in H.G. I met that humorous twist of the lip under the short moustache, the quizzical glance from impudent blue eyes, to which a lift of long lashes gave an almost triangular shape; that challenging air of the intellectual pugilist who esteems mankind muddle-headed and incompetent, but is ready to take on any sparring partner worth his salt.

The Wells's taste for modernity showed in the décor of the house; the long lounge had what seemed to me golden walls on which were electric candles in sconces, Regency style, and there was a pianola in a central position. It began to snow heavily; Jane looked out and said that under no circumstances must I go that night. Though we disagreed over pacifists, I was somehow reassured about H.G. by this encounter; I did not meet the family again for some years.

During this summer of 1916 Dot Wrinch rang me at Sutton to ask me to go for a weekend walking tour with her, Bertrand Russell and Jean Nicod, one of his best pupils. Russell, as I later learned, took great pleasure in long walks, and he used to go with his friends on the Continent. As he was not now allowed near the coast, the idea was to walk over the downs near Guildford, spend the night at Shere and go back by train to London on Sunday evening. Russell would take us to lunch on Sunday with his friends Bob and Bessie Trevelyan, who lived in that neighbourhood.

Dot joined the three of us in the train at Surbiton, carrying a large basket of very fine strawberries from her garden. The three mathematicians talked some shop while I walked silently, then they switched to philosophical discussion. After a sandwich lunch on top of Merrow Down we set fire to the empty strawberry basket. As it burned this served as a lesson on the changes in the appearance of things, and Russell's remarks about the table in *Problems of Philosophy*. Talk moved to the war: Russell deplored the unshakable strength of chauvinism and, turning to me, said suddenly: 'I am sure that you have, for instance, the utmost admiration for our great British Navy?' This was the time when the submarine menace was much in people's minds. The challenge gave me a jolt, I laughed and said that, well yes, I supposed that I did.

Russell began to tell us with emphatic repetition about the characteristics of Bob Trevelyan 'with whom we are lunching tomorrow' and his wife, and what we should or should not do in their presence. This was just in fun; and for Dot and me 'with whom we are lunching tomorrow' became for ever a tag we applied to Bob the poet. Russell took charge of our route, indicating short cuts to Shere, while Dot kept whispering to me that she was quite certain 'our dear Bert' was entirely wrong and we were in fact heading for Gomshall. Meantime I was observing him with Jean Nicod, a very brilliant young man, French and part-Russian, who would soon have to return to France and inevitably become liable for military service. Tall and slim, Nicod had a shock of very fair hair, very blue eyes, an extremely prominent nose, and a most pleasing large mouth from which issued careful slow judgments, often beginning with, 'We-ell you see . . .' By the side of Bertie Russell, climbing over the short grey turf on the slope of the down, I took stock of that profile which was to become so dear and so familiar to me for more than fifty years. The thick and rather beautiful grey hair was lifting in the wind, the large sharp nose and odd tiny chin, the long upper lip were outlined against the sky; of middling height, lean and spare, he moved with impetuous energy, but jerkily, not with the grace of an athlete. I noted later how his broad but small feet turned outwards; I used to tease him about them. My first impression was that he was exactly like the Mad Hatter. This reflection of itself indicated something beyond the ordinary human quality about him. T. S. Eliot had noted the faun-like element when he wrote: 'You see he has pointed ears, he must be unbalanced.' Great mathematical philosopher or not, here was also a mischievous sprite, enchantingly ugly, and this was how he first appealed to me, by that intuitive awareness which is the way we do on sight apprehend one another.

My conscious thought was of a man who must be much in need of sympathy and affection; he was being persecuted for his views and lonely, he had a gallantry that took chances and a spirit that tilted at windmills, both qualities which, in spite of better counsel, always compel my admiration. Neither then, nor later, was it the world-famous genius in Bertie Russell that I loved.

We landed up that evening in a tiny inn at Gomshall, where we sat by candlelight in a small parlour on our own. One fragment of our conversation had bearing on the future. Russell, prodding and entertaining as always, asked us what we most desired in the world. Nicod, who felt himself plagued with a very sceptical disposition, said he thought that he would like to be really absorbed and caught up in some great belief or cause; Dot, I think, also hoped that she would find something entirely absorbing to which to devote her energies. Conscious that my choice was a bit banal, but speaking with sincerity, I said that I supposed I really wanted to marry and have children. Russell took me up on this at once. Did I mean really marry, did I think marriage important? No, I said, not in the conventional sense, I had concluded that there was a good deal wrong with the concept of marriage and its laws.

In the train Nicod began to ask Russell's advice. He was in love, he said, with a young woman in France, and he could not make up his mind whether he ought to marry; there was the war and there was also the doubt whether marriage would interfere with his concentration on his work. Russell elicited just a few facts about the lady in question, that she was also a student and so on, and then whole-heartedly advised Nicod to marry her. After we had left Nicod, crossing Waterloo station, and by now less shy of Russell, I asked him how he could possibly advise Nicod to marry a girl, when he knew nothing whatever about her. 'When I am asked for my advice,' he said, 'I find out what the person is going to do anyway, and then advise him strongly to do just that.'

The war dragged on, life grew more grim and drab as the ghastly stalemate and sacrifice of young lives in France and Flanders continued; the submarines were taking a toll of our ships which was causing very grave anxiety. The allocation of food was not so well done as in the second experience of wartime blockade of our island; people began to feel the effects of the loss of essential fats and other necessities. When I saw my two clergymen uncles in the latter stages of the war, I was shocked to see how these rosy, well-covered men had shrunk. At that time I myself began to get tonsil trouble and a feeling of weariness; all of this contributed to general depression and debility, an underlying cause of the severe flu epidemic which raged when the war ended.

For me, however, in 1917 came a period of respite. Severe loss of food ships was one threat; a still worse one, from the point of view of fighting the war, was the sinking of the tankers bringing oil. By May and June 1917 these losses had swollen to terrifying proportions. America now came into the war. Accordingly a special mission was planned to ask the American Government to re-route some of their tankers across the Atlantic. My father was appointed its head. He felt a special duty in the matter for reasons which he explained to me.

In 1913, when he was at the Admiralty, the decision whether the ships of the Navy should convert to oil-burning had to be taken. The advantages were obvious—no filthy coaling, and also greater speed. There was one great snag: could we be certain of oil supplies in time of war? This was the problem that Winston Churchill, then First Lord of the Admiralty, put to my father. It was on my father's advice that shares in what was then Anglo-Persian Oil were bought by the Government. My father may thus be regarded as one of the founders of what is now the great empire of B.P., but I have my doubt whether he would have approved of the way it has developed.

No one had adequately foreseen the submarine menace; thus, in 1917, a Naval engagement could result in our ships finding no oil at all in the ports to fill their bunkers.

My father had an able personal assistant, but, in view of the submarine menace, he felt that he could not press her to accompany him to New York. He asked whether I, with a young woman who had been at school with me, would go. I was in a quandary. Anti-war feeling had been growing within me, I doubted if I would be doing right to undertake work in support while many pacifists were suffering for their beliefs. At the same time, things had not been going very well with my love affair. Completely forgetting what Russell had said to me about his practice when giving advice, I screwed up my courage to go and consult him. I saw him at his brother's house in Gordon Square, on the walls of which, as he once related with glee, some enemy had scrawled the words, 'That fucking Peace Crank lives here', a statement whose accuracy in every detail he considered beyond dispute. With his usual skill he drew me out to explain my doubts and my personal problem and then said that of course I must go to New York. Dot Wrinch told me later that she asked him how he could advise me to undertake war work, to which he replied: 'She is not, like us, fully convinced about the war, but, if she goes to America, she will find out what she really thinks.' In which he proved to be dead right.

My father, my former schoolfellow Gladys and I, with Robert Waley Cohen, representing oil interests, and his two women secretaries, set sail early in August 1917 on the Red Star S.S. *Lapland*. A thoughtful Government had given Gladys and myself each a dress allowance of £30: I could not have afforded any clothes for special occasions. Apart from stewardesses, we four were the only women on board. Crossing the Atlantic, unless on urgent business, was restricted, especially for women. We travelled in convoy and were never allowed to be one moment without our lifebelts beside us. Yet life on board was lively enough; among a mixed company of British and American businessmen and some Service officers, none of them, of course, quite young, we women had a scarcity value. I found myself the recipient of witty compliments and toasts at the dinner table. One sophisticated American businessman, lifting his glass to me, said: 'This young lady has a most interesting past ahead of her.' 'None of us will have anything at all ahead of us, unless we reach New York safely,' I retorted. Inevitably this anxiety underlay our gaiety and was in part the cause of it. At night I did sometimes wonder if my life, scarcely begun, was to end under the waters of the Atlantic.

On 5 August my father presided at a joint American-British dinner, the third anniversary of the outbreak of war, in which America had now entered. He was an excellent after-dinner speaker; he recited a poem he had written for this occasion, honouring America's devotion to the cause of liberty.

As ever, the Navy came first in my esteem: my constant companion was a Captain of the Merchant Service, transferred for war purposes to the Navy. He had been blown up by a submarine in the Mediterranean, though he and his crew had managed to get their ship to port. He told me that he had come to himself to find his men in the water and had sworn at them roundly for daring to leave the ship without their Captain's permission. He was the kind of daredevil who could have been a pirate. At this particular moment he was still convalescing from injuries received and had meanwhile been sent on a mission, into whose nature it was evidently improper to enquire. He was amazing good fun. We explored together almost every part of the ship, lugging our beastly life-jackets, laughing and discoursing about our views on life. It was unusual in those days for a man who had traditional and conventional ideas about women to meet one of the sex who was young, good to look at, but withal one of those bluestockings from Girton, with decided notions about women's rights and, into the bargain, outspoken in her advocacy of greater sexual freedom and aversion to marriage.

Since we found ourselves in agreement on most, if not all, of these subjects, the Captain and I were very partial to one another. He did me the honour to take me at my word, and one night, minus life-jackets, in mid-Atlantic, on the top deck and a folded heap of sailcloth, under a bright moon and scudding clouds, he took my virginity. In wartime life was made for living.

For the first time I saw the famous New York skyline as we came into harbour after a voyage untroubled by the submarine threat. In New York I suddenly burst out laughing in the taxi; there, walking in the streets, were men in the hats, suits, shoes, which I had so far seen only in films and in some way had never associated with real people. It took me a few days at least to believe that Americans were real and not part of some show.

It was great fun living in a suite on the seventeenth floor, and eating from tables wheeled in by waiters such food as we had not seen for some time. In practical ways Gladys and I were a help to my father; the way that we took to the gaiety of New York in the evenings must have been less agreeable to him. Plenty of our social engagements, of course, were official and for my father, including us only as his accessories; the Standard Oil men were lavish in entertainment and desirous of making a good impression on the British emissary. Their purposes, as we were to discover, did not entirely coincide with ours and, on some occasions, there would be a confidential whisper in my ear: 'What your father does not understand, dear young lady, is . . .', to which I would listen very attentively and then tell my father just what I thought they were up to. Once a box of exquisite underwear arrived mysteriously for me at the hotel; I returned it saying that it must be a mistake, and, when it came a second time, returned it firmly once more. My father had taught me very early that Civil Servants did not accept gifts; he himself at home would even send back braces of pheasants, no matter how 'high' they might be.

Our office was on Fifth Avenue at the British War Mission under Lord Northcliffe. I had told my father when agreeing to go to New York, that I had no desire to meet and shake hands with Lord Northcliffe, of whose politics I disapproved. On our first day at the office a good-looking, middle-aged man came in, bade us welcome and shook hands with us all—Northcliffe himself! We did not, in fact, see much of him. His eccentricity, which led to his recall, was already in evidence. On one occasion in the New York office he came in to warn Gladys and myself against 'careless talk'. 'There are persons,' he said in a mysterious, emphatic and pompous manner hard to convey, 'even in this office, who will report *everything* that *you* say and *everything* that *I* say, both to Washington and to London.' No doubt I owe to him the not very welcome M.B.E. with which I was decorated for my services in crossing the Atlantic on this mission at a time of danger.

New York was then in its heyday; a young woman in her early

twenties coming, as I did, from a country near desperation after three
years of war, could be forgiven for her astonished delight in the absurd,
coloured, changing lights of Broadway, the affluence of the shops.

A corollary to all this gaiety was not so pleasing. Having just come
into the war, the Americans were going through their time of bally-
hoo; in the streets flag-wavers were recruiting, or making strident
appeals for investment in war stock; troops marched and bands played
'Over there, over there'—all of this I would watch, grimly thinking
that they none of them knew what they were in for, nor did they guess
what our people had been enduring.

My father's task was to get those in authority to give the aid that
was urgently needed, so far as he could without revealing secret
information. We wrote to appropriate departments and to the office
of the President himself. We were referred to the official Petroleum
Executive. When we examined the names of the gentlemen members of
this body, it transpired that they were all oil men from one corporation
or another, Standard Oil predominating. We met A. C. Bedford,
President of Standard Oil, and with him visited Kansas City that my
father might speak publicly on the crisis, which, however, Mr Bedford's
speeches played down.

Reading press reports, my father exploded to me in private: 'Here
am I,' he stormed, 'trying to get these people to economize, to share
supplies and hardships with us, and now I read a speech by that fellow
Bedford telling the public they can have all the "gasoline" they want
and more!' I remarked to him that, to judge by our experience, the
assertion by socialists that governments were controlled by capitalists
seemed to be a statement of literal truth. In the back of my mind were
lurking the words spoken to me by the American Professor in the Harz
mountains: that there would come a time when the British Empire
would decay and then Germany and America would be the major
powers. To me it became clear as daylight that it was a matter of
complete indifference to these oil men if all our tankers went to the
bottom; the greater our loss, the greater in the end would be their gain.
There must be, I could see, many in America to whom it would seem
an advantage if we went under in the war, and that, at any rate, since
they had come into the war now, it was because they saw advantage to
themselves in doing so, and not, as we were deluding ourselves, from
a desire to help us, their beleaguered cousins.

Indeed, it was borne in upon me that these people were not our
cousins at all. They had developed into a foreign nation, had embarked
on a way of life that differed widely from ours and that of other Europeans. I had visions of the devastating uses which, in their general
indifference to the concepts and values that guided other nations, they
might make of their power; of just how dangerous their self-confidence,
indeed, arrogance, might become. I began to think of myself, by contrast, as belonging to Europe, a notion which, interwoven with my

leaning towards pacifism, led me into compassion, no longer for only my own people, but also for our enemies. Ultimately I could only see in the whole war a criminal folly, destroying all that was best of European youth, together with those values by which we in Europe had hitherto lived. The exodus of American artists and writers to Europe in the 1920s, and the present exodus of very many more, confirms my view. Then and now, these voluntary exiles seek something which may no longer exist, for, with the destruction of that entire generation, Europe lost something which has never been fully recovered, not only what was good in our inherent culture, but the power to alter and build upon it.

The natural sequence of generations is vital: each transmits some traditions from the past, evolves and creates something new and passes on its innovations to its posterity. A serious break in this chain brings about profound insecurity, and a resultant confusion in beliefs and conduct. During that war the young were left to be taught, not by those who were their fathers, but rather their grandfathers; women were not yet fully emancipated and could offer no fresh guidance; though some of them were fortunate enough to find husbands of their own generation, who survived the battle, others were almost broken by tragic widowhood, or perforce remained single; others, again, married older men. By all these means the traditional structure of our societies, with its national rivalries, its outmoded diplomacies, its faith in wars, its patriarchal authority, which that young generation should have modified and reshaped, was carried forward into a future where it did not belong and where it was to do even more, almost irreparable, damage.

More and more conscious of a generation gap, as of the gulf between the sexes, I was distressed and unhappy now in serving the errand on which my father had been sent. I was living, perforce, among elderly men convinced of the rightness of their cause, and, incidentally, of all its intrinsic prejudices; to them I could only appear as a young woman who had got hold of some notions about the rights of her sex which were obviously absurd, and who should be treated with patronizing, fatherly indulgence. It was impossible for them to believe that I really meant what I said; impossible for me not to resent the dismissal of my firmly held convictions as trivial nonsense.

One sample of the patriarchal attitude which angered me was an incident in a New York restaurant, when, lunching with my father, I, like him, lit up a post-prandial cigarette. At this the waiter placed before him a small card on which was written: 'The lady with you is requested not to smoke.'

While my father was moving about I was not really needed; I was able to return from Kansas City to go on a private visit to the home of the Professor and his wife who had been so kind to me as a schoolgirl in Germany. Standard Oil made all provision for my journey back with their usual precision and paternal care. It will scarcely be believed that, where I had to change stations, they literally had the red carpet out on the platform for me.

It was a relief from my public duties and some of my dilemmas to spend a few days in a New England home representative of traditional America. I received a warm and hospitable welcome but, rather to my embarrassment, I found that the Professor's wife had not forgotten her suggestion that I might marry one of her sons, of whom the youngest was still available. There was nothing wrong with the idea, he was a most pleasant young man; however, I never really knew what he thought about it, because, aware that it would not do, I prevented the affair from going further by explaining to him over a dinner in New York my views about feminism and the institution of marriage.

Presently our business took us to Washington, where I found the oppressive heat unbearable; we were also in Ottawa, and bidden to lunch with the Governor-General, the Duke of Devonshire. I have a recollection of the Service gentlemen at the Ottawa luncheon; why are aide-de-camps always such large persons, clad in khaki, booted, belted, red-tabbed, intimidating? At table someone with a little indulgent teasing turned to me and said, 'Perhaps this young lady would give sixpence to a starving German?' The young lady said that she would. There was a momentary silence, then some 'haw-haws', and they spoke of other things.

For some time I had made it plain to my father that I must now go home and return to my researches. Presently Northcliffe was to be recalled and my father appointed Head of the War Mission in his place. Arrangements were going forward for my mother to come out to him and bring Gladys's sister to replace me. An item of news made me anxious to be back in England; it was to the effect that Bertrand Russell was being prosecuted again for something he had published against the war. I feared that he would go to prison this time: I wanted to see him and tell him what I now thought about America and the war.

One day, while preparations were being made for my departure, the phone rang from Ottawa and, as I answered it, a voice said: 'Is that the hopscotch Queen?' There could be no doubt who was calling. My friend the Captain went on to say that he had learned I was shortly going home. 'How did you know?' said I, amazed. 'We have our methods. . . .' He suggested that it would be worthwhile to come up to Canada and go home by the *Olympic*, which we discovered would sail from Halifax, Nova Scotia, doing a rapid run without convoy. It was agreed that I should travel this way.

Once on board the *Olympic* we were told that our sailing would be delayed. In the event, we spent at least ten days marooned in Halifax under a grey sky, ringed with grey rocks, heather and scrub, a dismal place to wait in. But for me this was not at all tedious, since, as I might have expected, the Captain was on board on his way home, together with two or three other Naval officers and an Admiral. No one seemed to mind what we did, even to dancing the Highland fling on the deck. The Captain got hold of a launch, in which he and I scooted across the harbour, once visiting a wreck that was being salvaged; we climbed about the slippery sloping deck, peered into the green and to me terrifying depths, then sat down to eat with the salvage men in their shed. On board in the evenings I was bidden to dress for dinner and repair after the meal to the Admiral's cabin, which happened to be designed in Regency style, and where a hand of bridge was normally played. I have always resolutely refused to play bridge, but there would usually be an odd man out, who talked with me whilst I knitted or sewed.

As I watched these men, evening after evening, in that setting, their uniforms, the gold braid, the medal ribbons, their sea-haunted, clear-cut faces, their at times formal etiquette seemed entirely appropriate and, above all, reassuring. No matter what I had come to think about the war, sea-faring men could never lose their place in my heart. I was appalled to learn that we had some six hundred Chinese on board, going to work behind the lines in France. But it would have been useless to argue about the morality of shipping this human cargo; these were men on duty in their Service in time of war, in which, until that moment, I had been equally involved myself. The voyage passed without any mishap. Soon after this, a huge explosion in Halifax destroyed much shipping and many lives.

The experience away from academic life had unsettled me and I was tempted to get into some other job. My languages were an asset, I could have gone into Reuters; also there was some Government propaganda department where I went for an interview. I was ushered into a room and shown with pride a whole lot of fake pamphlets, including false copies of *Pravda*, intended for distribution—I fled from this in horror. In my absence the excitement of the Russian Revolution had occurred, but it had only just begun to have meaning for me. I soon saw that, whatever work I undertook, I would be involved in the war effort. Yet I had to consider my financial situation, for in the States I had been earning my living and I did not feel it right to go on being dependent on an allowance from my father. The salaries offered women at that time were, however, so low that I could not conceive how I would live on them.

Now I had some responsibility for keeping contact with my brother, who had been called up, and my sister Bindy, who was at College. Mary, after working for a time on a poultry farm in Surrey, had married Harold Unwin already in 1915. So I went back to my library and colleagues at University College, and was, on the whole, contented with that choice.

I went to live in Cheyne Walk, Chelsea, at the shabby end, then the home of working artists. From here I looked out on to the power station chimneys and Turner sunsets, enchanted blue twilights, and moonlit nights when the plane trees below cast black bars and patterns on the pavement. The first real place of my own.

Bertrand Russell had been prosecuted under the Defence of the Realm Act (commonly referred to as D.O.R.A., which was later a source of amusement to us both) for an article which he had written for the *Tribunal*, organ of the No Conscription Fellowship, of which he was Editor. Writings or actions likely to 'cause alarm and despondency', or offend our noble allies, could land you in gaol. He had been sentenced to six months in the Second Division, but had appealed. I had got back from America in time for the appeal, at which Dot Wrinch and I, as well as his brother Earl Russell and friends, were present. I believe that Lady Russell (author of *Elizabeth and her German Garden* and many other popular novels) was also there. Everyone was anxious that the sentence should be reduced, or at the very least that it should be served in the First Division.

Russell had become the object of hero-worship; his wit, his outspoken intransigence gave courage to lesser objectors against the war, and provided the sign and symbol of their faith in reason and tolerance. But he himself had, by this time, become somewhat disillusioned because of the insanity of mounting war fever and the utter lack of impression which, as he felt, he and his pacifist colleagues were able to make on the public, still less on the Government. At the very moment when the Government took action against him he had been on the point of giving up an agitation which, he had begun to feel, was a waste of time and energy.

Accounts of this prosecution always seem to me to miss the essential point of it, which was that Russell went to gaol for a joke, because the Government could not bear being made fun of. As we sat there in Court the Prosecutor read out the offending parts of the article: 'If the war goes on any longer,' Russell had written, 'the American troops now over here will be used against strikers, a practice to which they are well accustomed in their own country. I do not say that these thoughts are in the mind of the Government, I think there are no thoughts in their mind at all.'

At this we sympathizers in Court burst out laughing.

'Silence, silence,' said the ushers.

'I will read it again, m'lud,' said the Prosecuting Counsel with the utmost pomposity, and did so with renewed emphasis. At which we, naturally, laughed all the louder. On a threat to clear the Court we had to subside, then to watch the rear view of 'our Bert' as he stood, very erect, hands clasped behind his back, while the Judge told him he was guilty of a 'despicable offence', but all the same reduced the sentence to First Division.

I do not remember who was the Judge, but Frank, Earl Russell, apparently told him that the role of Torquemada did not suit him, which coming from Frank, with his domineering and aristocratic air, might have impressed even a Judge. Frank acted all along in a brotherly fashion; he himself had some problems because his wife Elizabeth, originally Australian, was the widow of a German Count with whom she had had four German children. On this occasion Bertie's friends gathered round him to wish him luck and say how glad they were that at least he would not have to sew mailbags. As is well known, he began to write *The Analysis of Mind* in prison and was well served by his devoted circle of friends, who made gifts to the prison library of such books as he needed. As I was not one of this circle, I left the Court unnoticed, glad that I had been able to be there and not expecting that I would be likely to see or speak to him again. I have sometimes wondered since what would have happened if he had tried sewing mailbags; he was utterly incompetent with his hands except when he held a pen.

Life in Chelsea suited me. I had begun to abandon bourgeois styles of dress. The modern hippies are no pioneers in marking themselves out by unusual apparel; it has always been customary for 'arty' people to dress for beauty or bizarre effect rather than for fashion. We made our own clothes, at this time peasant-style pinafore dresses of vivid cretonne, over a very bright, coloured blouse. Bright colours in furnishings and decoration were replacing the patterned chintzes and soft hues of the ornate Edwardian period, rooms were no longer cluttered up with all sorts of bric-à-brac, Roger Fry's Omega workshops made amazing carpets, Heals were there with new-style painted furniture, ornamented with a characteristic bright blue, red, green or orange.

I had made the acquaintance of a Belgian artist of the modern school called Marcel, the true bohemian type, corduroy jacket, flowing tie, broad-brimmed black hat, beard and longish hair and all. I could not do otherwise than find him fascinating, and he returned the compliment. In the intervals of my own work I sat for him as a model. Our views of life and morals were in tune, we ate together in Soho, or he would make a meal in his studio, teaching me how to make a real mayonnaise by adding the oil drop by drop. We were incredibly happy in each other's company, uninhibited and at ease. In his relations with me Marcel was all that I felt a human being should be—a warm and understanding friend, quite unpossessive, imparting to such a relationship his whole personality and evoking from his friend an equivalent response. Here— and this is possibly the great gift of artists to the world—was no rift between mind and body, but a full and whole reaction to the world and those within it. Marcel had sons who were still fighting in Belgium. One night, when I was to have a meal with him in his flat, a friend came to give him the news that one son had been killed in battle. I offered to go away, but he urged me not to do so, the best comfort I could give was to share his grief and to take him into my arms. Love is spoken of mostly today as if it were no more than a sexual encounter, yet there are a hundred and one reasons why people, especially women, may give comfort and solace to another in bed.

Like so many others towards the end of the war I had the prevalent influenza which killed millions. An acute depression followed it. I recall lying alone in my flat and then, when I could summon the strength, crawling out to post letters to some friends to the effect that I wished I were dead. That so many experienced this after the illness had, I feel sure, much to do with the state of anxiety, suspense and under-nourishment in which all had been living. I had suffered not at all personally in the war; none the less I did care and was deeply affected by the tense emotional atmosphere.

Now I learned that Girton had decided to award me a Fellowship for three years to pursue my researches; in the autumn, as the war drew to a close, I went back to Cambridge as a junior don, with all the liberties and privileges attaching to that status.

4

A Career or Love?

Being back at Girton and as one of the select few who sat at High Table was marvellous. I had an income of £3 a week, which could be enough then to live on given the advantage of a room and inexpensive board at the College. I still hankered after my old haunt of the British Museum, however, so I got a season ticket to London, then very reasonable, and had an added sense of liberty and independence.

Postwar Cambridge was quite a lively place on account of the demobbed young men flocking in to take up their studies; I have already told the story of their raid on Girton demanding the women for whom they had been fighting. I resumed giving help to Ogden with the *Cambridge Magazine*, and I took on the secretaryship of the Heretics. During the year I read them a paper on the 'Abbé Pluche and the *Spectacle de la Nature*', a study in eighteenth-century Christian apologetics and the argument from design, the manuscript of which I still have and at times read and marvel at my scholarship of those days. I wrote dramatic criticism for the *Magazine*, to which Ogden maliciously appended the signature M.B.E. At some stage I went to Buckingham Palace to receive this decoration, where we were marshalled and instructed in the etiquette and the paces forward and backward, and all proceeded in a long file on red carpet like pupils at a prize-giving, to the strains of the march from *Chu Chin Chow*.

With Ogden's encouragement I wrote for the *Mag* an article on my eighteenth-century *philosophes* headed 'The Right to be Happy'. This contained my attack on the lugubrious asceticism of Christianity. Father Conrad Noel was then Vicar of Thaxted, to which living he had been appointed by the famous Lady Warwick, who had become a socialist, and had several livings in her gift. Thaxted Church had become famous for the beauty of the hangings which Father Noel had introduced, for its processions and ritual, and even for his attempt to fly a red flag as well as the flag of Sinn Fein, in which he was frustrated by the Ecclesiastical Court. He had created in his church and the village the atmosphere of pageant and supposedly merry medieval life which it was then customary for G. K. Chesterton and High Churchmen to extol. Father Noel therefore attacked me in the *Cambridge Magazine*, asserting that Christianity was a joyful religion: the ritualists held that the mournful element derived from the Reformation and the Puritans.

I contended that medieval England was not joyful, but, on the contrary, dismal and dark, menaced by a Christianity that persecuted the dissenter and the slightest indication of free thinking.

Though this controversy was interesting enough, times were changing, and with the coming of peace, the passions aroused by the Russian Revolution, and the problem of how to deal with a defeated Germany, politics rather than religion was uppermost in people's minds. This had affected my view on policy for the Heretics. One of our principles was that we were not political, purely concerned with rational discussion and, in the main, with opposition to the dogmas of the Church. In the summer vacation of 1919 I wrote to Ogden about plans for the autumn:

> *27 August.* I personally don't think that the religious fight is by any means over and done with but very few people take an interest because they are absorbed by political problems. The only sort of anti-religious propaganda worth doing is among working class people I think . . . It seems impossible to keep free of politics without being ineffective. It is like the latter period before the French Revolution, when the religious battle had been fought, they all went into politics.

On 2 September I express 'a despair about the intellectual level of people in general and the relentless approach of class war'.

Clearly I had now begun to be aware of what socialism and the problems of the working class might mean, but I still did not think of joining a party. It would have been difficult for any intelligent person not to be interested in politics. From 1917 onwards the phenomenon of the Russian Revolution occupied the centre of the stage, even in the midst of the struggle to win the war. The efforts already begun in 1917 by our War Office and Foreign Office to combat the Revolution were little known to the general public until the war ended, but they were none the less strenuous.

In 1918 the Labour movement began to stir itself about Russia: a Council for Action was formed with Ernest Bevin and Margaret Bondfield among its members; later, Bevin's dockers refused to load the *Jolly Roger* with munitions destined for the fight against the Bolsheviks. The British Establishment was in a state of nerves, apparently fearing a revolution by soldiers returning to Britain. This notion, however absurd given the circumstances in our country at the time, was none the less very much in the air. I commented to Ogden on 2 September 1919: 'I wish we could all be Bolshevik quick and have done with it.'

In addition to political events, much had been happening in my personal life which contributed to my gradual movement into the arena of public affairs. I had become used to living on my own. The next thing was to find a place definitely belonging to me, where I could stay in vacations. Obviously this had to be near the British Museum,

C

in that part of London which was a sort of Mecca or Holy of Holies to intellectuals, Bloomsbury. The coterie of artistic, literary, political and professional people who congregated there has been often described, criticized and derided. I sometimes think, when I hear wholesale condemnation of 'ghettoes', what a loss there would have been to English life and letters if this particular 'ghetto' had never existed. Roger Fry and Wyndham Lewis at the Omega workshops, Ambrose Heal in Tottenham Court Road; Clive and Vanessa Bell and Duncan Grant pursuing art in Gordon Square, Keynes nearby revolutionizing economics; Adrian and Karin Stephen at work in the medical and psychiatric field; Lytton and the Strachey clan being incisive and witty; David Garnett writing, the 'Woolves'—Virginia and Leonard—writing and publishing; later also, Francis Meynell and Vera Mendel, my friend of College days, now his wife, founding the Nonesuch Press.

It was the thing to discuss art, to read Clive Bell on 'significant form', to dissect dogmas, to question traditional morals, to follow Russell into the analysis of matter and the analysis of mind. The politically inclined joined the 1917 Club in Soho, founded obviously to mark the year of the Russian Revolution, a place to which—it was said—the aspiring unknown repaired in order to meet the 'arrived' and famous, while the latter stayed away in order to evade such encounters. Destructive as their witty sallies may have appeared to the less sophisticated, the demolition work of this group was salutary; underlying it was a very positive outlook. Bloomsbury was a cradle of socialist thought, of sex equality, of a creative and non-possessive attitude in work, living and loving; of new theories of education and of much in modern psychology. Looking back, it interests me to note how intellectual pursuits, literature and painting predominated; much as it may have been enjoyed, there was less cult of music than today, when radio and record-players have greatly widened musical appreciation, albeit also with some disadvantages. Science, in comparison with the way in which it now haunts every moment of our lives, though exerting considerable influence on the theorizing of philosophers, made little or no impact on the Bloomsburies at all.

In 1919 I had the luck to find a top-floor flat at 24 John Street, in a row of good Georgian houses, which, despite demolitions, still exists, and to the door of which I still occasionally make pilgrimage. On the ground floor was a firm with two chubby legal gentlemen like Dickens' Cheeryble brothers, who allowed me to make extensive alterations, and even paid for doing the place up according to my taste. In all my life I have never met such remarkable landlords. I had the flat decorated in the bright, fashionable colours; Marcel came with me to Heals to choose the curtain material; for a wide Heal divan I incurred my first debt—of £10—for which I had to save; I explored the second-hand labyrinths of Tottenham Court Road; I was given some surplus furniture from home at Sutton, whence a friend, Reg Black, and I moved it to

London ourselves in a hired horse and cart, with much fun on the way. A small cane-topped stool was to acquire for me a sentimental significance; this and most of the furniture is still with me; I write now seated on an old upright Heal painted chair.

In my own flat I worked and entertained my friends. Once we had a New Year's Eve party for which Marcel made hot mulled wine with long sticks of cinnamon. Dot brought with her a Greek philosophy student called Demos. We descended to the street to hear the midnight bells, where we danced, draped in sundry Oriental covers and rugs from the floor. We ran no risk of disturbing the other tenant, a solitary man who was hardly ever there; the rest of the building was offices. But the front-door bell was capricious: if it did not ring in the flat, one might, as did sometimes happen, miss an important and welcome caller. There was no telephone.

In June 1919 my father resigned from the Civil Service and became a director of an oil company. He was also at one time President of the Institute of Petroleum Technologists. His long connection with petroleum business had made him very knowledgeable in all its aspects. Possibly his war experience had made him feel, as I myself had felt, a strong desire to be free of commitment to Government. Strangely enough, as he moved into the commercial world, I was waxing more intense in my opposition to capitalism and all its works. I argued with him about this step, reminding him of all his injunctions to me about the loyalty and integrity of the Civil Servant, and implying that he was not only selling out, but letting me down. But I am sure that for him personally the move was just what he needed. It was nearly forty years since he had passed his Civil Service examination: successive governments had had out of him their full complement of work, sent him on highly responsible errands all over the globe, counted on his tireless devotion to duty in time of war. True, they had at some stage shown recognition by making him a K.C.B.; he had been bidden to Court in gold braid, cocked hat and knee breeches; my mother had been presented, looking rather a darling in her long white satin dress, with the absurd three ostrich-feathers on her head. None of this really mattered very much to either of them. What did matter was that now, with the family grown up, and my father having only a few duties in the City, they would have more time to spend together. A block of shares compensated my father for loss of pension, and would provide for my mother and, eventually, for the family.

My father was merely one among many whose brains and energy made a significant and unassuming contribution to our history. For me personally—and for whatever contribution my own life may have made —what counted most was his enlightened views, in that period, on child-rearing and the education of women. I owe to him so much of what I was able to become. As a public servant he deserves to be remembered as Head of the War Mission to New York and Director of Munitions during the crisis in the war, but still more as among the few who foresaw the vital role that petroleum was to play in future. He used to like telling his story of the man who had been told that, when unconscious, it might be possible to discover the secret of the universe. Accordingly, having to undergo a minor operation, the man kept pencil and paper ready to write down his first thoughts on coming round. When he came to decipher his shaky script, it said: 'The smell of petroleum prevails throughout.'

Bertrand Russell, who was giving lectures in London and finding himself with an increasing income from his books, was sharing a flat with Clifford Allen in Overstrand Mansions, south of Battersea Park. He was presently offered, and had accepted, a five-year lectureship in Logic and the Principles of Mathematics at Trinity College, who now thus sought to make amends for their shocking treatment of him during the war. Clifford Allen had suffered a great deal in health from hunger-striking as a conscientious objector; Russell and he had become friends.

Many of Russell's belongings and furniture were still at Cambridge in store. As I was coming and going between Cambridge and London, Dot asked me on his behalf if I would bring up a small folding table. Russell's wish to thank me personally was the reason for his sending me a message inviting me to tea. I came there shortly after he had broken his collar bone when running for a bus, thus I found him sitting in a flowered silk dressing-gown, which gave him a very eighteenth-century air. They had an efficient housekeeper, Miss Haydn, who brought in the tea, and I briefly met Clifford Allen. We were left alone and talked of my experiences in America, of politics and pacifism. Then he asked me what had happened about my young man and in general my views on matrimony. On this subject by now I felt very sure of myself. I explained my disapproval of conventional and legal marriage, my belief in free love. He put a question as to what, in that event, should be done about children, to which I replied that they were entirely the concern of the mother, and fathers should not have primary rights over them. Russell gave one of his huge laughs, with his free hand slapped his knee in a very characteristic gesture and exclaimed: 'Well, whoever I have children with it won't be you!' I felt tempted to answer, 'Nobody asked you, Sir, she said', but refrained.

This was after the end of term, and it must have been about July 1919 when he invited me to dine with him in Soho. He was entertained by my talk about my studies—at the time I was fascinated by Malebranche, who 'saw all things in God'. Bertie said that he was now going away for the summer to Lulworth with Littlewood, his colleague and a mathematician, also from Trinity, but we would meet again. From Lulworth there came a letter to John Street, to which I replied. There came another, the correspondence continued. The odd thing about it was that, whereas my letters were as learned as I knew how to make them, his were nonsensical, with sketches of himself growing fat and lazy on good food and sea air. This cannot have gone on for more than two weeks or so, when there came a ring of my front-door bell—a Saturday afternoon, and had the bell not been on its best behaviour my whole life might have been different—Bertie was in my flat. I sat down on the divan and he on that little stool beside it, one knee over the other and a hand tucked between, the other hand holding his pipe, looking more like a goblin than ever, and said: 'I had some business to do in town. I am getting no work done. Can you catch the twelve-thirty on Monday?'

'Am I to understand that this is—?' He nodded.

'But I understood that you already are in love with a lady?'

He assured me that the affair was over, it had definitely come to an end. I did not know what to say but gave a half-promise that I would catch the train.

I was in turmoil. I knew that, however much I argued with myself, I would accept the invitation. But with what intention had it been given? Was this just an idea for a summer idyll on Bertie's part? Would it just be that for me? How far was this going to interfere with my own work and plans for the future? Down there at Lulworth they were a sort of college reading party; I could take my books. In October I expected to go to Paris, having persuaded the Girton authorities that study at the Bibliothèque Nationale would be useful for my work. Deep within me I cherished a secret purpose, which was, now that I had some financial independence, to use it and some of my time to get training in singing and acting for the theatre. Apart from this, I now had my own home in London, my College rooms in Girton, all that was needed for a start on a career which did not envisage marriage, but could be both interesting and rewarding. However, I did not at that moment think that Bertie had marriage in mind; Bloomsbury people did get married, but it was part of the code to regard this as not very important in sexual ethics and certainly that was basic in my own code of conduct. I held that one entered into a sexual relationship for love which was given and received freely; this might last long, it could also be very brief. No other motive but such love, which must involve awareness and acceptance of the other's personality, was to be tolerated. My code also ruled out poaching on another's preserves, which might cause the break-up of a marriage or other existing partnership. Bertie, as I knew, was married, but had been separated from his wife for many years.

In my sense of the word I knew that I had been for some time 'in love' with Bertie. Talking with Marcel about him I had said, '*Il est dangereux pour moi.*' Marcel was the most generous of men in all senses of the word. We had never intended to try and prolong our friendship by artificial means; I took it for granted that he would presently go back to Belgium.

And for him, without a doubt, any relation that no longer held its first inclination, flavour and beauty was, by that very token, at an end. After I took that twelve-thirty train on the Monday, we hardly ever met again.

All may or may not be fair in love and war, but certainly a lover embarks on an affair of the heart much as the general does a battle: '*On s'engage, et puis on voit.*' In this mood, for no other was really possible, I travelled down to Lulworth with Bertie. I had no anxiety about allying myself with his political views or way of life. I was convinced of socialism as of the need for peace and brotherhood, incensed at the brutality of capitalism and the post-war treatment of Soviet Russia. Part of my feeling for Bertie had always been a desire to comfort and make up to him in some way for the pain that he must have suffered from the hostility of the war-maddened herd. I had been rebuked at school for standing up for those who were in trouble for breaking rules or defying authority, an irresistible sympathy with the underdog which had been with me ever since I plucked the worms from under the gardener's spade. It is worth taking a look at this impulse, which psychiatrists will perhaps call masochism, or which in women may be dismissed as nothing more or less than maternal instinct. I believe this impulse to be much more than this, something utterly primitive, partaking of the very stuff of life itself—that empathy which one living organism may feel for another* in their mutual need for survival. All of us may possess it. But the tragedy of human existence is that this primary impulse is the very one that we seek to overlay and destroy by building abstractions, cultivating rivalry, aggression and hatred. Those driven by this impulse can take no credit for what is natural and common to all mankind, unless it be for not allowing it to be stifled within them. So, in our time, some of the younger generation, crying 'make love, not war', seek to pluck the human worms from under the grinding steel of a mechanistic and to them intolerable social system.

In our approach to life values Bertie and I were in tune. I was not aware, until later, that the inspiration of his intense and vulnerable sensitivity to the human condition differed radically from mine. But from the beginning I had perceived this quality in him and been drawn to it. Only half-conscious of this, I yet knew that a light-hearted affair was not going to be easy for me, the more so as my common sense, and certainly maternal instinct, prompted me to want to protect him from his own unworldliness. I was quite convinced that he did not know how to look after himself and, more than anything, needed some woman sturdy enough to take care of him. What a trap for an unwary loving partner is the appearance of delicacy or helplessness, whether in a man or a woman!

The Lulworth reading party was a delight. Littlewood and Bertie

* In an amateur film taken at our school is a shot of one boy drawing a bow. Behind him stands another moving his arm instinctively in an identical gesture

had somehow discovered a farmhouse standing back at the head of the valley, where they could book all the rooms for the summer and also the services of the farmer's wife. The University rule was followed: after breakfast we worked or occupied ourselves without disturbing others who were working; lunch was the student's meal of bread and cheese, salads and preserves; in the evening we dined, simply but very well. Bertie and Littlewood jointly managed everything and gave all the orders. In the afternoons each of our hosts saw to the entertainment of their respective guests; talk at mealtimes was always lively and ranged over almost anything. Our two mathematicians talked of space-time; it was, they said, much further in distance to come back from the Post Office than to go there—the return journey was uphill all the way. As we were all eating blackcurrant pudding with cream, Bertie saw fit to discourse about induction and deduction, and assured us all that we had no certainty that the sun would rise tomorrow. On this, Littlewood exclaimed, 'Good Lord, then I had better have some more pudding at once,' and rushed round the table bringing his plate to Bertie, who always served the dishes and carved the joints.

One of the funniest occasions at table was when we had an American visitor, who was an enthusiast for single tax and, for some obscure reason, wanted to see Bertie on the subject. Bertie had already begun to find it difficult to cope with people who sought him on account of his growing reputation. They were apt to turn up during the summer, hence, in part, the flight to Lulworth. He had replied to this gentleman that, as he was not in London, he regretted that he would not have the pleasure of meeting him, whereupon came a telegram: 'Can call upon you Monday, Tuesday, Wednesday, etc. etc.' So a date had to be fixed for him to come to lunch; he would have to take a taxi from Wool station to do so.

We all began asking Bertie questions about this visitor. Dot Wrinch was there and when we learned that he was a millionaire—possibly an exaggeration on Bertie's part—Dot had the idea of talking to him about some mathematical research for which grants might be useful. Bertie was of the opinion that he was more likely to buy up the republic of Andorra, in order to make an experiment in taxation. Bertie also divulged that he had once met the wife of this gentleman who had sent him a small book of her poems, which were actually in the house and produced for us to read. I got hold of the book, it was full of typical poetic diction. I found one poem entitled 'To one who lies by my side', which began: 'O thou that art too full of this world's meat and wine'.

Bertie then said that, although he had been intending to switch our dinner to lunch for the occasion, we must see to it that we had a sumptuous repast. Steps were taken to get in some beer, no chance of obtaining wine—we never in fact drank any liquor on this party, being quite merry enough without it.

The day came, the sound of the taxi was heard, a succulent leg of lamb with two well-cooked veg was about to be brought in, blancmange, stewed raspberries and cream stood ready on the table, the beer was at hand. We looked for a tall beefy fellow, there entered a small, lean, grey man.

'We cannot, unfortunately,' said Bertie, as we sat at table, 'offer you wine in this remote place, but we have beer and may I help you to some lamb?'

'No, thank you,' was the unequivocal reply. 'I am a vegetarian and a teetotaller.' Littlewood saved the situation by making some joke about a 'cold white shape' which we called blancmange, thus enabling us to burst into laughter. When lunch was over we fled, to leave Bertie to talk, though I think that Dot did try her hand at making tendentious conversation.

During the time that I was there we had several visitors besides Dot: Bob Trevelyan 'with whom we are lunching tomorrow', Clifford Allen, and Jean Nicod with his wife or wife-to-be, Thérèse. We invited C. K. Ogden; when he declined I wrote to him:

2 *September.* Life is good here, so happy that we fear the gods and want to cast rings into the sea like that fellow Polycrates. We have had some great arguments arising out of after dinner communal reading. I have to read to the assembled company . . . the men have to darn my stockings to compensate for my loss of time . . . There is something grand about B, to which one responds, dropping all cheapness away. This place is rather like the Palace of Truth, when people come here their real selves show and it's sad for them if they haven't any real selves. That's the effect of country life, you've less artificial support than in town and have to have lots of mental resource . . . I do believe all this isn't going to stop easily. I told you I could not be like a Jesuit about it . . . I asked B if he was bored and he said I was not at all dull except in Kits' sense of the word.

PS to an earlier letter of 27 August relating to a recent statement by Jos Wedgwood:

B and I have a grand idea. We think all the distinguished men in the country ought to write a letter to the papers after the manner of Wedgwood, saying that they have all been driven to sexual intercourse outside marriage and in future propose to ostracise all people who have NOT. Society could not turn down the whole lot of them.

Reading aloud, unhappily superseded now by radio and television, was, at Lulworth, usually concentrated on the short stories of Chekhov, in the little green books of Constance Garnett's translation, which Bertie had brought with him. When I protested at being allocated this duty, it was Clifford Allen who offered to darn for me; he alleged that he was a very domesticated person.

A fierce argument broke out between him and Bertie over the story in which a married lady descends on her lover, bringing her pots and pans to his flat, and taking him at his word when urged by him to leave her husband, although this was, as is so often the case in such liaisons, the very last thing he really desired. Allen thought her arrival a piece of trickery on her part, Bertie that the lover was an utter cad. Bertie got so heated that he walked about the room and threw up the window to get air. Allen at that time was a very independent-minded young bachelor, Bertie perhaps was thinking that it might be enjoyable if I arrived with my pots and pans. He had asked me if I would consider marrying him, if he got a divorce; I had said I did not want to marry but was going to Paris to get on with my work. He pressed the point, swearing that, in deference to my views about conventional marriages, he would never ask me to 'grace the head of his table', which he supposed was what I feared. Another time he asked me if I did not want to be a Countess. I then became angry for I thought this argument, which offended my own code, unworthy of him. The fact that he might one day become an Earl had positively never entered my head. Once, indeed, I burst into tears and asked him not to spoil it all.

I doubt if he ever realized just what he was asking of the person I then was. He was twenty years ahead of me in age and achievement; tributes to his brilliance were already international and now being swelled by admiration for his moral courage during the war. I was a young woman of deeply-cherished modern views, just arrived at independence and now desirous of spreading her wings; afraid of entanglements, suspicious of the wiles of men who were forever scheming to drag women back into the legal, domestic and sexual bondage from which feminist pioneers were trying to escape and deliver their sisters. Nothing in my upbringing had ever put into my mind the idea of planning to make a successful marriage in a worldly sense. I knew now that I had brains above the average, acting talent, a good speaking voice, some aptitude in singing and dancing: I wanted to make something of myself and my life, and had as yet no really burning desire to have children. Above all there was the fear of committing myself to a man who, as I knew, had only now ended one affair, was rumoured to have had another, but whom, knowing what I might be capable of feeling for him, I could never love lightly. Thus I might be absorbed, swallowed up entirely in his life and never be able to become what I aspired to in my own person.

Meantime, here was good company and talk, the sea and the sky. There was a valley near the farm which I named the Happy Valley; the grass was a curious yellow-green, it matched the huge green squares on the frock that I had made out of a tablecloth that looked like a chessboard. I would go out and lie hidden in the grass, filled with my present happiness. Bertie and I spent much time apart from the company; he would hire a boat, from which we would, at sufficient distance from the shore, dive naked; we walked the cliffs talking endlessly. I reproached him for not spending more time with his other guests; he agreed that I was completely in the right about this, but he did not propose to alter his ways. Sometimes we were all together. Littlewood was a magnificent climber, and used to terrify us by standing on one leg on the edge of a sheer chalk cliff, which we named Stork Point. Bob Trevelyan and Bertie were old friends and would exchange sly digs at one another.

'This house is full of noises,' said Bob, no doubt aware of the meaning of footfalls and doors surreptitiously opened and closed at night.

'Don't you wear your ear-stoppers, Bob?' asked Bertie, equally sly and equally aware.

Jean Nicod had managed to maintain his pacifist objection and survive the war, but only at the great cost of making himself ill and unfit, since in France there was no provision for conscientious objection. His health was undermined, with tragic consequences later. Just now he and Thérèse were happy and both delightful, Thérèse fair and grey-eyed, with French charm and elegance. She and I began a friendship which lasted all our lives.

I had one serious fright. As a keen swimmer I set out to swim across the bay; Bertie accompanied me, he was also quite at home in the water. But whether from cold or over-exertion, he stopped, crawled ashore and lay there apparently unconscious. Suddenly remembering my First Aid lessons, I began to rub the insides of his limbs so as to send the blood towards his heart. He revived and was soon all right. But I was more sure than ever that he needed someone with sense to take care of him.

In the midst of my Elysian bliss a telegram arrived for Bertie. Very much embarrassed, he came to me with it in his hand. He told me that Colette (Lady Constance) was coming down and that I must go away. So it had only been an amusing summer interlude: I packed up and went.

I came to my flat, which was bare of food, in the evening when it was difficult to get any. Not that this mattered much to me in my unhappy state of mind. Nor would I go out to eat—it was Peace night, people were celebrating, singing, dancing, the whole of London alive with a merriment which I could not share. In my grief there was only one element of comfort: I would not now have to make a difficult decision, and I would soon be in Paris. But before I left, Bertie was back in London. He came to me protesting that he had not deceived me, that he meant all that he had said. He persuaded me to Debenhams, where he bought me some exquisite things which I wanted to refuse but had not the heart to do so, because I knew that this was his way of making amends, and he did not understand that I was not that kind of luxury woman. With half of me I wanted to believe him, the other half was relieved to be still free: to Paris I must go.

5

Paris

Thérèse Nicod was in Paris working for some examination, and Jean, I think, was already in a teaching post. Thanks to Thérèse, I was at once established in a *pension* in the Rue de la Santé, opposite the prison. Such *pensions* in France, which cater for students and others not well-off, have always seemed to me better than similar establishments in England. The food, though simple, was good and well cooked; your room, though bare, had the essentials: bed, roomy wardrobe, a table large enough for writing, and a chair or two. The fireplace was a pleasant feature; it was possible to get just a few small logs and make a good fire. With a spirit stove I made tea, as my mother had done in Belgium, and I acquired a taste for drinking it without milk, which was an extra bother to buy and keep. There were, and are still, I imagine, very many of these bare rooms in Paris, some looking out on to grey courtyards with trellis and ivy, where only the morning coffee and rolls are served; you eat out, have your own key and lead your own life, no questions asked.

It is possible to be desperately lonely in Paris; it is also possible to lead a marvellous life, pursuing scholarship, painting, music and sharing your ideals and aspirations at nightly sessions with a few companions in the cafés of the boulevards. Cosmopolitan, transient visitors may frequent the Rotonde and the Coupole and have in mind an evening of drinking in a bohemian atmosphere. What the spiritual climate of Paris may be today is unknown to me, what I do know is that the traffic and parked cars on the boulevards have utterly ruined the physical background which, in the past, made Paris a city no other could surpass in the means to pursue a simple civilized life.

I have an old notebook of that short period. I find that it is stuffed with quotations from André Gide and Romain Rolland, references to the ideas of Clutton Brock, Gorky—all exemplifying an intense search for some sort of humanism capable of reviving ideals and rebuilding Europe. I reject science as a means of international unity and Esperanto as a universal language, which I describe as being the same as making everyone dress alike; standardized clothing and a universal language could make all people identical, a result which some would welcome. The notes show a great mistrust of the impersonal nature of science; I was 'certain that these studies that men get their teeth into, they never get their heart into'. I hold to Gorky's view that in the literary conception man is a responsible being and not a mechanism, as science shows him, and with Romain Rolland I see writers, who formerly served reaction, as now the people who should lead and be in the forefront of the enlightenment. It is through language and literary studies that we can come to understand better other peoples and nations.

In the book are notes for a three-act play and a comedy to be called *Love by Rote*, being the adventure of a *femme savante* who sets out to love by the book and finds that it does not work out as expected. The other play dealt with the clash of new and old morals: one of the characters, arguing with her brother, says:

> There was a time when freethinkers were at pains to show that their conduct was in no way affected by their noxious philosophical opinions. Think of the 18th century freethinkers. That's not so now. We must be candid about everything. Love, we think, must be as free as thought—when it is as fiery and as compelling and as clear— that makes us upstanding and fearless and impervious to social ostracism, gives us something that is definite and disciplined—why, there's no discipline so hard as an irresistible impulse towards sincerity.

I sketched notes for a satirical musical about concepts of God. In the medieval period God was to walk about in robes with enormous skirts and trains, whilst the 'maidens' were to sing 'O to be the humble wife of a valiant knight'. Galileo figured as the alchemist, and there was to be a chorus of priests and nuns, with a ballet of devils and cherubs. In the seventeenth-century scene God was to figure as a microscopic object at the top of a shaky ladder, Malebranche below with an enormous telescope constantly focused on God; Newton perambulating with a model of the universe, making the planets go round like an old man with a child's toy; Voltaire armed with a huge scythe to make hay of the argument from design. The intelligent, amorous Marquise sang:

> No more I languish in my bower
> Or pine in lonely Gothic tower
> I'm supposed to know a bit
> Philosophers admire my wit.

Newton enters to the chant:

> Mark the noble Newton comes
> Blow no trumpets beat no drums
> He blows his own trumpet best—

The Bibliothèque Nationale was not neglected; I pursued my studies there day after day. But I also found a master to train my singing voice, and would go to hired practice rooms which contained a piano. I would be found at two in the morning watching a dress rehearsal at

Copeau's Théâtre du Vieux Colombier. And I persuaded Michel St Denis, then one of the young producers at the theatre, who was later to work for the BBC during the Second World War and produce at the Old Vic, to let me attend its training classes. Copeau aimed at bridging the gulf between audience and actor, creating not illusion, but rather a harmony that abolished the critical factor. Only when this was achieved, in his view, could it be said that there was good acting. Realism, in his opinion, had the effect of intensifying illusion, rather than the reverse, by creating a separate, rather vulgar world. Copeau insisted that there was only one way to interpret a masterpiece. If you did not find the way, you would not be producing that play but some other. A theory that, perhaps, would scarcely appeal to some producers of our time.

In spite of political problems, Paris of the 1920s was a place fertile in artistic endeavour; in consequence it had perhaps more than the usual influx of foreigners. There were the Russian émigrés, and English and Americans escaping from what they felt to be a philistine atmosphere at home. One attraction may well have been the falling franc, which made it very economical for those with stronger currencies to maintain themselves in France. This proved an advantage for me, as for others; I was able to do and buy more than at home. This was the time of Sylvia Beach's shop, Shakespeare and Cie, which I visited but did not frequent; there was also the shop for classical Greek garments opened by the Duncans, and one would see Raymond, Isadora's brother, walking in sandals and handwoven robes. Many of their products were very beautiful.

However much I filled my days with work and varied activity—and I even began teaching myself Russian—the central problem of what to do about my relation to Bertie remained. My letters to Ogden, who was the only person in whom I confided, are the best indication of my state of mind. Soon after arriving in Paris on 26 October 1919, I wrote:

> I wonder if I can ever tie myself up. One minute I think I never can and the next that, after all, I waste my time and that I must yoke myself to something serious sooner or later, but it's jolly to be like the wind that bloweth whither it listeth, isn't it?

Both Bertie and I were aware that the scandal of a divorce might lead to his being unable to take up the appointment now offered by Trinity, to start in 1920, and that it would certainly mean for me the loss of my Fellowship and academic career. He was pressing for a decision and we had argued bitterly. In November my letter to Ogden says:

> How I wish I could see you. The position is that if I will only say yes and take on doing secretarial work for him so that he has me with him most of the time, the fracas will begin at once and he won't come

back [i.e. to Cambridge] as I don't imagine they will swallow that as well [as his political views], will they?

I got him to accept sans phrase for the moment after we had the row, as I am desperately afraid of the responsibility of preventing his coming back in case I shouldn't find a tie easy to bear. Then he'd reproach me, quite rightly, too. But if I won't play the dutiful wife, then he'll do nothing open unless there is a child coming, and would really prefer a complete break. Seen from his point of view that is perfectly reasonable. He is no longer quite young, and he has had enough of feminine caprice . . . is determined not to have any more nonsense. But I AM young, and the kind of slavery he wants me to accept is what he, at my age, would have emphatically denounced. I am perfectly willing to accept marriage with children, and he'll either have to risk marriage with the hope of having them, or else having one illegitimate and marriage after. If I don't have children, I must do some kind of work of my own. He wouldn't mind that if it did not interfere with my bottlewashing for him, but of course it probably would. I've offered to give up my present work and do something else to make a continuance of an irregular relation possible without interfering with his return. But he hates an irregular relation and wants absolutely surrender or a complete break. Either would, of course, damage me considerably in spirit. I do want to try and do what is best for his work and him without destroying myself.

Bertie had told me that the difficulty that had arisen between him and Colette was that because of her stage career she did not want to settle down to having a family. This was, in those early days of women's emancipation, a frequent cause of dissension between lovers. Women almost invariably got dismissed from posts on marriage; it was commonly held that a woman must choose between marriage and a career; men themselves, and Bertie was no exception, could not divest themselves of the old notion that to 'have and to hold' a wife in economic dependence was the right and proper course for any man worthy the name. What is more, sexual freedom for women was so condemned that any woman known to live freely would find it impossible to get work, except in a very few professions.

I had resolved from the start to do nothing that might prevent us having a child, the more so since he attached such importance to this. He was, of course, at that time of life when he wanted to take a wife and settle to a more domestic existence, natural enough at the age of forty-five. But to me, equally naturally, he seemed much older than he really was; I used to reckon how long it would be before he was 'really old' and I would have to spend my time in looking after him. In the light of subsequent events this is extremely funny.

Bertie was anxious to talk with Wittgenstein about the latter's philosophical theories. Since Wittgenstein was an enemy alien, he was not permitted, in 1919, to come to England. They therefore made an arrangement to meet at The Hague shortly before Christmas. Bertie asked me to join him there for about a week. I spent some interesting hours in the library at The Hague while Wittgenstein and Bertie argued in the hotel sitting-room. I do not know quite what the young man who accompanied Wittgenstein did with his time; he was a vague, shadowy figure, who spoke little, even at mealtimes. One day, on coming in to the warmth of the hotel from the biting wind, I found Bertie and Wittgenstein, one on each side of the table in our sitting-room, looking at a sheet of paper on which were two or three heavy pencil lines. Laughing, I asked them if this was all they had to show for a morning's work.

'Ah,' they replied, 'we have been discussing whether there are two things in the world, or three.'

This was the first time that I had met Wittgenstein, though not the last. In spite of all the learned comments that I have read about his work, I have never been able to think of him as other than the eager curly-headed—almost—boy, with the winning, shy smile, who would, none the less, argue most persistently, stretching out a hand, like a young child, and stabbing the air with his forefinger to emphasize his words.

These were pleasant, luxurious days, eating well in a warm hotel, and Bertie and I had some time to ourselves and a day or two left over after the others had gone. I had bought for Bertie a small Christmas present, for which I had gone to the expensive shops in Paris, St Honoré or even Rue de la Paix. It was a folder for notes, made of black brocade, with a pattern of golden birds. As I set out for The Hague I had realized, to my horror, that the birds were, quite unmistakably, STORKS! I just hoped that he would not notice. These symbols had nothing to do with it, but the visit ended with a scene about what storks represent which shook and distressed me unbearably. Bertie again pressed for a promise to marry, on which he would feel it worth while to seek a divorce. When I still refused, he told me angrily that if I cared for him I had no right to deny him children, and that I 'knew perfectly well' that, if he did not start to have them soon, he would be too old as they were growing up. I thought this totally unfair, since, after all, he could have had children during his first marriage if he wanted them so badly. Moreover, I had made it perfectly clear that I was, all the time, running the risk of a pregnancy, just because I thought it important that a man of his calibre should not be childless. To me the demand to have children *within* marriage was irrelevant. Curled up in an armchair he acted like a small boy in a tantrum, which, though it made me miserable, also made it more impossible to give way. There was no decision.

To make matters worse, he was departing to join Clifford Allen and Colette for Christmas at Lynton. My train left later and I had the unpleasant experience of being treated contemptuously by the hotel staff when I was unprotected. I was thankful to reach the French frontier, where the Customs officer grinned amiably and said: *'Rien à déclarer, belle aux beaux yeux?'* He might have said it to anyone, but at that moment it was balm to my wounded heart.

To Ogden I wrote:

December 1919. I am really very unhappy because I do not want to get married and yet I am given no peace. And I am too much in love to do my work the better for it. I must give up my Fellowship and take some job in which reputation does not matter and in which the work isn't damaged by affairs of the heart. I simply must go on earning my living unless infant turns up. Economic independence is my last weapon against him. He IS a terror. Rages like a small boy in a temper when I refuse to marry him. Og, do you think I could bear country life and a domestic tyrant even with a family? Am I an utter rotter not to put him entirely before myself and spend time making life easy for him? . . . I want to try the stage, not dilettanti new shows, but touring the provinces, hard work and no nonsense. It is the only thing my heart has ever been in, other than love affairs, and the more I have tried to stifle it, the worse it gets . . . He is made for a husband not a lover. . . I am afraid of the consequences if I cut myself free of him, both to him and to me, and yet he won't take less than everything from me. If I want any life of my own I shall have to do without him. And I don't WANT to give all my life to love, whether it is in affairs or in marriage, it's indecent. If only we were certain of a child. A merry Christmas to you, dear Og, I hope you get some holiday. . .

In Paris I was now more lonely; I had left the pension for a room of my own. Thérèse was not there any more and there were times when the company and place were not so pleasant. The bonne occasionally got drunk and would skate down the row of boarders like Charlie Chaplin on board ship: with a bowl of sloppy lentils or soup in her hand and her alcoholic breath, she could be quite a menace. But even alone in Paris I was never homesick; there was always something welcoming about its grey, tree-lined streets, the cafés, the Luxembourg, the galleries, the banks of the Seine. In the restaurants and cafés, the waiters and the Madame at the till would make friends with you, and see that you were well cared for without the least subservience. There was a simple restaurant near the library to which I went regularly for lunch. When, many years later, I returned there I was recognized and greeted at once as an old friend.

Once I was taken out to lunch at the Grande Chaumière by a French professor, who, on this occasion, taught me how pleasant it was to eat oysters accompanied by Vouvray. He was, it appeared, researching in my own subject. I realized that my efforts might well be amateurish in comparison; this was one more argument for giving them up. I wrote to Ogden that I thought of 'giving Bertie the push' and launching out into a theatrical career, since this research would be done anyway. The Professor was, in fact, Paul Hazard, whose superb book on *European Thought in the Eighteenth Century* was not published until 1946, two years after his death. There may have been good reasons for withholding so enlightened a book until after the German Occupation. For me it has become a bedside bible.

With the coming of spring Bertie came over to Paris, on his way to give some lectures at Barcelona; he had invited me to come with him and have a short holiday when the lectures were finished. In the week before Holy Week we travelled south; I looked forward to this, because I had never been to the Mediterranean coast. The clear light, the sunshine, the change of landscape, architecture, vegetation, were a delight —mimosa, olives, orange and lemon trees.

In Barcelona I was fascinated by the flower-market. Either side of the broad street were great baskets of flowers, glowing with colour, sweet and scented. Cheerful black-haired women stood beside them. On Palm Sunday morning when Bertie was making notes for a lecture, I wandered off to the cathedral. Never have I seen Christ's entry into Jerusalem celebrated with such gaiety and vigour. The whole congregation held long branches of dried palm, with which we went in procession round the cloisters, behind the priests and choristers. With our palm branches we beat on the floor, then raised them to wave wildly over our heads, all the time shouting, 'Hosanna! Hosanna!' It was most exhilarating, and gave the impression of a lively and vivid religion. But I had quite the opposite impression when Bertie and I went to the cathedral at Tarragona during Holy Week and came by chance on the ceremony of sanctifying holy water and oil. By contrast with the bright sun outside, the interior of the cathedral was so dark and gloomy as almost to seem sinister. Priests stood in two rows in the chancel and performed what looked like Sir Roger de Coverley, changing places, handing a vessel resembling a copper teapot to one another, and chanting 'Ave sanctum chrisma' like a magic spell. They then began the ceremony all over again with another vessel, this time shaped like a coffeepot. Suddenly my heretical and sceptical soul, in this aura of superstition, had a great revulsion against the whole system of repression, persecution and bamboozling of the people that went with it. I felt stifled, and hurriedly went out into the fresh air.

A Professor and his wife had charge of Bertie's visit: the Señora had arranged to drive with me in an open carriage to see something of the city. This was awful. She must certainly be well known in the town and, to be seen with me, who would turn out *not* to be the famous philosopher's wife, could cause her extreme embarrassment. The awkward task of explaining matters to this very charming woman had to be faced, but this seemed to trouble her not at all. She simply smiled and patted my hand, and ushered me out to the waiting carriage. If anything, relations after this became less formal: all four of us went to a fair together, and I noted quite a glint in the eye of the Spanish Professor when he looked at Bertie and me. I realized later that their calm reaction was not really surprising, since, in a Catholic country, there must have been many people of progressive views who found themselves obliged to live outside wedlock. And Barcelona was a far from reactionary place.

From there Bertie and I took ship for Majorca, for what was one of the most exquisite brief holidays of my life. For me its mood is best expressed in the poem 'To England from Abroad' which I wrote to honour my first glimpse of the South:

> When, like the prodigal I thankless part
> Proudly to leave your fog-enamoured shores,
> Spurning your perfidies of mind and heart
> Your murk and madness; dreaming of cool floors
> Of placid marble and the constant sun
> Whose exact finger on the yellow walls
> Prints oval cypress shadows one by one—
> Then, though with colour, clarity and peace,
> The warm South fold me in her tranquil arm,
> My thoughts, poor fretful children, will not cease
> To turn to some remote old English farm
> Afar on grey hills where the harebell hides its blue,
> With hazy copses girt, and violets and dew.

Both of us were enjoying a relief, not only from work but also from the political atmosphere in England which disturbed us. Bertie had hated the war and what it did to men's minds; now the reactionary policies, which saw to it that the tremendous sacrifices of young men's lives had been in vain, distressed him still more. The Russian Revolution had excited socialists in Britain, and the war now being waged against the Russians in their hour of turmoil and starvation infuriated them. No one knew quite what was happening in Russia, and no one was being allowed to go and see. The British Government were hostile to issuing passports for this purpose and the Russians, then certainly with good reason, were cagey about whom they would allow in.

Bertie and I had planned to spend the summer together. Now, in Paris, as we sat on a bench under the chestnut trees in the Avenue de l'Observatoire, he talked impressively of his great desire to see what was happening in the Soviet Union, of how important an event this Revolution was in history. Would I consent to visit Russia with him, and make this the start of our permanent life together? He was sure that the Soviet authorities would give us a visa, which he believed could be got from a representative they had in Copenhagen. I was still not quite ready to burn my boats, but did agree to go with him on this journey. I knew that this was the decisive moment in our relationship.

6

Bolshevik Russia

While I was thinking over and making my plans for our expedition to Russia, a letter came from Bertie. It seemed that a delegation of Labour men and women were to go, with the agreement of our Government, on a visit to the Soviet Union. Clifford Allen was one of the number, and others were Ethel Snowden (wife of Philip Snowden), the trade unionist Ben Turner, and Dr Haden Guest. Bertie found that he could be included, which meant that he would have better opportunities for seeing people and places than he would as an isolated individual. It meant also that I could not go with him. He has mentioned our sharp difference of opinion on this issue, giving as his reason for his change of plan the fact that he had learned of the dangers to health, especially from typhus, in the existing state of affairs in Russia, and did not feel justified in exposing me to that risk. I do not doubt that this may have been in his mind; but uppermost, I feel sure, as I did at the time, was the thought that this was for him a chance not to be missed.

On receiving the letter I went straight to London, for the delegation were to leave almost at once. I argued really angrily with him that he should hold to our original scheme of going on our own, and together. He had urged me, I said, and on his promise I had given another. Now neither would be valid. He was obviously upset at finding how much I minded what I felt was a breach of faith. Also, he had spoken so eloquently of the need to find out about Russia that I had become enthusiastic, my mind was now all set to go, and for me this was a painful anti-climax. There was, apparently, nothing that I could do, he had arranged to go, and that was that. Defiantly I said: 'All right then, if it is possible to go without the support of a delegation then I shall go by myself.' Suddenly he said that he did not want me to be frustrated in anything I might want to do by lack of money and he gave me a note for £100. He was bound for Newcastle, to cross over to Bergen, promised to write, and then, to delay the parting, took me with him as far as Grantham on the train.

Back in my room in Paris, I seethed and fretted and found it quite impossible to do any work. Bertie kept his promise and wrote to me about their journey: they were going via Stockholm, whence they would get facilities from the Russians. Finally I made up my mind. If they could get in via Stockholm then so could I. I told my friends Miss Burt and Mlle Reverchon, and somehow it got known to a few people what I was about to do. I was taken to see the family of Captain Jacques Sadoul, who, though in Moscow in an official capacity, had defied authority by supporting the Revolution and could not return to France. The family gave me messages for him if I should see him. A Swedish student called on me early one morning—I remember him vividly with his golden hair and beard—to give me some names and addresses of people in Stockholm whom it would be safe to contact in case I needed help. I packed up everything, gave up my room, and went to London to deposit most of my luggage in my flat. Armed with Bertie's letters as evidence of my bona fides, I went on board ship at Newcastle.

On the Norwegian ship, which was carrying just a few passengers, we sat like a family at the table with the Captain. One of the passengers was an Army officer who, surprisingly, was talking about seal blubber as a food. He turned out to be Major Orde-Lees, who had been with Shackleton in the Antarctic and had been marooned under a longboat for months on end. They had eaten seal blubber and they had then made plans for feeding the starving of the earth on this nourishing substance. Oddly enough, as soon as they came back to civilization, they wondered how they had ever stomached the disgusting stuff. He was now on his way to Stockholm to demonstrate at a show before the the King of Sweden the safety of parachute jumping.

In Stockholm I made contact with some Social Democrats associated with the local left-wing journal, but this did not much advance my plan. At an hotel I found two bearded Russians and asked them for their help. They were expecting to go to England, as also at that moment was Krassin, a leading Bolshevik who was about to negotiate with Lloyd George. They laughed a good deal and said it would be much better if I came to England with them. Somehow I found out where Krassin was and rang the bell of his flat. He opened the door himself, but was, naturally, uncommunicative and clearly preoccupied. He muttered something about a Soviet Consul. I took a chance and went to the Finnish Consulate, but at the last moment, when it looked as if some financial inducement was expected, I got cold feet and did not try for a visa. This was very lucky, since it would have been almost suicide to go via Finland on account of the White Terror.

Now and then I still saw Major Orde-Lees. The day of his display arrived and he took me with him to the show, saying that it would be a pleasure to have a friend and an Englishwoman on the spot to see the exploit. This was a very odd experience. He was not at all the strong silent Englishman. Though obviously a man of great nerve and courage, he was wiry and fidgety rather than calm. I stood on the edge of a great crowd and watched the seaplane appear high above. I could see the tiny figure on one of the floats and suddenly felt very much involved, as perhaps the only person in all that company who had any personal feeling for the man about to launch into space as a public spectacle. I held my breath, I almost had to shut my eyes until the parachute opened. There were some shouts and clappings of applause. Presently he appeared beside me. That evening, in an open-air restaurant by the water, of which there are many in Stockholm, I sat with Orde-Lees and the pilot of the plane, and one or two others, dining under the umbrella of the wide-open 'chute. A good time, as they say, was had by all.

Presently I met by chance in the hotel lounge a Finn with Bolshevik sympathies, who said that if I wanted to go to Russia he could arrange it. The next thing that happened was that I was introduced to Madge Newbold, who was to be my travelling companion, and provided with a tiny passport about two inches square, made of linen, with a red hammer and sickle on it. This I was to conceal about my person. We were to get ourselves enough food for a few days, and then go back into Norway and book passage on a steamer which took tourists to the North Cape to see the midnight sun. Madge was tremendously excited, for she was a dedicated communist, the wife of Walton Newbold, well known in left-wing circles in Scotland. She was small, very thin, and pale, and looked not unlike the I.L.P. leader Jimmy Maxton. Like so many communists whom I was to meet then and later, she was totally convinced and dogmatic, willing to make any sacrifice for the cause. I liked Madge and her spirit, her courage, her endurance. But her physical strength was not enough; I think she died quite young of tuberculosis.

It was near midsummer, an excellent time for the midnight sun. We walked the decks, in the tourist role, careful of our talk. The steamer called at various ports, rounded the North Cape, came to the small port of Vardö, and then turned back. Our instructions were to go ashore at Vardö and not to re-embark, but instead to go to a house where a local paper was published and there to ask for two men by name.

Vardö was a desolate spot, treeless, with a mere sprinkling of houses, obviously concerned only with fishing. Some nets hung drearily over lines and there were also fish hung up for drying—a fishy smell prevailed.

Carrying our small cases—I also had a portable typewriter—Madge and I made our way to the designated house and asked for the two comrades. We were told that they were not there. This was a ghastly moment. Had the entire plan miscarried? What should we do, abandoned motiveless in this forsaken spot? We turned back up the village street, wondering if we had better make haste to get back on to the steamer before it sailed.

As we went, two men came up behind us; grinning, they murmured, 'This way, comrades,' and, taking our cases, they conducted us—to an hotel! Here we were to stay until called for. Our relief at being taken care of was indescribable. The two comrades explained that tactics required that they should never be 'there' when asked for.

Presently, towards evening, a lorry came by and our luggage was unobtrusively put on it among other goods. Then our guides came for us and led us down to the sea, where a small fishing smack on which we were to embark was waiting. I was amused to see that a Customs officer was checking with the Captain what went on board, and that he had a paper with the hammer and sickle on it in his hand. On board were a young fisherman and an older one with a stubble of grey beard, and gaps between his broken teeth which were revealed when he smiled at us. The young Captain was taking his two children across. There was a large Swedish woman, voluminously dressed; her name, if I recall correctly, was Kata Dahlström. The boat had a small wheel-house, behind which was a bucket which served as the lavatory. It went with a pop-pop engine. So we all set forth under the bright mid-night sun. Kata took up a position lying on top of the hatch amidships, with the two children, and Madge and I disposed ourselves somehow on the deck.

As we moved out into the open sea it became quite choppy, and we found ourselves constantly rolling into the scuppers. There did not seem much that we could cling to, unless it were Kata's skirts. I began to feel queasy and I discovered a way down into a cabin where the old seaman made me a drink of what could have been either tea or coffee.

Soon we were in calmer water and in the harbour at Murmansk, where our first sight of Soviet activity was a small vessel of war, perhaps a frigate, which was flying the red flag with the hammer and sickle. Sailors on the decks waved to us; they had just strung out their washing to dry. All seemed quiet and peaceful under the summer sun, the surroundings of the harbour not unlike those we had left in Norway. Some comrades met us as we landed and conducted us to a group of temporary buildings. These, they told us, were part of what the British intervention forces had left behind when they withdrew—a most useful contribution, as they explained with smiles. It was 21 June, the true Midsummer's Eve. We were left to rest and presently sleep, for our hosts explained that they were going out to a Midsummer party.

Next day we met the local Soviet, and speeches of fraternity and welcome were made from a small platform; there was even a small band. After every few sentences of a speech and its translation, the band would strike up the 'Internationale', in which all joined heartily. Meeting after meeting at which I was present was conducted in this way, with the 'Internationale' the perpetual theme song, sung by full-throated, rich voices and accompanied by any instruments which happened to be handy.

I thought it would be fun to have actually bathed in the Arctic Circle, which I now did, escorted most discreetly by a young Red Army man. Surprisingly, the sea was warm, but a vast swarm of mosquitos attacked unless you remained entirely submerged!

We spent at most, I think, two nights in Murmansk and then the train was ready to take us down to Leningrad, or Petrograd as it still was. We bestowed ourselves in a compartment with wooden benches, on which I was able to sleep quite well with my typewriter for a pillow. The dilapidated engine ran on wood and its boiler was stuffed here and there with sticks and cotton waste. But the train meandered along cheerfully and fast enough, and when we stopped at stations, everyone descended to get hot water for tea, which always seems to be available in this way in Russia no matter what the crisis. Once a spark from the engine began to burn a hole in the rear platform of a carriage; the comrades and we put it out with tea.

The Russian landscape flowed by with birch and pine and the lovely monasteries and churches with their white onion domes, pictures of which I had come across, when a child, in a book of Russian folktales, thus they had for me an exciting, romantic quality. How marvellous was that journey! Madge and I ate sparingly of the food we had brought, made tea, picked birch branches and set them at the open windows to cool and refresh the air, chatted and occasionally burst into song. For here we were, we had really arrived in the Soviet Union, and it all seemed so simple and natural in this world which was looked upon with such horror in the West. The country through which we were passing was rather empty, marshland and lakes appeared between the forests. But we came in the end to a junction, it may have been Petrosavodsk. At this point there was shunting about and a carriage full of Red Army men was attached to the train.

Before long three or four of their officers were in our compartment to meet the English comrades. They brought with them tea and a tin of what they gleefully told us was British jam, another leftover of our Army. One of them spoke German. There followed one of those odd conversations, in many of which I played a part during my visit. Questions were translated into German and then by me into English. The theme was always, of course, the Revolution, Marxism, and what were the English comrades doing to further the cause? What, in fact, was happening in England?

At this date the Russians were convinced, as in fact was Lenin himself, that the Revolution must spread to Germany and so across Europe to Britain. Their country was in ruins, they were practically starving and Germany was in no better condition. After their bitter sufferings and their great triumphs, it was to them inconceivable that the British and German workers would not rally to their side; the day of world-wide revolution, they believed, must be at hand. Their ignorance of the circumstances and mood of the British workers was only equalled by the ignorance of the British about them. We had suffered considerable privations during the war and there was a rising mood of discontent among the people, but not sufficient, in spite of the fears of some in authority, to make a bid to overthrow the Government. But the Russians must have been aware that our trade unionists had at least set up the Council of Action to stop intervention against the Soviets and prevent the shipment of munitions destined to be used in the fight against them; thus far the spirit of international solidarity, broken by the war, had survived. Because of this they were now eating our abandoned military jam! I had only begun to learn about Labour politics from Bertie, and Marxism was to me no more than a name. There was, as yet, no Communist Party in Britain. But I became aware that in the absence of factual information these Red Army men rested their solidarity on revolutionary theory. The informed and militant section of the proletariat would inevitably arouse the workers, lead them against capitalist tyranny, and establish the International on the basis of the unity of the working class, which had thrown off its chains. To them a person like Madge was a representative of this spearhead in which they had faith. For hours in that train I translated back and forth this wishful thinking, in which I could see that Madge herself believed. Remarkable was the intense seriousness of our talking, the absence of light male and female exchanges. These were robust and handsome men: I remember the one who was brilliantly fair with great round blue eyes like a child's, the cut of his hair giving him the look of a medieval page. As they left the compartment he took his Red Army badge from his tunic and handed it to me.

In Leningrad (which I shall call it) we were taken to the Astoria Hotel and comfortably housed. It was probably the only such place where visitors could be received. A woman, Comrade Kingisepp, was in charge; she had an office with a telephone, one of the only lines working in the city. Under her was a sort of majordomo who proved very efficient. As I entered the lobby the very first person I saw was the American journalist, John Reed, author of the famous *Ten Days that Shook the World*. The Red Army badge was pinned to my dress.

'Where did you get that?' were his first words.

'A Red Army officer gave it to me,' I said.

'How brutal of him,' laughed Reed.

John Reed was tall and broad, and typical of the intransigent and generous American who supports an unpopular cause; they seem to act with greater commitment and less reserve than their English counterparts. Unfortunately I did not see much of him but I had one small expedition with him. He came by and called up to my window to come out, and he then took me on a launch on the river and into a park with classical statues and benches under the trees. He talked of the terrific struggles of the Russian workers and what the Revolution was to mean for the future. He had not much opinion of the Labour delegation that I was seeking; they had, apparently, gone on a trip down the Volga, but might by now have left the country. But here I was, none the less, and would now be able to see for myself. I must meet Angelica Balabanova and Alexandra Kollontai, the two great women leaders. Later that year, John Reed attended a Congress in Baku, where he caught typhus and died; he is, as is well known, buried in the Red Square.

I think it possible that I owe to this meeting and talk with him the fact that the Russians accepted me and allowed me to see and learn all that I could, and that I was saved from the suspicion and consequent misfortunes which befell other visitors at that time.

There was scarcely any traffic in Leningrad. It was like a large village. The usual services of a capital city seemed to have broken down except in such an oasis as the Astoria, where we stayed. I saw people going down to the river for water. There were great gaps in the roads where the wooden blocks had been torn up for winter fuel; driving about in one of the few Soviet cars was an adventure, as they swerved violently to avoid these holes. In front of our hotel was a huge pile of wood, guarded by soldiers. Our food was a clear indication of the desperate state of affairs. In the morning we had Russian tea in glasses, with one sweet-meat, spongy black bread, and a very small portion of rancid butter. At midday there would be thin cabbage soup and *kasha*—a sort of porridge—and something similar at night. With us were delegates from Germany and other countries, whom our Russian hosts welcomed and to whom they sought to show the achievements of the Revolution. We were all guests, no one was allowed to pay anything. No doubt the complete isolation and impossibility of currency exchanges accounted for this. None the less, there was something noble and moving about this hospitality to comrades in the midst of such severe hardship.

Many of us wanted to see the Putilov works, which were looked upon as the cradle of the Revolution in Leningrad, but Comrade Kingisepp, in the end, was not able to arrange this. We were taken to a new model bakery, which was at a standstill for lack of supplies of flour. But here was demonstrated to us with pride the efficiency of mechanical methods: the workers threw one empty baking tin after another to exactly the right spot on a huge tray which was then pushed into the great oven. There was a chute for the flour above a huge mixing vat. Anxious to impress us, our guide went forward and pulled the string that released the flour, and was at once covered from head to foot with what had remained in the bin. The silent machinery, the workers drilling themselves in industrial techniques, the pride in invention against the background of battle and hunger, had a pathos that moved me to tears. ' "It's all my own invention", said the White Knight'—this sprang immediately to my mind, and I wanted to say to the White Knight who stood there, 'Never mind, it *will* be in time for the pudding course.'

Leningrad itself, no matter what the state of its inhabitants, casts a spell of its own, especially in the light evenings of midsummer. The rivers, the many bridges, the ornate Winter Palace, the great houses bordering the rivers, the domes and golden spires, perhaps made a greater impression just because of the emptiness and silence. This city stood out, as it still does, as a great monument to the first introduction, by Peter the Great, of the culture of the West. But the spirit of the Revolution, abroad in the land, communicating itself, as it were, through the very air one breathed, was not at all of the West. It came from the uprising of an awakening giant, the birth of a new culture, and it was here, in these first days, that my enduring love of the Russian people was born in me, a love undiminished over the years, in spite of the changing attitudes of their Government.

My companion Madge had left for Moscow, to join other delegates, for it seemed that there was to be a Congress of the Third International. I was to be conducted to Moscow by a courier; he was a Jewish refugee from the United States, which, at that time, was in process of deporting known or suspected communists. The little man was nervous and fussy and anxious to do everything right. At the station there seemed to be no place reserved for me, and we were to spend a night in the train. There was a reservation for somebody called Stassova, who had so far not showed up. 'Never mind,' said my escort, 'Stassova you will be.' I wondered if this might lead to complications, but it did not seem to matter at all. We had an uneventful journey and a good night's sleep. In Moscow, with considerable difficulty, the courier got hold of a dilapidated droshky, transported me and my luggage and his own large parcels, which were destined for the Soviet Foreign Office, to the door of that building, then disappeared. I sat down on the bundles, reflecting on the absurdity of the situation. Here was I, an unknown foreigner, alone in charge of what might be very confidential documents, in the very heart of this revolutionary city. One or two young men came in and out of the building, looked at me in a puzzled way and then smiled, as if it were the most natural thing in the world to find a strange young foreign woman seated at their door. It was quite some time before someone came and conducted me inside; I had begun to be really nervous, for my escort did not reappear.

I was received by a young Jewish official. He was thin and pale and looked tired, but his large brown eyes were lively and kind. He was wearing a white flannel suit, such as is worn for tennis or cricket, which was very grubby. I thought this a bit odd, and then it occurred to me that obviously people would have to wear just what they might happen to possess, and certainly no one would be bothered about clothes at this juncture. His name was Comrade Rosenberg; I explained that I had intended to join the British delegation, but had been much delayed in arriving. I produced my letters from Russell as evidence of my connection with him.

'*Se perdre en Russie pour Bertrand Russell,*' he said, '*c'est une merveille.*' (To lose oneself in Russia for the sake of Bertrand Russell, what a marvel.) I would have liked to reply that my presence was rather due to rage and anger and a difference of opinion with the said Russell than devotion to him. He offered me a cigarette, one of those Russian ones that are nearly all cardboard tube. As we smoked, he remarked,

'*Mademoiselle, vous fumez comme une véritable russe.*' He then told me, what I had already guessed, that the British delegation had left, but that he hoped I would stay and learn about the Revolution. I asked if I could join the comrades who, I knew, were at an hotel called the Djelovoi Dvor. He regretted that this was not possible, since that hotel was reserved for delegates. But I could go to stay at a house for other guests, in the Haritonsky Pereulok. I asked what I should pay, but was told that whatever they had to offer was free. He then said that because of the number of visitors I would have to share a room with an American woman journalist. There were other journalists in the house also. Then looking at me earnestly he said: 'It is best to be careful what you say to bourgeois journalists.'

Realizing that some sort of warning was being conveyed to me, I asked no further questions, but thanked him for making it possible for me to stay. I was then provided with a '*propusk*', a sort of pass, which I was told would allow me to go anywhere and see anything, I had only to show it to officials or guards. A car then took me to my lodgings. This place, dubbed by the friends I made at the Djelovoi Dvor as the 'House of Suspicion', had belonged to a well-to-do Muscovite. It was now run as a guesthouse by a Commissar and his wife and contained a motley collection of people. Boni, the American of Boni and Liveright, was there some of the time. I was to share a room with Mrs Marguerite Harrison, an American citizen and journalist. It was quite comfortable and clean, there was a bathroom with cold water. And there were no bugs, which, as I learned from my friends, did frequent the Djelovoi Dvor. The food was exactly the same as we had had in Leningrad. Comrade Axionev, seated at the head of the table, presided at meals, and would make conversation in any one of several languages. He was small and bearded, with an ingratiating manner which I did not like. Indeed from the start I did not much care for the atmosphere of the place. Mrs Harrison was very pleasant and welcoming, like a typical middle-class American woman. I wondered what she was doing there.

After my first night I thought I would take a cold bath. This was refreshing and agreeable, but the door had no key, and just as I was splashing about in came a very tall gentleman, who at once apologized and withdrew. At breakfast Axionev presented the newcomer—it was Nansen, the explorer, who had come to help with relief. He took my hand, smiling, and said: 'But I have met this young lady already.' This tall Norwegian seemed to me the calmest, most wholesome and reliable person in the house. I was glad that he was here, but I determined to spend as much time as possible with the comrades at the Djelovoi Dvor.

Mrs Harrison showed considerable interest in my activities. What had made me come to Soviet Russia? Had I many friends among the delegates? How had I got into the country? I evaded her queries by coming in late, or pretending to be fast asleep until she was dressed and up in the morning. I had begun to grasp the meaning of being careful what one said to bourgeois journalists, for there was something about Mrs Harrison and her situation that was not exactly sinister but did not ring true. She herself seemed ill at ease at table when Axionev was present; under the guise of showing interest in his guests' concerns his remarks to her had a subtle menace when he spoke of a 'little walk' which she had taken that morning, as if he would make it quite clear to her that she was under observation. I felt sorry for her if she had somehow put a foot wrong with the authorities, but I was much more concerned with the delegates who had made their way by devious routes into the country, who were enthusiasts for the Revolution and who would be at considerable risk when they returned home. I did not want to say anything inadvertently which might do them harm.

'Mrs Harrison,' I said finally, 'you seem to have been quite some time in Russia. I have not asked you why you came or how you got into the country. Surely you know by now that these are not the sort of questions one asks people?'

There was good reason for the state of suspicion and nerves of the Russian authorities at this juncture. The Poles were attacking, and every evening some of us would go to the Foreign Office to get what news we could of the Polish war. Chicherin, the Commissar for Foreign Affairs, would come out on to the landing and give a brief communiqué and then depart again. The Poles were 'held', the advance was checked, the news was not too bad. At two o'clock in the morning the streets of Moscow were empty, silent and peaceful. I was often out alone late at night and was never stopped or molested for any reason. I had a sublime confidence in the good faith of the Soviet leaders whose courage I admired, and in whose revolution—though I was hitherto so unpolitical—I did believe. True, all of us visitors knew full well that there was an undercurrent of intrigue and of dealing with 'class enemies' and spies. We heard rumours of the arrest of a woman journalist, but could not get any details and were uncertain whether this was true.

It was at least a year after I had left Russia that I began to learn the true story of Mrs Harrison. She was later arrested as an American agent and there was strong reason to suppose that she was also working for the British Government. At the time I was in Moscow she was in a desperate situation; the Russians either suspected her or had found her out and they put pressure on her to do some intelligence work keeping under observation visitors to their country. It was said, though I do not know with what truth, that she then herself decided to denounce to the Russians persons whom she had found to be friendly to the Revolution. What is known is that she was involved in the arrest of Mrs Stan Harding, a friendly English journalist who had come hoping to send out favourable reports of the Revolution, because, as Mrs Harding later asserted, Mrs Harrison, whom she had met in Germany, was known to her as a spy. In her book, *Born for Trouble*, Mrs Harrison makes counter-accusations. Mrs Harding had, I believe, been removed from the house and, it may be, from the very bed which I had been allocated on my arrival. Both these women suffered long imprisonment, but were ultimately released by the Soviet authorities, and Mrs Harding received some compensation. Bertie was among those who helped her in her campaign, which was in part also directed against the Western governments for their activities.

Among the dedicated comrades in Moscow euphoria prevailed. The atmosphere at the Djelovoi Dvor was both pleasant and instructive. I found myself welcomed as a useful translator at the many discussions; I took my frugal meals with them, which no one seemed to mind, and went with them on various visits. Among them was Jack Tanner of the engineers' trade union from Britain, who had stowed away in the very ship which had brought the British delegation. There were the American Wobblies, too, members of the I.W.W. (Industrial Workers of the World), whose only comment on Mrs Snowden of the British delegation was, 'Gee, *that woman*!' We met and chatted with the Bolshevik leaders Zinoviev and Radek; and there was one exciting night when the masses assembled in the Bolshoi Theatre to hear a report from Krassin who had returned from a visit to Britain in a British battleship. How can one reproduce the atmosphere of impudence, mockery, confidence and steadfast courage that inspired listeners and speaker alike?

'I told these bourgeois gentlemen, this Lloyd George,' began Krassin, as he stated what had been the position of his Government. It was incredible to the politicians of the West that these Bolsheviks, who must be in a desperate situation, could be so dignified and intransigent: they would offer no apology for taking over everything, nor for repudiating the debts to foreigners incurred by the Tsarist Government. The bourgeois gentlemen would just have to put up with it. Those who were in touch and better understood the temper of the Soviets, such as Captain Sadoul, did what they could to persuade the West to deal with them—but all in vain, the interventions went on.

I sat behind Krassin at this meeting and a comrade translated for me. Everyone, whether Russian or foreign, was ready and anxious to tell me all about the aims of the Revolution. Marxism was expounded to me and the way in which, once the Revolution was established by the dictatorship of the proletariat, the State would presently wither away and the whole system would continue merrily for the benefit of the people. Suddenly it came to me that I was witnessing the coming to life of the eighteenth-century thought in which I had been steeped for the past year. These men were emulating the Great Clockmaker, the Architect of the Universe, and, just as He had set the planets in perpetual motion, so they would make a blueprint of the new society, based on industrial mechanism, in which each man or woman would find a place to work and contribute to the whole. Once set in motion, this new rational social system would carry on of its own momentum. It came to me also that this was *not* Marxism, but a sort of sublime heresy to Marx, in that it was not determined by economic forces, but rather *a priori*, emanating from the minds of the creators of the State, and shaping an industrial system to serve the idea, not the other way round. This too, I saw, was not the cut and thrust, the balancing of forces of democratic politics, rather was it a new religion, in some ways resembling the faith of my eighteenth-century divines, with their argument from design, though utterly opposed to any belief in a Divine Creator. Man, for the Bolsheviks, was his own master, the only creator, capable indeed also, of so changing himself and future generations, as to make possible the building of a new world.

At this time, and in the glorious mood which prevailed around me, I was inspired to believe that here was the creed which might civilize industrialism and tame it to be the servant of mankind. I conceived the idea of a book on the *Religion of the Machine Age*.

One question which, as a good feminist, I put to the comrades was: How would women benefit from this new system? They were vague on this point; they had, apparently, not given it much thought. Of course women would be 'free' like other citizens, but they supposed that they would go on as usual. Alexandra Kollontai, whom I had the privilege of meeting, had her doubts on this subject. She took me to see an exhibition, which had been designed to educate mothers. The mother and child, depicted on a series of posters resembling icons of Madonnas, illustrated the infant death rate in India and other countries; there were Black mothers as well as White on these posters. There was also a series of posters illustrating the proper care of a child. Madame Kollontai herself told me that the care of children and the matter of child labour were not immediately being considered by the men comrades; she had stressed the importance of ending child labour, but there were many who felt that this would have to wait until better times.

A congress of women was meeting in the Bolshoi that afternoon, to which she took me. Only three years had the Revolution been in progress, yet here was a packed hall of peasant women to ventilate their problems. Their reception of Kollontai amounted almost to worship. She did, in fact, look marvellous. She was a woman of taste and elegance, yet new clothes and style were the last things that could then be considered; there were no materials except perhaps the traditional coarse Russian linen. It was of this, in its natural fawn colour, that Kollontai's dress was made. But, from the high collar to the sweep of her skirt at her feet, it fitted perfectly to her figure. Her wavy dark hair was short, and, as she spoke, she held out her arms, lifted her chin and shook her short curls. She was an unforgettable, graceful, inspired leader of women. One after the other the women came to the platform to speak, with their young and eager, or old and gnarled faces, kerchiefs on their heads. And they spoke with the direct and simple warmth that I have now come to know in assemblies of women the world over, when, stirred by some common purpose, they open their mouths for the first time ever in public.

Though the comrades could not tell me much of what the Revolution would achieve for women, there is no doubt that it later outdistanced the so-called free world in the rights and dignity accorded to them, as well as opportunities to enter professions usually reserved for men. Though they have not yet reached completely equal status, the power and influence of women in the Soviet Union is still remarkable.

Even the enemies of the Soviet Union have had to admit the loving care which Russians give to their children. Already in 1920 this was evident. Crèches were being established, and also country homes for children, which spared them the hardship of the towns. Some schools were closed; it was found that many of the teachers were not in sympathy with the new régime, and time would be needed before teachers of the right views could be found and trained. In these early days the methods adopted in the schools were those considered advanced in the West; Montessori was followed and Dalcroze eurythmics. But I noticed that the dances and poems performed mostly related in some way to communism, and I heard a teacher deliver a long address on the duties of communists and the errors of anarchism. Deep-seated hostility to the doctrines of anarchism was a feature of all Soviet propaganda at this time.

Even as I watched the children I had misgivings about the future development of Soviet education.* The growth of industrialism, I feared, would inevitably bring with it greater regimentation in the curriculum and in conduct. The doubts which I expressed at the time have in part been justified. The free and easy style departed, and discipline, school uniforms and aprons have returned. But, as I have had an opportunity of seeing on subsequent visits, a creative love of children has continued undiminished, ensuring opportunities for their full and many-sided development, as well as self-reliance and a degree of independence. Only bigoted enemies of communism could fail to admit that the conquest of illiteracy, the raising of the cultural level of an entire people in the space of fifty years, is something perhaps never before achieved in human history.

But in the desperate situation of Russia at that time there was every reason for my fear that, as I wrote, 'the ideals of the Russian revolutionaries might go down before the logic of necessity'. They prided themselves on being hard, practical men to whom the full and human development of a child could seem a mere luxury. There was always the risk, as I also saw, that an educated élite, manipulating the dictatorship of the

---

* expressed in the chapter on 'Art and Education' I contributed to Russell's *Practice and Theory of Bolshevism* (Allen and Unwin, 1920)

proletariat, would dominate the more ignorant mass of the people. But there was a long, hard road to go before the more prosperous—and, to some, too bourgeois—Russia of today would be reached. Between now and then lay the marvellous work with the wild war orphans of such a man as Makarenko, and innumerable educational and cultural projects for children of all ages.

I could not avoid noting that communism was held and taught, not as a mere device of politics, but as an intense religious faith. As one who had come to scepticism, this seemed to me to have many dangers. 'This teaching of communism,' I wrote, 'however necessary it may appear for the building of the communist state of the future, does seem to me to be an evil in that it is done emotionally and fanatically, with an appeal to hate and militant ardour rather than to constructive reason. It binds the free intellect and destroys initiative.' It seemed to me likely that in both art and science a rigid censorship such as that of the medieval Church might prevail.

Communism has indeed shown itself as a severe impediment to the free flowering of the human imagination and intellect. But, one must add, the cruel repression of ideas unacceptable to those in power in Russia may be seen as evidence that more respect is shown there for the power of thought to change the world than in countries where new ideas, published freely, are boosted as novelties and as rapidly cast aside, or merely looked upon by the powers that be as a means of permitting the dissident to let off steam.

In 1920 I found a perplexing state of affairs in the Soviet attitude to the arts. I was myself much exercised as to what might be the effect on the arts in general of the approach of industrialism. There were two traditional streams—the aristocratic, as expressed in the ballet, painting, literature, architecture; and the peasant, which showed itself in the lovely wooden toys and dolls, carved and painted boxes, embroidered blouses and shirts. Industrial production was bound to do harm to handicrafts, as it had done in the West. There is no doubt that the preservation of the peasant-type work has been artificial and that its quality is inferior to that of former times.

None the less, on this first visit it was clearly evident how greatly the Bolsheviks in fact valued art and the artist. From the beginning they saw to the upkeep of churches, public buildings and museums; and to the artist, whatever his political beliefs, they gave anything they could in clothing and rations. In the theatre the old classics in tragedy and comedy, even the old-style operetta, were still being performed, as well as the superb ballet. As I sat in the theatre I was acutely conscious of the discrepancy between what was depicted on the stage and what was going on in the daily life of the audience. The art for art's sake thesis still seemed to hold, and art and politics were still in separate compartments. I commented in my contribution to Russell's book on Bolshevism:

There it stands, this old art, the purest monument to the nullity of the art for art's sake doctrine, like a rich exotic plant of exquisite beauty, still apparently in its glory, till one perceives that the roots are cut, and that leaf by leaf it is gradually fading away.

This was also the view of the more fiery Bolshevists, who at that time wanted entirely revolutionary art forms. They shaped designs for buildings, made avant-garde paintings, sculptures, poems. The curious fact is that none of this in the end found favour. The latest styles of painting in the West were condemned as decadent, such works of art hidden away in cellars, while 'socialist realism', resulting in literal portrayal, like that of our paintings of the Victorian period, ultimately triumphed. It would seem that a revolution in government and economics is easier to achieve than a revolution in taste.

Thus the Russian ballet has held the stage in its native country throughout the upheavals of wars and revolutions, while the great epic operas of Russian history still sound in majesty from the throats of her singers. It was the new art of the cinema, by reason of the genius of Eisenstein and others, which presently chronicled the epic of the Revolution—in *Potemkin, October,* and the story of agriculture in *General Line* and of transport in *Turk Sib.* History indeed returned powerfully in the films of *Ivan the Terrible.*

As I went to and fro to the Djelovoi Dvor, I would sometimes see Balabanova, a short, unassuming woman, her hair in plaits over her shoulders, chatting with the foreign delegates. I met also Emma Goldman and Alexander Berkman, who had arrived from the United States, and, as anarchists, were already feeling disillusioned with the Revolution. The Soviet leaders wanted to treat them with courtesy, and finally found nothing better to do than send them off by train to collect materials for a museum of the Revolution. Berkman was a slight, spare man; it was hard to appreciate that he had once tried to murder an American tycoon. Emma was what one might have expected, a broad, sturdy woman. I was to meet Emma again in London when she came there to inspire an anti-Bolshevik campaign, which Bertie and I then felt we could not support, so great already was the hostility to the Bolsheviks in the West. But I admired her as a pioneer among women, and I went to hear her speak at a lunch over which Rebecca West, young, slender and beautiful, presided with considerable grace and courage.

There were very many odd people to be found in the Djelovoi Dvor: I recall spending one evening with some gay Cossacks, complete with their black uniforms and boots, astrakhan caps and cartridge belts across the chest. They told me that they were planning to go down into Persia to 'make trouble for British Imperialism' and asked me if I would not like to go with them.

With faith in my *propusk* and taking the authorities at their word, I

D

97

wandered about wherever I liked. One day, with the knowledge that I had acquired of the Russian alphabet at least, I gathered from a notice that there was to be a play at some place which seemed to be occupied by Red Army men. I took note of the time and place and told Jack Tanner and one or two others about this, and suggested that we should go and see the play. So we arrived there quite unexpected and uninvited, but were none the less cordially received.

The play was called *Zarevo* (The Dawn)* and was performed on that Saturday night on a small stage in a small hall in an entirely amateur fashion. It represented Russian life just before the Revolution. It was intense and tragic and passionately acted. Almost the only comic relief was provided by the Tsarist police, who made one appearance towards the end, got up like comic military characters in a musical comedy— just as, in medieval plays, the comic character was Satan. The play's intention was to show a typical Russian working-class family. There were the old father, constantly drunk on vodka, alternately maudlin and scolding; the old mother; two sons, one a communist and the other an anarchist; the wife of the communist, who did dressmaking; her sister, a prostitute; and a young girl of bourgeois family, also a communist, involved in a plot with the communist son, who was, of course, the hero of the play.

The first act revealed the stern and heroic communist maintaining his views despite the reproaches of father and mother and the nagging of his wife. It showed the anarchist brother (as might be expected from the Bolshevik hostility to anarchism) as an unruly, lazy, ne'er-do-well, with a passionate love for Sonia, the young bourgeoise, which was likely to become dangerous if not returned. She, on the other hand, obviously preferred the communist. It was clear that he returned her love; both, in what seemed platonic comradeship, were serving their common ideal. An unsuccessful strike, bringing want, and danger from the police, together with increasing jealousy on the part of the anarchist, led up to the tragic dénouement. All violent action was performed off stage, which made the plot at times difficult to follow, but it seemed that the anarchist, in a jealous rage, forged a letter from his brother to bring Sonia to a rendezvous, and there murdered her, at the same time betraying his brother to the police. When the latter came to effect his arrest, and accuse him also, as the most likely person, of the murder, the anarchist was seized with remorse and confessed. Both were then led away together.

I did not consider that the play had much merit, apart from propaganda. But what was evident was how real it was for the audience; it seemed to establish a link with them as never in the professional theatre.

* this description is taken from my chapter in Russell's *Practice and Theory of Bolshevism*

After the play, all were in a mood for enjoyment, and we danced with the Army officers and shared some very slight refreshments.

There now arrived in Moscow Arthur Watts, on a mission of Quaker relief. He brought me a message from Bertie, to the effect that he was back in London, had been invited by the Chinese to go out to Peking, and was desperately anxious for me to come back in order to go with him if I would. On this his decision to go or not to go might depend. I repaired at once to the Foreign Office and explained this development.

'Oh,' they said, cheerfully, 'we will send you across Siberia to meet him in the East.' That region was then full of roving ex-soldiers and released prisoners; the Russians *may* have been serious in their suggestion, but I certainly was not. It was essential to get back to London, to find out from Bertie exactly what the visit to China meant, and to see whether the state of our relation to one another would really make it possible for me to burn my boats by resigning my Girton Fellowship, since this was clearly what such a departure with Bertie would mean.

But it was easier to get into Soviet Russia than to get out. I was told, with exquisite politeness, that I could not go back via Murmansk, since this was really an illegal route, designed for the true brethren of the communist faith. The way in and out for those on conventional business was through Estonia to Reval. And for this I would need an Estonian visa, which, I was soon to learn, was not easy to obtain for the odd traveller emerging from that dangerous Bolshevik land, who might be infected with communism.

Among fresh visitors at the 'House of Suspicion' was an Englishman named Mr Boon, said to have arrived from Siberia, and accompanied by a Russian woman. He seemed to me to be a very odd person to be in the Soviet Union at all at that time, for he wore patent-leather boots and on one occasion when we were both at the Soviet Foreign Office he told me that delay in getting out was very tiresome, since he feared that he would not be in time for the London Season. He assured me that there was a long queue at the Estonian Consulate, it would take ages to get a visa and indeed it might not be granted at all.

For one wild moment I had thought of staying on in Russia, now that I was there and learning so much. I knew I did care deeply about Bertie, but I was in no mood to be whisked out to China, which I had never thought of as an interesting place to visit. However, when I learnt that I could not go by Murmansk, I consulted Arthur Watts, who gave me a letter to take with me to the Estonian Consulate, which letter I was to return to him. At the Consulate, as I had been told, a long queue of people were sitting in the anteroom. There were, of course, large numbers who wanted, for one reason or another, to escape from the régime. Mr Boon was there among the applicants. I showed my letter, which was in Estonian, hence its contents quite unknown to me, to a young

99

woman receptionist or secretary. To my utter amazement, she exclaimed 'A-ah, *Pitka*' and ushered me forthwith, plus my passport, into the holy of holies. One glance at the letter and the Consul exclaimed in his turn 'A-aa-h, *Pitka*', beamed upon me and duly stamped my passport without question or delay. Emerging triumphant, I regret to say that I grinned maliciously at Mr Boon.

In the hurried preparations for my departure and Arthur Watts' preoccupation with his urgent business, I hastily handed the letter back to him without any further question. I had gathered, of course, that it must have been some kind of recommendation. It seems scarcely credible that it was only very many years later that I read in the *Evening Standard* of the death—I think—of a General Pitka, who was a prominent businessman in Estonia. It was through his firm that the Quakers were at that time importing supplies into the Soviet Union for the much needed relief for the starving. For years the magic of the word 'Pitka' in my life was an entertainment to Bertie, my children and my friends.

I sadly took leave of the company at the Djelovoi Dvor, but was not sorry to depart from the House of Suspicion. At table Axionev told us that, since there was no room in the house, poor Mr Boon had had to go and stay in a railway carriage at the station, from which the great misfortune had befallen him of the loss of his passport from the pocket of his coat. Axionev was Oh, so sorry, at the poor man's troubles.

I had not been blind to the sinister side of the Revolution; I had, in fact, visited the illegal market, the Sukharevka, where a pitiable crowd of desperate people offered anything and everything for sale, in order to buy some bread. I must have acquired some roubles, I cannot think how, but I bought there a typical embroidered blouse, and a skirt, woven, I think, of goat's hair, which I still possess. It seemed wrong to be buying such things from a poor woman, but at the same time right to try and save her from starvation. From the writings of Sholokhov, who has never been out of favour in the Soviet Union, it seems that in time the Russians came to tolerate and use the Sukharevka themselves.

Without untoward event I came again to Leningrad. I was given to understand that the railway carriage in which I was with my moderate luggage would be attached, after a delay of some hours, to the train which was to cross the frontier and continue down to Reval. I was not far from the Astoria, and I strolled up there to see and say goodbye to anyone I might know who was there. There indeed was Gilbey, of the Wobblies, and another comrade of his.

'Comrade, you cannot possibly leave the country at this moment,' they said, 'the Third International Congress is just about to take place. Tomorrow we are going to meet the train from Moscow, in which all the delegates will arrive.' At once they proceeded with me back to the station, removed my luggage from the carriage, put it into one of the station waiting-rooms, trying to make the Red Guards who were there understand by signs that we would come back for it later. The major-domo at the hotel received us with dismay, but, to my everlasting gratitude, he accepted the situation and agreed that I should remain.

So we came next day to greet the delegates and join with a cheering, singing crowd of many nations, to move with them in an untidy, enthusiastic mass towards the hall where the Congress was to be held. This is an experience which I shall never forget. As we went, we sang what has, I believe, been called 'The Song of the Exiles'. Here I can only recall that haunting music by giving the words which have been, at some time, fitted to it by English comrades.

> Comrades, the bugles are sounding
> Summoning us to the fray
> Bravely we'll fight for our freedom
> Boldly we'll hew out a way.

From time to time a familiar head with reddish hair, sharp, pointed, reddish beard and the Slav snub nose, would be seen among the crowd. Then there were resounding cheers and cries of 'Lenin, Tovarishch Lenin', arms were linked around him and he was carried forward in security and affection until the hall was reached. Here on every desk lay what was to become a feature of all such international congresses, a large imitation-leather folder—in this case with a red flag inset in the cover—filled with documents and reports, a pad and a pencil.

Then Lenin spoke. I do not know what he said, because, on this occasion, I could not expect a whispered translation, but I watched his restrained gestures, the lift of his head by which his beard would point straight at his audience. A man respected and loved and completely in contact with, and in control of, that great mass of people.

For the opening of the Congress the pageant of the World Commune was performed, which I described fully in my chapter in Russell's book; I have never seen any other account of this remarkable spectacle. It was performed on the steps of an immense white building that was once the Stock Exchange. In front of the building a wide road ran from a bridge over one arm of the river to a bridge over the other, so that the stretches of water and sky seemed to the eye of imagination like the painted wings of a gigantic stage. On each side, two battered red columns of fantastic design, that were once lighthouses to guide ships, were beflagged and illuminated, and carried the limelight. Between and behind them was gathered a densely-packed audience of forty or fifty thousand people. The play began at sundown, while the sky was still red away to the right and the palaces on the far left still aglow with the setting sun, and it continued under the magic of the darkening sky.

From slavery in chains to Kings and Queens, the drama moved through all the stages of revolution, culminating in a great mass spectacle as the 'Internationale', like a mighty trumpet call, sounded from ten thousand throats. The end of this pageant had the pomp and majesty of the Day of Judgment itself; it may have erred on the side of the grandiose, but this must be forgiven the organizers in view of the occasion for which they had prepared it. Nothing could detract from the beauty and dramatic power of the opening and many of the scenes. The effects obtained by movement in the mass were intoxicating. The first entrance of the masses gave an extremely moving sense of dumb and patient force; and the frenzied, delighted dancing of the crowd at the victory of the French Communards stirred one to ecstasy. The pageant lasted five hours or more, and was as exhausting emotionally as the Passion Play is said to be.

The physical and emotional strain of this long day spelt for most of us a sleepless night. I had sat with Jack Tanner throughout the performance, and we talked until dawn. I think none of the subsequent history of our lives ever obliterated for either of us the wonder of this shared experience.

The next day I was due to leave. I learned that the Cheka—the security organization—had become suspicous of the luggage unattended at the station; they had seized it. The pleasant little man at the Astoria, whom I have called the major-domo, had retrieved it, or else they had delivered it to him. He asked me to check my luggage over, to see that nothing was missing. Despite the scarcity of every kind of thing in the Soviet Union at that time, all was in perfect order.

The train, with a motley crowd of passengers, steamed on its way to the frontier; I sat back drowsy, sad, exhausted, wondering if I would ever see that astonishing country again. Several people were on edge, I noticed, doubtless some with good reason. One man asked me what I had been doing in Russia, and, probably with good intent, suggested that I should find some plausible excuse for my visit, such as having a sick relative there. I gave vague answers and determined that, at the frontier, I would do what I believe most British do in similar circumstances—say nothing whatever and appear perfectly calm. With a valid visa I saw no reason for difficulty in entering Estonia and, in fact, I passed the frontier guards without the slightest hitch.

In Reval I found a room at an address which had been given me in Russia, and set about finding a route back to London. I did not want to go via Stockholm, having skipped from there in a somewhat suspicious manner. I booked passage on a cargo ship sailing direct to London. Someone then told me that the British Consul was asking—it was thought—for me. I had not intended to call on him, my trip to Russia having been illegal. However, with my passage now booked, I went to the Consulate. There were telegrams and letters from Bertie, who was in great anxiety about me, a fact which I had not at all taken into account, having considerable conceit of my ability to take care of myself.

I assured the Consul, who was friendly and kind, that all was well and my passage arranged. He murmured something about difficulties of British subjects in Russia at that time and asked me if I had seen anything of a 'fellow called Boon'!

The ship was Danish, carrying a cargo of wood. So far as I remember I was the only passenger. I spent evenings on the voyage chatting with the officers and sometimes playing cards. We put in at Danzig, berthed at some distance from the centre of the city. Danzig was in a disturbed state; I saw a small procession carrying red flags meandering round the sand-dunes near to our quay. My hairbrush had got left behind when the comrades removed my effects from the train in Leningrad, so I thought that I would go into the town and see if I could buy another. I had not got far in the streets when I heard sounds of disturbance and even some shots. I decided not to proceed, but I stopped to read a notice in German pasted up on a kiosk. It said that, in the event of further trouble, the Allied forces would occupy the railway stations and important buildings in the city. When I got back to London I saw in a newspaper report that Lloyd George, replying to a question in Parliament, had denied that the Allies were intervening in any way in Danzig's troubles: one of my first experiences of the lies that statesmen tell.

At last we got away from Danzig and came with no further delay to Gravesend. But here to my distress I was told by the Captain that the ship must proceed to the port of London before disembarking or discharging of cargo could take place. I pleaded that it could surely do no harm if I were to land here. But what about Customs? Well, I urged, I had only a little luggage, were there no Customs men about? Presently a launch with some officials came alongside. I leaned over and called to them, laughing and waving my suitcase. Then the Captain put in a word for me, in spite of the fact that, as he gallantly said, he had hoped for my company a day longer. No one bothered about my luggage, and I came ashore, Third International folder with its red flag, documents and all—not that I think anyone would have taken the trouble to seize it at that stage of relations with Russia.

I telephoned to Bertie, who muttered the equivalent of 'thank God' and told me to come at once to Liverpool Street where he would meet me. In an hotel at the station where we spent the night, he explained that if we were going to China we must set sail within a few weeks and there was a great deal to be done in preparation. It was now 4 August 1920.

I learned that Clifford Allen had become seriously ill during the delegation's trip down the Volga, and that Bertie had seen him into hospital at Reval, and had then gone on to Stockholm. There he had wired to me in Paris and, getting no reply, he wired to some friends of mine there. Back came the message: 'She is in Stockholm.' He therefore sat down to wait in the hotel, from which he had written to me on his way into Russia, thinking that I must certainly come there. Nothing happened: he tried to make some enquiries and then, by chance, came upon the Finnish comrade who had arranged my journey. I had desperately wanted to get into Russia, he told Bertie, and indeed why not? It was excellent that the little comrade should see the country of the Revolution. Bertie, who was convinced that I would catch typhus and die, was horrified. But there was nothing to do but go back to England where he found the invitation to Peking awaiting him. He then got in touch with me as I have already described.

Now had come for both of us the moment of decision. The invitation to Bertie for a year at the National University of Peking was definite, a reply must be given, they had made his passage money available. He could, he said, pay my passage and had made up his mind that he did not want to go anywhere without me. I knew too, that I did not want to be parted from him, I was prepared to resign my Fellowship and enter on a permanent partnership. I did not want to go to China, not at all at that moment, but it was evident that there was no choice, since I could not ask him to give up what would be for him an important experience, nor could I suggest that he go without me. I saw Ogden at this time. I remember him saying that all sorts of interesting things were happening in China, how could I possibly hesitate, what with the time, the place and the loved one all together? It is possible that, but for Ogden, Bertie and I might never have married.

My dilemma was no different from that which faces many women deeply in love, who none the less have aims, purposes, perhaps a career, of their own. For me at this moment there was something more than this. I had had an intense experience in these few short weeks, received emotionally all the more since I had been alone. I had had the good fortune to be one person, uncommitted, not bound to any political allegiance, who had been able to get into Russia at this moment in history. I felt sincerely that in the Soviet Union I had seen a vision—a vision that I would accept to have been almost mystical— but in the political sense a vision of the making of a future civilization. I, with my unpolitical fresh eyes and the background of my studies, was —and I really felt this—the only person in England who could interpret the true essence of what was happening in the Soviet Union. To do this was a mission which I felt called upon to perform, in order that I might contribute something to the making of peace between East and West.

I knew that the trade union and Labour element on that delegation simply hadn't a clue; the communists were in blinkers imposed by their ideology; and here was Bertie, usually so right about most things, reacting like an old-fashioned liberal to a great people in torment and travail to bring forth their future. My mind was seething with the book that I wanted at once to sit down and write. When he saw how much I disagreed with him about Russia, Bertie very generously accepted in his own book a chapter which I wrote at white heat when we were in Paris on our way to China.

The opening chapter, written in 1921, of my projected but never completed book on the Machine Age was called 'The Soul of Russia and Body of America'. Here is a very brief résumé of it that only inadequately recalls the passion and flavour of that time.

The 'body' of America, during my visit of 1917, had appeared to me as an 'immense, impressive mechanism' in which producing goods, developing resources, speeding transport were being mistaken for the goal of civilization. This machine was being endowed with a message 'to be carried to the uttermost parts of the earth, to be taught, if need be, by bullying or at the point of the sword'. Other nations, trying to rebuild after the war, could see with misgiving what they themselves might become, as they looked to America, 'this excellent body, this shell of a state, and the soul of man walking mournfully through it, seeking an oasis, not hoping to find a home'.

The Chinese I had seen fearful lest the development of industrialism in their country would make them as 'horrible and degraded' as, watching the war, they had felt us to be. But of what I had seen in Russia I wrote: 'She is a country just emerging from the medieval ages of faith into the valorous adolescence of the Renaissance. Her thought is burning and her courage high. Honour and glory, faith are for her words still charged with meaning, scepticism has not yet dimmed her ardour, nor materialism blurred her soul . . . she still breathes the air of Shakespeare and has not known the caustic age of Voltaire.'

I was convinced that accepting economic determinism, as Marx had done in his analysis, was the source of the lack of ideals, the barrenness, of civilized purpose in the West. Utterly wrong were those who maintained that only out of a developed industrialism would the spirit of socialism and communism arise. On the contrary, the challenge of Russia was unanswerable: 'You have the body, but where is the soul?' Were we not the 'puppets of material forces, that we had allowed to grow at random and that now . . . threatened to engulf us in hideous destruction'? Were we, the pragmatists, right, or they, the *a priori* idealists, who saw communism as a 'whirling heart of fire, that must first consume ancient evils and then, cooling, transmute itself into the crust of material expression, creating industrialism anew, a thing, it may be, of undreamed power and beauty'? In Russia was a civilized purpose that could subdue and direct industrialism. Which would win, industrialism or the spirit of mankind? I described an idyllic vision of how the spirit of Russian communism and its 'twin brother' Western science and skill might leap like great waves towards one another: 'So they met at last, soul and body, and went springing skywards in a clear, green pyramid of joy. The filth of factories and the grime of poverty were washed away and everywhere there emerged a new and smiling world.'

7

To China

Among the preparations for our departure for Peking was the necessity of providing evidence for a divorce. Bertie insisted that, whatever I might think about marriage, he wanted to be free in case I might find myself pregnant, a risk which I had never attempted to avoid ever since our life together had begun. I had also to let my parents know that, back from Russia, I was about to depart again on a longer voyage. Their astonishing confidence in me was unshaken. They were at all times concerned for me and my welfare, and they must often have been worried. But they preserved an outward calm and matter-of-fact acceptance of my activities. Informed that, instead of remaining in Paris, I had been in Russia, my father said: 'Oh, what sort of an hotel did you find there?' At that I could not begin to tell him of my adventures, even had there been time for the recital. Both he and my mother knew that Bertie and I were attracted to one another, thus our decision did not really come as a surprise.

Bertie informed his solicitors of our stay together at the railway terminus hotel on my arrival from Russia. But when they went there for information they were told that no such young lady had been there! While we greatly appreciated this tact, it was not quite what we required at that moment. So we went next to the Charing Cross Hotel, and took pains to see—I think by my unpacking my Russian blouse and skirt—that the chambermaid would remember us. Later she was asked to look from the window, in order to recognize Bertie on the platform of Charing Cross station, where he, not to waste time, was occupied in swearing an affidavit. Later, when the divorce proceedings became public, the *Express* referred to Bertie as 'having succumbed to a sordid affair in the Charing Cross Hotel'. We delighted in this description of a love affair which was, in fact, conducted on a journey round the world.

Meantime I had to see about my passport and visas. The authorities treated me with a courtesy and respect which would not now, I think, be accorded to sympathizers with communist régimes and illegal travel. They issued me with a new passport, and, with a sly smile, handed me my old one, with its Soviet visas, saying that perhaps I would like to keep this as a memento.

At last we were away and en route for Paris. Bertie had told me that the French liner, *Porthos*, on which he had booked our passages, was in fact delayed for two or three weeks to be disinfected on account of a case of plague. But he thought that we should not ourselves delay, but say goodbye and spend the waiting period in Paris, where we could be free to talk and enjoy each other's company. We went to the Hôtel Louvois, which I had noted as quiet and, I thought, reasonable.

Here, in a sense, our married life began. I can remember how, in the morning, turning over sleepily in bed, I became conscious of Bertie sitting bolt upright and wide awake beside me, and how I thought rather desperately: 'This is how it is going to be for the rest of my life, this is what being married means.' It is true that in all our married life, Bertie was always 'brightly intelligent' at the moment of waking, at once tackling his letters and the newspaper, a characteristic which I presently found endearing rather than the reverse. Once, however, at the Louvois, I missed him from my side during the night and found him on the small balcony star-gazing. He was troubled, he told me, over whether he should publish his book on the Bolsheviks or not, and he had been asking the constellation Cassiopeia for guidance. This does not imply any faith in astrology; he was merely emulating Pascal and Kant in communing with the starry heavens. We had been eagerly discussing our separate experiences in Russia. I wrote my chapter, and the book went to the publisher.

Letters and journals came regularly for Bertie, and it was then, in the weekly *Nation and Athenaeum*, that I found the fragment of a very beautiful poem by Wilfrid Owen, which he later incorporated in *Strange Meeting*. Because it somehow symbolized then for me the partnership on which Bertie and I were embarking, this is the version I prefer and have quoted and carried with me to the present day:

> Earth's wheels run oiled with blood, forget we that
> Let us turn back to beauty and to thought.
> Better break ranks than trek away from progress.
>
> Let us eschew men's minds that are brute natures
> Let us not feed on blood which some say nurtures
> Be we not swift with swiftness of the tigress.
>
> Wisdom is mine and I have mystery
> Beauty is yours and you have mastery
> We two will stay behind and keep our troth.
>
> Miss we the march of this retreating world
> Into vain citadels that are not walled
> Let us lie out and hold the open truth.
>
> Then, when the blood has clogged their chariot wheels
> We will go up and wash them from deep wells
> Even the wells we digged too deep for war.

For now we sink from men as pitchers falling
But men shall raise us up to be their filling
The same, whose faces bled where no wounds were.

We had leisure those days to talk of many things, including our future plans. Bertie told me that when he first received the invitation to Peking, he thought that it must be a mistake, or, since the letter was signed with the name Fu Ling-yu, that it might be a hoax. But when, on request, Peking had sent his passage money, he believed in the project. But he had no idea what it would all be like, we were both embarking on an adventure. Meantime we paid a hurried visit to two friends who expressed astonished interest in our recent Russian adventures—Thérèse and Jean Nicod, both now teaching in the lovely peaceful town of Cahors. Between us and them was an abiding affection, to which that pleasant reunion belongs. Not so many years later, at news of the sudden death of Jean, Bertie and I left London at once for Geneva to try and comfort Thérèse.

At last we were on our way from Paris to Marseilles. Two suitcases containing our hot weather garments, accidentally left in Paris, were being sent on. In Marseilles Bertie proceeded to the *Porthos*, while I undertook to get the suitcases from the station and join him later. My task was not so easy as it seemed. At the station the officials demanded 'les tickets' before the cases could be handed over. These should have arrived by post, I explained, but they had not yet come to hand. French officialdom was adamant. No receipt tickets, no luggage. In a vast space underground at Marseilles station are acres and acres of luggage of all sorts and descriptions. One gets the impression that every traveller to and from the port must have deposited and lost some article belonging to him there. Otherwise, where on earth did it all come from? Descending underground, thankfully I saw our two suitcases, near the entry. To get them I saw that I must put on an act. I was looking attractive enough, and wearing a rather fetching wide-brimmed hat of yellow organdie, lined with dark blue. Gesticulating with hands and arms in the approved fashion '*Mais voyons, Messieurs*,' I appealed, '*le grand navire français Porthos va partir. Mon mari est à bord. Nous partons pour la Chine, nous avons tellement besoin de ces bagages*.' I managed great distress and even a few tears, for I was really afraid that officialdom would defeat me. However, pride in the French Merchant Navy and French gallantry won in the end. They released the cases.

Finding no taxi, I got hold of a horse and cart, and, perched up beside the driver, set out for the quay. En route, to my horror, a taxi collided with our cart, but not seriously. Now both drivers began an altercation which looked as if it might long continue. Once more I appealed that the great *Porthos* would not wait, and so came finally, plus luggage, to an anxious Bertie. When he heard my story he gave one of his great laughs and assured me that he would never have succeeded as I had done. A suspicion came into my mind that he had deliberately allocated this job to me with this in view.

On board we found that we had plenty of time, for, when we sought to arrange for two deckchairs, we were told that the steward in charge of these had not yet arrived himself. We expressed some surprise, at which with a shrug of his shoulders the deputy murmured something about the charms of his superior's 'petite amie'. For us this set the mood of a voyage on a French liner, by contrast with what would have obtained on a P & O ship. French cuisine and the courtesy of the French hotelier and restaurateur, an informality and acceptance of individual idiosyncrasies made us feel that the journey would be entirely enjoyable, as indeed it proved to be.

As we passed into the Red Sea, we thought that Jehovah had not chosen the most pleasant spot on Mount Sinai for His dwelling-place and the origin of His Ten Commandments. The heat was, in fact, worse than we had expected; many of us slept on deck on two deckchairs, and, as the ship tacked deliberately, there would come a soothing breath of wind. We wondered if we could have taken this liberty on a British ship. In the early morning, as the sailors swabbed the decks, they would move gently and quietly around our chairs, and tenderly pick up the fallen tassel of a dressing-gown.

From Colombo I wrote to my mother:

We are through the bad heat now . . . I can manage to write more comfortably. Everybody says the heat was worse than they ever knew it. We thought at first this was the usual tale to comfort us, but one of the passengers who has been through a great many times says he has NEVER known it so intense. Our head cook died of it. He went from the hot kitchen to the ice house, took a chill and was dead in a few hours. The Chief Steward got knocked up and two soldiers raving with it. B was badly affected one night. I thought he would be delirious and kept bathing his head and neck and fanning him. I got a very bad headache and some trouble in my tummy, but now we are both very fit indeed.

The *Porthos* carried a number of official Frenchmen, as was natural, but we did not find them interesting on the whole. I wrote:

Colombo, 19 September. There are no very nice people on board except a French Commodore or Admiral (not quite sure which) and his family. The family are delicious, two girls and a boy all in their teens, and all full of energy and fun, splitting with laughter over the oddity of the rest of the people most of the time. They watched B and me laughing and last night they came and asked B to adopt them, because he and I had the same way of laughing that they had. B was quite touched. They are almost the only people on board that treat him like a human being and not a professor. Everybody else is terrified and thinks he must be very learned and pompous. It is so funny to me, because I never thought of him as learned or pompous. When I was introduced to Lady O [Ottoline Morrell] she tried to impress on me that he was such a genius and I almost said I hadn't noticed it. B thinks of course, that I am a genius too and that is why I don't notice how odd and remarkable he is, but I doubt that. I should not, however, be at all surprised if he were to become Emperor of China. Will you come on a visit to our Imperial Court, if so?! Choose a time when it is NOT hot in the Red Sea. When we arrive, we have to find house and buy furniture and engage a few dozen servants. It is all going to be most tremendous fun. They will put articles about us in the Chinese papers and then all the nice Mandarins will come and call.

My love to all of you, you are such darlings.

This is not so conceited as it sounds. Bertie and I pursued our courtship with badinage and teasing, and Bertie, for his part, never hesitated to use flattery, the traditional male weapon; in fact, I doubt whether all his life he could resist flattering any attractive woman. 'The ladies, God bless 'em!' In spite of supporting female suffrage and emancipation, Bertie adhered to the then male view that a woman's mind could not be equal to that of a man. One of the greatest compliments he ever paid me was to say that he never needed to 'talk down to me' in a discussion, as he invariably felt with other women. This does not, of course, apply to his specialist subjects, like mathematics and philosophy, in which I had no pretensions. Nor did I in any sense presume to put myself in a class with him in intellectual attainments.

I do not now recall how we managed to meet Ottoline Morrell during those hectic days before our departure, but my very first experience in meeting many of Bertie's older friends was the way that they would patronize me and imply how lucky I was to be chosen by this great man. I knew full well, nobody better, how great a treasure was Bertie's company to me, but I did think that he also got something out of it all. What is more, at the time I wrote this particular letter, I was in a very truculent mood. Our dispute about Russia had continued on our voyage, and persisted even in the intense heat of the Red Sea. I have a very clear recollection of one discussion (I was wearing one of my new white dresses, with a series of net frills from waist to hem), when Bertie was reiterating his anxiety about freedom and democracy in communist Russia. I retorted, almost with anger: 'Why are you worrying? Industrialism will make an end of democracy, it is a system that can only be run by oligarchs or a dictator.'

'How can you, sitting there, an elegant young woman, come by such ideas?' was Bertie's reply.

Out of this exchange, in a very hot climate, came probably the germ of our book *The Prospects of Industrial Civilisation*. And over the years I have seen, in Hitler, in Germany, Russia, and in the West, the fulfilment of my melancholy prophecy, engendered by that torrid discussion.

Bertie thought it a good idea to sleep a night ashore when possible. At the hotel in Colombo we were very much in a British atmosphere, as also at our next port of call, Singapore, where we landed only briefly, but had time to drive about and notice the very English style and layout which we, as a colonial power, had imposed on the town. This was specially interesting, in that it differed so much from the French style which we were to find in Saigon.

I helped the delightful French teenagers, and others, to dress up for a fancy-dress dance which was to take place on board ship. I transformed Bertie into an ancient Chinese philosopher of 2000 B.C., copying from a picture in a history book which he had. I borrowed a scarlet embroidered robe, fan and Chinese shoes from one of the Annamese Mandarins, and managed to concoct the strange hat of the Sage. Bertie could hardly eat his dinner for taking care of three long wisps of black beard stuck on his chin, and the Chinese could hardly eat theirs for laughing; the dignified Annamese (now Vietnamese) also enjoyed a joke. We, quite improperly, dubbed our ancient Sage Fu Ling-yu. In my peasant garments I was Bolshevik Russia, only born yesterday.

This dance caused us to fraternize more with our fellow voyagers. There was a Russian, with whom I danced very vigorously that evening. And there was a Chinese Professor Liang, who was friendly and courteous to us as to others, but seemed to keep himself much to himself. We invented fantasies about him and said that he expanded both in dignity and self-assurance as he neared the East. In actual fact, so far as we were concerned, he did blossom when we reached Saigon.

Bertie and I were induced by our fellow passengers to give some account of our recent visits to Russia, at that time of course an extremely controversial matter, but of intense interest, since so few had been there. We were listened to with attention and tolerance, except by a few, who included a repressed official type of Englishman. People had been fed on stories of rape and violence and nationalization of women and so on. When I said that I had walked about Moscow at any time of the day or night safe and unmolested, many snorted and the Englishman ejaculated, 'Tell that to the marines!' But Mrs Marguerite Harrison, who had little reason to love the Russians, in her book *Born for Trouble* stresses this very fact of the safety with which she went about the city at the same date. I never learned who this Englishman was, but he did, apparently, take it into his head that Bertie and I were unsuitable persons to be let loose in China, and he made some attempt to avert this catastrophe, but without result.

When we were in Saigon, we went to a small zoo, where there was a lazy crocodile or alligator dozing in his pond while people tried to torment him into action, which angered me. There was also an elephant beside the pond, demanding buns, which one was evidently required to buy from his keeper, which we dutifully did. Behind us, however, came our English friend and enemy from the *Porthos*, immaculate in his white suit. Imperiously he waved aside the request to buy a bun, whereupon that elephant, with uncanny aim and speed, deluged the poor man with dirty water from his trunk. I cannot say that we deplored this blow to British prestige.

Saigon [so I informed my mother] is a French town in Cochin China —very rich fertile country, but all swampy and full of mosquitoes and malaria. They live by growing rice and the Europeans look fearfully wealthy and too comfortable. The town is delightfully laid out, with boulevards and cafés, just like Paris, but yet one cannot feel that part of it to be real. The swamps and native huts and tropical thickets are so close at hand, and give one an unhealthy nightmare feeling. The rooms at the hotel are full of lizards, which eat the insects and are probably harmless, but none the less one does not enjoy sleeping in their company.

As Bertie and I lay under our canopy and mosquito netting at night, I could not sleep for horror of those lizards. Bertie began to soothe me by reciting poetry, most especially Keats' sonnet which begins 'When I have fears that I may cease to be', which I have, since that day, always preferred to the more famous 'last sonnet'. How often in Cornwall have I looked upon the 'night's starred face' and watched those 'cloudy symbols of a high romance', which are a feature of Cornish skies, and been transported back to that tropical night—in what for me was already the sinister city of Saigon—and a tender memory.

Once I went down to the edge of some swampy water, in the dark, listened to the chirping of crickets, the distant sound of the native people away in their huts. And I wondered about them and what they thought of their destiny and the Europeans. Bertie and I watched the French men and women as they came out, driven in their rickshaws to the cafés for the evening apéritif, as the air cooled. They all seemed to look pale and unhealthy, not, somehow, belonging. The women were elegantly dressed, pale too, like exotic orchids. Once in the mid-day sun we saw an elderly, plump woman being pulled along, followed by rickshaws containing children. She looked fit and cheerful, we thought it might be that her absorption in useful work had made her so. We went to some sort of operatic show at the theatre; lizards crawled up the proscenium and bats flew out from the wings. We also saw an Annamese play, which featured very rich clothes and very little action, but the audience sat in rapt attention.

The Chinese life in Saigon was vital and cheerful, in sharp contrast with that of the Europeans. Cholon, the Chinese quarter, or town, situated on the outskirts of Saigon, was full of life and colour—I remember the fat jolly butcher, with an exposed belly, like a Buddha, sharpening and brandishing his knives under the flaring torchlights. Here Professor Liang did his blossoming with an invitation to us to dine with him. I described the evening to my mother:

Just outside Saigon is the Chinese town Cholon and we went there to see the streets and shops and to have dinner with Professor Liang and some friends of his in Saigon. It was in a real Chinese restaurant in a little room on the first floor of a corner house, and it opened out on to a balcony on both sides. Just below were all the shops and bright lights and noise and chattering people, and not far off clashing cymbals and beating tom toms outside the theatre. We ate with chopsticks, several dozen courses and they all laughed to see us try to manage them. We had two singing girls to entertain us and real green Chinese tea in tiny Chinese cups. The Chinese in Saigon are rich as they really cultivate the rice and there is a Chinese Chamber of Commerce. When they heard that we were there and going to dine with Professor Liang, they engaged the next room to ours and invited us in to drink champagne and solemnly welcomed us as the friends and benefactors of China. The table was all decorated with garlands of tropical flowers and leaves, bright colours and queer intoxicating scents and they all stood and drank solemnly while we sat, after the singing girls had poured the champagne and put ice into it. Mr Liang introduced us as Professor Russell and the Very Intellectual Miss Black. We were quite overwhelmed . . .

After Saigon our voyage was easier and more ordinary. Our interesting French friends had gone ashore; Hong Kong, which we were only able to see briefly, was very 'sane' and British in its superficial aspect, after the nightmarish thoughts that had assailed me in Saigon. At long last the *Porthos* was alongside at Shanghai. Packed up and ready to disembark, we leaned on the rail and hopefully scanned the quay for some of our Chinese hosts to greet us. Between us and the shore buzzed a depressing, unwelcoming cloud of horrible insects. Other passengers were going ashore, but still no sign of any reception committee for us. Turning to one another, and recalling Bertie's misgivings at the signature on his invitation, we burst out laughing and simultaneously exclaimed: 'Fu Ling Yu!'

Well, here we were, and Bertie having so far defrayed our expenses, we had nothing left, and not the least idea where we were supposed to go. Still laughing, Bertie told me to look in my handbag for the last dollars; he had been teasing me en route about the way change got to the bottom of my bag, and was, at times, useful when we needed a small amount of cash. Eventually, and before long, our Chinese friends arrived, having got wrong information about the ship's arrival. We were soon in a pleasant Chinese hotel and had no reason to complain of the attention bestowed upon us.

For the first time I heard speeches in Chinese at a Shanghai meeting to welcome us—the strange singing lilt of the tones, and here in Shanghai also sibilant sounds. As is well known, spoken Chinese varies from one province to another. We found that we were not to proceed at once to Peking, which Bertie rather regretted, for he had been invited, as he understood, to lecture at the University there. Now began a round of visits and a tour up the Yangtse. In Shanghai we were taken to the Commercial Press, an impressive publishing venture, which was bringing out translations into Chinese of modern books. We were interviewed, photographed, our remarks published in the local press. Most foreigners at that date, not taking the trouble to read or speak Chinese, which was, in any case, a formidable task, were largely ignorant of what the Chinese were reading and writing. A great many 'dangerous thoughts' were flying about. A well-known comic story is that the Chinese printed the Communist Manifesto in the middle of some Bibles, which was never discovered by the earnest white missionaries who distributed the Holy Word.

In Shanghai there came to us Chao Yuen-ren, who was to be interpreter for Bertie's lectures, and who had been sent for from the United States, where he had been for about ten years, because he was deemed to be the one person capable of this task. He travelled with us on the train up to Hangchow. I remember him leaning out of the window beaming from ear to ear; he told me that it was an incredible delight to smell the scents of his own countryside once more after so long an absence. Mr Chao became a part of our lives; more of him later. As with most Chinese, it was impossible to guess his age, he seemed at this time like a postgraduate university student.

Three days beside the lovely lake at Hangchow did give us a breathing-space, though all the time we were now meeting people. We enjoyed the simplicity of the Chinese hotel beside the lake, but made the acquaintance of the hardness of Chinese beds, which were no more than a cane mesh stretched on a wooden frame. Our Chinese friends, we noticed, brought their padded bedrolls with them. In the distance somewhere we could hear sounds of some entertainment going on, shouts of 'Hao Hao' in applause, and a persistent phrase of what I must call music, 'te tum, te tum, te tum, tetetum', repeated over and over for hours and hours, always followed by applause. Our friends told us that this was a circus and the phrase accompanied the final feat of one turn. It may seem absurd, but this phrase punctuates my whole impression of the first visit to Hangchow, monotonously, though not disagreeably. The lake and the mountains were exquisite. Bertie and I were specially delighted with an 'Enjoying Rain Pavilion', typical with its four pillars and tiled roof. Here one could sit in the dry, and watch the rain sweep across the lake; on the roof were little effigies of birds and other creatures who take pleasure in wetness. I visited Hangchow once again, when I was at a Women's Congress in 1956. We stayed then at a newly-built hotel, only just finished, which had none the less managed to keep a Chinese style and not ruin the corner of the landscape where it stood. It had every modern comfort and luxury.

Bertie and I were taken back to Shanghai and thence up to Nanking, where he lectured to the Science Society. Then by boat up the Yangtse to Hankow and from there to Changsha in Hunan, back to Hankow and finally from there by train to Peking. Somewhere on this trip I remember us being carried in sedan chairs, up and up through bamboo groves to a temple on a mountain. I was amazed at the height of the bamboo trees. Chinese scenery at once fascinated me; I discovered with surprise and delight that Chinese pictures were not fantasies, but really depicted the landscape. I wrote to my mother from Peking:

2 *November 1921*. Chinese scenery is perfectly divine, delicate as Chinese pictures, with distant, misty mountains always in view. And the Yangtse is, I imagine, quite one of the most beautiful rivers in the world.

There are indeed, few more romantic sights than the Chinese junks, with their great sails, gliding rapidly past downstream.

The waterfront at Hankow, with imposing modern buildings, banks and suchlike, contrasted with the burdened coolies loading junks along the quay, and still more with the medieval, curly, tiled roofs of Changsha and the glimpse which I caught on the river bank of thatched sheds, beside which a woman was beating out rice-husks with a flail.

On top of our tropical journey we found this excursion tiring; Bertie had to speak several times in each place to vast audiences of Chinese students, whose eyes looked as thirsty for knowledge as parched ground for rain. I spoke too, about art and education in Russia, and about women's education, sometimes to big mixed audiences and sometimes to women. In my letter of 2 November I wrote:

Everywhere we are treated like an Emperor and Empress, indeed it becomes terribly fatiguing to be so looked up to. The Chinese papers report and describe us every day, what we look like and what we wear and so on, and photographs all the time. B is represented even on a cigarette advertisement, with his finger held up as in benediction, looking like an Ancient Sage. He is never seen in this attitude in real life, thank the Lord.

For me it was quite an ordeal to be called upon to make speeches, but it was also here that I was able to learn how, since every few words were followed by the translation, thus allowing one time to think what to say next.

In Changsha on the night of the eclipse of the moon, at a banquet, Bertie referred to the tale of the Chinese Emperor who had executed his astronomers for not keeping due watch on the eclipse, whereas the common people had played their part by firing crackers, lighting fires, beating gongs, in order to frighten away the Heavenly Dog about to devour the celestial orb; for, even as we feasted and addressed our Western wisdom to the assembled intelligentsia, outside the populace were once more fulfilling their traditional duty. As we were carried in sedan chairs to go aboard our river steamer, on all sides the crackers were going off, the gongs were beating and the streets were thronged with a mass of people yelling themselves hoarse. Deafened by the awful din, we were sure that that Heavenly Dog must have been stricken with terror.

Only after Bertie's death did I learn that his exquisitely appropriate joke on that occasion reached only those who knew English: it was not translated, Mr Chao having given way to the local interpreter. What is more, recently, on Mr Chao's request, I had to recall to him what the joke was. Among those who heard Bertie at one of the meetings in that neighbourhood was Mao Tse-tung. He was critical of Bertie's contention that communism could be brought about without the dictatorship of the proletariat and seizure of power, by the education of all classes. This was, said Mao, not feasible, since money and all educational weapons are in capitalist hands; children will thus perpetually be educated in the capitalist tradition, unless a sharp break is achieved.*

At last we arrived in Peking, where I felt very remote from the making of blackberry jam, to which my mother's first letter referred! I wrote that we were now relieved to be able to settle down to studying Chinese conditions, reading and writing. I conveyed a message from Bertie that my parents should no longer call him Mr Russell, and at the same time told them of his Chinese name Luo Su, this being the nearest the Chinese could get to pronouncing Russell. The characters which represented it meant, we were told, 'simple oyster'. I have always thought this expressed very well Bertie's subtle and evasive way of responding to the Chinese repeated requests for advice about their future.

'We hardly ever see Europeans,' I wrote at this time, 'and when we do, we are glad we don't meet them often, because the kind you meet out here all seem villainous or frivolous or both, barring the missionaries, who are good but dull.' In fact our encounters with missionaries were somewhat embarrassing, both for them and for us. Bertie and I were determined that there should be no pretence of our being married, or of a platonic relationship. On our Yangtse trip this caused trouble, which we at the time could not have foreseen, and which our very courteous Chinese hosts did not explain. It was suggested that in Changsha we might stay at the mission, but, because this would have

* see *The Political Thought of Mao Tse-tung*, Stuart R. Schram (Penguin, 1969), p. 296 ff.

meant our separation, Bertie and I opted for an hotel. This, as our friends well knew, was likely to be infested with bugs. A woeful night was spent by us all; we were deeply sorry when we understood the discomfort that our rigid principles had imposed on our friends. No doubt the missionaries, though perhaps offended, were also laughing. And it must be said that we never again met bugs in the whole of our stay.

Once in Peking our days were fully occupied. We now met the sponsor of our visit, Liang Chi-chao, who was a progressive, literary, and extremely cultured man, who had been in bad odour before the 1911 revolution. He was now financing, almost entirely, I believe, the scheme for bringing professors from the West to lecture at the National University of Peking. Professor John Dewey and his wife had been in residence now for a year and had also been invited to stay longer. The Chinese had been deeply shocked to see the Europeans, who constantly sought to impress with their superior morality, engaged in savage warfare, one of the results of which had been the revolution in the great neighbouring country of Russia. They themselves, it is true, had done away with their centuries-old imperialism and now had a constitutional monarch in the shape of the young Emperor who lived a secluded life within the Forbidden City, being taught how to be constitutional by an English tutor, Mr Johnston. But there was no real group, or body of opinion, capable of leading the nation out of its confusion brought about by events in the modern world.

For some years Chinese students, in part through use of the Boxer indemnity funds, had been sent abroad, with the result that they adopted much of foreign cultures. Peking National University had been founded in the hope of rearing generations of educated Chinese whose cultural basis would now be their own country, albeit a more modern curriculum and culture. At the same time, according to Chinese tradition true wisdom and guidance could come only from Great Sages, who taught, not a religion, but the way that a man should live in the world. There was Lao Tse and the way of Tao, but more influential and completely interwoven with the patriarchal system was the teaching of Confucius with its detailed code of conduct. Some new great philosopher—so ran the hope—would guide the country and set its feet on the path for the future. Such men as Dewey and Bertrand Russell had been cast for this role by the liberal intelligentsia. In 1920 future developments in China were unclear. But on 4 May 1919 there had been a revolt and demonstration by the students of the National University, which is now honoured as one of the first great events of the People's Revolution. This ferment of ideas thus already existed among the students whom Bertie had been invited to teach. At about this time Mao Tse-tung was employed as a librarian at the University in Peking. The Great Sage to come was, as yet, obscure.

Liang Chi-chao was courteous, civilized, delightful. The mystery of Mr Fu Ling-yu was solved in the person of Professor Fu, a tall Northern

Chinese, young and handsome and of extremely fine presence. There was the brilliant and witty Hu Shih, the earnest and sincere V. K. Ting, the geologist, who worked with Teilhard de Chardin.

The oddest mixture of cosmopolitan society was at that time in Peking. There were, of course, the legations of foreign governments, all involved in their various intrigues for further dominance over China; there were the businessmen frankly out for exploitation; and there were the missions, of which the Americans did most for education and medicine: they had founded the Peking Medical College, with its fine, green tiled roof, Chinese style, and the University of Tsing Hua, outside the city. Now and then we met Mr Johnston, tutor to the Emperor. He was what one called an 'old China hand', one who had come to love the country so much that he never wished to leave it. One of the most comical sights I remember in Peking was Mr Johnston, in formal dress, top hat and all, being carried in a sedan chair with great pomp and ceremony, through the gates and courtyards, beneath the yellow tiled roofs of the Forbidden City, to pay his respects to his young pupil on the occasion of the Emperor's birthday.

Our relations with the conventional people, what nowadays is called the Establishment, were equivocal. Strictly we were beyond the pale, we were living in sin, opposing many of the cherished beliefs which our fellow countrymen were seeking to impart to the Chinese. At the same time the Chinese were so obviously delighted with us, and our doings were thus so much the talk of the town that curiosity to meet us would overcome the stern duty of ostracizing us. Clearly it was galling for those who extolled the Western custom of monogamy to be slyly reminded by some Chinese grandee that 'their most eminent philosopher had arrived in China accompanied by his favourite concubine'. But to the young Chinese our stand on sexual morals had real significance. They were struggling to free themselves from the toils of a patriarchal system and ancestor-worship, which not only arranged marriages but still gave parents the right to authorize the execution of a recalcitrant son or daughter. While we were in China the more courageous of the younger generation more and more asserted their right to marry for love, and would celebrate their union with a simple ceremony, calling this a 'Russell marriage'.

Those first weeks in Peking did involve, as I complained to my mother, a great many social and formal calls. The American Ambassador did not hesitate, but invited us to lunch; the British were rather more reserved, even a trifle furtive. I had never acquired the habit of, nor taste for, formal social occasions, and I am sure that I must at times have given offence. The truth was that I found the superior attitude of the Europeans towards the Chinese intolerable. Official people lived within their four walls and knew very little about what was happening outside their own social circle. The British had a small racecourse to occupy them and the usual round of lunches, dinners, teas and functions. I remember being asked whether I was teaching my students English language and grammar at the University, when we were in fact discussing the economic interpretation of history. There was, too, the diplomat who took pleasure in meeting the Chinese, but complained that, when he wished to whisper sweet nothings into the delicate ear of a Chinese beauty, it was disconcerting to have her reply by asking whether he had read Keynes' *Economic Consequences of the Peace.*. That should have opened his eyes— or ears—but such hints certainly had no results in a more intelligent British policy towards the Chinese question.

Bertie had been invited to teach the Chinese, and we both wanted to get to know them and understand their problems. Chinese visitors would announce their imminent calls, but they would rarely arrive at any stated time or make their call of any stated length. They would sit beside the cup of china tea which etiquette required, discoursing elegantly. We would never dare to drink our tea, in case this should be the signal that we wanted our visitor to depart. It was evident to us that we were in a pre-industrial civilization, in which the exact measurement of time was of little importance. The pre-industrial nature of the people had also struck me on the railway journey to Peking, when I had noticed the peasants trying to jump on and off a moving train and falling, through lacking our acquired habit of following the movement of the vehicle.

Impressions of the beauty of that old civilization flooded in on us. It was distilled from the dignity and manners of our Chinese visitors, who would bow, hands folded in the sleeves of their long black satin robes; it spoke through the white marble steps and balustrades, the figures of lions and dragons, the shops with their exquisite silks and embroideries, ivory, porcelain and jade.

From the hotel where we were at first housed, Bertie and I had to decide whether, like some foreigners, we would live in a modern-style flat. We hankered after a real Chinese house. Bertie was dubious at first, but I undertook to find and furnish a home for us within a fortnight. He gave me some money and left me to it. In that house, whose every feature is as vivid as if I lived there only yesterday, I spent the happiest months of my whole life.

Chinese houses are designed for a very private life. The streets in Peking as I knew it then, were no more than narrow tracks between grey walls, in which at intervals a gateway surmounted by a tiled overhang would appear. There were Chinese characters on the wooden doors. In our house, 2 Suei An Buo Buo Hutung, there was a first small courtyard, with one room whose wall backed on the street; on each side—East and West as the Chinese would say—were kitchen and servants' quarters. Then came a screen beyond which was the second courtyard. A separate screen stood in front of the opening entrance to this court, and you entered round it, for it kept out the evil spirits, who can travel only in a straight line. East and West in this second court were the two rooms in which Mr Chao came to live; the main part of the house faced south with three steps and a narrow veranda which we embellished with pots of flowers. Here were four rooms, one of fair size, the others small. The bedroom was almost entirely filled by a double bed, thus we had a dressing room; then there was the study where Bertie worked, and the very small room off that, which was mine. The door, by which you entered straight into the main room, had some glass panels, as also did the lower part of the windows, but the upper part was of lattice lined with rice-paper, and the only way to let in fresh air was by rolling up a small part of this paper. There were lattice and rice-paper shutters to fit the lower windows, if required. The veranda, of course, had the typical round pillars, and the roofs were of the lovely Chinese tiles in grey. We had a tiny annexe in which was an earth closet that was cleared daily and kept scrupulously clean. The Chinese use of human excrement for manure, instead of pouring it all into rivers or the sea, is well known. Like most foreigners we had been advised to beware of fresh salads, or other products which might infect our non-immunized bodies. No bathroom, of course, but the luxury of a hot bath in your bedroom.

The design of the house provided a suntrap, so that, however cold it might be—and Peking winters are bitter—it was not easy to guess the wind and temperature outside our own little court. Chinese houses were, I think, warmed by charcoal braziers, or hardly at all, but we had small stoves, which our Head 'Boy' would stoke to such heat that we began to fear that he received a 'squeeze' from the sellers of coal.

With perhaps justifiable pride I boasted of the speed with which I got us into that house, of dealing with Chinese workmen, bargaining, engaging servants, planning the colour schemes. Everything had to be acquired: linen, cutlery, china, kitchen equipment, as well as furnishings. I did the dull buying in the mornings while Bertie was working, and then in the afternoon we would go to the junk-shops outside the city gate and bargain on our fingers for Chinese chairs and tables. In the vogue for foreign fashions the Chinese were furnishing in what we called boarding-house style—furniture stained light oak, which, apart from a modern bed (which was, however, pretty hard), we could not endure. Armchairs and stuffed sofas acquired by the foreigners seemed to us equally out of place. Chinese-style chairs were hard and stiff backed, but I sought for comfort with cheap cane couches softened with cushions of lovely silks. We bought an old Chinese sofa, of very dark brown redwood, smelling good, a sort of Buddhistic smell, our friends told us, the kind of sofa used for smoking opium, they said. But soft blue silk cushions on its fine cane surface gave us the comfort to lie and dream without need of the drug. A tall camphorwood press with shining brass fittings soon scented our clothes.

Workmen came and fitted the traditional yellow woven straw matting on the floors, which were then covered by wonderful hand-woven carpets and rugs, whose size, colour and pattern we could order for ourselves at the workshops where we could see them being made. One of these, a vivid yellow, lies even now on my bedroom floor. We asked for a translation of the characters on the two panels of our street door. 'Poetry and learning endure for ever, and honesty increases the family', we were told. 'Well,' said Bertie, 'you must be poetry and I learning, and surely, since we are honest, the rest may follow.'

We now lived, as I wrote to Ogden, in 'disgraceful luxury, four men-servants and my maid for sewing and mending'. These were the male cook, two rickshaw boys, and the Head Boy who in his long, pale-blue robe, with his delicate hands and movements, was a paragon of an upper servant, with authority over the others, except that we sometimes saw the cook for special orders. One never knows to what extent the devotion of such a servant is real or simulated; he is at hand to minister to your every comfort, to see that you take your medicine if you are ill, to watch over and know everything. Did a rickshaw boy offend some-how, this overlord would draw himself up with dignity and say, 'Master, I have *blamed* him.' Once when I was looking for some change in the small drawer of a table, supposed to be almost secret, the Boy came behind me, hands folded in sleeves and smiling gently, and said: 'Only one dollar there, Missy, he bad.' He was scrupulously honest himself, and proud. Once we asked him who, he thought, would win if the Chinese were at war: 'Chinese man, for certain', was the un-hesitating reply.

Foreigners who did not know Chinese were almost entirely in the hands of their servants. When we were bidden to lunch or dinner any-where, we did not know where, nor how to get there. We placed ourselves in our rickshaws and were carried like parcels, according to the direction given by the Boy. What is astonishing in view of the way the Chinese had been treated is the extent to which the foreigners' confidence in this very Chinese integrity was not misplaced.

This luxury gave both Bertie and me the leisure to do what we most desired, which was to prepare our work for the Chinese, do our own writing and thinking, but most of all to continue with the exchange of ideas and exploration of each other's personality in which we had been engaged now for six months or more with no sign of boredom and with a strong wish not to be distracted by outside events from our growing love and intimacy. I had burned my boats and embarked on this adventure, and thus, with barriers down, I loved Bertie with adoration and almost worship. He was lover, father-figure, teacher, a companion never at a loss for a witty rejoinder or a provoking bit of nonsense. Paternal though he might be towards me, I was, in spite of being so much younger, maternal towards him. My feeling that he was not tough, but needed someone to watch over and cherish him, persisted— a deep female pride that without us the male can never accomplish or survive.

Not only our house, but the whole city was a romantic setting for our love. Palaces and temples of great beauty were set off by the very bright sun and clear sky; there was the colourful life of the streets, the oddness of this cold, dry desert of the north where even camels were to be seen. After our day's work we would walk for a while, and Bertie would observe how remarkable it was that with this immense journey through space-time we should arrive back at our own front door. I cannot describe this better than in a poem I wrote at the time:

Twilight Walk, Peking

In the dusk we walk together
Through the busy streets the rickshaw pullers pass
And boys with bamboo poles
Balance their wares and cry them with a song
Whose twisted rhythm nor begins nor ends,
But, like a fragment of some secret fairy music
Breaks all unlearned from their astonished lips.
The tuneful bells
On the rich carriages of wealthy men
Ring sharply through the darkening air.

In the broad street
That East to West through all the city goes,
The sun that's dying and the rising moon
Have met and mingled;
Twined their honey tendrils over green roofs of temples,
Flooded all the ground with misty opalescence;
Lent a wistful veil of beauty
To shapes and faces passing at this shadowy hour.

House lamps are lighted;
Through soft lattices
They too are spreading honey-coloured light;
The square lamps on the fruit stalls
Encircle with a band of orange ribbon
Golden persimmons, yellow pummeloes,
Black-eyed and roguish children bargaining for pea-nuts;
Coveting millet candy,
Weighing their coppers slowly like their elders;
Women are gossiping, old men are smoking,
The cookshop boy is singing as his dumplings boil.

'What peace and loveliness are here,' I said,
You smile and nod your head;
And coming home, our eyes,
That were o'erfilled with beauty,
Brimmed and wept.

Bertie now took delight in teaching me about many things, history, philosophy, even Einstein. He stimulated and encouraged me as he would have done any able pupil. I could comprehend fairly well his theory of 'events' in *The Analysis of Matter* on which he was working. I stretched my mind to follow as he tried to make me understand something of the modern physicists' view of matter, and how Einstein's space-time upset the Newtonian universe of my eighteenth-century researches. There were moments when I dimly grasped the significance of Einstein, as he explained to me that matter was not solid lumps hurled about by dynamic forces, but that 'things take the easiest path through space-time'. This glimpse of the post-Newtonian cosmology and the dissolving of matter coloured my subsequent thought, and, together with what I drew from the way the Chinese thought and lived, shaped my view of the world and how I should live within it.

The joy of living side by side with Bertie was that he was never superior, he was always such fun; he would provoke you into clarifying an idea by some sly comment and seemed as pleased with what you said and wrote as with his own work. I was no docile sponge: the argument about Russia and the potential of industrialism went on. There were ways in which I contributed to his thought; I think that I helped to keep the old-fashioned liberal in him at bay, and enabled him, so to speak, to go on from there. For him science and philosophy were something pure, above the battle, like mathematics. He would not admit the thesis that I was developing about their relation to, or influence on, the way men thought about politics. When he wrote the *History of Western Philosophy* I think that he had come to accept some notions like mine. In general, of course, the term philosophy is loosely used. What the young Chinese of 1920, like many ordinary people, wanted of a philosopher was that he should give some general interpretations, principles and guides to action. This Bertie would have called political and social philosophy (or science, perhaps); technical philosophy, the speculations of academic philosophers, was a different thing.

As a respite from contemporary problems we would read poetry aloud, or from Mainucci's *Adventures at the Court of the Great Mogul*, or *The Travels of Messieurs Gabet and Huc in Tartary and Tibet*, long books which Bertie had packed specially for this purpose. We chuckled over the preaching of the two Jesuit missionaries to Chinese nomads, who, when the good fathers thought them on the point of conversion, would nod their heads sagely and remark: 'Ah, religions are many, but reason is one.' Not only did we live in our growing love and intimacy; we were both in an exalted frame of mind. I tried to express in a poem the relation of our personal love to serving the troubled world; it concluded:

And they are knit in love whose passions shed
This mystic radiance, who dare lay their head,
'Neath Heaven their canopy, the Universe their bed.

Bertie had been dragged out from his ivory tower in Cambridge by horror at the slaughter of the young in war. Now he could see that concern for human beings could not stop with this one protest; he was taking into himself and seeking to remedy all the troubles of the world. I now felt that my own sense of mission since the Russian visit could be joined to his, and that together there might be much that we could accomplish.

Bertie was now lecturing on the Analysis of Mind once a week, with a weekly seminar class on this in English, and a fortnightly one in Chinese through an interpreter. On Sundays he had a popular course to help the understanding of technical philosophy. In the New Year he was to give a series of lectures on Social Philosophy. In preparation for this I gave six lectures on Political Thought and Economic Conditions. A Society for Studying Russell's Philosophy had been formed. Week by week I was called upon to speak to the women students on women's education, professional life, socialism, marriage, and to meet them for discussion. A letter from a woman student which I happen to have preserved gives some idea of their problems. It is written in a very clear hand.

Peking University

Dear Madam,   16 Dec. 1920.

Permit me to have the liberty to write to you without a previous introduction. Though I am a stranger to you yet I am a friend, and I have a strong belief that you have an interest on the women's movements in the country. Therefore your opinions to this concern are undoubtedly valuable; so I unhesitatingly proceed to write to ask you about your opinions on following questions:—

1. We are believers of women's rights and equality with man and to accomplish this we believe that the only way is through education, but at present the control of the board of education of this country is in the hand of a group of conservative almost corrupt men, which conditions allow not radical change. How would you suggest to us to introduce a system of general education for girls and to elevate their education?

2. The women's right is a good matter. But when we propagate the idea we are sure to meet with difficulty from the authorities of the school or the government. How shall we get at the thing most wisely?

3. It is our hope that you will also write us an essay which we will gladly publish in the 'Woman's Review' on any subject you choose which I am sure will benefit our fellow countrywomen greatly.

4. We hope you will also write an essay specially expressing your opinion on the question of love and marriage, to be published in the same magazine.

With sincere wishes for your health and happiness.
I remain yours truly
S. P. Young.

Needless to say I responded as best I could to such requests, and in their turn the women students gave me a most beautiful satin scroll on which was embroidered in black silk some old Chinese characters, and there was an inscription describing the merits of the Very Intellectual Miss Black at one side.

While there were students whose interest in philosophy was genuine and who carried ability to pursue it, Bertie complained that on the whole they seemed to want to suck up knowledge rather than to use their minds to think for themselves. Already there was talk of asking him to stay another year, but he felt that his subject and style of teaching were not suited to what seemed to him elementary work. Of course what they wanted from him was political thought and advice, and when we both spoke about our views on religion to the philosophical society, they were delighted. At this, I wrote to my mother (16 January 1921): 'All the missionaries got into a great state and are now making speeches all over the place in reply. The Chinese simply love this, they enjoy watching the antics of rival European factions, and B and I enjoy providing this amusement.'

As we got to know the students better, the ferment set up by the Russian Revolution became more evident. Students, we learned, were coming and going across Siberia; there was as yet no Communist Party, this was formed a year or so later. We also learned one odd fact, that there was difficulty about communication with Moscow, because either in Omsk or Tomsk some question of appropriation of funds had arisen and whoever was responsible was hindering visits lest he be found out. Gradually we both became convinced that the only way in which China would ultimately defeat the foreign capitalists would be by going communist. Bertie in fact so advised his official diplomatic friends on our return to England, but he was not, of course, believed. What also gradually became clear was that communism, so far from being suited to an advanced industrial society, was just what was needed where industrialism was in its infancy, since it could then be developed by a state controlled by the people and not by private enterprise. Nor would there exist a powerful and rooted system of profit-making capitalism to overthrow.

In contrast to our peaceful life in Peking, elsewhere in China people were dying of famine. The foreigners organized some relief and were shocked at the apparent indifference of the Chinese. My parents, who had sent us Christmas fare, were worried at the reports of famine. I explained to them that this was not like a war shortage, 'but an old-fashioned medieval famine which only affects the actual district and then only the country folk. People here are horribly callous about relief. They leave their neighbours severely alone, even when they are dying. At home we succour the starving, but then we also do all we can to hurt our neighbours. The Chinese just remain placidly indifferent. I think the attitudes are about equal in their results.'

The so-called Chinese indifference, as I came to understand, rested on their knowledge that the hunger of their people, first in one area, then another, was like a bottomless pit, and as yet they had found no general remedy. Then, too, they lived close to and were almost part of their soil, and fatalistic about their closeness to death. On the other hand, while living, they were very much at home in the world, seeking no mystical escape route, displaying intense sensuous enjoyment in their art, their music, their theatre, their hospitality and food.

We had many pleasures: we danced the night away on New Year's Eve at the Peking hotel, and savoured many delightful meals at Chinese restaurants. Nowadays the Chinese classical theatre is appreciated by Westerners, but I record that the English and Americans I spoke with in Peking described it as barbarous and horrible caterwauling. I was fascinated by it and had the pleasure of seeing the famous Mei Lan Fan in some traditional female roles—no women performed. It was like what the Shakespearean theatre may have been, in that the square apron stage stood out, the enthusiastic audience chewed melon seeds, ate oranges, threw the husks and skins about; steaming hot wet towels for wiping faces were also thrown from hand to hand. Fights between the ordinary soldiers in the plays were marvels of acrobatics, and the strutting warrior generals with their thick-soled shoes, their backs a nest of small pennons, hurling their defiance from behind absurd symbolic fortress walls, had a highly artificial savagery that was the reverse of barbaric. It was not easy at first to take the shrill operatic singing, but you could eventually appreciate it, as did the vociferous audience. In fact our modern pop singing is curiously similar. The conventions were odd, too. In one play a young wife was accused of murdering her elderly husband; so modest was she that she had not observed who it was that came through the window and did the awful deed, but she feared that it might have been her lover whom, seen in the street from her curtained litter, she had wanted to marry. A wise judge resolved the mystery by imprisoning the lovers together and listening in to their agonized exchanges: the true murderer turned out to be some low fellow, a tailor or some such, out for blackmail or revenge. He bore the unmistakable sign of his low and probably immoral character by the white symbol plastered across his nose.

A serene pleasure of these days, just for the two of us, was to go on Monday, which was our day off, to the Temple of Heaven, with sandwiches and hard-boiled eggs. We took with us Shakespeare and— diabolo, at which I enjoyed practising my skill. We sat on the marble steps in the bright sun, gazing at those heavenly blue roofs and scarlet lattices, with only the carved birds and a few rooks in the arbor vitae to keep us company. We needed such rest, for both of us were often unwell in spite of our first good reaction to the cold northern climate. The bitter winds searched through fur-lined coats, and I was often below par. Bertie was always susceptible to bronchitis. At times he teased me with being ill from boredom at the visitors that I disliked; the only way to keep me in health was to preserve me from their wearisome company. It was true that I was restless; when I had finished my lectures, I thought of travelling up to Chita, for which my sewing woman was making me some warm, padded trousers. Chita was in Outer Mongolia, a whole province that had just been lost to China in a most bizarre fashion. It had been ruled by a Hutuktu, or Living Buddha; these, in Chinese custom, were allowed to marry. This Hutuktu loved wine, and also a young wife, whose Bolshevik sympathies led to his overthrow and the establishment of an independent communist republic, which it would have been interesting to visit. Meantime Bertie and I were both looking forward to the spring, when in May the plan was for us to go up the Yangtse gorges to Chungking, to visit Canton, then Japan and come home via Canada. None the less, I had an itch to know what was going on around us now; there were little wars and rumours of wars. Life went on as usual in Peking; the educated Chinese continued in their tradition that war is a low pursuit fit only for greedy war-lords and the vulgar; they often indicated to us that there was very little that they could do about the state of their country.

In January we gave two parties for our students, a mixture of the sort of party with games that my family and I so much enjoyed organizing at home, and the Chinese style. We played blindfold 'tailing the donkey', which was drawn on the screen designed to frustrate evil spirits; I wonder what they thought of it? There was dancing and singing, firecrackers and fireworks. The courtyard, warmed with braziers, was lit with Chinese lanterns, some with a legend of welcome to the students in Chinese characters: 'It was,' I wrote, 'so beautiful, the court with the little red white lanterns swaying, and the red fires glowing, the curly old roofs for a background and overhead a brilliant starry sky.'

When the mail and the newspapers came from home our peace and happiness were broken. The Bolshevik book was out and, as might be expected, was severely criticized. To support the Russian Revolution was essential to the left and not to do so unequivocally was looked on as a betrayal. The *Daily Herald* with George Lansbury and George Young attacked, H.N. Brailsford was displeased, *The Liberator* in New York with Max and Chrystal Eastman was also on the warpath. Bertie was distressed at their lack of understanding, and their gibes at his 'Whig ancestry'. Other people have ancestors, as he intimated to me bitterly, and he felt like having a go at them on similar grounds. *The Liberator* wanted a reply from him; he was burdened with work and I wrote one for him which he fully approved and supported by a personal letter to the Eastmans. They refused to print the article, and Bertie, in anger, wanted to send it again over his own signature, but I dissuaded him, realizing that their attitude was not surprising since I was quite unknown to these people. For myself I was infuriated because I was not in England to confound the critics and had not been able to write that book which, I felt, would have promoted understanding. I was intensely angry with Claire Sheridan who had got into Russia, as I felt on the frivolous project of doing busts of the Bolshevik leaders, and had written what I thought a most harmful book, called *Russian Portrait*; among her other misdeeds was that she had said in her diary that she did not regard the Chinese as her brothers.

I unburdened myself to Ogden:

Peking, January 1921. We learn from Allen and Unwin's announcement in the *Nation* that our book, according to the C Mag is likely to become a standard work. We are left wondering what standard works you class it with—the Bible and the Koran? . . . Getting the book done and in shape was a terrible scramble . . . We never ceased talking and worrying since I landed from Russia, night and day. We are still at it. Many times the MS for the Russian book was nearly destroyed . . . The added chapters, written in Paris, were the product of our joint agony over the whole business.

Criticisms like that of George Young are therefore hard to endure . . . He and B discussed a good deal, and he ought to have found some better way of meeting B's arguments than misquotation and saying: 'Shut your mouth there's a war on.'

It's funny that Wells can say the same things as B and everyone bursts out in admiration. But then of course Wells does not suffer from aristocratic ancestry . . . A good deal of Wells's articles [are] likely to produce a good effect, but I just cannot bear the sniffy superior tone of it all. It is just as bad as that of the typical British diplomat, who from his warm and comfortable home ejaculates: 'Dear me, those Russians have no sense of humour', forgetting that he's starving them. Nor does there seem to me much humour in people who send battleships to blockade Russia and then address whining petitions against their destruction by Russian submarines. What impressed Wells most about Russia was that England would be awful without telephones and WC's I think. So it would, but what would be awful about it, would not be the inconvenience, but the fact that with the collapse of industry the hope of a socialist commonwealth collapses also.

The critics' lack of historical perspective, their dogmatic Marxism while they kept on prating about being scientific, exasperated me.

All these people are so stupid with their political make-up. Even B was. It was I who got it into his head that industrialism was infinitely more important for countries like Russia and China than the particular creed that administered it. The whole point about practical science and the industrial system it has produced is that IT and it only makes a tolerable life of work and leisure possible for everyone. Where you do not have machinery you must have slaves, —communism cannot be administered without industrial organisation. It is funny that people at home seem to be forgetting all this in the fight between capital and labour, and presently, after a long and bloody battle, they'll find themselves sitting amid the ruins of the industrial system, a thousand leagues further from communism than they were at the start. I told you when I was in London that relapse into barbarism in Europe was not at all a remote possibility and I'm more than ever convinced of that fact. Just a little more war and a blockade from a hostile USA and there we are. Every thing I said in my chapter about art and the practical problem is borne out by what one sees here in China. I can see Asia as a magnificent industrial state, but I cannot see it anything but nominally communistic, for ages to come. How can you get communism immediately, with no material basis for communal living, with foreign capitalists in possession of your ports and all important industries, and not a single soul in the country who can be trusted with money? Notwithstanding idealists can have visions of an immediate reign of communism it can be no more than a religion both in China and Russia yet . . . As a religion it may have the advantages that religions do have for states in the making, that of binding people into a community and giving them an expression of herd feeling. It is amusing to see the West supplying the East with a religion for a change. Maybe when the time comes, the East may be able to return this doubtful gift with re-civilisation of barbarous Europe. Hard work being a heretic in these days. Marxian religion is quite attractive and so simple . . . Eastman prates of a new aristocracy. It makes me sick. They can all see from analysis of the capitalist what possession of power does to a man's mind, but they imagine themselves so perfect that they would not be affected in the same way. Besides, the tyranny of a doctrinaire may be far worse than that of a fat capitalist . . . I get absolutely crazy at the lack of understanding of the scientific outlook in all these people who talk so proudly of science . . . Communism could come in simply and scientifically without all this metaphysical twaddle and dogma, but it won't. We shall all have to subscribe to the materialistic conception of history, to forget that the whole purpose of the movement is to give education and freedom to more people, not to take it away from everybody . . . To say that there are *Non*-materialistic causes of things is a dreadful heresy. And the absurdity of the whole thing being that pure scientific thinking and no material cause at all, started the world off on this tack.

Sweet Og, love us still. Soon we may have no friends but Lloyd George and we don't want him.

The letter continues in frivolous vein with some account of Bertie writing articles for Japan, of which a mild one on patriotism was none the less censored by their Government.

> We learn that the blood of the young Japanese 'was boiled with enthusiasm' when they read the article. As we send one article per month we fear their blood will be all boiled away before we get there to lecture in July . . . Sometimes we skip for exercise in our courtyard. I want to photograph B at it, but the fellow eludes me. He says I shall send it you for the CM [*Cambridge Magazine*] entitled 'Thought in China is advancing by leaps and bounds.'

The articles written for Japan were to be the basis for the book on *The Prospects of Industrial Civilisation*, which Bertie had begun to write, which we discussed together and looked upon as our joint work. It was not possible to evade these problems as one looked at the political world, both East and West. My depression about Europe deepened and I was not always so sanguine about the need for industrialism in undeveloped countries. To my mother on 15 February 1921 I wrote:

> Vast budget of belated papers and press cuttings. News from England with the exception of your letters and one or two others B gets, always comes like a blast of madness and fire into our peaceful existence here. The struggling and yelling and spiteful writing—all people on a shipwrecked liner . . . each pushes and stabs at the other, each offers some new way of saving the whole shipload, but always only with the secret design of saving his own skin. That, sweetheart, is what Europe looks like to us from here. And as for America she represents the grinning pirate, standing by without assistance, ready to salve the property when the lives of all the property owners have been lost. I am filled with hatred for money, for battleships, for industry, for factories, for the grind, grind, grind of the machine on all our creative instincts, grinding out the good and putting power in the hands of evil. Comfort is bought at too high a price. Let us scrap industry, even if we go ragged and hungry, and lift our hands and square our shoulders and say at least we are men now, not cogs in a diabolical machine of destruction.

At this distance in time our distress may seem exaggerated, but post-war Europe was indeed in a bad way, and we had both recently come from the world-shaking experience of the Russian Revolution. Bertie, still affected by his isolation during the war, now felt isolated even from those who should have been with him. I wanted to champion and defend him: it was about this time that I had an absurd dream, in which we were both in a small boat being carried along in a violent flood. I knelt in the bow, trying to fend off obstacles that might sink us. Bertie was standing up haranguing the troubled waters, above the tumult. 'Was that a good speech?' he called. 'Yes, my dear,' I shouted back, 'but do you think anyone heard it?'

In my waking hours, however, I made for him a not very good but tender poem.

To an Idealist in the Present Time

Let my love be to thee, my Life, an hidden shelter
Not from the winds and storms that tear the hearts of men,
Not from dark dreams of bloody tumult and the welter
Of staggering tyrant realms that shall not rise again.
For thou art but ennobled by this pain.
But from the snaky bitterness that creeping, stealing,
Coils round the heart that needs must tread the lonely way,
Till cold death fright him. Thou, my tenderness thy healing,
Shalt keep thy spirit armoured for the nobler fray!
For thou must speak that truth which conquers pain.

We presently entertained a very welcome visitor, Eileen Power, who was on a Travelling Fellowship and full of amusing gossip about Cambridge where 'nasty rumours about Dora Black were going about'. Eileen replied that she was staying with the nasty rumours.

I had some very decided views about women and their education which I expressed to my mother when I learned that Miss Jex Blake (Kits) was retiring from being Mistress of Girton. I wrote that I loved her and thought that Girton needed her, as a strong attitude about women was essential to cope with their disadvantages in the University. I might even have aspired—as I said—to be Mistress of Girton myself, though I knew this to be impossible. Bertie often teased me about this, he said that I had the right kind of forceful nose. I objected vigorously— as I still do—to a ladylike education for women, I wanted them to be strong and free, 'not taught to intrigue for marriage, and specially they ought not to be able to give up serious work when they marry, unless they have several children'.

Mr Chao, more correctly styled Chao Yuen-ren, was a very pleasant colleague to have living in the house. He was very helpful with advice, as well as being available for translation at lectures, in itself quite a heavy task. Bertie and he enjoyed cracking jokes, for Mr Chao had a great sense of humour. He had translated *Alice's Adventures in Wonderland*, the jokes of which apparently chimed with what amused the Chinese. With Hu Shih he was trying ways of writing the Chinese spoken language phonetically. Foreigners always complained of 'those antiquated Chinese characters', not realizing that this writing could be understood by those who spoke in the very many dialects, just as numbers are, or as Latin served for common communication in the Middle Ages. Dialects interested Mr Chao, and his keen ear caused him to make fun of the refined speech of English diplomats. Why, for instance, did a gentleman whose name was Rose call himself Röse?

We noticed that our Mr Chao became a bit absent-minded, even sad, for him most unusual. Presently Bertie found out that there was a certain Yang Bu-wei, with whom Mr Chao had fallen in love. It also transpired that Mr Chao had been betrothed by his family, when still no more than a ohild, to a young woman, whom, also according to custom, he had never been allowed to see. This was one reason why he had stayed away from China so many years. Release from this engagement would not only cost him money in compensation, but would also mean that the young lady was not supposed ever to marry anyone else.

Yang Bu-wei—for me the fabulous and indomitable—was a qualified doctor, who, when she met Mr Chao, was engaged in setting up the first non-missionary hospital in Peking and was also the first to be giving birth-control advice in the city. Before then she had lived an intransigent and dangerous existence, through the time of the Boxer rebellion, the revolution of 1911, when her brothers were at risk of their lives for cutting off their pigtails; she had witnessed executions, been head of a girls' school, and had finally got to Japan to study medicine. She had broken the engagement to which her family had pledged her, was actually threatened with death by an uncle for doing so, but had stood firm and not even given an undertaking not to marry anyone else. Wise counsels from her more enlightened grandfather had protected her. The 'uncle' was, in fact, her true father; she had been given to her real aunt and uncle, who were childless, at birth, and had been reared as a boy till she was thirteen. She wrote her story;* it should be required reading for anyone who really wants to understand what it meant to be a young Chinese—and a woman—in all those years before the People's Revolution of 1949. One generation had virtually to exhaust itself in the fight against ancestor-worship and all that it entailed; it needed another to rise and accept the suffering required to set their country free and build it on new foundations.

Mr Chao was negotiating for his release from the old engagement, but had not enough money to complete the bargain. Bertie offered to lend him £100. He secured his freedom and also a promise that the money paid should be used to give the rejected young woman a modern education.

As what were called 'new-thinking people', Yang Bu-wei and Chao Yuen-ren planned how to break with the traditional Chinese marriage ceremony. Friends suggested that it was advisable to have at least two witnesses and some sort of document as a sign of legality. Accordingly, Hu Shih and a woman, Dr Chu, friend and colleague of Miss Yang, were invited to dinner with the young couple at a private address.

* *Autobiography of a Chinese Woman* (John Day, New York 1947)

Here Mr Chao produced a statement that, for the information of relatives and friends 'the wedding would have taken place at 3 p.m. Mean Solar 120 E Standard Time, June 1, 1921'. The next day the Chinese paper *Ch'en Pao* had a headline, 'New Style Wedding of New Style People', and this kind of simple ceremony, or rather no ceremony, was increasingly adopted by the Chinese of modern views.

Since Mr Chao was bothered as to whether he could repay the loan, Bertie told him not to worry, but if and when he ever had the money, to pay it to me. In 1947, at the first session of UNESCO in Paris—that section of the United Nations which owed its very existence to the insistence of the Chinese—I met Mr Chao, who was on the Chinese delegation. He insisted on repaying this loan, which by then I had completely forgotten, as well as that repayment was to be made to me. Some friendships are long-lasting; I still occasionally hear from Yang Bu-wei and Chao Yuen-ren, who continue to address me as Miss Black.

Early in March, in the treacherous spring weather, when the sun increased in warmth, but winds were still bitter, both Bertie and I had a sort of 'flu and cough. I was better, but Bertie was running a temperature and for the moment I postponed any thought of my journey up north to Chita. Meantime I was able to see, as very few foreigners could, the ceremonies of the Spring Festival in the worship of Confucius. Since I doubt whether this celebration still takes place, it is worth quoting a letter in which I described it:

It is very impressive like priests celebrating Mass. It takes place in Confucius's Temple, in a vast white courtyard with dark arbor vitae (trees of life) each side, very old sacred trees. At the end of the courtyard is a flight of marble steps leading up to a raised space before the main temple. This temple has three wide doors. The worshippers, in their ceremonial dress, which is magenta, purple and dark blue, embroidered with bands of gold and their strange hats with square flat tops something like mortarboards, and their black satin boots, with thick white soles, stand in front of the doors on the raised space. Some stand below in the court. There are lots of 'choir boys' in bright blue robes with flowers. Half carry long pheasants' feathers set in short poles (I never saw such long feathers, about four or five feet long), and half little narrow painted shields with pointed tops, and toy axes.

The music plays and they chant. Perfectly lovely old Chinese chants, accompanied by magnificent instruments, bamboo pipes painted scarlet, and flutes, and great drums like red barrels mounted on red stands.

The little boys perform various ceremonial antics and the worshippers prostrate themselves. At a given moment the central door of the temple flies open and presently the chief priests go inside and read and chant holding the sacred books as Roman priests do the Gospels

133

at Mass. Finally they carry out some ceremonial boxes and tablets covered with writing . . .

The funniest thing was a little crouching tiger made of wood, like those toy beestes one buys at home, about the size of a cat, with a ridge of bristles, or something like bristles, on his back. When one chant ends and another is about to begin, a man beats the tiger's head with a stick and then scratches the ridge on his back with the stick several times. Everybody found this very amusing. There was nothing solemn in the occasion, the Chinese do not take the worship seriously and have not done so for a long time. There used to be a Ministry of Proprieties that directed such things. Now the Ministry of the Interior takes charge. We were with someone from the Ministry of Education, he seemed to think it quite suitable that that body, which is very up to date and invites over people like B, should NOT be in charge of these antiquated ceremonies also.

This letter also gives a brief glance at Chinese children:

. . . you would love the Chinese babies. They wear so many wadded clothes that they can't put their arms to their sides and they waddle along like little tubs on wheels. Their hair is done in dozens of tiny plaits that are twisted with red silk and stick out all round like quills on a porcupine. There are a lot of babies always about in our street and they have learnt somehow to say 'hullo' and I am greeted all along by 'hullo, hullo,' in little piping voices as I walk or ride down the street.

Bertie's health was better, but the intense cold of some of the Chinese lecture rooms was far from good for him. Some friends invited us to go with them for a weekend break to the Western hills, a favourite resort, not far from the city, with woods and temples and even hot springs. Mr Wang, a sturdy and lively man, who had been, I think, Governor of Honan, until kicked out by the military, and Mr Fu were of the company. They arranged to take us by car. On the way we paused at an ancient pagoda, which looked rather dilapidated and almost seemed to lean. But it was possible to go up it for the view, which Bertie and I did. Our Chinese friends remained below. When we asked them why they replied that, seeing the pagoda might be far from safe, it was as well that there should be witnesses as to how the famous philosopher died.

At our destination, so far as I remember, we were housed in ground-floor rooms well heated by stoves, and the dining-room was nearby. We were eating a meal on arrival and understood that we were also to dine later. As we ate, I laughingly exhorted Bertie not to eat too much, or he would lose his appetite for the next meal. He answered that he did not propose to forgo present pleasure since one did not know what the future would hold, he might not even eat that next meal. He did not.

After a while, we both went to swim together in the hot spring. When we came out, in our room Bertie began to shiver violently. I wrapped him up and piled quilts upon him, and the fire was stoked up. All to no avail, the shivering got worse, he seemed to be getting delirious and it was evident that he was seriously ill.

Our friends could hardly believe this, he had seemed entirely himself when we set out. I said that we must get him back to Peking at once: they doubted if this was possible, for the city gates would be shut at sundown. But it was clear that this was no place to nurse a sick man. Accordingly, the two Chinese drivers and I, with Bertie wrapped up in the car, started on the return journey, leaving behind our friends, who, I think, really thought this a false alarm.

The car went on well enough, then suddenly, going up a hill, the engine stalled. We were out here alone, in this wintry countryside, a keen wind blowing. I was in a panic, but knew I must try and keep calm. I ran to the top of the hill, luckily it was not far. I then signalled to the two drivers that we must together push the car. They got some big stones and so, inch by inch and yard by yard, we shoved the vehicle along, putting the stones beneath the wheels to hold it. At the top the drivers knew enough to do the right thing, they let the car go and we all prayed for the engine to engage. Spluttering, we came on to a bumpy bridge, I was gasping with fright in case we stalled again. There was no chance of help from any passing car. But all went well and the road to Peking was now flat.

Alas, the gates were shut, and nothing but some high authority could open them. In the gatehouse I was desperate, but there was a telephone. Bertie now became conscious enough to say that we must reach Mr Chao. Somehow those gatehouse keepers and the drivers were able to get the number and get through. Mr Chao, who knew that Bertie had gone off gaily and quite well, would at first not believe his ears, until he heard Bertie's unmistakable voice. It could, after all, have been a trick to lure him for some reason to the city gate. But now he hurriedly got a rickshaw and our passports and rushed to the rescue. The gates opened; we drove home, and from there by stretcher and ambulance we got Bertie, now quite delirious, into the German hospital.

He had double pneumonia: in those days there were none of the drugs which now make this no longer such a dread disease. You simply nursed your patient and tried to keep up his strength and waited for the 'crisis', when the lungs would clear and temperature fall, or failing that he would die. There was a very good elderly doctor at the German hospital, which had an excellent reputation, and also a young doctor Esser, who had somehow got himself out to Peking, where no Germans were supposed to be allowed to come from postwar Germany. He was one of the people whose optimism helped me through this time. At first I was at the hospital till late in the evening and then went home, not to sleep, but to bang my head against the wall in despair. As things got more hopeless, they made a bed for me in a corner of the hospital corridor. Presently the Americans at the Peking Medical College offered their help. They had a pneumococcus serum, which was the right one for the germ, but no one really knew whether it would kill or cure. However, it was given. Bertie's temperature ran so consistently high that Dr Esser would say to me, '*Na, das hält kein Mensch aus*' (No human being can stand that), but in fact expressing admiration at Bertie's endurance.

I was utterly absorbed in the battle for Bertie's life and only learned later of the concern friends had shown at what might be my situation, if Bertie died, leaving me isolated and penniless. Professor and Mrs Dewey saw him at an early stage and made some financial arrangement, but I do not know what this was. A bank book, I think, was put into my hand, but I was barely conscious of what was said to me, and I put it aside to think about it later. Meantime I felt quite unable to leave Bertie's bedside, and helped the kindly male German nurse to care for him.

Towards the end of March everyone seemed to be giving up hope; a deputation of students and scholars waited upon me at the hospital and I received them at the door of his sick room. They stood there, in their long black satin robes and black caps, with folded hands, bowing, troubled and anxious. They asked if they might be permitted to enter and hear the philosopher's last words. Bowing in my turn I answered gravely that, if it were possible to do so, I would admit them at that time. But I was certain that their philosopher would not die but survive. Shortly after this the Japanese press reported that Bertie had died on 27 March and this story went round the world. Mrs Dewey also took a fatalistic view, but from a different angle, when she spoke to me of the 'self-determination' of the lungs in such a disease. On Easter Eve she, with real kindness, prevailed on me to come to her flat, take a hot bath and try to sleep. It was useless; I had a fixed conviction that I must be with Bertie on Easter Day, for, if he lived then, he would recover. In the early hours, a rickshaw was called and I returned to the hospital. There he was, frail, face and hair dead white against the pillow, but the breath of life still in him.

I wrote to my mother on 13 April 1921:

Sweetheart,
    You'll be troubled at my not writing for so long—and well you need be. I have just dragged Bertie back from the very brink of death. He got double pneumonia and every soul gave him up but himself and me. And he only lived by the strength of what we are to each other. He has been ill for nearly a month now and I have been with him night and day, and now, with the pressing danger over, for the whole twelve hours a day. We succeeded in getting a very competent English nurse for night duty, it wasn't easy, because

nurses and doctors here are terribly overdriven, there is a smallpox epidemic and a great deal of lung disease of sorts . . . We gave him an anti-pneumococcus serum, which possibly saved his life. It is a recent discovery—it is a terrible kill or cure thing, for the battle between the germs runs the temperature higher than the pneumonia. They had to give oxygen too. He ran a temperature between 104 and 107 for three weeks and a bit *without stopping*—two nights he was up to 107 at which people normally die, and the heart was missing beats—as one counted the pulse it would go one two three—stop—four five six—and you knew that stop might be forever. The worst days were Easter Eve, Easter Sunday and my birthday [3 April]. On my birthday afternoon the doctor came in and was certain he was dying. I held violets to his face because he loves them best and every time he smelt them the delirium would leave him for a moment and he would cry.

It has been a most terrible time. I do not know how I myself am still alive, every minute has been agony and doubt and I have had next to no sleep. I swore he should not die and shook my fist at the foul universe, and I rejoiced all the time to find that he did too. All through he knew me and me only and could only talk sense to me. He says only my face was clear, the others blurred and spiky. He says that at one point I spoke to him boldly and said he must fight or he would go under and that from that moment he set his teeth and held fast to my love and fought. I never saw such magnificent courage and defiance of life and death. His delirium was full of wit and he would smile ironically and tell the doctors he was never better in his life, when we all knew he might slip away the next moment. He ate *everything* I gave him. He would just look up and say: 'It is necessary?' and then swallow it down desperately. He says he felt every spoonful full of my iron resolve to save him and he meant to do his part. It has been wonderful even through all the suffering, to feel how we were fighting together and how nothing could terrify us. I never tried to deceive him about his state, nothing but clear knowledge and a resolve to fight could have saved him.

You cannot think what a man he is. I hope you will be able to know him well, when we come home (which may be soon now, as he can't finish his work here) because he is just sublime, with the greatness of our greatest English poetry—you cannot detect meanness or egoism in him however hard you try. And he does not know what it means to humbug himself or others. I am so glad of him and so glad to have saved his life. I could not have returned to England and faced people who loved him and said that I let him die.

The slow climb after the critical days has been terrible. We could not tell if the strength that was left after the sharp battle was sufficient for building. But to-day for the first time the doctors have looked less grave. They say the right lung is nearly clear, and if so the left will clear more quickly now. Both lungs were nearly full up with the filthy pneumococci—damn their filthy souls—but now there are not many pneumococci left in the sputum.

Do you know . . .

> Hey nonny no
> Men are fools that wish to die
> Is't not fine to dance and sing
> While the bells of death do ring?

It is one of Bertie's favourites and to-day I repeated it to him with others that he knows by heart and so does not find tiring. Bertie was just like the spirit of that poem all through the bad time and I know of nothing more glorious than his smiling in the face of death. I felt it too. Our Chinese sewing woman had been making him silk pyjamas and one pair was ready. And while I was mourning over them and thinking I would put them on him when he was dead, I took more silk from the cupboard and said to the 'Amah', 'Make him another pair.'

I am still nursing from 7am to 7pm and it needs all my strength . . . Please do not be worried now. The bad time is over and you can think of us both convalescing—for I feel as if I had been near death too—and telling each other how wonderfully we fought and how great a thing our love is.

Dr Esser romantically called that recovery the slow climb of a weary man up a steep stair, and referred to me as a *Kraftmensch*. Unremitting watchfulness was needed; there was plenty still to contend with. Once there was a dust storm, we had to line the window cracks to keep it from seeping through. The spring was on its way—a time of incredible beauty, when the bare, dry, brown landscape suddenly breaks into the delicate green shimmering of the willow leaves. The courtyard of the hospital, outside Bertie's window, had tall acacia trees, which were presently in bloom. With relief in my heart I turned, as I did in those days, to writing poetry.

Death and Birth

We have come through: our battered spirits lie
Folded upon your sick bed in a close embrace.
No more the unwearying chase
Of Huntsman Death
With foul hot breath and pack of fears full cry
Hounds on the quarry and our broken heels
Falter and faint, but onward, onward fly.
No more my heart with sickening anguish reels
And throbs, and will my cracking bosom tear
As that pale steed comes on with bloodshot eye.
To rest—Ah rest

O God, we sink to rest
Ambushed and safe as they go panting by.

Now let me wrap thee in the cloak of love
To keep thy weary body warm,
Scarce let us breathe or move.

Quiet, quiet be our souls
As winds and waters stilling with the calm of even.
My eye, with purple lined and washed with tears
Now once more rests in thine,
Searching those pallid depths where stirs unseen
The memory of such things as only thou couldst ever know nor
    ever speak
But I may half divine.

Between our eyes
Peace lies
From thee to me breathing and hovering
As on some far-off sacred night of Spring
The lilac mist
Enveloped bush and tree
Shrouded us as we kissed
And awestruck fell to gazing silently
No sound but dripping trees and the dim cuckoo echoing.

Quiet, quiet be our souls
Between our eyes
Peace lies
From thee to me breathing and hovering.

O white acacia swaying in the blue
O white acacia swaying to the sun
Sing of my love returning from the grave
Frail and resplendent as your crested wave
O white acacia tossing on the blue
O white acacia nodding to the sun.

Sing warm and quivering air,
Through those green boughs and through this shining room
Wrap and enfold him, living, on his bed.
Wrap and enfold him there
As I, with golden mist of love and tears
Do sheathe him fair.

O world of things in bloom
O blest advancing Spring
Dear Love, that art not dead—
Sing, white acacia sing.

Other elements besides the skill of German and American medicine and an English night nurse contributed to Bertie's recovery. Among the friends we had made were three representatives of the new régime in Russia, who, unrecognized by anyone official, were serving their country as best they could. There was A. Hodoroff, correspondent of the News Agencies Russia, Delta and Rosta. He was a tall, dark man with a handlebar moustache and a ferocious air. When you talked to him about his opponents he would twirl the moustache and exclaim: 'If we do not keel zem, zey will keel us.' He was, of course, not as bad as he liked to sound. Then there was M. Yourin, not so tall, very fair, blue-eyed, with corn-coloured hair, reminding me of the soldier I had met in the train. Yourin was the chief of the three. Ivanov, short and rather delicate-looking, was the intellectual. I had some interesting discussions with him about our book on Russia, when he came to call after Bertie was out of danger. He gratified me by liking my chapter, I think genuinely.

While Bertie was desperately ill, these men had delivered to the hospital, as often as necessary, whipped cream and champagne. How they obtained it I do not know, but I sat hour after hour with my finger on Bertie's pulse, giving him sips of champagne and spoonfuls of the cream. Sometimes they sent flowers, and on my birthday a huge basket of them, scented and beautiful; among these were the violets which gave pleasure to the sick man. The Bolsheviks had chauffeurs and a car or cars; they later insisted on calling at the hospital and taking me to dinner or supper with them, saying that I should not spend the evening alone in my house. They hinted very delicately that they could help me out if I needed money, which I as delicately declined, not wishing to be accused of taking Bolshevik gold.

The first evening that I dined with them there were a number of other guests, the table groaned with Russian *zakuski*; we had sucking-pig twice, and I don't know what else. I thought this grandeur excessive, when my country was starving, but as a guest I refrained from comment. Drinking Bertie's health and mine they would say: 'He will not die, he is necessary to the Revolution'—a sentiment which they repeated often, and which matched my own mood better than anything else said to me at that time.

The next time I went to eat with them, there was nothing on the table but the familiar old cabbage soup and *kasha* and bread. 'You see, comrade,' they explained, 'when we are alone, and not entertaining guests, we eat as they do at home. We know that this is something you will understand.'

We naturally talked of Russia, of the Revolution, of what I had seen. Once M. Yourin was telling me of the many peoples and languages in the Soviet Union, whom it was necessary to bring together. I said that surely they ought all to be taught Russian first of all. M. Yourin was shocked; on the contrary, the policy was to study and keep the languages alive by getting them written down. '*Mademoiselle*,' he said reproachfully, '*vous êtes plus royaliste que le roi même*.' After supper they drove me home, dashing round those narrow streets at an alarming speed.

The time came for Bertie to be moved back home. Convalescence had not been easy: his nurse, trained expert though she was, had ultra-conventional views, a good deal of snobbery and much Christianity. She doubted whether it had been right for her to come and save the life of an influential unbeliever. Bertie, in his weak state, found her talk about God unbearable. He did not wish to be ungrateful, but he did want her now to go. For a time I went back to sleep at the hospital and helped out instead.

When we brought Bertie home we installed him on the soft blue cushions of the big divan: the servants had made great preparations, and over the divan hung various toys, including the Chinese glass mobiles that tinkle as the wind blows. He had to remain quietly in bed because, possibly from camphor injections, he had some poisoning in one leg—the doctors called it perhaps a necrosis, but definitely thrombosis. Bertie said that what with 'necropolis' and 'trombones' in his leg, he had the graveyard and the last trump all complete. He lay there for more than three weeks, long-suffering as ever, but glad to be home and able to gaze at the many flowers with which the servants had filled the courtyard. We found that they really did love us and were glad to help, because they said we 'had a good nature'. I asked if cook could make a cake for his birthday on 18 May. When it appeared, large, chocolate-iced, on it was written in white icing: 'Dear Sir, Mr Russell, happy your borthday, May 18 1921.' As the cook did not know a word of English he had had to practise for hours to set down the inscription devised by the Head Boy.

Soon we both had an added reason for rejoicing. I had wondered why, at the worst times in the hospital, sick with anxiety, I had found myself capable of eating the large German meals, often sauerkraut and all. I had never fainted in my life, but now, helping the doctor to deal with the abscess in the leg, I came near to doing so. Suddenly it occurred to me to wonder when I last had a period. Thinking it was all probably just overstrain, I went for an examination. When I brought home to Bertie the slip of paper on which Dr Esser had written 'gravidas incipit' he could hardly believe it and was beside himself with joy.

Now of course letters to my mother were full of nothing but the excitement of the coming child, our journey home, and endless reassurances to her and my father not to worry at our not being married, and to wash their hands of the whole affair if it displeased them. The news was imparted to Ogden with somewhat less sentimentality.

31 May 1921 . . . apparently while Bertie was doing his utmost to die, my body was engaged in preparing him an heir, which person we may expect to appear in the flesh—that is as a separate entity—at the end of November next. So now withdraw your taunts about taking up with the aristocracy and congratulate us both! We are almost beside ourselves with delight and excitement. I feel like singing the Magnificat all day, but I don't want Bertie to respond with the Nunc Dimittis! Of course it is just like Bertie, who so hates the heroic view of life, to do things in the most dramatic manner possible, get me with child, and then lie at death's door for a month. Mercifully I did not know at the worst time, or else I should have been still more desperate, not because of being left with the child, but because of the tragedy, if Bertie, who has so longed for a child, had not lived to see it. He's still in bed, but if you saw him as he contemplates the prospect, smiling from ear to ear and laughing 'like an irresponsible foetus' [one of Ogden's words for him] you would exclaim many times 'isn't he a dear?', that, as I remember being your favourite expression about him . . . Bertie regrets not dying here. They were going to give him such a grand Chinese funeral—and they ARE grand—and bury him with the poets and emperors near the Western Lake, Hangchow, one of the loveliest places in China. He would have had a temple in the hills and become a god. And I rather regret having lost the opportunity of appearing in bronze as his disciple, sitting in a lotus, specially as, giving birth miraculously to a child afterwards, I should have been a second Madonna or Kwan Yin.

Kwan Yin is a Chinese goddess whom I greatly respected. Originally male, I believe, she represented the principle of active benevolence in the world; later a female, she came to stand for maternity and appeared with a child. Among my most cherished possessions is a small ivory figure of her with child and Chinese toy rattle, which was a gift to me from Dr Esser in remembrance of our joint share in that grim struggle for Bertie's life.

Blessed by Kwan Yin, we were now recuperating. To his delight Bertie achieved one of his ambitions, to read his own obituary; the papers said that 'missionaries in China might be forgiven if they heaved a sigh of relief at the news of Mr Bertrand Russell's death'.

Over the date of our departure hung a question mark: would Bertie be well enough to travel before my pregnancy made it inadvisable for me to do so? Any idea of lecturing in Japan was abandoned, but we still planned to go that way and sail from Yokohama to Vancouver. With optimism we booked our passage, and, when we came to fill up the forms which asked were we single or married, Bertie, not knowing if his divorce had come through, wrote 'don't know', while I decided that 'both' was the correct answer. In fact, though we did not learn this until much later, the divorce went through on 3 May 1921. The solicitors, at the rumour of Bertie's death, had been uncertain whether to proceed with the case, but fortunately Lord Russell doubted the rumour and told them to go on, with the remark: 'My little brother wouldn't do a thing like that without letting me know.'

To leave Peking saddened me. We had really not been able to do enough active work; I knew that there was a great stirring of life among the students, and we had looked forward to seeing much more of other parts of China. Selling furniture, packing, arranging for the packing and despatch of some of the furniture, rugs and curtains that we wanted sent home, must have been a bit of a nightmare, but my letters gave no hint of this. The greater anxiety was to spare Bertie fatigue over the necessary farewells. In the end a farewell meeting was arranged, at which he would speak only briefly, for there was a real risk to his heart for some time to come. I was to prepare a longer address, so that the students should not feel deprived on this last occasion. Frail as he was, Bertie made a point, having almost risen from the dead, of saying unrepentantly all that he said before about his rational disbelief in religion. The missionaries' brief respite was over.

My own speech, printed entire in the *Japan Chronicle*, too long to include here, was addressed to the youth of China. I have often wondered whether Chairman Mao may have heard or read it; it does contain some prophetic insight. I warned them against reliance on the wisdom of foreign 'sages'—'The real solution to all your troubles lies in the courage, the hearts and the brains of your own people.' I spoke of the usefulness, but also of the dangers, of science, of the bankruptcy of old systems of religion and ethics, both in their country and mine: 'The problem for you, as for us, is to forge a new ethical system in which we can believe and on which we can base our social and political life, some system which will control and subject the industrial machine and the mechanical discoveries of science.' I touched on the future for emancipated women and even on limiting the population, urged them to raise the 'banner of a new humanism', since 'to perceive ideals and not live for them is, in so dark a time, a treachery to mankind'.

Bertie, with hardly any flesh on his bones and with shins like a knife-edge, could now walk a short distance with the help of a stick. At last, to my relief, I was able to get him safely on board ship for Japan, and concentrate my energies on our personal problem, which was to get us both, without disaster, through the long journey home.

With a view to a quiet journey home, since Bertie was still so frail, we sailed from Tientsin to Moji and Kobe, planning to pass quickly through Japan and embark at Yokohama for Vancouver. Eileen Power, whose plans were elastic, kindly came with us that far. Any thought of passing once more through the Red Sea was obviously ruled out. We thought to keep our route secret, but we had reckoned without the Japanese, whose blood had been for so long 'boiling with enthusiasm' over the great philosopher and his utterances. We had, of course, cancelled lectures in Japan, and written to explain Bertie's state of health. I was disposed to be annoyed with the Japanese journalists for their news flash reporting Bertie's death, which had certainly caused distress to his many friends and supporters in more than one country. As we soon learned, Japanese journalism prided itself on equalling or sur- passing the Americans in smartness and on-the-spot efficiency. In spite of our efforts, what I described as 'fifty million' reporters and photo- graphers turned up at Moji, as well as two men from the very journal for which Bertie had been writing, who came on board to travel from Moji to Kobe with him.

Very early in the morning one of the ship's officers came to me and said that there were a number of journalists waiting to interview Bertie. I explained that he was far from well and was undertaking no interviews or work while in Japan. To emphasize this I wrote on several sheets of paper, 'Mr Bertrand Russell having died according to the Japanese press, is unable to give interviews to Japanese journalists', and, in my dressing-gown, went into the corridor to hand these to the several reporters waiting there. They muttered 'Very funny, very funny', drew in their breath, but, when they saw that I would not give way, they retired. I did, of course, try once more to make them understand how monstrous it was that a man in such a delicate state of heath should not be allowed to travel in peace.

Later on we put in at Kobe. As we leaned on the rail waiting to dis- embark, we saw that the whole quay was a mass of people marching with red banners. We wondered what this might mean; someone stand- ing nearby said, 'Probably it is for you', at which we both laughed as at a good joke and impossible suggestion. But, to our amazement, as we came ashore, this was indeed a large-scale greeting for us. In fact it was also a skilful piece of opportunism. The Japanese Government was at that time thoroughly repressive in its opposition to socialism and what were described as 'dangerous thoughts'; in consequence all demonstrations were forbidden. But Kagawa, a Christian Socialist, realizing that the arrival of a distinguished foreigner would put the authorities in a difficulty, had used the occasion to organize a turn-out with which the police would hardly dare to interfere. We were soon among friends who showed us the town, including the poorer quarters and the bathhouses.

During our transit through Japan I was above all else concerned with trying to see that Bertie was spared worry and fatigue. I had also to have some regard to my own state for the sake of the baby to be born. We visited exquisite Japanese temples, including Nara, and once we were required to take part in a tea ceremony, which involved squatting, Japanese fashion, for what seemed an age, while there was mixing and grinding, until finally a mixture looking like fine spinach emerged. In my pregnant state I found the squatting on the floor very trying, and wondered how Japanese women could endure it.

In the train en route, as I think, for Tokyo, I leaned back in an open carriage with seats along the sides, to snatch some sleep, and woke to find a Japanese photographer trying to take a picture. The worst moment in this duel with the press was when we arrived in Tokyo station and were about to descend a flight of steps leading down from the platform. Suddenly a flash went off and I almost missed my footing and would have rolled down the stairs. Bertie was white and literally shaking with rage, in defence of me and the unborn child, and, as I got into the car waiting for us, he shouted loudly and pursued the press with his stick. Somewhere there must exist a photo of the one time in all that great pacifist's history when he was moved to threaten violence.

Police surveillance was unpleasant and extremely dangerous for the Japanese of socialist views. As we opened the door of our room in the hotel, Bertie and I found grey-silk robed gentlemen suddenly effacing themselves. We met and talked with the socialist Miss Ito, her small nephew, and one of the left-wing leaders, Osugi, all of whom, as we learned later when we were back in England, were, literally, strangled by the police.

A talk with Robert Young, Editor of the remarkable *Japan Chronicle*, gave us both great pleasure. But, in the main, we were anxious to be gone, though we regretted how little we were able to give and receive from our Japanese friends on this visit.

One day when we were at lunch in our hotel in Tokyo, I was called to the phone. A voice kept saying something like 'Awdeliss, awdeliss'; finally I understood to my amazement that Major Orde-Lees wished to speak with me. At once we asked him to join us at lunch. Bertie, who had heard from me all about his exploits demonstrating parachutes to the King of Sweden, was anxious to meet him. But our conversation at lunch was drowned by a terrible, metallic booming and banging, taking place somewhere in the hidden purlieus of the hotel. Orde-Lees, saying that he could stand this no longer, went to investigate. He presently returned, having found that nothing could be done about it, since the perpetrator of the outrage was out of sight and earshot *inside* a huge boiler. Bertie laughed and remarked that the 'man of action' had, it seemed, been unable to achieve more than the intellectual with his 'masterly inactivity'. Orde-Lees, who was a man of many talents, was in Tokyo in some advisory capacity to the Japanese Armed Forces, in which skill with mechanism was, as yet, not always very far advanced.

At last came the moment when the pair of us, unhappy at the political climate of that time in Japan, and both not feeling fit enough to cope with the exuberance of supporters, or the sinister atmosphere of Government repression, were able to proceed to Yokohama to take ship for home on a Canadian Empress ship. This sailing from Yokohama was my first experience of the drama of the departure of a great liner: friends on the quay, flowers, farewells, music, and from ship's deck to shore innumerable paper streamers which drew apart in brightly coloured festoons as the ship got under way.

I looked forward to relaxation on board. But this was not a very pleasant voyage. We could not, of course, have a cabin together, being unmarried, which made it difficult for me to look after Bertie properly. I was not feeling too good at times myself, and was stirred to suppressed anger by the not very friendly way the stewardess would hint that she knew quite well what was the matter with me when I lay down for some extra rest. I rather think that we were cut by most of the conventional people on board, but we were little aware of this. It is a fact that we talked with no one except Eileen Power and Mischa Elman, who sought us out and with whom we spent agreeable days walking and discussing. He seemed not to care to fraternize with our fellow travellers and murmured something about not intending to give them a concert which they wanted of him.

Crossing Canada by train both of us gathered strength in the temperate climate, and on board ship for Liverpool we were pacing the decks in true sea-going fashion. My pregnancy was by now noticeable and, as we walked arm in arm, I remember gratefully how an elderly woman smiled at us and congratulated me on my cheerful mien.

8

Marriage and a Home

We came ashore at Liverpool. Of course it was pouring with rain: standing on the quay to greet us was my mother.

I never loved and admired my mother more than I did at that moment, as she, such a modest and retiring person, tried to find words for what she wanted to say in this awkward situation. That we both looked well and happy reassured her at once, but on the train for London she wanted to know where we thought of going, of which, of course, we had not the slightest idea. Bertie, with affectionate courtesy, said: 'Surely Lady Black, you did not imagine that on arriving home I was about to abandon your daughter?' Soon they were on the best of terms and my mother was telling him to 'keep Dora in order', which she asserted she had never been able to do.

Oddly enough, I cannot now remember where we stayed at first in London; I think we went to Clifford Allen's flat in Battersea. But within a few days we were both at a thatched cottage on the edge of the marshes at Winchelsea, which Dot Wrinch rented and had generously vacated for us.

The baby was likely to be born before Christmas: a permanent home had to be found. Reluctantly I had given up the idea of getting the floor below my own Bloomsbury flat, which seemed less suitable now, but Clifford Allen was about to be married and it was possible to take over his flat. A builder had been given full instructions about redecorating, when, out of the blue, the landlord refused to give his consent for the transfer of the lease, although according to the usual jargon it 'could not be unreasonably withheld'. There was no doubt whatever that this was a 'politically motivated' refusal, due to Bertie's wartime pacifism. But this was August and there was not much time to spare for argument or legal action, and both of us were a bit low at this point from the after-effects of constantly 'keeping up' under strain. Bertie was frustrated and angry; I feared for his health, but thought it best to concur with his going up to London to see what could be done. His dear friend the lawyer Charlie Sanger had come to visit us and we both thought action was best for Bertie, apart from practical considerations. Anyone who has seen Bertie in one of his rages against injustice and victimization can guess just what he was like at this time. Soon he returned in triumph from London, having bought a freehold house, 31 Sydney Street, Chelsea, for his child to be born.

Next, what about marriage? Bertie's solicitors had asked for the decree nisi to be expedited in order that the child might be legitimate. Personally I was indifferent to these legal considerations, but I was faced with a serious dilemma. When we saw Bertie's solicitor together, he beamed on me and said (considering the risk of miscarriage), 'Take her home and keep her in cotton wool.' Remembering the fight for Bertie's life in Peking, the risks run in Japan, the crossing of two oceans and a continent, I was convulsed with laughter. But it now depended on me whether I should legitimize this child or not. I had no doubt whatever that it mattered enormously to Bertie that we should do so. Physically he was still a shadow of his former self, and I could not bear to shock or hurt him. I had by now realized that I might be disinheriting a future Earl; I wondered what the embryo might think about this and felt I could hardly prejudge the case for him. Even for a daughter the matter would not be very different. More than this, I now felt that Bertie's and my partnership was solidly based and long-lasting, a relation that, of its nature, warranted marriage. Later, when people asked me why, with my views, I did finally consent to marry, I used to laugh and say: 'Oh, of course it was because of the title.' But some of the agony of the decision is in a letter which I wrote to Rachel Brooks, a missionary with surprisingly unorthodox views, whose friendship we had enjoyed in China, and who had, with others, admired the stand on marriage and sex which Bertie and I were making:

Nobody could be more disappointed than I was over the marriage. For my own part I felt it had no justification, and I was infinitely happy when I believed the divorce would come too late to make it possible. B.R. thought differently, and people who criticise me ought to bear in mind that the baby had two parents, to one of whom (B.R.) he was the long-desired exquisite miracle, given when it seemed as if everything was to be taken away, and as such to be guarded from every faintest shadow of danger or harm. B.R. has always held that children are the basis of marriage, that a certain promise of stability in the relationship should be given by both lovers when the child arrives. I do not agree with this view and would not have given way to it had B.R. been a younger man . . . I shall certainly never quite recover from the feeling of disgrace I had in marrying. There is however no doubt that any academic work would have been closed to B.R. or myself, if we'd not married; that I could have done nothing whatever but cook and clean house and care for the baby—all of which I don't scorn—but I happen to have training and interest in other work . . . I think that puts the case more or less as B.R. sees it. Being younger, I'm for blundering and breaking through, probably to disaster!

... I have a RIGHT to have a child if I wish without my neighbours peeping and trying to starve me and it. I wish you would let those people who were interested in my experiment know some of what I say here. I do not like to feel I have let people down, even though I have!! Only at least they do know that I never feared unpleasantness or abuse of myself.

So, under pressure of Bertie's health and aristocratic feelings, and the knowledge that he did not support my view, the decision was taken. In the light of subsequent events the legal nature of that marriage was, for me personally, little short of a disaster.

However, one day, we came up to a registry office in Battersea, myself now rather large in a black cloak, and, with Bertie's brother Frank and Eileen Power for witnesses, we were married. Frank and Eileen arrived there first and Frank alleged that the Registrar was on the point of marrying them, when we came in the nick of time; and I got teased because I had a bunch of sweet peas I had picked and wrapped in newspaper, which they maintained was my bridal bouquet. The Registrar wished Bertie 'a happier experience' and we all went and had tea at a local café. Bertie and I went back to sit under the apple tree in the Winchelsea garden. Presently Frank came to stay for a few days and the cottage resounded with the loud Russell laughs from the pair of them. By now I had a most horrible toothache, but the local dentist whom we visited said that nothing could be done to pull the tooth in pregnancy. I resorted to vinegar and pepper and brown paper plasters on my cheek.

Bertie had learned that Joseph Conrad, whom he greatly admired, was living not very far away, somewhere near Canterbury. We decided that it would be pleasant to go and visit him. Accordingly, we meandered about in trains for what seemed a long journey and finally arrived for lunch. Jessie Conrad, large, and, I think, partially crippled, took pride in preparing the food herself. Conrad was always most punctilious in his respect and support for his wife and did not like being invited anywhere without her. He himself, bearded, had the head of the sea captain, but his dress, pearl tiepin and all, and manners, were those of a Polish country gentleman. I remember there were brocaded gilt chairs in the room in which we were received. My toothache was bad and I took little part in the talk at table. Later, I walked in the garden with Conrad along a grass path with a richly planted herbaceous border backed by a wall of red brick. I remarked on the peace and beauty of his home. 'It is so,' he answered, 'and my wife loves it. But for myself I dislike living where I cannot see the horizon.' Though I am not a seafarer, this struck a deep chord in me, for all my life I have felt the same. I said something about marks on my face due to drastic remedy for toothache, and said this explained my seeming perhaps unsociable, whereupon Conrad took my hand and said earnestly, 'I think you are a heroine, I would find it unbearable.' Our son was named John for his great grandfather and Conrad for Joseph Conrad who was his godfather though not in god. At that time I had a long romantic letter from Conrad, which unfortunately is lost.

I got help in my toothache trouble from Bertie's dentist, who said that not to extract teeth during pregnancy was nonsense. He came to my parents' flat, gave me gas and took it out. So another of the arguments for not sparing a woman pain in child-bearing went west. The old wives used to say you had to lose a tooth with every baby. No doubt modern diet dispels this superstition too.

Came the day when we finally moved into 31 Sydney Street. A strange assortment of furniture from various locations converged upon the house. Our rugs, a table or two, some embroideries, and silk and satin curtains had arrived from China; Bertie had a walnut dining table and chairs, a bed and a fine plain wardrobe, which he had acquired from Wittgenstein, who had designed these himself. Crate-loads of Bertie's books appeared, some things from his flat, and from mine, including the Heal divan which was my pride—a wide single, or narrow double, bed, which we both found adequate for the whole of the years we were together.

It was a typical terrace house, three floors and a basement, French windows giving on balconies on the first floor, back rooms which could be thrown into those in front. It acquired a certain distinction by the odd bow window jutting out, as from a medieval castle, from the ground-floor front. This was to be Bertie's study, and presently he was to be seen, day after day, framed by this window, sitting so quietly at a small table, turning over page after page of neatly written manuscript. Once, during an election, some small boys threw tomatoes through that window; they missed, but the philosopher did not even raise his head.

In the early days of our occupation, he worked amid piles of books littering the floor, and even noise from the carpenter, who was causing floor to ceiling book shelves to grow about him.

We slept in our drawing-room on the first floor; it was amazing how everything seemed to fit and grow together, the large blue Chinese rug blended with some lovely, heavy mauve curtains patterned in silver, which came from Bertie's flat. The top floor was for day and night nurseries, small, but adequate.

Very pregnant as I was, I sat in a chair on the pavement indicating to which floor articles should be taken as they were unloaded. Passers-by naturally found this sight intriguing.

Chaos within was gradually reduced to a semblance of order; William Blake engravings graced the narrow hall, Bertie's bust of Voltaire, on its special strip of blue brocade, stood on his mantelpiece; his ancestors—as he said—spiritual and temporal, Leibniz and Spinoza, and sundry Russell Lords, found space upon the dining-room walls.

We had to engage servants. In these days, only the very well-to-do are staffed and cared for as was customary between the two wars for people of quite modest means. Chelsea was a very conservative borough, with some expensive houses; in the meaner streets were the poorer population, many of whom lived by 'service', trained and genteel, lace curtains at their windows. It was not difficult to find dailies. But how they would quarrel with one another, how refined spinsters proved to be secret drinkers, and cooks would cheat on the books, or be found almost dead drunk in the kitchen when cooking for a dinner party—all this the inexperienced housewife had to learn. Far be it from me to decry the love and loyalty in service that one human being can give to another, perhaps understood too little in these days, but the class basis of 'service' as it used to be too often poisoned the relations between master and man, mistress and maid. In the event, servants and staff played a bitter role in the story of our family, a fact which to me has some historical as well as personal importance. However, when the class question was out of the way, people who first came as staff, or in a domestic capacity, later became my life-long friends.

Neither Bertie nor I knew what to do about doctor and nurse for the confinement. His sister-in-law, Countess Elizabeth Russell, came to our rescue. Her brother Sir Sydney Beauchamp was a first-class gynaecologist, and Elizabeth insisted that no one but he should take the case. After examining me, and bearing in mind what this birth meant to Bertie in his anxious and delicate state, he decided to induce the child about a month early. Even so, it was a forceps delivery, and I think that John did not do too well out of the bargain. As I lay there on the top floor on 16 November 1921 in the bed that had been Wittgenstein's, giving birth, the bells of St Luke's Church at the end of the street were ringing in practice, but to me at that moment they rang for my son.

John has always carried his father's image on his features, but, in those first few weeks, the likeness of that diminutive face was almost absurd. As some of Bertie's friends flocked in to see the baby, one woman stood by the cot laughing heartily.

'Why,' demanded Bertie with some asperity, 'are you laughing at my son?'

'Why? Because I never thought to see that face twice.'

Elizabeth came in to cheer and entertain me with her wit, remarking that she 'liked everything about men, except where beds came into it'. (She had had five children.) One day only Bertie's physician Dr Streatfeild came, and I sensed an atmosphere of strain. But presently, when the gynaecologist Mr A. H. Richardson appeared, they had to break it to me that Sir Sydney had been knocked down by a bus and instantly killed. At such times one stupidly thinks of omens: John's father had nearly died when he was conceived, and now his birth was shadowed by a death.

A. H. Richardson was at that time coming to the top of his profession; I was, in fact, very fortunate, for he agreed to deliver me on the three occasions that followed. He also officiated at the birth of the Queen and Princess Margaret. We had a mutual friendship and understanding which I greatly valued.

One of the servants took the opportunity of John's birth to steal some articles, which included Bertie's top hat. Bertie chuckled and said that he could not, as a socialist, possibly prosecute for the theft of a top hat. So far as I know, he never acquired another.

Bertie had told me that, in the circles in which he had moved, in which top hats were de rigueur, it was the custom for ladies, after giving birth, to drive out with their spouses in a 'barouche-landau'. He thought it would be fun not to deny me this compliment, with the result that, one fine morning, a suitable equipage, with top-hatted and cockaded coachman, appeared at the door of 31 Sydney Street. The Hon. Mr and Mrs Bertrand Russell, elegantly attired and amiably conversing, were to be seen on their festive drive through the streets and parks of London.

The next six years at 31 Sydney Street were packed so full of social and political life that I now wonder how we had time and energy for it all.

To begin with, Bertie had neither job nor money; he sat down, amid domestic confusion, while his son was being born upstairs, to make a living for his family by writing. Stanley Unwin had backed *Principles of Social Reconstruction* in 1916. *Roads to Freedom* had followed in 1918, then came the books on Bolshevism, on China, and in 1923 our joint book on *The Prospects of Industrial Civilisation*. The reputation of Bertrand Russell and the house of Allen and Unwin rose together in a remarkable partnership.

We were never rich then, life was a bit hand-to-mouth, but we enjoyed what must be described as an upper-class life. I did not have to clean or cook, nor look after the baby except when I wanted to do so; in the early months my chief duty was to get home from engagements in time for breast-feeding.

Chelsea was a most agreeable place to live; the King's Road was not then garish, but an ordinary, good shopping street from Peter Jones at one end, to the World's End pub at the other, the latter a centre for open-air politics. Many good friends lived in the area; the Sangers were in Oakley Street, Sybil Thorndike and Lewis Casson in one of the squares, Desmond MacCarthy was always blowing in talking incessantly; A. N. Whitehead and his wife lived near, as did their son North, with his wife and son, who was born just after John and who shared with John his first birthday party, at which both showed considerable resentment at the existence of another baby.

There were dinner parties out and at home, quite simple, but sociable and with good talk; there always seemed to be streams of visitors by the fire in the study or up in the first-floor room; Arthur Waley, whose pale, narrow face, gentle voice and exquisite Chinese poems we loved, was never shy in our home. Bertie delighted in the poem about the cockatoo, which Waley applied to him, and the greeting to a firstborn:

> I, through intelligence having wrecked my whole life
> Only hope the child will grow up ignorant and stupid,
> Then he will crown a tranquil life
> By becoming a Cabinet Minister.

W. B. Yeats came, and T. S. Eliot; among political friends, the L'Estrange Malones, Hugh and Ruth Dalton, Harold and Frida Laski were not far away and frequent visitors.

Ottoline Morrell came too, in her taffeta and pearls: when John was a toddler, he found her fascinating, and would stand by stroking her dress. Once he looked disappointed as she rose to go, whereupon Bertie told him she must go home to her husband. 'I suppose,' said John sadly, 'he is a big man.' Callers also came to us from overseas, Americans and Chinese. I remember vividly Count Karolyi, for whom I not only had much affection but also admiration for what he had tried to do in Hungary and for his book, *Gegen eine ganze Welt*.

I was taken to lunch with the Shaws. Possibly it is not strange that my most vivid recollection of this meeting is not of Shaw, but of Charlotte and her relation to him. With what surprise, in the pleasant large room in the flat at the Adelphi, I met in Mrs Shaw the image of my former headmistress, erect, gracious, somewhat forbidding! An eager young poetess arrived carrying a bunch of wild flowers: Mrs Shaw placed them in a vase in a distant corner of the room. We sat down to lunch. Charlotte and I faced each other in silent communion as the wit and laughter of our two irrepressible, brilliant husbands sparkled and crackled across the table. I recalled Ann's 'go on talking' from the end of *Man and Superman*, and reflected on the wives of great men. As we left, Shaw remarked that the poetess had intended to read him her poems all afternoon. But she had already vanished; Charlotte had seen to that.

I have a dim and awful memory of being taken to dine with Lord Sheffield (a Stanley); a night of pouring rain, red carpet across the pavement and a manservant with an umbrella. A guest at table remarked that it was raining and terribly wet; 'If it's raining, of course it's wet,' snapped his Lordship. Each time I tried some topic of conversation it was subtly indicated to me by my neighbour that 'that was not likely to interest his Lordship'. I realized where Frank Russell had got his formidable character. Bertie always used to say that the Stanleys were alarming: their mother was a Stanley.

There was a time later, when Bertie, baby John and I went to visit his eccentric old Aunt Agatha, who insisted on seeing us one at a time. For me she had put a photo of Bertie's first wife on the mantelpiece, and she said: 'Ah, when I look at you, I think of poor dear Alys.' She was a malicious old lady; Frank Russell, who also had more than one wife, once remarked to her, 'Why, Aunt Agatha, you're always a wife behind.' But she did admit to Bertie that I was good-looking.

And then there was Bloomsbury, of whose denizens and influence I have already given some account, and many of whom I now met. Bloomsbury people dined with one another, gave parties, discussed, dissected, argued with brilliance and elegance; every aspect of Victorianism was being taken to pieces. The Russian ballet—*Three Cornered Hat*, *Good-Humoured Ladies*, Massine, Lopokova, Karsavina, were all the rage. Some also went to dance at the Cave of Harmony, where Harold Scott and Elsa Lanchester offered a cabaret which sang satirically of bourgeois tastes and aspidistras, while Elsa, for the first time, I think, dug up sentimental Victorian songs such as 'Please sell no more drink to my father', rendering them with a subtle twist of mockery. Mary Merrall, Franklin Dyall, and Raymond Massey would come there and give brief sketches. The postwar desire to enjoy life and its sceptical tone have caused the 1920s to be dubbed frivolous and irresponsible. 'Dance, dance, dance little lady' they sang in the Noël Coward revue.

In fact, as I have indicated earlier, the reverse was the truth. Underneath their banter and analysis most of these people held positive views, were members of the Labour or Independent Labour Party and of the left-wing 1917 Club. My friend Vera, of Girton days, no longer the devout Countess Kathleen figure, completely modern-minded, was collaborating with her husband Francis Meynell in the Nonesuch Press at their lovely Georgian house in Great James Street. Francis was to the left, associated with George Lansbury in the *Daily Herald*'s defence of the Soviet Union; he was also an expert on printing and type; famous editions of the poets issued from their press, while Bloomsbury delighted in the wit and games of the Nonesuch *Week-End Book*. Freud, sex and marriage were topics of constant concern. But political views which had been unpopular during the war now came into their own; in the elections of 1922, 1923 and 1924, Labour steadily gained ground, the previously despised Ramsay MacDonald became the leader of his party and in 1924 the first Labour Prime Minister.

Bertie, with *The Analysis of Matter* and *The Analysis of Mind*, his repartee, his social conscience, was part and parcel of all this movement. He belonged to the I.L.P., which he said I should join; Clifford Allen was moving into prominence within that party.

Bertie had promised me that if we married, I would not be required to 'grace the head of his table'. But inevitably I was drawn into this social and political round. Many of Bertie's friends were much older than I: to an extent which I only realized later, I was shifted out of my own generation. Presently I found friends of my own age, but for many years I felt indefinably apart from them. Bloomsbury dinners were alarming to a novice; the talk was allusive, often learned, exchanges swift. Modesty required listening rather than talk; in any case it would have been difficult to get a word in edgeways, but I enjoyed observing people. Once when we dined with Keynes and Clive Bell in Gordon Square and the talk was about the ballet, I referred to a rumour that Madame Lopokova was about to run off with a Russian general. Keynes repudiated this impertinent suggestion with some warmth. On the way home I told Bertie that in my opinion Keynes was in love with Lopokova. Bertie asserted that this was quite impossible, Keynes was not interested in women. However, not long after, they got married and were, I believe, extremely happy.

Among the Bloomsburies I liked best was Leonard Woolf, who came quite often to Sydney Street. Virginia I saw only once in the distance at some gathering. Woolf's constructive work was not enough valued in his lifetime: I was so glad that he wrote his autobiography, a valuable record for history.

Bunny Garnett and the Meynells gave very good parties, and Bunny was in part responsible for a comical incident in which I was involved. This was at a time when I was busy with politics and came from some conference late to a Bloomsbury party. Bunny plied me with drink in order to 'catch up', but I was a bit overtired. Presently Oswald Mosley, whom already I distrusted politically, began dancing with me and pulled me out on to the landing. I was promptly sick on the floor. Next morning, waking up beside Bertie, I began laughing and explained that the merest hint of advances from that quarter had, it seemed, triggered off this instant result.

When I recovered from John's birth, I had no thought of taking to politics. My ambition was still the theatre, as it had been from childhood. It may seem odd that with such a husband, a pleasant home, a lovely baby, and a whole society of interesting people, I should have wanted anything else. But it is necessary to understand that my generation were the heirs of women's agonized struggle for the vote. Not, in fact, until 1924, was I eligible, at thirty, to cast my first vote in an election, and then I had the pleasure of voting for myself.

My mother's generation had been content with a life bounded by home and family; the women of my generation asserted that they were capable of something more than this. They sought an identity that was not submerged in that of a husband; there was a good deal of argument about not changing names on marriage. When, for instance, letters began to arrive at Sydney Street, addressed to the Hon. Mrs Bertrand Russell, such was my ignorance of the titled world that I went to Bertie and said that this must be a mistake. But this was, he assured me, the correct way to address me. I said that I would have none of it; Russell I had agreed to become, but Mrs Dora Russell was to be my name. Bertie of course, did not mind, and in time I managed to prevail with correspondents and the press, but my annoyance was great when, on the cover of my first book, for the sake of publicity, stood the Hon.

Mrs Bertrand Russell as the author's name. The book has, in fact, been entered in some library catalogues as written by him!

Women also sought economic independence, but most vital to us, I think, was to prove our capabilities as individuals, not merely as wives, mothers and daughters. And we needed to belong to ourselves, not to fathers or husbands. The story of Isadora Duncan's life shows very clearly how her drive to pursue and perfect her art made it impossible for her to settle down even with a devoted and wealthy lover, or indeed to remain permanently with any one man.

Our objection to legal marriage, however, was not in the main the wish to practise 'free love'—though we did not rule this out for those who might be so inclined—but to the nature of the marriage law as it then was. It gave rights of property and possession of persons and, by treating infidelity as a crime, encouraged marriage partners to pursue one another with jealousy, suspicion, hatred and revenge masquerading as virtue and righteous indignation. It derived from ecclesiastical diktats according to which sex itself was a sin, to be endured only for the procreation of children. In practice the law was a morass of subterfuge and evasions imposed by its severity, well satirized in *Holy Deadlock* by A. P. Herbert, whose gallant forays over the years finally brought about some divorce law reform.

The claim of Bloomsbury to shaping the future lay as much in its views on sex, the marriage laws and women's life in this aspect, as in political power and economics. Poems in vogue were Andrew Marvell's 'To His Coy Mistress', Donne's

> Whoever loves, if he do not propose
> The right true end of love
> He's one that goes
> To sea for nothing but to make him sick.

and Blake with his urgent pleas against the caging of love:

> And priests in black gowns
> Were going their rounds
> And binding with briers
> My joys and desires.

Bertie would often quote Blake, and Bertie's famous distinction between the 'possessive' and 'creative' impulses of mankind became the gospel of many of the younger generation. Husbands should not 'possess' wives, nor wives husbands, parents should not 'possess' their children. Not 'possessing' here had a deeper and more psychological meaning than the usual argument about property rights in marriage and the family.

The efforts of men and women of my generation to strive for these ideals in human relations and for women's emancipation brought conflict and even tragedy into our private lives. But this has been the burden of the story, not only in this country, but wherever in the world the battle for women's liberation has been fought.

Bertie, who had stood as a candidate for Women's Suffrage, thought it right that I should have a career. But at this time, early in 1922, we were both of us more concerned about our son. John had not been doing too well after the first month or two. I had devoted myself to breast-feeding, but, due to 'first-baby' inexperience, and anxiety, I had not succeeded very well. I was desperately anxious to do my best for John, and there was no question of undertaking any work until his need for breast-feeding should be over. My feelings were hurt when a specialist, whom we consulted about possible bottle-feeding, told me abruptly that I could 'perfectly well go on feeding him myself'. He was, I think, under the impression that I was one of these society women who shirked this duty. Doctors were still in those days very dictatorial towards women, especially to mothers, as I was soon to find out in some of our political campaigns.

However, Bertie felt that he, like John, might benefit by getting out of London and away from the pressure of visitors, at least for a part of the year. So I got hold of a thick book of properties in the West Country, to let furnished and/or for sale. Studying this exhaustively, I asked Bertie if he wanted Devon or Cornwall. He said the latter, and also that part of Cornwall that was not lush with trees and vegetation.

The house agent, Mr Treglown, drove me out on a chilly grey day in March 1922 towards Land's End, to a house called Sunny Bank, belying its name by standing rather stark in brown stucco and awful, dark red paint, surrounded by about a quarter of an acre of rough grass and a few evergreen bushes.

It was a plain, roomy house, the sort of house for a family, or for friends to visit, furnished with light oak as holiday houses are; it had three of the best and most cleverly planned attics. To the north, south, east and west lay farm, moorland and seascape. It faced south and in the distance I could see the blue-grey line of the sea; to the north the moorland hill, which I came to know as Chapel Carn Brea. The valley was the seat of what was then the Eastern Telegraph Company (now Cable and Wireless), and they had already desecrated its rural beauty by a row of suburban villas for staff and a dull-looking official building for students. But beyond these stretched the tangle of bracken, and between granite cliffs a beach which, when we saw it later in sunshine, was the whitest I have ever seen, all of fine broken shell and no grit. Across the inlet stood Treen Castle with the famous Logan Rock.

As I stood on the half-landing looking out on a view of fields and cows, like a flat, modern painting, and down from there into the hall, it suddenly came upon me that this house could and should be our home. On my say-so, Bertie took the house for the whole summer.

When I moved our small family of baby John, servants and luggage down in that early spring, there were hardly any motor cars; we had none, and our luggage—pram, cot, trunks—was brought out by lorry. One bus daily met the train and took people to the Land's End hotel, but none came to Porthcurno. We cooked by coal range or oilstove, our light was from oil lamps, whilst a row of candles stood on a chest on the landing to light us and visitors to bed.

The house had been well designed: a deep concrete tank covered the roof of the back kitchen; from this and the well, with the use of a hand-pump, came our water supply, which flowed through taps to bathroom sink and toilet. But when, in high summer, the rain supply failed, 600 pumps were needed to make a bath; swinging the pump was quite good rhythmic exercise. It is worth mentioning here that only since the 1960s have we had a main piped water supply.

Bertie had some lectures in London that first year and came down later. I walked the two miles by footpaths to Trevescan Corner, where he got off the Land's End bus. As we walked back together I suddenly had a fright that he might not like the house, for which the entire responsibility had been mine. As we came in sight of it he remarked, 'My dear, it's just the sort of house I like.' No doubt, with his unfailing courtesy, this is what he would have said in any case. But, as it proved, we had not been a month in the house before we knew that we must make it our own.

It was a funny house: from a distance it looked as if it would leap up into the air. We decided that we must find a way to settle it down, so we presently made a sort of terrace and lawn, and had a porch built, with round pillars, that owed something to Chinese inspiration. The house lay open to wind from every quarter and to the Atlantic gales. It simply could not go on being called Sunny Bank. We named it Carn Voel, after a headland at Nanjizal that likewise proudly fronted the storms from the west. We also dreamed, though we never achieved this, of building a square pavilion, Chinese style, perched at one corner of the garden, which would be entirely enclosed by glass and so would, in emulation of the 'enjoying rain' pavilion at Hangchow, be called the 'enjoying wind' pavilion.

That first summer we were getting to know the place and generally making do with what we had. Yet Bertie, who had fled for quiet, enjoyed inviting friends. Littlewood and others of the Lulworth reading party came, and were so delighted that Dr Streatfeild and Littlewood presently built themselves a house not far away. Vera Meynell, who had been intrigued by my adventures round the world, of which, I believe, she had not thought me capable, wanted to take a look at this marriage to a distinguished man. Her comment on us living in 'simple domestic bliss' and in a house 'actually called Sunny Bank' suggested that we did not quite come up to her expectations.

We talked much that summer about bringing up children: Freud was beginning to bite deeply into the thought of intellectuals. Prospective parents took seriously the danger of a child becoming too deeply involved with father or mother. Moreover, if early teaching and impressions were so vital, then was the average person really fit to bring up so delicate and important a creature as a child? Bloomsbury began to suggest that children from an early age should be entrusted to 'experts'. I remember that Vera advanced this theory, as we looked at John, and that I replied by saying that such experts did not exist; in fact we might have to learn to be those experts ourselves. Probably this was the moment when, unconsciously, the notion of starting the school was born.

Like most parents, Bertie and I were infatuated with our firstborn. John throve on Cornish milk and air from the start and was soon cheerful and sunburnt. I wanted to understand something about his development and was fascinated to watch him, as he lay in his cot, slowly discovering that he could consciously move his own hands: he would bend one finger after another, gazing solemnly at the movement with his big brown eyes.

Bertie, too, was robust again, sunburnt and happy. It was the thing among Cambridge men at that time to dress shabbily and go on long walking tours—'these Whigs,' H. G. Wells once said to me, 'love striding over their barren moors'. Bertie, in a loose flannel shirt and baggy grey trousers, with a peaked cap pulled over his sunburnt nose, looked, as I told him, like an old boatman. Roger Fry came down with the intention of painting Bertie's portrait, but was dumbfounded and indignant to find his countenance no longer 'sicklied o'er with the pale cast of thought', but rather beefy. He was dubious about the success of his effort; I think he rather blamed me for the transformation and I doubt if he ever quite forgave me.

Meantime Bertie and I unrepentantly lay in the sun, swam as early as May, tramped all round the marvellous West Penwith coast, and thought nothing of pushing John in his pram four miles across country to Sennen Cove. We delighted, too, in the footpaths, then wide grass paths stretching across the fields from granite stile to granite stile; no farmer in those days would have dreamed of ploughing them in.

Bertie had been receiving letters from Wittgenstein, who had given away all his inheritance because he did not want to be bothered with money, and was teaching in a small country school at Trattenbach, Austria. He wrote that the people of Trattenbach were the vilest in the world. Bertie replied that most men are vile, but that he could not accept the proposition that they were viler in Trattenbach than elsewhere. But Wittgenstein came back with the assertion that no men could be more vile than the Trattenbach population. It seemed that their only idea of the teaching of mathematics was money sums, whereas Wittgenstein had other notions.

Wittgenstein could not yet come to England, so Bertie and I managed somehow in that year, 1922, to visit him in Innsbruck. Inflation in Austria was at its height, even to replace a broken jug could cost a fortune. The whole place was full of ghouls and vultures, tourists profiting by the cheap currency to have a good time at the Austrians' expense. We all tramped the streets trying to find rooms in which to stay; Wittgenstein was in an agony of wounded pride at the state of his country and his inability to show us some sort of hospitality. In the end we found one room, in which Bertie and I occupied the bed and Wittgenstein a couch. But the hotel had a terrace, where it was pleasant enough to sit while Bertie discussed how to get Wittgenstein to England. It has been suggested that they quarrelled on this occasion; Wittgenstein was never easy, but I think any differences must have been over their philosophical ideas. Bertie never ceased to take trouble over furthering Wittgenstein's career; they met and he stayed with us more than once later. The circumstances of the time made this a troubled meeting.

Another event of that summer was the first dispute between Bertie and me, remarkable because not only was it so small a matter, but also because I cannot recall that we ever really quarrelled about anything so long as we were together.

Bertie asked me to tie up a parcel for him. As I happened to be busy I suggested that he might tie it up himself. 'I have never,' he said with great dignity, 'tied up a parcel in my life and I am not going to begin now!' With equal dignity I replied that I had not married him to tie up his parcels. Deadlock was avoided and face saved on both sides by our guest at the time, the gentle Charlie Sanger, who, smiling broadly, performed the menial act himself. It was, in fact, Bertie's constant claim that he had never been able to do anything useful with his hands, except to hold the pen with which he wrote. Nothing in his upbringing in an aristocratic milieu had encouraged manual dexterity, and no doubt he came to feel that what he did with his brain was ample compensation. 'From each,' after all, 'according to his ability.'

So there, in Cornwall, Bertie would sit as usual all morning at his table by the window, writing with his intense concentration. He had said that here I should have that 'room of my own' for work, on which Virginia Woolf had insisted as a symbol of woman as a person with a chance to achieve something in peace. In London I had no such refuge, but even here I found that the cry of a child would disturb, and the maids had no hestitation in coming to me with their problems, so long as I was in the house. Later on, after my daughter's birth, I rented a black hut on the cliff, to which I retreated with sandwiches after breakfast. Here, with nothing but a table and chair and the sky and the sea, preoccupations would presently fade and my own thoughts and emotions begin to rise. In the afternoon I would see the children arrive on the beach and go to join them and Bertie. The evenings, after time given to the children, would be spent in a civilized social manner, reading or

Sir Frederick Black K.C.B.

Lady Black

The author, aged eighteen

'For Professor Bertrand Russell with sincere compliments of the Society for Studying Russell's Philosophy' (Peking). On the author's left is the interpreter Chao Yuen-ren, and on Bertie's right Professor Fu Ling-yu

With John Conrad, three weeks old

Bertie with John and Kate, 1928

A candidate and his supporters, Sydney Street, 1923. *In the foreground left to right:* Stella Browne, the author, Bertie

The author with the Penzance General Strike Committee, 1926

Lunchtime at Beacon Hill School: John is on the extreme left, Kate on the extreme right

Left: Griffin Barry in war correspondent's uniform. *Right:* Bertie with Kate *(left)* and John at Hendaye, 1931

Telegraph House

The author arriving in New York for a lecture tour early in 1928

Paul Gillard

The author on the porch of Telegraph House suckling Roderick, with John, Harriet and Kate

Pat Grace

discussing by softly-shaded lamplight, and a fire if it was chilly. The very moist air in that sea-girt place was quite a problem, solved years later for me by electricity. But in those early days we often had to put our garments under the top blanket at night, or find them damp and uninviting to the skin in the morning.

Cornwall soon began to snare me in its magic: I wrote eloquently to Rachel Brooks of its combination of wildness and fierceness with delicate luxury, of Atlantic winds sweeping the sky of clouds; of the spring blossoming of the great granite cliffs, like 'some bleak old Gulliver caught and garlanded with dazzling ropes of flowers by Lilliputian imps'. There were days of dense sea mist too, eerie with an unearthly greenish light, the sinister effect enhanced by the booming (in those days) of the foghorns with notes from middle to deep bass, from headland to headland, fascinating for a moment, but nerve-racking when lasting for hours. Bertie and I noticed that the Cornish seemed disinclined for work in this special sort of weather; we felt that they then suffered, as we did, from Celtic melancholy.

I wrote:

Blue, white, grey are the clouds,
And patches of grey and silver are made on the sea
And paths of blue and pearl for the ships to go.

Blue, white, grey is the house
I have made on the hilltop,
Where the clouds shall go over and winds shall blow
And we shall gaze on the sea.
Children and lawns and flowers shall blossom about us.
When we die, may we sleep in love;
Perhaps in the winds our thoughts will speak to our children.

Let people say
They were fearless in life and loved beauty
Therefore these souls are worthy
To cleanse and ride with the majestic sea
And to speak and wander the world with the murmuring winds.

9

Politics and the Cause of Women

In the autumn we were back at Sydney Street, John well established in health and ten months old. I began to feel that I might perhaps now turn from domesticity to work of my own. Bertie had no wish to stand in my way. But for me the matter was no longer simple. I had been known to a small circle as of some academic standing, when Fellow of Girton: all that was destroyed when I set out for China.

Now, though more in the public eye, I was the newly-married wife of a very distinguished man and mother of his son after a romantic courtship. I already began to notice that visitors—and this practice was continuous and specially characteristic of the women—would call ostensibly to make my acquaintance, or to meet us both, and would then address themselves solely to Bertie, treating me as the dispenser of tea. Every wife of a famous man has reason to fear the wiles of predatory females. But just now this was not the issue.

My book *The Religion of the Machine Age* had been begun, but I had been bitterly disappointed to find that even Ogden had not understood its basic thesis, for he had cut out the passage which first outlined it in a controversial piece I had sent him from China and which he summarized in the *Cambridge Magazine*. I had reproached him for this, saying that I thought I had here an original idea.

The general argument in these paragraphs was that men tended to shape their political systems according to what they believed about the attitude of their God. After sketching the medieval notion, I went on to say:

Since Newton, religious thought has tended to take refuge in the notion of the First Cause; God becomes merely a clock-maker or cinematograph operator turning a handle, no longer closely concerned in individual lives, or with individual desires. He is the impersonal origin of the laws by which the Universe is regulated, laws which are strictly impartial and no more favourable to man than the rest of creation. I believe this to be the instinctive religion of the average modern mind; though not formulated as a dogma, it dominates the imagination. With it goes a passionate belief in the solidity and importance of matter, likewise derived ultimately from the Newtonian gravitation theory. Good, or rather goods, come to that man who sufficiently understands the working of natural laws to achieve material prosperity by their means.

The modern theory of the State derives, like the old one, from the current religious conception. It envisages the ruler, or group of rulers, as scientific winders of the clock, who construct society according to certain fixed laws regulating the distribution of matter, in complete disregard of ranks and classes, prayers of individuals, or received moral standards. This, I think, is what is meant by the exclusion of the 'ethico-deific argument'.

Instead therefore, of a 'divine right' of kings, we have, as it were, a 'mechanical right' of kings and opposition to the mechanism is an abominable heresy. Criticism of men like Lenin is as absurd as criticism of the impartial First Cause, since they are no more responsible for the social upheavals involved in their clock winding, than God for the earthquakes occurring in His well regulated universe. Further, to object that the State was made for man and not man for the State, is as antiquated a superstition as the pretension that the Universe was made by God as a comfortable dwelling place for humanity. All that we can do, in both cases, is to sigh and wish that the Creator had spent His time in anything but creating.*

In the Lent term of 1922, Bertie and I had made a flying visit to Cambridge to read joint papers to the Heretics. Bertie refused to go on his own in the autumn before John was safely born, but suggested that it might be entertaining if we were to go together. The topic was industrialism and religion; Bertie dealt with traditional religion in an industrial state, and I put forward my idea of the industrial creed. There was a great crowd, who all adjourned from the hall to Kingsley Martin's rooms at King's to continue the discussion. I first became aware of Kingsley on this occasion on the point of 'preserving the tiny spark of reason' in mankind. I had the impression that my thesis was not well understood; this is confirmed by a passage in Ivor Montagu's recent memoirs, in which he is critical of Bertie's paper but makes no mention of mine. Since one of my arguments was that, though poverty should be conquered, it was a mistake for socialists to lay too much stress on the possession of material goods, it was not likely that Marxists of those days would agree. I had written:

The time will come when it is universally recognised that oppression in the interest of economic inequality is as absurd as oppression in the interest of some particular belief about God and the future life. But this will happen more surely and permanently by propagating disbelief in the importance of property than by disciplinary redistribution of it. Because that redistribution must depend, in the last

* open letter to *The Liberator*, New York 1920, from China

resort, on the general will of the community to accept it. It is capitalist industry that is the persecuting religion, and its central dogma the importance of private property and wealth. Communism should aim at creating a society of men and women to whom that doctrine is merely laughable. To them economic justice will be instinctive, they will desire economic justice, as they will desire developed industry, not as an end in itself, or as a means to communal luxury, but as a means to the higher development of the community. If communism concentrates only on goods and the mechanisation of life, and if it attempts to establish itself by dragooning majorities with fire and the sword, it thereby submits to the machine, adopts the capitalist dogma and the capitalist method, and proves itself to be no advance of science, but merely a further phase of this persecuting religion of industrialism, from which we hoped it would free us, and from which free thinkers will have to liberate the world some hundreds, perhaps thousands, of years hence.*

Nowadays there is a constant stream of books and articles discussing the effect of industrialism on thought and belief and trends in State education. We have even reached the point of doubting the wisdom of affluence and a constantly rising standard of living, whilst latter-day socialists have become increasingly corrupted by productivity and the profit motive. Nationalized concerns are no longer public services, but profit-making corporations outside the control of Parliament or people. What is more, to be a heretic to the machine god can land you in prison or the lunatic asylum, and this not only in the Soviet Union.

With hindsight I must now regret that I allowed myself to be discouraged, to think that no one would understand what I was trying to say, and that, in any case, they would simply believe that all my ideas were derived from Bertie, who, as it happened, did not at all agree with me on this one. None the less, I had to live in the shadow of his reputation.

I was in no way jealous of him, this would have been absurd. My love for him was almost worship, and I would go to his defence whenever he was attacked, with whatever ammunition I could muster. He was equally loyal to me and always encouraged me. However, I did not tell him how I really felt about my work, but privately decided that I must turn to my old and chief ambition, the theatre, in which no question of rivalry between us could arise.

Before ever I went to Paris I had put out feelers about the stage and I knew Norman MacDermott, who later had the distinction of putting on Noël Coward's *The Vortex* when others were afraid of the theme, and who was now producing at the Everyman Theatre. During my Paris stay he had once offered me a part in a bank holiday open-air show, for

* open letter to *The Liberator*, New York 1920, from China

164

which I was tempted to return. Now I was able to get associated with what he was doing at the Everyman and I was allowed to understudy several parts. During the winter 1922–3 he put on Shaw's *Philanderer*, in which I actually played Grace Tranfield for one week. There was a Christmas show, *Brer Rabbit*, in which Raymond Massey blacked up to play Uncle Remus, and I went on in a minor part; Margaret Yarde was among the company and Jean Cadell, who played in *At Mrs Beam's*. We would sit in the basement by a roaring fire—they were all very kind to me and I knew that this was really the sort of atmosphere that I loved. Later I got on at the Old Vic, where Robert Atkins was producing, and did my part of the rhubarb, rhubarb of the crowd in *Julius Caesar*.

But before all this came a very strenuous interlude. The coalition in Parliament broke up and the Tories went to the country. This was a great chance for Labour, which had gone under badly in the Khaki Election of 1918. Disillusion with the Government had been gaining ground. Bertie was asked to stand for Labour in Chelsea; although there was no chance of winning so Conservative a seat, the campaign would be short and sharp, not much waste of his time and perhaps worth the publicity to the movement, as well as stiffening up the local Labour people.

So for the time being I was a candidate's wife and began to write to Bertie's friends and to Ogden in Cambridge to raise the money for the campaign, to which we could contribute very little. Sir Samuel Hoare was our opponent and the general feeling among the local Tories was that it was impudent of Labour to be butting in. It was not easy to secure the booking of halls or committee rooms, and there was definite discrimination; but, secure in our possession of a freehold house, we defiantly opened the gate of the steps to our basement dining-room, and hoisted placards across the first-floor balcony. Many helpers flowed in to address envelopes; I had to produce a letter in support, with a picture of John and me. I was here, there and everywhere in the borough, on a soapbox outside the World's End pub, canvassing in the working-class streets. The press, of course, became interested; they ran stories about literary and artistic Chelsea, quite ignoring the fact that these were only an infinitesimal part of the local electorate. In those days before television, elections were such fun; there were crowded meetings both indoor and out, sallies from heckler and speaker. We got out a leaflet showing the voting record in the House of 'Sammy', as we all called him, which showed that he had voted for the tax on beer but against the tax on sparkling wines. His supporters would endeavour to reply, and when they began 'As for beah', an echo would come back 'Ah, beah, heah heah', and 'What about them sparkling wines, Sammy?' Rumour had it that someone at the World's End had thrown fishes' heads at Sir Samuel's car, which, of course, we 'deeply deplored'.

Saklatvala was an Indian communist candidate in Battersea across the river; Bertie made a point of appearing on a platform with him. Saklatvala was in fact the first communist M.P. We had help from many of the Labour intellectuals, like the Daltons and the L'Estrange Malones; there was a great packed meeting at the Town Hall when Harold Laski, brilliant and learned, fired off his rapid sallies like firecrackers. It was suggested that I should produce our son at a women's meeting. Thus John made his first appearance on a public platform, sitting in the arms of his nurse behind me and the chief woman speaker. As she proceeded I noticed that, although there were no special jokes, the audience were smiling and even nudging one another. Turning, I saw that John, inspired by the occasion, was perfectly repeating the speaker's gestures with his arms and remarking 'Ah Ah Ah' in emulation of her eloquence. I asked his nurse to remove him, and he departed waving his goodbye to responsive admirers.

I confess that the count and the declaration were for me thrilling moments. As I watched those piles of voting papers in that, my first election, I felt tense excitement. We put the vote up by near five hundred, and, as we went on the balcony of the Town Hall for the declaration of poll, the lively crowd outside was, as might be expected, rather for Bertie than his opponent. The Town Hall faces Sydney Street and, emerging from the front door, we were swallowed up by our supporters and almost carried by them back to our own front door.

It was a great election: Labour representation, to the astonishment of the press, was more than doubled; it came back as the second party and, at its first meeting in Parliament, elected the pacifist Ramsay MacDonald as its leader.

For me personally in the election had come the intoxication of the acclaim of a great crowd of people and the knowledge that I did have the power to move and even inspire them.

Now there was time, through the winter, for me to pursue my acting career. I cared a great deal about this and was more convinced after finding that I could 'hold' an audience, that given a real chance, I would make a success. Shaw's *Saint Joan* was in rehearsal; I longed to ask Sybil Thorndike, who had grown up alongside my mother in Rochester, if I might not understudy in her company. But I felt that this would be impudent presumption. About this time Lewis Casson came to see Bertie for advice: he wanted to give up the stage and, a keen Labour supporter, perhaps adopt a Parliamentary career. I was amazed that anyone in what I held to be a glorious profession should ever dream of leaving it. And I am glad that he did not, having delighted in his and Sybil's performances for so many years. We went to see *Saint Joan* and visited backstage afterwards, chatting with the Cassons and others of the company; the young Laurence Olivier I remember sitting on the floor by Sybil and expressing great admiration for her performance.

Understudying meant being at the theatre every night from 8 p.m.

to 9 p.m., which of course involved renouncing evening social life in which Bertie and I might have wished to participate together. I did, however, persevere in my efforts until the end of the season. By March, though, Bertie was impatient to get away with John to Cornwall. I followed after putting the London house in order for tenants. Then came another blow to my theatrical hopes; I became pregnant again.

Ogden, who had always been pressing me to write instead of dissipating my energies, was now urging both Bertie and me to sign contracts for books, and I did agree to write about my adventures in Russia and China, though in fact those particular books never got written. On 30 April 1923 I wrote to him, 'Farewell to the theatre for many months, *won't* you be pleased, baby expected at Christmas.' The rest of that letter is rather pathetic. Much as I loved John, I evidently at that time regarded having a baby as a tiresome interruption of more important activities. Although I intimated in this letter that after this baby I 'will not be expected to do more', I knew I was facing the end of my theatrical ambitions and sought to boost my morale by enumerating other achievements to justify my existence.

'If I have two babies and three books and one garden and two houses in order by my thirtieth birthday, I shall feel I have done well.' So, too, I had written my mother from Peking that I had 'helped to save one life, started another, and begun writing a book'. Women's Lib will well understand this state of mind.

Ogden was perfectly right: all my life I have tried to do too many different things. I wonder if this is not a perpetual dilemma for women. A man enters on a job or profession, needs to stick to it to earn his living, and is unlikely to have to change it on marriage. For a woman marriage presents not only practical problems, but she finds herself emotionally pulled all ways, and tends by tradition and impulse to put the needs of others before her own. What is more, opening her eyes on the world, she feels intensely responsible for setting it to rights. Arnold Bennett, when he made his witty contribution to feminism, called his novel *The Lion's Share*, indicating what a 'hell of a lot' modern women were undertaking.

This second pregnancy gave me more trouble than the first. Somehow it set up pressure on the sciatic nerve; I was in pain most of the summer and spent nearly two months lying down most of the day. Concentrating on writing was almost impossible; into the bargain I was offered a part to go on tour in *R.U.R.*, which had to be turned down because of the 'blighted baby'. Nevertheless, it was this summer in Cornwall that I started to make the garden, in the teeth of discouragement from the locals, who opined: 'She'll not make a garden there, not with all that wind.' This summer too, we had a boat. We had done much rowing at Lulworth, but the tides and sea off the Cornish coast were a totally different matter, and we only used the boat inshore along our beaches.

Bertie had given me some capital and the house in Cornwall was in my name, but in the main I was dependent on him. He wrote steadily. *The Analysis of Mind* appeared in 1921, followed by *The Problem of China* in 1922, and our joint book *The Prospects of Industrial Civilisation* in 1923, in which I had a half share. Bertie had agreed to do a very short lively book, *Icarus or The Future of Science* for the new To-day and To-morrow series which Ogden had started with Kegan Paul.

Unfortunately for our peace of mind—and body—in November of 1923 Mr Baldwin, who had become Prime Minister on the death of Bonar Law, suddenly decided to go to the country on the question of protection. We were in no mood to fight another election, but felt it would be faint-hearted not to do so. Polling day, 6 December, was not only near to Christmas, but about three weeks before my baby was due. But I set to work to organize our committee room and took part in the canvassing; when I now and then met a very pregnant working mother she would say that she doubted if she would be there on polling day, and I would pat my equally large belly and say that I could not count on it either.

Our vote went up again; throughout the country it was a famous election. Labour polled four-and-a-half million votes, increased its numbers in Parliament from 142 to 192, carried 'no confidence' in the Tories with the help of the Liberals, and by 22 January 1924 Ramsay MacDonald was Prime Minister.

My Kate, with great good sense, bided her time, let us have a peaceful Christmas and appeared on 29 December. But the campaign did take toll of the health of both her parents.

Bertie was concerned about endowing the future of his two children and he had decided to go on a lecture tour in America after the baby was born, but he briefly delayed his departure to give time to get his breath. I can never think of that leave-taking without a pang: I see his desperately unhappy face at parting from the three of us as he gets into the taxi and drives away, and I stand feeling equally forlorn at our front door. Living and working together day by day, very much in harmony about our beliefs and purposes, we had become almost part of one another.

Fortunately lecture tours are not so very long, and I meanwhile had plenty to keep me busy. Kate got measles, to the anxiety of her absent father and present mother; John had to be spirited away to the care of his grandparents to escape infection; and, with a young and not very competent nurse to help with the baby, I had to deal with Bertie's affairs in his absence and was already involved in the beginnings of the birth control fight.

The credit for pioneer work in the campaign to lift the taboos on sex and birth control in that generation must be given to Margaret Sanger in America and Marie Stopes in Britain. *Married Love* by Marie Stopes was a much read and much criticized book. Bertie and I used to laugh at some of its passages, as for instance that a woman might allow her body to be seen by her husband 'in the clear water of her bath'. As we had a very inadequate gas water-heater and mostly had to share our morning bath, Bertie would say that the correct procedure was for me to step into the 'clear water' first.

Marie Stopes had established the first birth control clinic in Britain; the whole question of informing women, especially those who were poor, about methods of contraception, began to be discussed. Early in 1923, Rose Witcop and Guy Aldred, both on the left politically, were selling cheaply a pamphlet by Margaret Sanger explaining about sex and contraception in terms which, it was thought, uneducated women would understand. The police seized the pamphlet for destruction as obscene. The report of this made me exceedingly angry, for I could not see why information which a middle-class woman could get from her doctor should be withheld from a poorer woman who might need it far more. In actual fact, ignorance about contraception and the importance of family limitation was then fairly widespread among all classes.

Bertie agreed with me that we should take some action; I contacted Maynard Keynes, who agreed to go surety with me for an appeal; St Loe Strachey was prepared to give evidence at Quarter Sessions and we briefed St John Hutchinson K.C. In conference St John Hutchinson indicated that the police were probably aiming at the diagrams which showed a finger placing a pessary in the correct position. 'It might not,' he explained, 'be the finger of the woman concerned.' Not having a sufficiently 'dirty mind' this had simply not occurred to me. But undoubtedly, because of women's ignorance and shame about their sexual parts, the diagrams were really important.

At Quarter Sessions, however, the magistrates refused to hear evidence, saying that they could make up their own minds. It seemed to me that what worried them most was the question and answer in the pamphlet, 'Should a woman enjoy sexual intercourse? Yes, she should.' What would be the effect of this information coming to the knowledge of their wives and daughters?

We did not expect to win this case, but to ventilate the question: the battle was now joined. So far as the pamphlet itself was concerned, it was permitted to appear, minus diagrams, after the Labour Government came in the following year.

But meanwhile, how was the working wife and mother to get advice which she might desperately need? In a letter to the *Nation and Athenaeum* Bertie indicated that treatment of birth control in print 'would become impossible', to be firmly rebuked by Marie Stopes in a letter to the same journal,* maintaining that it was not the pamphlet but the 'method of publication', the 'manner the Aldreds handled it,' which the magistrates found objectionable. Margaret Sanger should have issued the book herself through her own publishers. In other words,

* *Nation and Athenaeum*, 3 February 1923

made it available only to the better-off and dissociated it from left-wing politics. We did not differ from Marie Stopes in the important central aim, namely to make birth control 'respectable' and remove it from the aura of rubber-goods shops and sniggering. That this concern led to political action did not, I think, appeal to her.

Sundry requests began to be addressed to maternity clinics for birth control advice, which was always refused; the policy of the Ministry of Health being to threaten with dismissal doctors or health visitors who gave such advice, as well as indicating that grants to health centres might be withheld.

With the coming of the Labour Government, those of us who saw the issue as political began to feel that this obscurantist attitude might be overcome and that to achieve nationwide permission to blend contraceptive advice with maternity care would be an immense boon to overburdened mothers.

Together with others I began to sound out Members of Parliament, doctors and medical officers who were favourable, and public men who might bring pressure to bear. I found considerable support from all sorts and conditions of people. The Independent Labour Party was especially inclined towards us: hence I once invited the Clydeside M.P.s, Campbell Stephen and Jimmy Maxton, to come to tea and discuss the matter. To my amusement they refused, implying that they did not wish to be accused of hobnobbing with the aristocracy. I replied that, since they insisted on my meeting them at the House, I would not guarantee not to come with the intentions of Guy Fawkes. I did meet them and other M.P.s of differing parties, including a lunch with Duff Cooper, who assured me that he would support our movement with vigour.

The Clydeside accused us of wanting to throw the baby out with the bathwater: they were, naturally, resentful of the attitude of the Eugenists, who implied that the working classes should not breed because they were of inferior stock. It was perfectly true that, owing to women's ignorance, the workers had the largest families. The modern threat of overpopulation had not yet dawned, Malthus was then rather at a discount, and the workers argued that they should have more money rather than less children. We Labour women fully agreed with the more money argument, but asserted that, even if we lived in Buckingham Palace, we would not want a baby every year. The health of the mother, the contention that only wanted children should be born, were the bases of our campaign. In dealing with doctors I was shocked to find that they would not sterilize or give contraceptive advice, even after several Caesarean deliveries; they would even tell me that a half-starved mother could produce a perfectly healthy child. Would not, I suggested, a properly fed mother produce a better one?

We enlisted the help of H. G. Wells and Julian Huxley, who both gave publicity to our demands. H.G. helped us with funds; my visit to him to discuss our work was the start of a long friendship which, despite my misgivings about his wartime views, placed him for me among the greatest and most intriguing personalities of our time. I appreciated his wit, his cheek, his outbursts of temper at his adversaries—this was a real person. H.G., as is known, saw contraception as a means to the sexual liberty of women, for he—like modern young people—treated sex as (in his words) 'one of these compliments we pay each other'.

I began to study official reports on the health and death rate of child-bearing women. In these it was admitted that many 'miscarriages' were in fact illegal abortions; I discovered that the death rate of mothers giving birth varied very greatly from one area to another; in heavy industrial towns it reached as much as nine per thousand births. We found that the *average* death rate of mothers was then four to five per thousand births. By contrast the death rate of miners from fatal accidents was 1·1 per thousand miners actually engaged in mining. Leah L'Estrange Malone and I then coined the slogan: 'It is four times as dangerous to bear a child as to work in a mine, and mining is men's most dangerous trade.'

We now organized a deputation to the Minister of Health of the Labour Government, Mr Wheatley, who, unfortunately, was a Roman Catholic. There has always been a considerable Catholic vote for the Labour party, and at this time, in 1924, Catholic opinion was in constant ferment over the Stopes-Sutherland libel case.

We prepared a petition for the Minister, and a statement which described the cases of mothers of tubercular and syphilitic children, of abnormally large families, and of several Caesarean operations.

The deputation met Mr Wheatley on 9 May 1924. It was introduced by F. A. Broad, M.P. Accompanying him were Dorothy Jewson, M.P. for Norwich, H. G. Wells, Dr Frances Huxley, and other doctors, Mrs Jenny Baker of the Dr Stopes Constructive Birth Control Society, representatives from the New Generation Society, birth control clinics, Labour Women's Sections; Dr Sloan Chesser gave us a statement which was read.

Our claim that it was four times as dangerous to bear a child as to work in a coalmine came as a shock to our supporters: as we mounted the steps to the Ministry of Health, H.G. said to me: 'Dora, are you sure of your facts about this?' 'Perfectly sure,' I replied.

Dr Frances Huxley spoke for us, as did H.G., who described the Ministry's policy as 'aristocratic', treating working-class women merely as materials for breeding. I supplemented these statements.

We asked two things: one, that in institutions under the control of the Ministry, birth control advice should be given to those mothers who desired it; and two, that the doctors at welfare centres should be allowed to give such advice when they considered it medically advisable. Both pleas were rejected by the Minister, who gave as his reasons that State- and rate-aided institutions could not, on such a matter, be permitted to give this advice by administrative action—the authority of Parliament was necessary. Where contraception was necessary on strict medical grounds, the patient must go to a private doctor or hospital. Our deputation had not expected to receive any other reply, but our secondary aim, publicity, was secured in full measure. The national and provincial press buzzed with reports of the deputation; the Catholic—and other—papers stormed into opposition to our immoral proposals.

We saw our next steps clearly. Mr Wheatley had referred us to Parliament, to Parliament therefore we would go. But first of all we would obtain the verdict of the Labour Women's Conference. Several Women's Sections had sent in resolutions on birth control; as a member of the Chelsea Women's Section I was in charge of one. It was my first conference: I was excited and nervous. I dressed for the occasion in a scarlet jersey long-waisted dress with a short cape tied at the throat with dark blue braid to give myself confidence. Mrs Jenny Baker, an elderly woman, we agreed, should move our amendment in the maternity debate and I was to second. In a narrow corridor of the Holborn Empire, where the Conference was to take place, I was confronted by Dr Marion Phillips, Woman Organiser of the Labour Party, tall and to me appearing massive and terrifying. 'You must,' she said, 'withdraw this resolution.' 'I cannot, Dr Phillips,' I almost stammered, 'I am instructed by my Section to move it.' 'Sex should not be dragged into politics, you will split the Party from top to bottom.' 'Dr Phillips, this is a burning question for all mothers, I think that tomorrow you will get a surprise.' This interview revealed to me that the Labour Woman Organiser existed, not so much to support the demands of the women, as to keep them in order from the point of view of the male politicians.

The next day, 14 May 1924, Mrs K. Bruce Glasier moved the resolution of the Standing Joint Committee of Women's Organisations on motherhood, which demanded paid absence from work for women for six weeks before and six weeks after childbirth, improvement of maternity care, and some form of payment to non-wage-earning mothers. Our addendum, moved by Mrs Jenny Baker, said:

This Conference, while in no way criticising the views of those who for scientific or moral reasons are opposed to the practice of birth control, expresses the opinion that the Ministry of Health should permit Public Health Authorities to provide, for those who desire it, information on the subject of birth control, and that, in cases where Local Health Authorities desire to give such information, the Ministry of Health shall not on that account withhold the usual grant.

Mrs Baker urged that the need was urgent, and citing tragic cases, asked whether mothers had not the right to prevent more misery being brought into the world.

According to the report in the *Daily Herald* of 15 May I said:

Rich women are able to obtain the information from Harley Street specialists; it is a crying shame that the same advice should not be made available to every working mother who desires it. If a rich woman wants to limit her family for selfish reasons, surely a woman who has had 15 confinements, or a tubercular mother who cannot bear healthy children, should have that same advice. The matter is one of public health, and must not be left to quacks, abortionists and non-medical people. Help should be given and given now.

One mother of eleven opposed, and was greeted with hostile murmurs from the delegates, but despite urging from Mrs Harrison Bell, a formidable lady in the Chair, there was virtually no other opposition. Why, said one delegate, should a woman go on bearing like a fruit tree forever? Our addendum was carried by one thousand votes to eight. Several women M.P.s, Dorothy Jewson, Susan Lawrence, Margaret Bondfield, as also Ellen Wilkinson, were on the platform to listen to the debate. Next day the *Daily Express* supported the mother of eleven in a leader headed 'Motherhood Menace'.

We now formed our Workers' Birth Control Group to make clear that we were working in and with the Labour Party and did not share the views of the extreme Malthusians, or the Eugenists' notion that the poor were inferior stock. We were well supported by a few Labour M.P.s: Dorothy Jewson was our President, Vice-Presidents were W. M. Adamson, Major Church, Ernest Thurtle, F. A. Broad, H. G. Romeril, S. P. Viant—all Labour M.P.s.

Our very active Committee was composed, among others, of Frida Laski, Joan Allen (now Lady Allen of Hurtwood), Dorothy Thurtle, Leah L'Estrange Malone, Alice Hicks, Margaret Lloyd. We met, like our election workers, in the basement dining-room of Sydney Street. But we had many other active supporters, Mrs Jenny Adamson, Stella Browne in Chelsea, Janet Chance in Hampshire and others all over the country, who acted as corresponding members and co-operated with us for political action.

The nationwide furore of comment and controversy, questions and debate in Parliament, debates in great numbers of local councils, innumerable meetings, are evidence of how large a contribution we all made to the enlightenment and liberation of women—and men too, on a subject hitherto shrouded in shame and secrecy. Marie Stopes' libel action at this date stirred immense public interest, but our work went down to the grass roots and made ordinary people begin to see that here was a pressing social and political problem. Those women pioneers were a lively and intrepid group with whom I spent many rewarding hours. We were of all sorts, intellectuals, middle and working class.

Dorothy Jewson and I were often fellow delegates at the Women's Conference; as a single woman she showed courage in dealing with a topic then so shocking as sex. Lady Allen of Hurtwood became well known for all her work for children; Margaret Lloyd—a cousin of Bertie's —also devoted her life to left-wing and women's causes. Dorothy Thurtle, daughter of George Lansbury, supported and egged on her husband in all that he did for us. Leah L'Estrange Malone was an astute politician and gave good advice; Alice Hicks, wiry, indefatigable, was the best type of active working-class woman. Rose Witcop, seller of the Sanger pamphlet, tall and beautiful, had the presence and dignity of Deborah the Judge, who 'arose a mother in Israel'. Frida Laski and I were close: she had a forthright contempt for the smug and sanctimonious arguments of our religious opponents, which I shared.

The supporters of abortion law reform, Alice Jenkins, Janet Chance and Stella Browne, were at times an embarrassment to us; I did not disagree with their views, but overcoming prejudice about contraception was our first target. Janet Chance had a reassuring respectable air, but Stella Browne was a holy terror. She made no bones about raising the abortion issue in meetings and, wisps of hair floating from her untidy coiffure, would resist all efforts of a Chairman to put her down. Though I feared harm to our cause, I did glory in her intransigence. Dogged persistence by women over many years has brought about abortion law reform in Britain. Alice Jenkins, whom I did not know so well, lived to see realized the cause for which she fought so long.

Mr Wheatley had stirred a hornet's nest: all through 1924 we buzzed and stung. In June, H.G.'s syndicated article raising the issue was headed the 'Serfdom of Ignorance', in another he threatened that the intellectuals would leave the Labour Party. We found the pages of the *Daily Herald*, the *New Leader*, the *Manchester Guardian*, the *Nation and Athenaeum* open to us. Mr Wheatley had said women should seek birth control advice from hospitals; in a letter to the *Herald*, Frida pointed out that our Group had investigated this possibility and had found that hospitals were neither equipped nor willing to do this service. The doctors, too, got on their high horse and, in their journal, asked who was Mr Wheatley that he should tell them where and what advice they should give. When he told the National Council for Combating Venereal Disease that the community should not rely for its health on 'uncontrolled individual action—in the matter of health we are all socialists now', I was immediately after him to point out publicly that in the health matter of birth control he had deliberately referred us to private enterprise. When he addressed the Baby Week Conference in July, Bertie and I in a joint letter from Cornwall, widely published, charged him with hypocrisy so long as mothers and their babies suffered ill health or died, when contraceptive advice and help might have saved them. Meantime Dorothy Jewson and Ernest Thurtle were harassing him with questions in the House.

When I left for Cornwall after the Women's Conference I undertook the care of baby Kate and John myself. The nurse engaged when Kate was born had been too young for the responsibility I had to place upon her. That was a glorious summer of sunshine almost from dawn to dark, and I recall the beauty of the early morning light when I got up to give Kate her feed. Both children flourished and Bertie had returned from his lecture tour not at all overtired. But I was definitely suffering from the strenuous political work undertaken so soon after Kate's birth, and the extra responsibility during Bertie's absence. In spite of the exquisite weather, for three weeks I was ill with tonsillitis. We presently had to engage a new nurse for the children.

It was, too, a very political summer and, even out of town, we could not avoid following events. Ramsay MacDonald had recognized the Soviet Government, and, after the French invasion of the Ruhr, had attempted to begin peace negotiations and reconstruction in Europe through the London Conference and Settlement of July and August. He went on to plan for treaties with Russia and even for a loan. His government was only in power by reason of support from the Liberals, who now began to be restive. Our birth control campaign continued unabated; I wrote many letters and an article for the *Socialist Review*, and was away, finally, to the I.L.P. Summer School near Scarborough in August.

My ill health had something to do with the intense anger and frustration which I felt at the attitude of the opponents of our modest requests on birth control. Mother of John and a babe only a few months old, even I, like others present, had been astounded at the fury against child-bearing displayed by the delegates to the Labour Women's Conference. Here were women fiercely repudiating what had been preached at us as the noblest fulfilment of our womanhood. And the preachers went on to tell us that we were immoral, obscene, crude and clumsy materialists, lost to all sense of the spiritual aspects of the relations of men and women. How little scope there was for this last in the lives of working mothers I found out as I listened to their stories, and later I learned still more as I went about the country speaking on this question.

The 'Very Intellectual Miss Black' now received her true political education. Feminist indeed, I began to wonder if the feminists had not been running away from the central issue of women's emancipation. Would women ever be truly free and equal with men until we had liberated mothers? Demanding equality and the vote, women in the Labour movement had argued that there should now be no distinction between men's and women's questions, a view which I had more or less accepted until I came up against this issue of maternity. What rights had the working-class mother? Dependent on her man's income, she yet had no claim to a share of it; she must bear and attempt to feed and care for every child born to her; left in ignorance of the functioning of her own body, she must accept with gratitude the charitable help from the maternity clinics and the patronage of health visitors and the middle-class women who came to 'weigh the babies' at the clinic sessions. Yet was not this woman, and her children, the very foundation stone and future of our race and nation? How come then that our religious leaders and politicians could despise, neglect and oppress her?

'To me those are materialists,' I flung back at our enemies, 'who leave the shaping of our destinies to the chance activities of matter; those are spiritual who seek, through science or art, to realise their dreams in the material world. To the first class belong the preachers of resignation and submission to all the natural ills of mankind; to the second, those who hold that we not only may, but must, learn to control through politics and science the destinies of mankind.'*

We were trying to set sex free from the stigma of sin, we saw it as an expression of the union and harmony of two lovers; our adversaries' dogma demanded that sex be indulged in only for the procreation of children. Yet this very creation of new life they hedged about with taboos and excessive suffering. I became ever more hostile to religious teaching, seeing it as the negation of life; what is more, it was the basis of our whole economic and political structure. Like Voltaire I cried: '*Écrasez l'infame!*' One of our successful campaigns of that year, through letters to the press signed by eminent persons, prevented Charles Trevelyan, then President of the Board of Education, from giving more public money to the denominational schools.

Only gradually over the years did I reach the conviction that the trouble with traditional societies is that they completely neglect the views and needs of women. At this stage I simply felt the urge to champion the oppressed mother, and, disgusted though I was with false sentiment about the noble act of childbirth, I could yet visualize the bearing and rearing of children as a creative activity hitherto little understood or practised in the world.

Nor was I, of course, the only person to glimpse this vision. Margaret McMillan had begun her nursery schools, undertaken in a socialist, not a charitable spirit; Eleanor Rathbone, noting the plight of large poverty-stricken families, began the campaign for family allowances; she was also responsible for furthering legislation on inheritance, to prevent men from disinheriting their wives and children by caprice.

The Summer School of the I.L.P. of 1924 was significant in that its discussion booklet not only contained me on birth control, but also Eleanor Rathbone, and it covered more general issues as well, such as nationalization of land and other resources, which were causing concern to the capitalist press.

This I.L.P. meeting had considerable press coverage; the Prime Minister, who, as a member of the Party, had hoped to attend, sent a message of apology; in the Chair was the young Clifford Allen, greatly admired for his ascetic good looks and his courage as a C.O. during the war. For the next few years, he was, as it were, the life and soul of the I.L.P., an adept at raising funds, open-minded and inveterate

* *Socialist Review*, August 1924

in his stimulation of discussion, but inclined to caution as regards the Party in action. With a Labour Government in power, any deliberations by its Prime Minister's Party attracted attention. We had thus been given an excellent opportunity for stating our birth control case.

In my speech to the I.L.P. I made clear that for me matters that affected women as mothers were in a real and lasting sense women's questions, though, apart from this, we should not differentiate between the sexes. Making our usual plea based on the risks to life and health of child-bearing, I none the less added the comment that there seemed no reason for demanding an increasing population, nor could the Labour and Socialist programme of housing, education and endowment of motherhood be fundamentally carried out without reference to population growth.

That Summer School, despite the austerity of the accommodation, was most agreeable; those who took part were among the intelligent and eager in the movement, there was an atmosphere of idealism and hope. Miles Malleson and I rendered a dramatic reading of Ernst Toller's *Massenmensch*, translated by Vera Meynell and issued by the Nonesuch Press.

The I.L.P. had been the educational driving force within the Labour movement: with MacDonald as he then was, at the head, and with this strength behind him, there was good reason for optimism. There need be no rift with Soviet Russia, the communists, like the I.L.P., were, to begin with, affiliated to the Labour Party. Had this united action and drive continued, the whole course of history in Europe might have been very different, no Cold War, perhaps no Second World War. But already came the move to exclude the communists, which, though I differed from them, I regretted, since it seemed to me that our reactionary opponents, though they might have their differences, always managed to preserve the unity of Church, Army, Landed Gentry and Big Business.

It was this very combination which, a few weeks after the Scarborough meeting, brought down Ramsay's Government on the trivial issue of the withdrawal of the prosecution against a communist—the famous Campbell case. On the evening of that momentous debate in the House, I stood outside Parliament with Frida Laski. Presently Lord Haldane crossed Palace Yard, a tall figure in a black cape or ulster, to be greeted by us at the corner. 'Well,' said he, in his deep authoritative voice, with dramatic emphasis, 'the Government has fallen. It remains to be seen what the country will say to 'ut!' And as delegates to the Labour Party Conference that October, we heard our Prime Minister, with a rousing cry of, 'To your tents O Israel!' send us forth to do battle at the polls.

To the campaigner of the 1920s politics was a passionate and dramatic affair. All the same, a general election every autumn was an ordeal demanding in time, money and energy. Bertie had felt that he did not want to stand yet again, but fortunately the local supporters were unanimous in wanting me to stand in his place. Naturally, I was excited and proud to be in a position to fight for a seat in Parliament, young as I was. I knew there was no chance of winning, but I could carry on my crusade for social justice and the rights of women.

This proved a very tough election for Labour. The other two parties made pacts not to stand against one another when this might let a Labour candidate in; we were all smeared as Reds, and, at the last moment, the notorious Red Letter was launched, purporting to be by Zinoviev, giving his instructions to his 'comrades' in our movement.

In mid-campaign the Foreign Office suddenly despatched to the Soviet Government a strong note of protest against its subversive propaganda in Britain, producing this Red Letter as evidence. At the very same moment the *Daily Mail* carried the story. Here were we candidates defending the policy of a treaty with Russia, MacDonald was our Foreign Secretary as well as our leader and Prime Minister—had he seen this 'Letter' and authorized this note? The whole thing was neatly timed to catch the Sunday papers and with polling day following hard on the weekend there was no chance of an effective rebuttal, unless some word came from MacDonald himself, and he was down in his constituency in Wales.

Out on our own, we had to do the best we could. I put two and two together; if Ramsay had known about this and authorized the note to Russia, would he have had it despatched at the precise moment most likely to damage him and his Party in the election? Then how came the *Daily Mail* to be obviously 'in the know'? Already, with my small political experience, I had no illusions as to the sort of dirty work we might expect from our opponents; Bertie and I had faced some personal abuse in the previous campaigns.

Without hesitation I went on the platform and denounced the whole thing as a forgery, deliberately planted on, or by, the Foreign Office to discredit the man who was both the head of that department and Prime Minister. And, forgery or genuine, I said, the Foreign Office could not escape responsibility, first in ending the note at this juncture, and second in the leak to the *Daily Mail*. Had not someone been guilty of a breach of the Official Secrets Act? If, on the other hand, someone had communicated the thing to the Foreign Office and also to the *Daily Mail*, then quite clearly it must be a forgery, on the assumption that the Foreign Office was acting in good faith and not responsible for a leak. I noticed that when I repeated these remarks outdoors at the World's End, there were cetain gentlemen taking notes of what I said.

Bertie was as deeply concerned as I about the Red Letter; we discussed with others the possibility of him making a public statement about one of the Foreign Office men whom we thought suspect, with the object of drawing a libel action, so convinced were we that there had been a clever plot which we ought to try and expose. I even had a word with Rakovsky, the Soviet Chargé d'Affaires, at a Soviet reception about this possibility, but the plan was too complicated and of doubtful value; it was at once abandoned. The Red Letter remained a mystery for about thirty years; the forgers finally owned up, proving that the Conservative Party had been involved, and vindicating those of us who had never wavered in our accusations.

But the poison had done its deadly work. Despite a big increase in its vote throughout the country, Labour lost the election. What was worse, the Party continued dubious about the genuineness or otherwise of the Letter, and the next year saw the decisive rejection of the Communist Party. MacDonald's equivocal attitude about the Letter shook the faith of his I.L.P. followers, who already feared that his liking for upper-class society was weakening his drive towards true socialism. To those who launched the Red Letter it may have seemed at the time a good joke—as so much underground work is apt to appear to spies and intriguers—but to me it stands as an historic disaster, indeed a crime.

In my own contest I had, in all the circumstances, done well; about twenty-five years later I was told by an elector who had supported me in that election that I had gained the highest vote ever obtained for Labour in Chelsea. But I was pretty tired, and, during the contest, had also been worried because Bertie was ill with bronchitis and a threat of pneumonia. And I was now advised to have my septic tonsils removed. Dr Somerville Hastings, Labour M.P., did this operation and to my surprise, as I was about to step up to the operating table, announced to the nurses that now they would see how a socialist would stand up to the ordeal. But perhaps it was only to put me on my mettle. I can only say that I found a confinement less agonizing than the pain that follows such an operation. At first I feared that I would not be able to control my voice, so vital for speaking campaigns. But this soon righted itself and, to the horror, as I later learned, of Dr Hastings, I was away to the Newcastle area to speak about birth control with the throat only just healed.

For me personally 1924 had been a great year. There had been enough drama and platform appearances to satisfy my theatrical instincts. I had begun to earn a reputation as a convincing and moving speaker, whilst the press controversy had given me malicious delight in detecting my enemies' weak points and replying in brief, sarcastic sentences. I suppose it would be said by psychiatrists that I had found a constructive outlet for my aggression. However that may be, all my life I have enjoyed this kind of controversial pamphleteering, begun in that exciting year.

Ogden now intervened to check my too active career with an opportune suggestion. He persuaded me to write a short book for the To-day and To-morrow series, in reply to a very anti-woman book, *Lysistrata, or Woman's Future*, by A. M. Ludovici, which he had just published. Bertie had also promised him another of these squibs. The amount of our advances was very modest, but, as Bertie cheerfully remarked, they would pay for our joint convalescence. We went away, in winter weather, to the Valley of the Rocks Hotel in Lynton to write these books.

Our room, high up, gave us a view over grey rocks, sky and the bright brown of wet bracken; it had a small high grate with hobs, in which we had a fire; we sat either side of this, most contentedly scribbling. Bertie was writing *What I Believe*, for him a not too difficult task. In this, my first book, I hardly knew how to begin, or if what I set down was of any worth.

The little tracts in this series made play with classical allusions and titles. Opposing the traditional Christian view of the status and ignorance proper to women, I called the book *Hypatia*, who was a lecturer at the ancient University of Alexandria, and was torn to pieces by the early Christians. Such, I thought, would be the fate of my book. Once started the book began to write itself; I had that wonderful experience that can come to writers, of setting down thoughts and emotions of which one was, until then, unaware. My theme was the sex war and the many disabilities suffered by women, deprived both as to citizenship and education. But it was women's right to sexual pleasure and liberty which provoked most opposition. *Hypatia, or Woman and Knowledge*, to give its full title, was published early in 1925; I gave Bertie a copy for his birthday inscribed: 'Age cannot wither him, nor custom stale his infinite variety.'

Suddenly, down in Cornwall, I began to receive telegrams asking for comment and interviews. The *Sunday Express* review had described this as a 'book that should be banned'; consequently, to the joy of the publishers, it sold 600 copies in a week. The attack upon marriage, the assertion of women's sexual freedom, some further remarks that men might advocate polygamy, but women were polyandrous, provoked this storm. A woman reviewer—this not at all to my surprise—asked: 'What has feminism to do with mothers?'

The fuss over such mild assertions of women's sexuality must today seem very much 'old hat'; and the book has a romantic style and lack of cynicism that are not in conformity with our age. But its basic thesis that love and understanding between men and women is the true force of creation, that the whole purpose of life and politics should be to build a finer race of human beings and a better world, is as far off attainment as ever. The book became widely known and translated in many countries; in Calcutta in 1954 an Indian Professor took the little book from his shelves and, bowing formally to me said: 'You have an undying place in the history of feminism.'

In that summer of 1925 I rested from writing and politics, beguiled more and more by the mysterious charm of Cornwall. Day after day we would lie on the white sand, steep ourselves in the green and purple water. The garden began to prosper, I started to grow tomatoes in my greenhouse; John was toddling about and playing with his father, fishing with my whole ball of string in my watering can. A cow got in and made hoof marks on the new lawn; in a rage I came to the window of the room where John was with his father, thus alarming John by my angry expression and words. 'Mummy,' Bertie carefully explained to his small son, 'is angry with the cow.' 'Mummy is angry, she is angry with the cow. John is not a cow,' replied John with equally careful logic, delighting his father with this evidence of his reasoning powers, at the age of four.

We had planted a tree lupin: there would be nights of full moon shining on the sea, still and warm, the scented lupin glowing pale yellow like moonlight itself, the bell on the Runnelstone sounding dimly in the far distance; on Sundays the bells of the church at St Levan would come to us upon a gentle south-wester.

We had begun to know our neighbours. The Cornish are independent, self-reliant, hardy in the face of wind and weather, simple in their tastes, yet with a fine sense of shape and colour, and great imaginative capacity, which can still harbour a number of ancient rites and superstitions. The postmistress in the valley was a most formidable person, who would bite your head off if you expected her to deal with you in any way until she had done with the morning in-coming post, but this was only a front. Her father, Charlie Matthews, was the man who had built our house. He ran a bus once a week—the old Tol Pedn bus—to take us into Penzance to do our shopping. This was a neighbourly business and great fun. We would dump our many parcels on the pavement by the bus for the return journey, whereupon Charlie would scratch his head and gaze upon them, and scold us and demand how we ever thought he was going to get all that on top of his vehicle. We also enjoyed the services of Mr Hall the carrier, who called daily with horse and cart, and later on with a motor van, and would go to Penzance to do any small shopping for us. The Prowse family, father and sons, ran the lorries that fetched and carried for the farmers, as they still do to this day.

Mr Matthews cultivated a small garden, which was the admiration of all for what he could produce in vegetables and flowers, tending every inch of soil with love. He went fishing from the fishing rocks, with tremendously long bamboo rods, which he kept in his loft along with the potato sets. He was one of those also, who took charge of the local Sports every August. Charlie Matthews lived to be ninety or more, alarming his relatives by insisting on chopping up wood at that great age.

I was, I think, one of the first women in this country who wore shorts. Down in Cornwall at least, they did not then exist for women. I used to buy a roomy pair of men's grey longs and cut them off short. In and out of the sea, carrying babies under each arm, up and down the slippery rocky paths, skirts were out of the question. Once, when we took the children to the Sports, for John to run, if he would, I was wearing my shorts. Joking, I asked Mr Matthews if I could run in the ladies' race. 'Yes,' said he, 'if you were dressed like a lady.' Home I went and returned in a skirt, came in second in a race with young seventeen-year-olds, and won two silver-plated vases. The Sports records are still preserved locally, and recently one of my neighbours reminded me of this event of 1925. Traditionally now, our family always takes part in the local Sports, unless none of us are here.

As a young girl of about seventeen Daisy came to work in our house. As the years went on, she became one of my greatest local friends, an association of more than forty years. She left us to marry Matthew the postman, not an easy husband, though he became much loved and respected by his neighbours. Matthew liked the company of his cronies over drinks, sometimes imbibing after hours at midday. His duty was to collect the afternoon post in Treen. The Treen postmistress, tall and spare and very prim, once came to remind him as he went rolling down the street. 'I don't care for the G.P.O., nor me King nor me country neither,' said Matthew the Cornishman, and the letters remained uncollected. Bertie and even the prim postmistress put in a plea that then saved his job. Later he was working on the land, at which he excelled. Once I let my house here for three years to Daisy and Mat, on a shake-hand agreement; we never had the slightest quarrel and the house was never better cared for.

Close at hand, at Polgigga, was a village smithy, and, up a narrow flight of steps, above this, the local shoemaker. The latter was in the perfect tradition of cobblers, thoughtful, to the left in politics, inclined to scepticism, small and slight in stature. Joe, the blacksmith, on the other hand, was, appropriately, a 'mighty man': we all enjoyed watching him shoe a horse; he would also make for us eel hooks, with which we hiked out sand eels on a falling tide, using them as bait, or fried like sprats. Both cobbler and blacksmith have vanished into that lovely traditional past.

Carn Voel saw many visitors: Frank Russell came, and was astonished because I made him a birthday cake, which he *said* no one had ever done before. Miles Malleson came with his new wife, the young doctor Joan, expecting her first baby. Joan had long legs like a young colt, and would plunge into marshes after flowers. I loved them both. J. B. S. Haldane came with his wife Charlotte, just after his battle with Cambridge University about the accusation of 'moral turpitude' on account of her divorce. Ronnie, her son, was with them, and I could not help feeling some anxiety for him, with such a dominant personality for a stepfather. Charlotte was lovely, with her waist-length mane of black hair.

Though there was plenty of intellectual discussion, Bertie and I were delighted with simple things. One morning, when we were dressing, I looked out of the window and noticed some young heifers behaving oddly in the field opposite. They appeared to be chasing a young bull, who dashed into the next field and hid behind the hedge, too young, no doubt, to be of use to them, or he would not have been there. The shyness of the male pursued by females made us both laugh heartily. At breakfast, Ottoline, who was then with us, asked what the joke was. We both felt a trifle diffident about explaining its bucolic nature.

Somehow I managed to tear myself away that summer to attend the Labour Women's Conference in Birmingham, where our birth control resolution was once again discussed. We carried this overwhelmingly once more, asserting that birth control was an essential part of maternity care. I telegraphed the result to Bertie with the words 'Deborah arose', indicating that mothers were on the warpath. In the autumn, the Labour Conference itself, which I did not attend, got away with an Executive recommendation that birth control should not be a party political issue. The reference back was moved, because this did not meet the demand of the women, and was lost only narrowly on a card vote, 1,053,000 votes being recorded against the Executive, after a rapid closure of the debate.

The battle of the Workers' Birth Control Group went on: back in London, with others, I was harassing M.P.s. We had also begun a campaign of approaching local authorities direct, Medical Officers of Health and so on. Sponsored by our Parliamentary Committee, Ernest Thurtle, in February 1926, introduced a Bill in Parliament to enable local authorities to spend money on giving birth control information and advice. This was, as might be expected, defeated by 169 votes to 84, 45 Labour members voting against, in spite of the clear lead given by the Labour women. But we had friends in the Lords, where a Motion by Lord Buckmaster, '. . . that His Majesty's Government be requested to withdraw all instructions given to, or imposed upon Welfare Committees for the purpose of causing such Welfare Committees to withhold from married women in their district information when sought by such women as to the best means of limiting their families' was, on 28 April 1926, carried by 57 votes to 44, in spite of official opposition from Mr Baldwin's Government.

We got out a leaflet giving the names of Labour M.P.s who had voted for or against Mr Thurtle's Bill, and urged our supporters to tackle them. The I.L.P. conference supported us. Much to their annoyance, we carried the war into the enemy's territory by visiting the constituencies of Labour men who had voted against us, and we held meetings for their women. I went to the area of Consett and Chopwell in Durham: here I visited the miner, Steve Lawther and his wife, who sponsored my meetings. Their lodging was very simple. Mrs Lawther, pregnant at that time, had to carry coals up several flights of stairs and cook on an open grate. Then Alice Hicks and I were away to Mother-well, to take the Reverend James Barr M.P. to task. I took with me a whole bale of pamphlets of information about birth control written for us by Dr Maurice Newfield. Strictly speaking, these should not have been carried as passenger's luggage, but the railwaymen at the London terminal merely grinned as they said: 'We know you, Mrs Russell,' and bundled it into the van.

Motherwell had a steelworks, where John Wilson, who was our host, was employed. He and his wife lived in a flat with the typical 'butt and ben' beds in the kitchen-living room. There was one other bedroom, where they housed me and my great bundle of pamphlets; the rest of the family, those few days, somehow managed with the butt and ben. Peggy, their daughter, later came to help at our school. I liked that staunch Scots Labour family immensely. I was taken to see the 'steel wark', where the great red-hot bars, alarmingly gripped in massive tongs, sailed over our heads, and I was, as always, filled with admiration for the men who work day after day in such places.

John Wilson took the Chair at our birth control meetings: I can still see him, his head slightly bowed, shy and apprehensive at approaching this subject which, to so many, was taboo. As I was always to find, once the ice was broken, women spoke out about their sufferings and needs. It struck me that women in Scotland were more under the thumb of their menfolk than in the south, which I regretted, as I liked to consider myself as of Scottish origin. One middle-aged woman whom we canvassed, telling her that she would find the meeting interesting and ought to support the movement, refused, and when we stressed that she was on her own and had no young children to keep her within, she said: 'Och, nae, Jock wudna like to think I was oot of tha' hoose.'

The Rev. James Barr hit back with immense vigour, attacking Bertie and myself as middle-class infiltrators into the Labour movement, and as atheists; my book *Hypatia* was expressly condemned. The *Motherwell Times* of 23 April 1926 carried lengthy retorts from John Wilson, myself and also from Walton Newbold (Madge's husband), who had previously been a Parliamentary candidate in Motherwell, but was now living in London. Interesting points in Newbold's letter are that he affirms that birth control will become a 'first-class political issue' and further he 'challenges the notion that in economic science is all salvation. Biology has its place along with other sciences.'

Early in 1926 I was also down in the Welsh mining areas. When I came home from these excursions I presently developed a rash which turned out to be scabies. For this I insinuate no blame whatever to kind and courageous hosts. A mere handshake—of which I must have had thousands—can start the thing up. Bertie and I had to suffer the unpleasant cure together. I was often unwell after brief absences to speak. My Irish cook Hannah remarked: 'Ye always takes ill when ye're away from yer ouwn bed.' She would mother and cosset me and I was very grateful to have at last domestic care on which both Bertie and I could rely.

I was not, in actual fact, away from home for more than a weekend or so at a time. Our campaign went on from the basement 'den' at Sydney Street; we had won the support of resolutions at the Railway-women's Guild Conference, the National Union of Societies for Equal Citizenship, and the Co-operative Women's Guild Congress.

The campaign among local authorities was impressive: Edmonton Council, after declaring in favour, sent a letter to all other authorities urging them to do the same, supported by the names of a Labour and a Tory representative. This, and our efforts, provoked widespread public discussion, reported at length in the local press. By the spring of 1926, eighteen local councils were in support,* as also were the Maternity Committees of Bath, Camberley, Camberwell, Gloucester, and Smethwick.

How important was public discussion and debate is shown by Julian Huxley's review (in *Nature*, 26 September 1925) of a report by the Special Committee of the National Council of Public Morals on 'The Ethics of Birth Control'. He wrote:

This is a curious publication. The spirit in which the Committee approached its task may be judged from the introductory remarks of the Chairman, the Bishop of Winchester. In these he says that many people regret the public discussion now given to such topics as birth control, and that 'in large measure the Committee share that regret'.

It is this attitude which is in itself a serious matter. Here is an invention—the mechanical and chemical control of conception—which is one of the few important biological inventions made in historical times. The discovery of anaesthetics and that of various methods of killing or weakening the action of harmful bacteria, are the only others that are in the same street with it. It points a practical way to a final satisfactory control by man of his own evolution, since the only other regulators of numbers, which are not merely pious wishes, are war, pestilence, famine, or overcrowding. Yet a serious body of public men regret, decades after its widespread adoption in practice, that it should be DISCUSSED.

Julian also poked fun at the Rev. Canon Lyttelton, who had taught him Classics at Eton, for his minority report opposing birth control in toto.

While writing these very pages I could not help reflecting that, even now, in spite of Edwin Brooks' 1967 Act, which allowed local authorities to do what we were fighting for in 1924, and, in spite of further wide-spread provision of contraceptives and advice, so many young women, especially the unmarried, profess ignorance as a reason for their

* Battersea, Bethnal Green, Blaydon, Buckinghamshire, Chester, Chester-le-Street, Croydon, Edmonton, Gelligaer (Wales), Hammersmith, Hull, Knaresborough, Mitcham, Portsmouth, Shoreditch, South Shields, Sunderland, Wolverhampton

pregnancy. Following the reform of the abortion law, many also seem to look to abortion as the remedy, which they then do not find easy to obtain. Virtual intimidation of medical and lay people against birth control is still carried on by the Roman Catholic Church in Ulster and elsewhere. Meanwhile world conferences summoned to deal with the population question, or the desperate world food situation, find no solution and evaporate in nationalist or ideological bickering.

In April we were back in Cornwall. Quite other serious political events demanded attention: the Baldwin Government had instigated the trial and imprisonment of twelve Communist Party leaders, including McManus and Wal Hannington. Protest came not only from the Communist Party, H. G. Wells being one voice. In the spring of 1926, the left-wing leaders safely under lock and key, the miners were threatened with a cut in wages—a CUT, be it noted. Backed by the famous Triple Alliance of railwaymen, transport men, with Bevin's dockers, and their own miners' union, the miners refused to take the pay cut: they were locked out; the printers refused to print a leader in the *Daily Mail*, the pent-up anger of the postwar years burst out; the General Strike was on.

My first impulse was to help the cause of the workers in any way that I could. But what was possible out here in this remote place? Was anything happening in Penzance? We had deliberately refrained from having a phone installed. I got on my pushbike and rode, up and down dale, the nine miles to Penzance. I went down to the harbour, and there I found a man sitting on an upturned boat. Rather nervously I asked: 'Are the men out down here?' 'They are.' 'Do you think they are likely to go back?' 'Be fools if they do.' 'Could you perhaps direct me to the Strike Committee?'

That body of men received me kindly and I told them that they had the full support of Bertie and myself. Next day, Bertie and I made them a joint visit, hiring a car to go in, and of course gave something towards the funds. The men who waited on us in the London–Penzance railway dining car were there, delightedly fraternizing and shaking hands. It was said at the time that Walkden, the leader of the railway clerks, was so delighted at his men's solidarity, that he would march up and down his office singing 'The Railway Clerks are out on Strike' to the tune of the *Red Flag*.

Bertie and I talked about the situation; I, as usual, itched for action and wanted to know what was going on all the time. Bertie, who was writing his book on education, said that he felt that there was nothing useful he could do, but I could, by all means, go ahead and help. Most days after that I could be seen cycling in to St John's Hall, where we encouraged the strikers to assemble, so that they could receive reports of any news, listen to speeches, sing at times, and generally express their solidarity. We did some marching around the town; to my amusement the dockers, who could lift and heave with a will, found all this walking a wearisome exercise. I was made a member of the Strike Committee, the only woman on it. It was an expression of remarkable unity, Labour, I.L.P., trade unions acting together as one.

When they found I could speak, they asked me to go out to various local meetings. George Thomas, a young engine driver, had a motorbike with a sidecar. More than once we took to the open road, in the fresh invigorating winds that move eternally over Cornwall. Up at Hayle, they said, there might be some weakening. I wondered what to say to Cornish brethren, when suddenly I found myself reciting Milton's *Samson Agonistes*:

> Oh, how comely it is and how reviving
> To the spirits of just men long opprest
> When God into the hands of their deliverer
> Puts invincible might
> To quell the mighty of the earth, th'oppressor,
> The brute and boistrous force of violent men
> Hardy and industrious to support
> Tyrannic power, but raging to pursue
> The righteous and all such as honour truth . . .

In St John's Hall, finally, we listened on the radio to the sell-out by Bevin and his colleagues. Caught by the argument that a General Strike was 'unconstitutional' and dreading to push on to the point when resistance became a revolution, they called the whole thing off and left the miners to face owners and Government alone. It was a sad march that we all made round the town and out to Marazion, to begin negotiating against victimization, that might lose many their jobs; there were many among us who knew just what this capitulation— with no terms demanded—might mean.

When the miners increasingly felt the pinch, we, like many other people, had two miner's daughters to stay with us. I did what I could to make them feel at home. They were about eleven or twelve years old, and, as might be expected, they were always on their best behaviour. The lock-out dragged on: presently A. J. Cook came down to Penzance to speak and with him his secretary, Nancy Adam. He was a passionate speaker, who exhausted himself in oratory, but was deeply moving in his sincerity. They both came out to stay the night with us after his speech. I had just had some rooms redecorated, and we put A. J. Cook —who was a large man—in our large bed in the best of those good attic rooms, the beams of which had been painted—oddly but appropriately enough—in a very vivid scarlet, which I had had specially prepared. To this day I have seen to it that those beams have remained red in honour of the man and the time.

Not until 1959 did I see George Thomas again, after a showing of the film of *The Caravan of Peace* in Penzance; I recognized him immediately.

In the 1960s he received a special medal for his work in various sections of trade union organization, and I was among those invited to the ceremony, together with other old comrades of the days of the General Strike. Recently too, the National Union of Railwaymen decided to have their conference in Penzance and the local men invited me to their social evening so that Sir Sidney Greene and I could meet. These are among the 'souvenirs' that I greatly value.

During the summer of that year I was writing my second book, *The Right to be Happy*. Bertie, in addition to the book on education, was preparing the Tarner lectures on the Analysis of Matter for Trinity College in the autumn. When we came back to London in the third week in September, I had completed the last chapter of my book, but was still expressing a wish to get on with *The Religion of the Machine Age*.

The next Labour Party Conference—in Margate that year—was imminent. Our Birth Control Group were planning a definite onslaught to make the Party understand that the women meant what they said. On 9 and 10 October I was at the Grand Hotel and here we held a meeting of our caucus, women who had come from Women's Sections all over the country. Taking the Conference agenda, we looked to see at what points it might be possible to raise our issue. A plan was worked out by which one of us would get up at any one of these points. It was agreed that I should move the reference back of the paragraph in the Executive's report dealing with the question. We had no idea how we stood with the unions and the other delegates, but we had done a great deal of spadework. A story is told that, in the room next to the one in which we held our meeting and which had some shut communicating doors, Jimmy Thomas, of the N.U.R., heard us plotting and was so impressed that he resolved that we should have the N.U.R. vote. But I doubt if there is the slightest foundation for this pleasant and amusing tale.

At the Conference itself, everything went according to plan. The 'squibs' went off, thus exciting interest; then came the reference back, with Bob Williams in the Chair. I did not speak long, but made my usual points about the dangers of child-bearing relative to men's dangerous trades, women's rights to choice; I concluded by appealing to trade unionists on behalf of the 'ancient and honourable Trade Union of Mothers, to which I belong'. Following the discussion, Bob Williams was about to give me the right to reply, which, strictly, is not in order on a reference back. James Sexton, one of the Liverpool Catholic M.P.s, got up and shook his fist and shouted, 'Don't let her speak again!' On that I stood on my chair and bowed and waived my 'right'. The vote was taken, I think the miners and N.U.R. settled it; in any case, we won the day. By that vote the Conference endorsed the demand that the Labour Party should espouse what its women were demanding, that birth control advice should be given at health centres as an integral part of maternity care. H. G. Wells sent me a postcard on which he

wrote: 'Referred 'em back, hooray! Bertie thinks, I write, but you DO.'
He used to describe me often as his 'man of action'.

In the event, our victory was a hollow one. Labour was not in power,
and the fear of the Catholic vote was a potent force; the surrender of
the General Strike had badly shaken the nerve of the Party. Indeed, I
think that it was that year that the revolutionary hopes and mood of
the Party were lost forever, and reformism took their place. At that
same Conference Oswald Mosley delivered a speech with an elaborate
peroration. He was very warmly applauded. To me there was an element
of deliberate play-acting in his oratory, which I felt to be insincere.
I was disappointed that others did not seem to detect this.

For myself, though, I had become somewhat disillusioned with
Labour politics. Hypocrisy over birth control had been followed by
lack of courage in the Strike. Once or twice in these years I had thought
of a political career, and had had the notion of asking the Party to let
me stand for St Ives constituency, or for one with a chance of success.
Herbert Morrison wanted me to stand for the L.C.C.; he said he would
be glad to have me in his team there, and 'handle me'; those were his
words. But I realized that such a career would mean being a great deal
away from home, that it could scarcely fit in with the pattern that Bertie
and I had made of our lives and those of our children. I also now had
further opportunities for writing.

In Chelsea had come to my door a dark-looking foreigner who asked
for Mrs Bertrand Russell. Inviting him in, I replied that I supposed he
meant my husband. 'No, it is you,' he said, 'if you are the author of
Hypatia.' That anyone should call on me on account of my work could
not fail to be exciting, but my excitement increased when I learned that
he was a Spaniard from the Madrid paper *El Sol*, who wanted from me
fortnightly articles of a thousand words on any topic that occurred to
me. This marvellous assignment began in 1926; *El Sol* never once
queried anything I wrote, and payment was invariably prompt. I
continued for at least five years and only ended it when too much
occupied with other work and cares. In Cornwall there were days when,
after lunch, having only decided during the morning what to write
about, I would type madly, and then dash downhill to catch the vital
four o'clock post. It was then that I acquired the journalist's habit of
chain-smoking, and had to take to a pipe and a very mild tobacco
because the smoke got in my eyes. But for very many years now, I have
been a reformed character and non-smoker.

In this year too, I began to be involved in public questions, outside
party politics. I was invited to attend the Congress of the World League
for Sex Reform in Berlin, organized then, if I remember rightly, by
Dr Moll. Dr Norman Haire, who was to attend on behalf of the
American Birth Control League and International Birth Control
League, got in touch with me, and there began an association between
us on sex reform which continued for several years, as I will presently

relate. On birth control itself the political point was being somewhat lost, as more and more people began to organize clinics, which were supported by voluntary subscriptions. Although I recognized then, and still do, the help given to women in this way, I did not feel that this was my field of work; so strong was my conviction that this was an inalienable right of women on which Governments should take action, which they would never do so long as the work was done for them by charity. I also thought that research on methods was needed, for which there must be Government funds. Further, clinics faced opposition from religious objectors, who even tried to prevent them from appealing for money.

In 1926 we held a wonderful communal Christmas. A party assembled at the Valley of the Rocks Hotel, Lynton, composed of: Miles and Joan Malleson and their small son Nicky, Vera and Francis Meynell, John Strachey, Cyril Joad and Doreen, Clifford and Joan Allen and small daughter Polly, Bertie and myself with John and Kate and our nurse, with whom I undertook to help care for the children. The large octagonal room at the hotel was put at our disposal with, needless to say, a huge log fire. Here the children, and those who liked their company, rampaged with their toys at stated times, Cyril Joad a trifle sarcastic about parents and their menagerie.

When the children had gone to bed there was much interesting talk, spiced with wit from Bertie and some from Joad; there was plenty to discuss: the results of the General Strike, where to go from here; sex and marriage law reform; the rights of women; as well as more philosophical discussions around Bertie's work and the topic of education in which the parents of the three-, four- and five-year-olds were now interested as a practical issue. Bertie got me to read part of *The Right to be Happy* aloud one evening; I had the manuscript with me for revision. He thought well of the book and wanted to see how others reacted. Joad said it was romantic nonsense, but John Strachey that it was extremely interesting. Though I say it in this context, I was never one of those who appreciated Joad. Kingsley Martin had a long friendship with him, he acquired a great reputation with his 'it depends what you mean' on the famous radio Brains Trust, and he was certainly extremely attractive to women. For me mentally and physically he was a negative quantity. But I thought well of one of his achievements, which was the attempt to bring together the various reformist societies under the name of Federation of Progressive Societies and Individuals, the F.P.S.I., which later resolved itself into the Progressive League, but did not succeed in its original purpose. I think that it was in part because he was one of those who aped Bertie's style and sallies, that I did not much like him.

John, just five, dark and a trifle pale after a tonsil operation, contrasted with apple-cheeked Kate and Polly, with their straight wisps of very fair hair. Nicky, too, was fair, chubby and curly haired. I enjoyed their company almost as much as that of the grown-ups. John was very sociable, but Kate a trifle shy, which was surprising, because she was extraordinarily verbalized. She was once heard remarking, when lying in her pram, under two years old: 'Last year I used to dive off the diving board, I did.' Was it an echo of something she had heard said and already wished to emulate? But it was her very own words that she spoke aged about two and three months, in a cold April, riding in her push chair:

> The North wind blows over the North Pole,
> The daisies hit the grass,
> The wind blows the bluebells down,
> The North wind blows to the wind in the South.

There never seems to have been a time when Kate could not read. But John, too, had a lively, enquiring and logical mind.

Bertie and I spent much time with the children and by now we had practically made up our minds that perhaps the best thing we could do would be to start a school. There was so much in modern psychology and social attitudes that was not being brought to bear in education. The Labour Party was in favour of better schools and more education, but had never addressed itself to the question of what the content of education in a changing society should be. Bertie said to me that inevitably I would be spending much of my time and energy on the care of children and it would seem a waste to restrict my activity only to our family, though we did then hope that it would increase. What is more, we both felt that we would still have our holidays in our Cornish home and thus, in every way, this plan would fit the needs of the children and ourselves and perhaps make some contribution to the theory and practice of education for a society of the future, in which we both believed.

Presently Bertie learned that his brother Frank wanted to let Telegraph House, on the Sussex Downs near South Harting, and he began negotiating with him for it. It has often been said that Bertie was over-persuaded by me to start the school. But he was writing his book on education, his thoughts at that time ran entirely in that direction, and he was, in addition, passionately devoted to his children, and anxious to give them the fullest opportunity of escaping from the kind of upbringing to which he himself had been subjected. Nor did he, at that time, wish his son to go to a public school.

The winter of 1926-7 was thus the last that we spent in our home in Chelsea, at which I felt some sadness, but I was fully occupied with all the preparations that would be necessary, if we were to open the school, as we proposed, in the autumn of 1927. The manuscript of *The Right to be Happy* finally went off to the publishers. I was obliged gradually to withdraw from the birth control agitation, and, for the time at least, from politics, which was less of a deprivation to me since I had lost much of my faith in our leaders. It might be that education was something more fundamental to which one should turn one's hand.

But before leaving the wider political arena I was involved, though my part in it was very small, in one more important event. I had never lost my association with affairs in China and was in contact with Chinese in London, at one of whose anniversary dinners George Lansbury and I both spoke. Now, in the spring of 1927, came the rising of the Chinese in Shanghai, during which the Kuo Ming Tang, hitherto the movement of progress in China, turned on and virtually massacred their communist supporters. The tragic story of that rising has been told by André Malraux. Our Government, fearing that the foreign concessions were in danger, was sending troops against the Chinese. I was roused to great anger and even said I would go and sit down to obstruct them marching to a London terminus. Hastily we formed a small committee of Bertie, Brailsford, Francis Meynell and W. N. Ewer. A considerable Trafalgar Square demonstration was held; George Lansbury and I appealed for the liberation of the Chinese from foreign interference. It was, unhappily, no more than a gesture of sympathy. But when, in 1956, I visited the Revolution Museum in Shanghai, I found that it had not gone unremarked and unappreciated by the Chinese people.

Soon we were to depart for Cornwall, with my faithful cook Hannah and a delightful young governess to look after the children, who were both to be part of the staff of the school. I would have to come up during the summer to see that all was ready for the family to move into Telegraph House in September, as well as arranging for other staff. One day a surprising visitor called on us in London: Mrs Rosengolz, who at that time worked at the Soviet Embassy, where her husband was the Chargé d'Affaires. She told Bertie and me that she had understood that we were opening a school. 'Why yes,' we said, 'but in the country and not until September.' 'I wish my son Valya to come to your school, but at once, please. Can he not now be with your children?' The plea was insistent and Mrs Rosengolz was obviously so much worried about how to do her work at the Embassy and give proper care to her son that, in the upshot, Valya travelled down to Cornwall with us all. He was, I think, between the ages of John and Kate, who were both delighted to have a companion. He was dark, with curly hair, tall for his age. Kate began to flirt with him and would say enticingly, 'Valya dear, Valya dear.' He was protective to her, too, quite plucky on rocks and in the sea, so long as you did not offer to help him. He did not like to rely on anyone else.

This was to be no easy summer. I was presently in trouble with brother-in-law Frank. We had arranged for the time being to share his chauffeur and wife, who were at the moment taking care of Telegraph House. They had children and the man wrote to me for his wages. Meaning no harm, I replied that if he did not receive them from Lord Russell I would send him some money. At once I was threatened with a libel action by his lordship, and got rebuked by Bertie's lawyer Crompton Llewelyn Davies, who pointed out to me that I had insinuated that Lord Russell could not pay his just debts, and had to smooth the whole thing over.

Next came a telegram from Mrs Rosengolz, to say that she must come down at once to see us. She arrived: it seemed that there had been a police raid on their offices—the Arcos raid—they were not certain if they could remain in the country and presently it might be necessary for me to bring Valya to London. She was in much distress: her very handbag had been searched. Bertie and I felt furious at the absurd, extreme suspicion with which the Russians were being treated in our country, but before long I was on my way to London with Valya.

John and Kate were also furious at the departure of a companion they had become fond of. Their father explained that it was the British Government who did not like Valya and were sending him away. 'Then we must get rid of the Government,' they said.

'That is not easy, it needs a general election.' Bertie explained carefully what a general election meant.

'That will take too long,' was the children's verdict.

'The only other way,' said Bertie, 'is the use of physical force.'

In those days Force as a breakfast food was much in vogue: Sunny Jim and all that. Presently I found John and Kate with an old lemonade bottle in which they had mixed up a concoction of leaves, water and goodness knows what else. This was physical force to give to the Government. When I said that I thought it did not look pleasant enough to tempt the Government to take it, they got a label and named it 'Food for the Gods', which, they felt sure, a powerful Government would be unable to resist. I never was able to see Valya again, but Mrs Rosengolz was most kind to me later when I visited Moscow.

The most important thing for me, apart from preparing for the school, was the publication of *The Right to be Happy* in England and America. This book was, in a sense, my manifesto against that religion of the machine age whose growing power and influence I so much dreaded. I had more and more come to believe that the dualism of mind and matter was at the root of what was false and dangerous in Western philosophy and religion. What sort of a person, basically, was a human being, and by what motives driven? Suppose we treated the human being as not divided, but as a whole organism. What then would be our primary needs and how far were these at present served by our social and economic system? The Chinese, for instance, seemed to suffer no dualism of mind and matter, nor a desperate striving to purge themselves of sin.

I saw little to choose between the medieval emphasis on the primacy of the soul and that of the rationalist on the primacy of reason, since both drew man away into a world of abstractions, suppressing or ignoring the very impulses that gave life, that could indeed

G

193

turn to destruction but, given the chance of normal functioning, were, in themselves, creation. It struck me that Christianity, even from Christ himself, attached to the individual, apart from his family, tribal or biological background, a significance which had in the end led to the modern type of egoism, which resisted the loss of personal advantage or submersion in the generosity of sexual or parental love. I envisaged a 'mechanical synthesis' which would make both in Russia and in the U.S.A. a blueprint for society and the manufacture of human beings, based on the Newtonian cosmology and Descartes, and the psychology of Pavlov and the American behaviourist Professor Watson. My suggestions for the foundation of society were what I called the primal rights of man, springing from the biological organism: food, work, knowledge, sex and parenthood.

There is much in *The Right to be Happy* which, in my view, is as relevant today as when it was written. However remotely, it foreshadows the views of advocates of the 'alternative' culture and society, and of Desmond Morris in *The Naked Ape*. My remark, 'Animals we are and animals we remain, and the path to our regeneration, if there be such a path, lies through our animal nature' shocked T. S. Eliot, who evidently failed to understand what the book was about. Ecologists of today would find themselves in sympathy with many of my sentiments: I speak of the 'quality' as opposed to the 'quantity' in life; I suggest that a group of men and women who seek and find the 'right road to conquering ourselves and our environment' could, by their speech and action, show that 'this way of life can be practised by all and is capable of being the foundation of a society'.

The title of the book came from my articles in the *Cambridge Magazine*, but also from a statement of the Hon. and Rev. E. Lyttelton, Headmaster of Eton, to the effect that: 'Children go to school impressed with the belief that they have a right to be happy, that God will give them a good time. This is the perversion of true religion, self-denial and obedience.' (*Evening Standard*, 14 October 1925.) On the fly-leaf as one of the Sayings of Luo Su, I put a sly remark of Bertie's: 'Good wine needs no bush and good morals no bated breath.'

Published in the autumn of 1927, the book had a considerable success in England, but a very much greater one in the United States, where it was extensively and favourably reviewed. I received a number of letters about it; Lewis Mumford was one of those who were appreciative. The American publishers presently urged that I should come over and lecture there on the strength of my book and were prepared to pay my passage over. But Bertie had already undertaken a lecture tour that autumn in the States: getting ready for opening the school was taking up my thoughts and my time, for I would have to face the first term of the school alone. None the less we were able to arrange for a tour by me after Bertie returned.

There is a beach near Treen Castle called Pedny Vounder, which for Bertie and me was always the 'inaccessible', because, when we first looked down on it from above, with its marvellous sandbank and pools at low tide, we thought that there was no way down to it. It became our favourite place, where one could, in those days, mostly be entirely alone. Bertie would keep note of the tides and, during the spring tides, everything had to be adjusted so that we and the children could enjoy this beach for the longest possible time. Only just lately I came across, scribbled in an old notebook, a poem I wrote about our bathing there. It expresses joy in our growing children and in the sea, and something of what was moving me when, in the black hut on the cliff, looking down on that beach, I wrote *The Right to be Happy*.

Green salty waves
From thigh to shoulder leaping
Browning our arms, straightening our legs
To Titan beauty;
Brown naked bodies of my boy and girl
Held close amid salt kisses
As the water sways us.

Sea people are we, born and nurtured of the sea
Back to our element when moons are new or full
And tides come, more than ever swift and grandly washing us
  in foam.

So once our ancestors, flung high upon the shore
Found, not expected death
But sentient painful mortal life
For watery immortality . . .

Yet still this mortal blood
Salt with the tang of that which gave us life
Yearns back for conquest of its ancient element
Draws near bewitched to the eternal sea
Changing and changeless
Breeder of mystery.

So we may believe
That on some day when white and piercing rays
Fuse with a water, jade and burning blue,
And foam beats on the milky shore in ecstasy
A mortal diving deep and faithfully
Shall never die
But live forever
Knowing all
And part of thee
O glorious god, creator and destroyer
Mighty sea.

Or on a night
When white and honeyed moon
Piercing thy deepest hollow
Leans down and calls
The black and purple waves, to rise in sapphire train
To dance and follow;
Then, taking wings, like grey gulls from the granite
So every human sea-enchanted spirit
Flies out forever free in darkest space
Then sinks his rapt and star-transfigured face
To final rest in thee.

Idle and mystic dreams
'Tis better far
Than on such night to kiss the wandering star,
To drink immortal life with mortal breath
And through love's ecstasies to conquer death.
For human blood immortal sea life bears
And to its seed bequeaths a myriad years.

10

Turning to Education

Telegraph House stood on the West Sussex Downs, very near to the highest point called Beacon Hill. It had been one of the stations for signalling by semaphore from Portsmouth onwards, originally quite a small building. Frank Russell added a library and the square tower with windows facing north, south, east and west, which gave the whole house a somewhat Italian look. It stood out clean and white against a background of blue sky and cloud and the yellow green of the downland. The views from the tower over The Weald to the north and seawards to the south were superb. There were several hundred acres of woodland, with old yews—almost prehistoric in character. The long drive had been planted by Frank with copper beeches, which in the spring had their exquisite golden-brown leaves, but these in summer and autumn became a rather gloomy sort of purple. Hedges of ordinary beech about eight foot high sheltered the tennis lawn. But in the main there was little formal gardening, and beyond the wide front lawn the wilderness began. I had been there for a weekend with Bertie to visit Frank; it seemed a place in which children might be healthy and happy. On that occasion, though, there was driving rain from the south-west, and my chief recollection is of Frank Russell expanding into a large armchair with small, shaggy, white dogs climbing over him, as he chatted amiably with his brother.

It must have been a great wrench for Frank when economic necessity forced him to let his house. Bertie has written in his autobiography that, in his opinion, his brother never really forgave him for occupying what had been for Frank a little paradise. That may well be so and I think that some of the resentment became also directed towards me. However, to Bertie and me at this time, the thought of a new dispensation at Telegraph House, with the place full of happy children, was most attractive. Now and then I had misgivings and asked Bertie what we should do if the school were a failure, on which, with that lovely, cheerful recklessness that characterized him when he was taking a chance, he said: 'Well my dear, then we shall at least have a very nice house.'

There was an immense amount to do to get the school ready for opening: seeing to the colour schemes for painting and distempering; pleasant lino to be laid on dormitory floors; small divan beds, made specially by the blind, to be installed, as well as tables and chairs in bright colours and various small sizes, for class and dining room; the furniture from our Sydney Street home, which was being sold, to be brought down and set in place; not to mention crockery, cutlery, stationery, classroom equipment, blankets and linen. The tower room was to be got ready for Bertie's study. It was decorated in a rich dark blue paint and cream to match the three Chinese rugs which he cherished; there was room, too, for the spiritual and temporal ancestors on the wall space: here he could be above the battle as and when he chose.

I was to and fro between London and the house, dropped in at the 1917 Club to eat, had a bed at a communal Bloomsbury flat. Bertie and I, as is clear from what I have already written, left each other free as regards possible sexual adventures. I knew how women, especially in America, were apt to court him, and I had been courted for some time by an agreeable young man in London. I told Bertie that I might spend a night with this young man at this time, and in fact did, not regarding it as of any importance, as I believed the young man did not either. At the 1917 Club one day I found a scrawled ill-spelt note saying that I must come home at once to Cornwall. It was from Hannah, my Irish cook. I came home in a great state of anxiety to find Hannah mounting guard over the two children and refusing to let their governess come near them because she alleged that she was sleeping with 'the Masther'. A distraught Bertie had met me at the station. I could not help being upset: an affair in one's own home with someone in charge of one's children is specially wounding. And I felt let down over all the work I was doing for the school: it looked, too, as though at one blow I was to lose the school cook and member of the staff on whom I had most counted.

Bertie had an aristocratic attitude to servants, which I had always minded, on this occasion more than ever. But the situation had to be dealt with. To a Hannah weeping on my shoulder I had to explain that, though I loved her for her loyalty, we did not feel quite the same way about these things. I would have to let her go, because she and 'the Masther' could hardly get on after this. And to the governess, who was a charming girl, I simply said that her job at the school was *not* cancelled. But it was necessary for us all to move up to Telegraph House now, although it was not quite in order, because there at least were some domestic staff to cope, while preparations for opening the school went on. There were no stormy scenes, or violent recriminations. We all went on with our various jobs, as planned; Bertie remarked, on seeing what had so far been accomplished at the school house, that he had not realized all the work it had entailed. Soon he left for his lecture tour in America to be home in time for Christmas, and in September the school duly opened.

This is not a book about the school, which would require one to itself. None the less, it is necessary to give some brief account of what the venture was about. The impression too often given is that it was a wild place run by crazy amateurs. Not only were we both academically qualified, but we had been studying modern psychologists and theories of education; during 1926, Bertie had been engaged in writing his own book on the subject. We knew about Freud, Adler, Piaget, Pestalozzi, Froebel, Montessori, and Margaret McMillan. Once we took John and Kate to spend half a day at the McMillan open-air nursery school, while we talked with her and studied her ideas in action. We had looked into the various methods for teaching the three R's that were in vogue, but we did not think that the object of education was to decide the mould into which the child was to be poured and did not believe in educational materials designed to fit this purpose. Thus the Montessori material, much of which was to teach number, reading and writing, we thought too rigid; we preferred the McMillan style of providing the child with all kinds of materials by means of which it would find its own way. Nor did we think it was necessarily a good thing for a child to read and become bookish and academic too early. There is a period of doing, feeling, observing the world and his fellow citizens—the concrete before the abstract—apparently almost completely lost to sight by our planners today, when it seems that children are to be stimulated to read, write and do sums even before they leave the nursery school.

Beatrix Tudor Hart was to be the chief member of our staff; we had also a trained matron. Dr Maurice Newfield, who had been active in the birth control campaign, advised me about the medical and first-aid chest and was to be, though not residing all the time, the school's medical adviser. Part of our plan, too, was to see that the food was really good and in accord with what we could learn about the best views on diet. We arranged to fetch every day, from a farm some distance away, a big can of T.T. milk. We now acquired our first motor car—a dark brown Austin Twelve.

Almost at once it became obvious that, in this remote place, it would be difficult for parents and visitors to find somewhere to stay. We therefore rented a roomy, pleasant house in the sheltered village of East Marden. Sylvia Pankhurst in fact came for seclusion to write a book there and stayed for quite some time, with her son Richard, who was a day pupil. Richard, as I recall him, was a very determined small boy; we used to say that he was the only male who succeeded in bullying his intrepid mother.

Many of the principles on which the school was founded are now current theory (though certainly not everywhere current practice), and must seem like platitudes. But in 1927 it was not accepted that even young children could be allowed to be nude in each other's presence, and should not be scolded for 'playing with themselves' as masturbation was decently called. We did not 'teach sex', we answered questions on this, as on all matters, as honestly and correctly as we could. Measures of self-government and a school council, especially for such young children, were a great innovation. It might be accepted that the older pupils of a school, especially a boarding school, should have some responsibility and authority in making rules and seeing that they were kept. We thought, on the other hand, that by that age the authority of superior and older persons would have become ingrained. The time for freedom and absence of discipline was much earlier in life, when a bit of rampaging could do no harm and children could learn that orderly behaviour ultimately arose out of living together, and not from the commands handed down by the authority of parents and teachers. Democracy could only spring from practising it early, and democratic action was not to be expected from young people brought up under a close authoritarian system. Common parlance now, this, and the source of some lively demonstrations by present-day children. According to our view, freedom given and understood early enough would result in a natural evolution to maturity and self-discipline. Severity and repression of the old type, however, almost certainly carried with it in adolescence, disturbance, confusion and the necessity of revolt.

There were only one or two educators at that time who were as radical as, or even more radical than we in our school. A. S. Neill, who died only recently, and is now world famous, left his pupils entirely free as to whether, or what, they would learn. Our pupils were also free not to come into the classrooms or workshops, but it is obvious that a man like Bertie Russell attached considerable importance to offering the opportunity for intellectual studies. Geoffrey Pyke, in Cambridge, had opened the Malting House where a group of children were presided over and studied by Susan Isaacs, in a small community that could hardly be called a school, since its principle was to see just what children would do and find out in freedom on their own. Dartington Hall School was as yet not in existence.

With regard to Freudian and other psychiatric theories, we thought that knowledge of these might be applied in education in a preventive sense, rather than, as they then were, merely curatively. For instance, provision of good nursery schools might well be a better means to children's mental health than the Child Guidance Clinic which, by treating a young child as a patient, could induce hypochondria or self-importance. One of my own experiences, when I later ran the school without Russell, was that a trained nurse as Matron is not always the best person to keep children in health, because she is too much concerned with, and accustomed to, people in illness.

Freedom, discipline, punishment are perpetual topics of discussion and dispute among educators. Our present 'generation gap', as also the argument about degrees of severity in the treatment of prisoners, question the rightness or wrongness of the policy of the so-called 'permissives'. The free school's theory that early practice of democracy would produce mature and self-disciplined adolescents could also mean that they, in dealing with their elders, would be more conformist, or at least that the generation gap would not be wide, because there would be less occasion for the sharp revolt induced by an authoritarian system. Yet today on all sides the revolt against authority in home and school, and against the very foundation of the State, seems widespread and growing. Within the family I believe that parents who have reared their children on progressive lines, genuinely treating them, not as property or as vehicles for parents' own frustrated ambitions, but as individuals whose aims and purposes a parent can help, or at least not hinder, find that the generation gap is almost non-existent.

The wider issue of public ferment and protest is more complex. Some young people, especially at the primary stage, have been educated on progressive lines, but the majority have still been subject to authoritarianism. Whatever may be the virtues of the individual parent, the older generation as a whole are seen, after two devastating wars, to be simply engaged in remaking systems and policies which, to the clear-eyed mature young, are manifestly intolerable. The breath of freedom is in the air, the free spirits join forces with those who have been repressed, unions are formed even by children, and the demand comes at student level, and among adults too, at grass roots level, for greater participation in decision-making, an extension of democracy beyond the narrow limits of the election of parliaments. If democracy in our school and in others contributed even in small measure to this result, I can only rejoice.

Following the rise of the Labour Party it seemed reasonable, in 1927, to expect, or at least to hope, that co-operation for the common good might gradually replace the competitiveness of capitalism. Hence we did not foster competition in our school, on the contrary. Nor is it true that children are naturally competitive, unless egged on to be so. It would take too long to explain the various ways in which we and the Council dealt with rule-making and rule-breaking. Physical punishment was, of course, not permitted, and we sought to mitigate aggression among the children themselves. If an adult uses violence on a child, the child will naturally assume that he, too, has the right to use it on one smaller or weaker. The Council once earnestly considered what to do about children hitting, which they called 'sloshing', one another. One child proposed that the Council should make a rule forbidding 'sloshing'. Objection was made to this on the ground that such a rigid rule would certainly not be kept. Finally a resolution was passed as follows: 'This Council disapproves of sloshing as a method of settling an argument.' Thereafter when a quarrel broke out, one might see children run up to the belligerents exclaiming 'This Council disapproves' etc. And in most cases this intervention was effective. Indeed in the prevention of war between nations the United Nations has so far not got beyond the method arrived at by our children.

The first Christmas at Telegraph House—or Beacon Hill School—

was very happy. The first term of the new venture was safely over. It had not been easy, with so much to organize and co-ordinate. I had had to be away for a short time for an urgent operation to remove a small fibroid from one breast which the doctors categorically refused to let me postpone in spite of my urgent plea that I could not leave the school. I was terribly afraid, but fortunately tests for cancer were negative.

We had seasonable weather that Christmas, a foretaste of what it could be like living up there on the Downs. We had a visitor who left to catch a train on Boxing Day: as our chauffeur returned from the station, calling for the daily can of milk on the way, it began to snow so heavily and to drift between the hedgerows that he was only able to reach a point about a mile from the house, staggering home from there, blue with cold and waist-deep in the snow. The car remained covered roof-high for nearly a week and the milk was with difficulty dug out half frozen. Loud cheers greeted Ben Glue, gardener and handyman, when he battled his way to us next day from East Marden.

Bertie was back from his lecture tour, there was the Christmas tree and singing 'O Tannenbaum', we were all together. But I had to get ready my lecture notes and suitable clothes for my own departure early in the year. It had seemed foolish not to take advantage of the opportunity to enjoy the success of my book in the States and earn some more money. That departure was a traumatic experience for me and, as she herself was to confirm to me more than forty years later, for my small daughter Kate, who was then just four. As I drove away the last sight was Kate's little round face through the window, white and with anxious eyes. The crossing on the *Aquitania* was exceptionally rough, but I did not suffer, I was more incommoded by the shipboard reporters and the bewilderment of arrival in New York. I suddenly felt desperately lonely and homesick. I had had to leave the school work which I had begun to find absorbing, and colleagues whom I was getting to know, as well as placing the burden of the school for the time being on Bertie, though he still had for company the young governess, now teaching, who, as we had agreed, should stay for the school year.

Almost immediately I had to face a large crowd for my first lecture: for the first and only time in my life I completely lost my voice. Luckily a visit to a throat specialist and, I suppose, recovery of my nerve, put this right just in time. My speaking voice in and outdoors I had always regarded as one of my great assets. The lecture, I felt, was only a moderate success. There were interviews, articles to write, cocktail parties. Cass Canfield, then one of the young partners at Harpers, and his wife, showed me great kindness.

There came letters from home, amongst them a large sheet of drawing paper, on which Kate had drawn a ship and lines representing huge waves, and put 'Mummy love from Kate' in shaky capital letters. Someone must have told her I had a rough passage, or perhaps she merely used her imagination. I could not help crying over this letter and wrote a poem of which I can now recall only the beginning and the end.

> I have answered the letters and written the articles
> The papers say they want
> And now I take your letter little flower.
> So large the paper and so small the ship
> You drew to show what took your mother from you.

It ended

> Here in tall buildings in an alien land
> I watch my heart across the mountainous seas
> Flutter about you like a hungry bird.

My lectures were to deal with education and also topics drawn from the books *The Right to be Happy* and *Hypatia*. Chiefly my audiences were interested in advanced views on sex and marriage, but at that date there was much less freedom in speaking about sex in the States than at home in England. But there seemed to be more broken marriages and divorces. I remarked that in England you might say what you liked on these topics so long as you DID nothing, whereas in America you might DO as you wished provided you did not speak of it. People seemed to want me to be daring and outspoken and at the same time were scared if I was. Nor was I flamboyant enough in dress and manner to fit the image they had made of me. One of the so-called 'sob sisters' said to me once: 'I don't *get* you, Mrs Russell, you seem to me more like a conventional married woman, how come you have these views?' Ordinary married woman or not, the ladylike culture of the women's clubs terrified me—scrubbed white oak tables and cabbage salads, and my talk at times preceded by a salesman's chat about some food delicacy. I should, of course, have known, as my more experienced and sophisticated husband did, that a lecture tour in America was 'show business', designed to entertain like the rabbits out of the conjuror's top hat, rather than to inspire or inform. Bertie was the ideal performer for this act, his wit and turn of phrase enabled him to put over an outrageous idea in such a way that his audience would be amused, convinced by his argument only if they wished to be so. This is praise of him rather than criticism, for in that way he must have spread much enlightenment during those many weary tours of his, just as Voltaire's satirical methods helped to demolish the ancien régime in France.

Like Candide, I was too naïve; the powers that were perceived only too well that I meant what I said. I had one lecture, 'Should Women be Protected?', which covered a number of aspects of the subject: the vexed question of night work and certain jobs for women in industry, the many taboos that beset the education and life of young women; as also my view that the whole institution of marriage had been devised by men for their own protection, in order that they might be certain of the paternity of their children. That traditional marriage was a protection for wives seemed to me a pretence.

I was invited to speak on this special topic of the protection of women in the University of Wisconsin, whose President then, Glenn Frank, was considered to be enlightened. It also contained the Experimental College conducted by Alexander Meiklejohn. The Experimental College embodied at university level some of the ideas on freedom in education which were stirring in schools like ours. Already in America it was felt that modern industry and technology were undermining not only traditional teaching and subjects, but also traditional codes and beliefs. What sort of young American was desirable, what should be the aims of America itself? The plan was to give the student considerable freedom of choice in subjects and methods of work, to aim at a liberal education, above all to awaken and stimulate *intelligence*.

To the amazement of my sponsors the liberal-minded Glenn Frank forbade me to speak on sex questions to a mixed audience of students within the University precincts. The organizers determined that the meeting should, none the less, take place. Apparently with some difficulty, they in the end secured a hall. The Meiklejohns had me to stay. A quite extraordinary tension made itself felt as we entered the hall for the meeting. The Chairman spoke quietly and with lowered head of the rights of free speech. It was almost as if the audience expected a lynching. I was dismayed, for I felt that my discussion of the many aspects of my subject, in the face of this mood of passionate protest, was bound to be an anti-climax. At the very least they had perhaps been hoping that I would advocate universal free love, orgies on the campus, and the abolition of female chastity. It all went off peaceably enough, and, if they were disappointed, no one said so. President Glenn Frank was made to look absurd by the rather academic nature of my lecture, though I in no way shirked the issue of women's rights to birth control and sex experience, the archaic nature of the marriage system, and discrimination in employment.

Although I viewed the position of women in perspective, in which sex was only one part, the sensation-mongers were determined, as they always are, to make much of this aspect of my message. The Hearst press took up the matter of Glenn Frank's veto on my lecture, and from then on I was pursued by Hearst reporters wherever I went, who tried to trap me into statements that they could blow up with great headlines, as indeed they managed to do. Back in New York, one of my friendly visitors was Anna Louise Strong, with big but none the less keen blue eyes, who pressed me on the details of my Protection of Women speech in order to find out just what had been offensive. I spoke at Dartmouth College: the emanation of masculinity that seemed to issue from rank upon rank of vigorous young males in that amphitheatre was almost overpowering for a lone female.

One evening I was invited to dinner by Mrs Dorothy Harvey and her sister, who were friends of my husband, and were among the artistic and intellectual circles of New York. We were arguing the woman question and I was, I think, upholding my view that women should not play up and live by their femininity. The company seemed to disagree; in any event I heard a very pleasing male Irish-American voice chime in in my support. Its owner was Griffin Barry, a freelance journalist who had, though I did not know it at that time, been in the Soviet Union in 1920, was a friend of John Reed, with whom he had crossed the frontier from Finland, and had also rendered assistance to George Lansbury in his interviews with Soviet leaders, as Lansbury was to indicate in his book, *My Life*, published in 1928. Barry had been in trouble with his own Government over his Soviet adventures.

Griffin and I found that we had much in common and we began a love affair that was to have far-reaching consequences for ourselves and others. He was not a tall man, and was what is called well-proportioned, with deepset blue-grey eyes and a broad face and brow that spoke of his Irish ancestry; handsome in the Celtic style, seen likewise in Scottish Highlanders, romantic heroes of my childhood. And that voice had the charm of one who might have kissed the famous Blarney stone. Both of us were romantic devotees of the free love code and did not at this time attach special importance to this encounter. For myself, feeling isolated, I was glad to have found a friend.

Whatever my personal feelings, there was no lack of sympathy, scattered over the American continent, for the ideas I was advocating. And there were Americans, like Judge Lindsey and his wife, and Horace Kallen, who were concerned with opposition to traditional religion and with sex questions, and who suffered persecution for their ideas. I had a certain amount of fan mail, of which samples have been preserved. Some of it was sincere and encouraging, but much patronizing and patriarchal.

One person whom I hoped to see, but did not, was Rachel Brooks. Months later I received an emotional letter from her which implied that even she—owing to her religious commitments—had hesitated to associate with me in the glare of unfavourable publicity—'I couldn't get into New York that last day. How much was due to the YMCA job and how much to my emotional stirrings—I don't know. But anyway, I am out of the job now—fired—so I might just as well have had the party for you. One might as well be oneself.' She had sent a telegram and ordered some toys for my children to be sent to the ship when I sailed.

I was glad finally to be back at the school some time in March, with the Easter holiday and then the summer term to come. We found that we did not see eye to eye with Beatrix Tudor Hart about methods, and we parted soon, but quite amicably. This was, to some extent, a disappointment, because we had looked on this association as the start of a partnership. Like A. S. Neill we found that we had perhaps more support from American parents than from those at home. Quite a number of American children had come to the school: in consequence we planned to end the summer term earlier than in most English schools, in order that the children should have a sufficiently long period at home then, since they would be with us all the rest of the year.

We were surprised and disappointed—though no doubt we should not have been—that the school in our own country was treated in either a frivolous or hostile manner. The Bloomsbury circle, from whom we had expected support, with some exceptions, looked upon us as a joke and would dine out on invented tales about the school, some of which unfortunately began to be repeated as if genuine. We were not troubled by the press at first, but when we were, it became a typical experience for some journalist to come, ostensibly in friendship, and then go away and write us up in a sensational style with a slant that was damaging, but yet not always quite actionable. We could not see what was wrong or so remarkable about what we were trying to do for the children in our care, to us it all seemed natural and obvious.

Bertie was always busy writing; he acquired an excellent secretary and began to dictate a good deal. We had spent capital from the sale of the house in Chelsea on the school, and the first year showed a heavy deficit on running expenses. Bertie planned a lecture tour in America for 1929, I was earning a bit from my books and articles and was able to finance Carn Voel, the house in Cornwall. Like most people who were involved in idealistic causes we were both beset with demands on our time and energy.

With Norman Haire and others I had been at the International Sex Congress in Berlin in October 1926. Those of us on the left were not in agreement with the sponsors of this Congress: we had met Magnus Hirschfeld there and visited his remarkable Institute where the results of researches into various sex problems and perversions could be seen in records and photographs. We actually met two people whose sex had been changed by operation. Hirschfeld was a most courageous pioneer; with him was projected a World League for Sex Reform, the English section of which was started by Norman Haire with myself as Secretary. This had involved committee meetings at Norman Haire's in Harley Street, and plans for a Congress in London in the near future.

But at the end of the summer term of the school Bertie and I sought a brief holiday together and, with John and Kate in safekeeping with friends in Switzerland, we went to Locarno, intending to collect them to spend the rest of the summer in Cornwall. Suddenly a phone call informed us that John had become mysteriously very ill; a panic night train journey took us to his bedside. A poignant memory for me is that, after a night of such agonized anxiety that he was almost incapable of dealing with practical details, Bertie's first words were: 'It's all right,

John, Mummy is here now.' John certainly looked ghastly pale and ate nothing, but he did recover fairly quickly. He asserts that he had eaten a bad peach, but I think that the doctor was at first afraid of meningitis.

A further complication was that Griffin Barry was arriving in Europe and wanted to see me. Bertie of course knew about this and insisted that, in spite of everything, I must see him, if only for a brief visit. We were thus together for a short time in France, when we also called in on George and Mary Slocombe, and I saw for the first time that exquisite place Les Andelys, and stayed in the lovely old hotel Chaîne d'Or, on the bank of the Seine, at a curve of the river, overlooked by Coeur de Lion's castle. George Slocombe was one of the group of journalists associated with George Lansbury and his *Daily Herald*, and was a striking figure: tall, handsome, redheaded, affecting a wide-brimmed Quartier Latin hat. He had a charming, dark-haired wife, Mary. Francis Meynell, another of that circle, with Vera, happened to arrive, touring France. This was the kind of party that Griffin greatly enjoyed, for the purpose of intelligent conversation and argument, which, with an Irishman's love of skirmishing, he would stimulate with provocative comment. Roving journalists are a special breed; professionally they cannot afford, and temperamentally dislike, any ties. A youngish man, like Barry, especially an American, could live by some well-paid articles in the heavier reviews, or temporary assignments abroad, with only occasional bondage to a newspaper.

Griffin and I found interest and pleasure in each other's work and company apart from sexual attraction. For both of us it was a refreshing occasional interlude, and neither of us at that time (and I, it must be said, never) even considered the notion of a settled married life together. Nor did Bertie and I consider ourselves 'married' in the conventional sense, an attitude which, as I have indicated, was then quite common among left-wing people and still is. We had made John and Kate legitimate, but Bertie often said that this had been the sole purpose of our marriage, and further, that we should continue to conduct our lives according to our own moral code, not troubling about legal 'matrimonial offences', since we would never need, whatever happened, to bother about a divorce.

The latter part of the summer I was happy to be back in Cornwall, writing my articles, having fun bathing with Bertie and the children, entertaining occasional visitors. We cherished this private family refuge from the more public life and responsibility of the school. None the less a stream of our visitors, mutual and otherwise, came there for brief holidays over the years. I recall Tagore seated solemnly on the lawn in the sun, in serious discourse; Mr and Mrs Chao had come; and once, when we were walking to the Logan Rock, the official guide pointed us out, as objects of local interest, to no less persons than Sybil Thorndike and Lewis Casson, with the result that we enticed them and most of their family to tea at Carn Voel.

When the Chinese poet C. H. Hsu went bathing with us all in Cornwall, we noted with amusement that his creamy skin was lighter than the rich brown sunburn of our entire family. Hsu's own family, well off, had imposed on him a traditional education, which meant learning the Chinese classics, sitting beside the old family tutor, who never changed his clothes and had not even been washed at birth. After his father's death, Hsu told us, it fell to him to give the funeral instructions when the tutor also died. Should the corpse be washed? 'No, bury him complete' was Hsu's reply. This able and charming young man, to our great sorrow, died in an air crash in the 1930s.

Bertie had published *Sceptical Essays* and was writing *Marriage and Morals*. He was more and more sought after for popular books on the issues of the time; what is more, the financial burden of the school was heavier than we had expected. We consoled ourselves with the thought that we at least had our bread and butter and our children's education thrown in. We were also hoping to have another child of our own; Kate was now five years old. I was deeply immersed in the whole subject of the nurture and education of children, as also were such pioneers as Marie Stopes and Sylvia Pankhurst.

I had been thinking of writing a book on the 'making of the modern child', inspired as I was by the vision that our children were in fact the future of humanity, an idea that for many is now a mere commonplace or slogan, but which was something quite new in a world which still looked on children and their education as destined to carry the traditions of their elders and the past. I was happy in the thought that, in my own maternity and the school, I had found creative work which might also be of use to society and, besides, did not involve rivalry or discord between Bertie and myself.

At the school we were sharing the burden in harmony. The staff enjoyed Bertie's comments and witticisms at table and at the weekly staff meeting. But the responsibility of the entire care of young children and of finance was very heavy.

We hoped so much to have another child and, if we had had the good fortune to start one during this year, the whole course of our lives might have been very different. My love for Bertie had never wavered or altered. I believed, and I think rightly, that at that time he was as devoted to me. But we were both working extremely hard and with little time for relaxation. Bertie's severe Victorian upbringing and the intensity of his intellectual concentration had inhibited him sexually; he had in fact told me at the very beginning of our relations that he was dubious of ever begetting a child. Yet we had two and I was desperately anxious to give him another. I took advice to see if anything had gone wrong with me, but there was no reason, apparently, why I did not conceive. I suggested to Bertie that he might perhaps also seek advice, but he was unwilling to do so. Gossip has put upon his alleged numerous love affairs an entirely false interpretation. I believe that he always hoped that a sufficiently strong attraction to some woman would overcome his disability by spontaneous, natural means.

Early in the year 1929 fate took a hand by visiting the school with a highly dangerous influenza, whose infection, in an incredibly short time, flew straight to the ears. We watched over the children, every child received the best we could give in medical and nursing care. Cruelly, as others recovered, it was our own two who contracted mastoid trouble, which, in the days before penicillin, involved operating. As I comforted John with the promise that the germs would be conquered, he looked at me with his big, serious brown eyes and asked: 'What happens if the germs win?' On a freezing night we drove down to Petersfield for his operation, John in my arms. Looking up at a brilliant starry sky he said: 'I have been thinking how poor people are', by which I knew he meant the frailty and insignificance of human life. We took Kate to London for specialist advice and eventually an operation.

This terrifying experience put great strain on us both. At Easter we went with our children to Ventnor to recuperate. And here, from a small boy sitting on a bench on the front, Bertie contracted whooping cough, for him a serious illness, but from which he made a remarkably quick recovery.

As if serious troubles were not enough, we had to endure the battle of the telescope. Unknown to us, Frank had left this article in the attic of Telegraph House. We searched, found and carried it down to Harting to be called for, according to his instructions. He then began to sue us for alleged damage to the said telescope. We replied that we were 'unwilling bailees', not even having known of its existence. We could not believe that he was serious, but he carried the case right up to the hearing at the local County Court in Midhurst, when, with us and all the appropriate legal gentlemen present, he wrote to say that a debate in the Lords prevented his attendance. Nodding their heads sagely, the magistrates opined that doubtless his Lordship was much occupied with business of national importance. This was my second experience of a Russell's frolic with the law. I was to have more later.

As A. S. Neill also found, visitors to an experimental school can take up a lot of time at weekends. Once Sinclair Lewis and Dorothy Thompson, not long after they married, drove through our gate trailing their caravan. We liked and admired Sinc as a person and writer, but were a bit dubious about him camping on our school's doorstep. Sensing this, saying he could see they were not welcome, he turned his vehicles sharply and began to drive away. Running with all speed down the flinty drive, I assured them that no discourtesy was intended. We had a few amusing days in their company. Sandy-haired, angular, awkward, restless as quicksilver, Sinc was an amazing character. To be at a party with him was hilarious; having drunk well, he would sit cross-legged on the floor pouring out a stream of his fascinating nonsense.

The World League for Sex Reform was progressing: Norman Haire's secretary did a great deal of the work for me, but I had occasionally to go to committee meetings in London. Norman Haire, a well-known gynaecologist, was a flamboyant figure, a lover of opulence. His consulting rooms in Harley Street were richly furnished with Chinese carpets, scarlet, black and gold lacquer cabinets, Chinese porcelain. He shocked people by his brutal frankness about birth control and sex. 'Sex, for the proletarian,' he used to say, 'is fourpence and find your own railings.' Through him I met Jack and Ingeborg Flügel, who were to become two of my dearest friends. A brilliant writer and lecturer on psychology, Jack was also a warm, generous and understanding person to whom one could go in time of trouble. Ingeborg was a marvellous hostess; all discerning people were delighted to be included in her parties.

Our movement acquired more members, among them a lively and handsome young man, Bob Boothby. Our organization was not 'party political', but I, as a socialist, felt that we were a bit too middle class and ought to be doing something to help those proletarians about their sex. At one meeting Bob Boothby got up and accused me of dragging the class war into the organization. I responded hotly, while Jack Flügel, in the Chair, restored us to harmony. Plans for our forthcoming conference in London went ahead. I continued also some connection with the I.L.P. and the Labour Women's Conference.

Bertie was making plans for a lecture tour in the autumn of 1929. Meantime I heard from Griffin Barry that, for an organization in the U.S.A. called the Open Road, he was to lead a small group of tourists to the Soviet Union in the summer holidays. I wanted to join it; it would be interesting to see Russia nine years after my first visit. I would not be away long, and we would have great pleasure in each other's company.

Accordingly I found myself on 24 July 1929 at midday at Mills Hotel, London. With Griffin Barry and Susan Paxton, a young woman who was assisting him, we were in all a party of ten. There were four elderly American ladies and one elderly American gentleman, and a young Englishman, Lewis Cohen, a member of the I.L.P., employed at an estate agent's office in Brighton called (to Griffin's and my delight) Reason and Tickle. With Lewis was a girlfriend. Lewis became later very wealthy, a staunch Labour supporter, patron of the arts, and Mayor of Brighton; he died not very long ago.

This was my first experience of the intrepid elderly American woman touring the world. These women must have been at least seventy, or near it; at the time their venturing on extensive foreign travel, especially to Russia, astonished me, though it would no longer do so now.

At Hull we embarked on the *Oberon*, a ship of French construction but run at that time by the Finns. All the ladies besieged Susan to get single-berth outside cabins; Mrs C wanted to know why there were not more of these even on big boats, and thought people ought to be able to travel how they liked, if they were willing to pay for it.

On 29 July we came to Leningrad. The faces of the frontier guards were grave, and, I felt, a trifle contemptuous. As our train went through flat wooded country I noticed naked brown babies and children sunbathing. Griffin was in one of his prodding moods, implying, to my annoyance, that I was full of prejudices, which may well have been true. At the moment I wanted to sit silent in the third-class carriage smelling again the strange odour of the Russian people, watching their wonderful faces, differing so greatly because marked with real experience.

At Leningrad station we were met by new Ford cars, of which our guides were obviously very proud. So of course one of the women in our party had to say that she wanted to ride in a droshky. At the Hotel Europe—queer, grand, large and dilapidated—I felt like a caretaker living in the Duke's house in his absence. But it had a charming roof garden. I found the town gardens and squares beautiful but melancholy and romantic with neglected long grass. Leningrad still had a mournful air. Both Griffin and I were pretty tired and quarrelled endlessly about our relationship. In this weary, low mood I found myself very receptive to impressions. It fitted well the evening concert given by an elderly orchestra in the Garden of Rest and conducted by an 'Honoured Conductor' of the Republic, small, shabby, with unbrushed hair and a puffy little cherubic face with a large mole and an affectionate smile.

The visit to the Pavlov Institute was very rewarding. Dr Gant, ill-shaven, lantern-jawed and with enthusiastic eyes, showed us round. Contempt flickered over his face occasionally at foolish questions put to him. We saw the kennels and the observation rooms with all the appliances for stimuli. These rooms had very thick, carefully constructed walls. Spironsky, who had a humorous, pockmarked face and close-shaven hair, casually and exquisitely dissected the brain of a dog as he talked to us. He showed us the pituitary gland and, tracing out other parts of the brain, he said laughing, 'This is what he dances with, this makes him angry', etc. A dog—he told us—can adapt himself to living with only half of his brain. They were trying to find out the function of a sort of gland that connects the two hemispheres and what happens if you sever it. This experiment was not yet completed at that time. Asked how they looked after the dogs who had been operated on, Dr Gant replied scornfully, 'Better than the patients in the hospitals.'

Near to Leningrad Griffin and I, on our own, visited a children's country home that was called, I think, the Red Ray. On a hot summer's day we found this place delightful. The children were diving into a lake, others were looking after the smaller ones, some busy with domestic jobs. It had the feel of a community run by and for the children.

In Moscow we had those interminable sessions on education, social welfare, the marriage laws, with which so many delegations to the

Soviet Union have become familiar over the years. Very severe measures were being taken to end prostitution, which was now prohibited by law. More severe laws were proposed for use against men who frequented prostitutes. Intense re-education was clearly the order of the day, but the fate of the 'hopeless' cases, who could be sent to the Solovetsky Islands on the White Sea, sounded ominous. However stringent the attack on prostitutes, the marriage laws in those first years after the Revolution were more lenient than they later became. Before marrying, a man and woman had to declare that they were free of venereal infection, and the penalty for a false declaration could be a year in prison; for actually infecting a marriage partner, up to three years.

Divorce, at that time, was by mutual consent. But, if one partner did not consent and refused to come to the bureau to agree, the divorce would none the less go through. If there were children, then payment for them was by mutual agreement, though, in the absence of one party, the authorities would make the necessary decisions. Even if a wife was earning, a man must contribute to the upkeep of his children until they were eighteen. Normally a child would go with the mother in divorce; she would help with its maintenance, though not legally bound to. If, however, children remained with the father, then the mother was expected to pay towards their maintenance. What is more, in a childless marriage, if the wife was earning, she must, on divorce, help her ex-husband financially for six months, if he needed it. There were blood tests in cases of doubtful paternity, and the calling of witnesses.

Abortion was not illegal. If a woman desired an abortion a panel of doctors could decide if it should be allowed. If permission was given, then the abortion would be performed free and with due leave from work with pay. But a woman could herself decide in spite of the medical judgment. In that case she would herself have to find the money (about £5) for the operation, and would not necessarily get her paid leave. The period of absence for a woman having a baby was two months, and, at the place of work, she would have a break every three-and-a-half hours to suckle her child in the factory nursery.

We were shown a most interesting short film about abortion. It depicted the distressed mother going for a backstreet abortion, and showed by diagrams the risk of perforation, haemorrhage and death. Then we saw the mother who sought good advice, and the care and safety afforded her in a sound surgical operation. The film went on to show, however, how women who did not get rid of their babies were helped by clinics, nurseries, and medical care at an actual birth.

I was immensely impressed by this film. Remembering the colossal ignorance of their internal organs that I had found among women at home on my birth control crusade, and the obscurantism surrounding the whole topic, I thought how remarkable and excellent it was that women should be taught in this direct and simple manner about conception, pregnancy and the giving of birth, a matter of supreme importance in the lives of probably the majority of women. I said that I would very much like this film to be shown in my own country. And of that more later.

Miss Spitzer at the Education Department gave us an exhaustive account of Soviet education. Its underlying principles she defined as first of all not to treat the child as an 'object'. Pupils and teachers were 'comrades' in the upbringing of the child; there was self-government in the schools. School programmes were not abstract but took account of real life now and in the future; every child had to learn to do some socially useful work. One very interesting piece of information was that there were 170 nationalities in the Soviet Union teaching in their own languages; of these fifty per cent also taught Russian. Some of these languages had not been written down before; there were some thirty new written alphabets.

This was, of course, still a very live period in Soviet education: co-educational, experimental, trying out some of our advanced Western theories and not yet hardened into a State system. What the Russians had been doing in those nine years, in training teachers, and getting children into school, was phenomenal. We still had every reason in the West to admire much of the Russian achievement; I had long wanted to have a Russian teacher in the school, not only to teach the language, but to bring with him or her a breath of this new approach to life. A famous film that was often shown in the West was a story made on the work of Makarenko, who had set about finding and reclaiming the thousands of orphans of the Revolution and civil wars, who lived in holes and corners as vagrants and thieves. I had read also Makarenko's own books, which threw a searching light into that period of Russian history.

On this visit I was given a special opportunity to see one of similar colonies, which was under the direction of what was then, I think, the O.G.P.U. Mrs Rosengolz who, when at the Soviet Embassy in London, had wanted her son Valya to come to our school, came to see me. Her husband was now high up in one of the Soviet State enterprises; she was practising her profession of medicine and said that she found it more satisfying than diplomacy abroad. I was invited to swim at one of the new bathing establishments on the Moskva, where I met Rosengolz himself—in a bathing costume. Mrs Rosengolz offered to take Griffin and me to this co-operative colony in the country, and drove us out in an old Rolls-Royce over rough, dusty roads to what had been a monastery, romantic onion domes and all. The church was now used as an assembly hall and there the community's orchestra played for us. We understood that here, as under Makarenko, members of the community could, so to speak, contract in, when they would have food and lodging and other necessities, taking their share in the work. The community had its farm, fields and livestock; but it also had workshops in wood and metal. One of the interesting facts about the original

Makarenko community was the immense prestige which industrial development acquired for the pupils, who, though they would assist the local farmers with advice and work, really despised agriculture and were only too ready to rush off to the factories in the towns as opportunity offered. It may well be that this has been one serious defect of the whole Soviet development.

Here, in this community, they were making bicycles, and no doubt other artefacts of the machine age; I saw tanks in which metal was suspended for silver or copper plating. But the Superintendent of the establishment, a huge, burly, genial man in uniform and boots, led me into a shed where, leaning on the barrier, he gazed with rapture at some immense white pigs, which had been imported from England. His love for those pigs was clearly a great thing in his life; he said he wanted many more of them. I asked if members could leave the community. Yes, they could, it was not to be regarded as a reformatory. But times were not easy and an individual on his own seeking bread and work would not have too good a chance.

Mrs Rosengolz told me then of the early days of the Revolution in 1917. Her husband had been one of those who made it, and was in the Kremlin. She herself, with her small son, lived some distance away in another part of the city. The Bolsheviks were quite uncertain whether they would hold power for more than a few weeks. Every day she went on foot across the city, to see if her husband and his comrades were still alive in the citadel of power.

By February 1937, according to the Moscow diary *Mission to Moscow*, published in 1942, of the American Ambassador Joseph E. Davies, Rosengolz had reached the high position of Commissar of Foreign Trade, and was living both in the Kremlin and in his dacha outside Moscow, where Ambassador Davies was entertained to lunch to meet Marshal Voroshilov, Mikoyan, Vyshinsky, and Rosov (then head of Amtorg in New York for trade with Russia). Rosengolz seems to have taken the lead in discussions about financial transactions, including the vexed question of the repayment of Russian debts. Only a year later, March 1938, Rosengolz was in the dock with Bukharin and others, found guilty of conspiracy with Germany after apparently confessing to passing information, condemned to death and shot. Ambassador Davies seems to have swallowed hook, line and sinker the official story of these treason trials. When, in the end, the war with Germany broke out, he admired the Russians for having discovered and executed their 'fifth column' in time. Much more was revealed later about Stalin's purges, especially of former revolutionary colleagues.

I will never be persuaded that Rosengolz and his wife, who had borne the brunt of the early revolutionary struggles, the starvation and agony of the civil wars, the frustration and ostracism of representing their Government in a hostile country abroad, would ever have been guilty of betrayal of their revolution.

What happened to Valya and his mother I do not know, but I still have two letters from her. After a severe illness she wrote in the spring of 1930, inviting me to come and stay with all my family in her new apartment, and explaining why I had not yet been sent the Russian teacher I asked for: a real friendship that might have borne fruit but for the brutal preludes to the 1939 war.

A faint uneasiness hung about me all the time on this expedition. It may have been the American atmosphere of my fellow tourists, but something was communicated to me in the very air of Russia itself. I did not expect to find the morning glory of revolutionary fervour; this was the period of vast reconstruction, involving grinding work. And revolution meant a break with the past, surely, in every respect. Yet, it came over me that there was a continuity in human life which could not be arbitrarily broken and my old fear of the industrial machine revived. I remember saying to someone that, pleasant as the trip had been, I would not be sorry to get back to my own country where there was some sense of 'biological continuity'.

11

Storm Clouds

There are periods in human history when, without apparent reason, at first imperceptibly, the movement in one direction goes into reverse. The change occurs not only in the economics and politics of the time, but even in the motivation of individual lives. Of course no one is exempt from the effect of the basic structure of the society of which he is a part; some may become richer, some poorer; more, or less, free. I mean something more than this, something 'in the air', a mood, an atmosphere, which affects the ideas and conduct of individuals, almost unknown to themselves.

> There is a tide in the affairs of men,
> Which, taken at the flood, leads on to fortune.

But there is also ebb tide. After the General Strike of 1926 in England, in the disillusion that followed, such a change already began to set in. Cracks in the Labour movement widened. But it was the economic collapse in America in 1929 which set in motion the wave of unemployment, anxiety, uncertainty that affected the rest of Europe. From then on, though very few can have been aware of it, there was a steady deterioration in the hope for a better world. Within four years came the Reichstag fire and Hitler in power in Germany; the Civil War in Spain in 1936. At the end of those ten years, we were at war with Germany ourselves.

My uneasiness in the Soviet Union perhaps presaged the antagonisms and purges which were soon to occur there; I may also have become increasingly aware of how irreconcilable was my view of private and public morality with that still held by the majority at home.

When the crisis came, large numbers of people were, of course, directly affected by economic losses; for others, whose lives, in most respects, seemed to go on as usual, there took place an unconscious polarization of thought, for some back to the status quo, for others forward still to a forlorn hope for the future. Looking back, something of this sort seems to have happened to the attitudes of those with whom I was most intimately concerned.

Through the summer of 1929 we all contentedly made our plans for the future. Bertie's lecture tour in America was to be in the autumn,

I would carry on with the work of the school; Griffin Barry had put by and invested enough for him to live modestly in Europe freelancing. I acquired a small top floor in Bloomsbury that might be used by any of us when in London.

Just before school term the Congress of the World League for Sexual Reform, for which Norman Haire and I had been working, took place in London from 8 to 14 September 1929. Presidents of the League, whose full title was 'The World League for Sexual Reform on a Scientific Basis', were August Forel, Havelock Ellis and Magnus Hirschfeld. There was a very large International Committee, on which Norman Haire, E. S. Jerdan and I sat for England. Literally every country in Europe, except Portugal, was represented; included in the Committee also were British India, Canada, Egypt, Iceland, Liberia, the Malay States, the United States, Latvia, Argentina, Chile. Alexandra Kollontai sat for the Soviet Union, and sent a message to the Congress. Among other eminent people who sent messages and letters to the Congress were Aldous and Julian Huxley, and Hugh Walpole; Judge Ben Lindsey from the U.S.A.; Henri Barbusse, Paul Morand and others from France; Freud regretted that it was not possible for him to come or send a paper, but rejoiced at the number of important personalities who would participate in the Congress.

The number of those actually present was 350. If anyone wishes to know who were the standard-bearers of progressive opinion in the chief European countries at that date, the index of the participants is a reliable guide.*

Remarkable, in view of how women were to be treated under the Hitler régime, was the number of courageous, intelligent, professional women from Germany: Drs Helen Stocker, Hertha Riese, Maria Krische, Marthe Wolff. In quality and quantity the entire German contribution was impressive.

Russia sent Dr A. Gens, whose paper was a thorough account of abortion in the Soviet Union; Dr G. Batkis dealt with their problem of prostitution; there was also a paper on the Soviet marriage laws from Dr Nikolai Paschooserski, Professor of Law at Kiev University, who was unable to attend owing to illness. To my delight they also brought with them the film about abortion which I had seen. From Russia came also a letter from Professor Bonner, Chief of the Department for Social Diseases of the Commissariat of Health, who wrote: '. . . the experience of our country—the first Socialist State—has clearly shown how quickly the legal, moral and religious traditions which are insurmountable in bourgeois society can be destroyed by a social revolution.'

I stress the friendly co-operation of the Russians precisely because there was little in the political attitude of the West to encourage them;

* *World League for Sex Reform Congress* (Kegan Paul, 1930)

also because Professor Bonner's remark illustrates a significant feature of this Congress and indeed raises the vexed question of the value and influence of political and legal action in social and sexual reforms. Even now it is too little recognized to what extent such reforms were brought about in Russia by radical and courageous legislation.

In our Congress the contributions were nearly all designed to inform and influence public opinion rather than to organize political action for the ends which we thought desirable. It is therefore noticeable that, on the contrary, the *political* aspect was the subject of my own address of welcome. I emphasized how effective had been the *political* action of organized bodies of women on the subject of birth control. But, on the whole, my learned colleagues contented themselves with describing the existing state of public knowledge and practice, exposing the inhumanity of the laws without envisaging any serious organization to change them.

Apart from Oliver Baldwin and John Strachey, no Members of Parliament are listed among the Congress supporters; John Strachey's family connections with Lytton Strachey and Amabel Williams-Ellis would have brought him there as well as his own sincere convictions. I think it is accurate to say that there were, otherwise, no active politicians at this meeting. Personally, I had diverted my energies from the political side of the birth control cause, perhaps lost touch with the M.P.s who supported us. But the wide gap between this great volume of cultural opinion and political action may well have contributed in no small measure to the subsequent inroads achieved by reaction. Perhaps this is always so, perhaps a truth still neglected: those who form and lead social and cultural opinion cannot afford to be 'above the battle' in politics, whereas the politician who excludes their vision and despises them as cranks and intellectuals is both short-sighted and irresponsible. In this matter the politician bears the greater blame, for the cultural prophets do in the end protest and pressure him, but they are not the holders of power.

Norman Haire, Jack Flügel and I co-operated in the preparations for the Congress. Both were delightful colleagues. Norman, though often criticized, was a very loyal friend and intensely sincere in his views on sex questions. He had an infectious, bouncing vigour that came over well in his address of welcome to the Congress in which he described how he and I, at first pessimistic, began by enlisting 'names' such as H. G. Wells, Arnold Bennett, Bertrand Russell, Hugh Walpole, until 'other people were less hesitant in supporting openly what they believed in privately. The list of supporters grew like a snowball that rolls down-hill . . . many people gave their names when they found that we were backed by a lot of other respectable people.' Jack Flügel's address of welcome was delivered in Esperanto. He indicated that sex affected all aspects of human life, individual, family, social, economic, national, even peace and world civilization.

Magnus Hirschfeld formally opened the Congress with his Presidential Address. He recalled his visit back in 1913, when he had met with William Bateson, Edward Carpenter and Havelock Ellis, as also that the meeting, in the Albert Hall, had been interrupted by the Suffragettes in opposition to Sir Edward Grey. He endorsed the women's agitation, and insisted that the complete equality of men and women was not only social and political but had its basis in the findings of sexology. Hirschfeld, whose work in this field is justly famous, touched on sexual abnormalities, which he preferred to regard as biological variations, rather than pathological cases. Having regard to the state of the law, such definition enabled doctors better to protect and care for the sexually deviant. He issued an interesting warning against using marriage as a cure in deviant cases, which could do much harm especially to the other party to the marriage. He concluded: 'In a life-long fight against ignorance and injustice in sexual matters I have had as my motto: "Per scientia ad justitiam." This aim has not yet been attained. But it shall be attained. The power of truth, once it has been recognised and spoken, guarantees that it shall be so . . .'

I cherish a vivid memory of this eager little man, with a shock of wild grey hair, dashing hither and thither, consumed with glowing enthusiasm for his ideals. I record this here to his memory in thanks for the enjoyment of our brief collaboration, and because, after Hitler came to power, Hirschfeld's life's work at the Institute in Berlin literally went up in smoke.

The first paper at the Congress was Cyril Joad on 'Sex and Religion', the last Bernard Shaw on 'The Need for Expert Opinion on Sexual Reform'. In between came—from British women—Vera Brittain on 'The Failure of Monogamy', Marie Stopes on 'Birth Control' and a further paper on the 'Impediments to Publication' of information on the subject; Naomi Mitchison on 'Intelligent Use of Contraceptives'; my colleagues of our birth control agitation, Janet Chance and Stella Browne, on 'Marriage Education' and 'Abortion'; Barbara Low on the psychiatrist's angle on 'Sex Education'; Ethel Mannin on 'Sex and the Child'; myself on 'Marriage and Freedom'.

Among the men contributors, on various forms of censorship in literature, the theatre, films, were Laurence Housman, John Van Druten the playwright, Ivor Montagu, George Ives, Desmond McCarthy, and Bertrand Russell on 'The Taboo on Sex Knowledge'. Miles Malleson argued for a 'New Positive Morality', Jack Flügel spoke with insight on 'Sex Differences in Dress'. Bernard Shaw, as always, drove home his telling points under the guise of entertaining nonsense. He claimed expertise in sex for himself as a playwright, since 'the theatre is continually occupied with sex appeal . . . as a costermonger has to deal with turnips; and a costermonger's opinion on turnips is worth having.'

A joyous lark of the Congress was the showing of the Russian abortion film. Obviously it would not pass the Censor. Norman Haire and I arranged a private showing in a studio at the end of someone's garden and special tickets were issued to bona fide members of the Congress. As might be expected, the press pestered Norman and me with enquiries; we were even shadowed on the day of the event and had to do some more or less skilful evasion, leaping in and out of cars amid much giggling. Much as the film was appreciated, our audience did not see the full version, but one which had been shown in Germany. Although unskilled abortion was shown, the exposition of skilled abortions done under the new humane laws, as also the care given to mothers and the babies which *were* born, were omitted. Evidently in Germany, said Dr Marthe Wolff, a German delegate, it had been decided that people were 'sufficiently advanced to see the *wrong* way, but not sufficiently to see the *right* way.' My own recollection of the film in Russia confirms this. Dr Wolff had herself seen the film in a club of a trade union of domestic servants, waiters etc. in Rostov on Don.

At a business meeting of the League on 14 September, several favoured the Soviet Union as the next venue for our Congress. The Russian Government would provide all facilities, and there was much that we could learn there. But a great deal of work needed to be done in Britain and the U.S.A.; a previous visit to a communist capital might prejudice further efforts in the West. In the end the International Committee plumped for Vienna in 1930.

Drs Gens and Batkis of the Russian delegation came down to visit our school. Our methods did not differ widely from what was then the practice in Soviet schools. But one thing did impress them, our 'lab' in which we acquainted quite small children with science by the 'magic' of simple experiments. Dr Gens's speciality was maternity care. To my surprise and pleasure, he said that he had a folder of press cuttings and information about our Workers' Birth Control Group, the only group in bourgeois society with which their Government and experts could agree.

To me this Congress had meant more than I can say. It had begun to outline those things in which I ardently believed; it had, moreover, expressed an internationalism that went beyond mere politics, and kept open the channel between us and the Soviet Union, still blocked by the politicians. We had passed resolutions on marriage and divorce, sex and censorship, sex education, birth control, abortion, prostitution and venereal disease, which might serve as a basis for a tolerant and humane society, some of which have even yet not been fully realized. But we had, as Hirschfeld urged upon us, 'broken through the conspiracy of silence'.

Besides our Russians we had many other visitors to the school. I think that it was after Bertie had left for America that autumn, or during the summer term when he was away for a weekend, that Beatrice and Sidney Webb and Bernard Shaw arrived at the school one afternoon on a surprise visit. The Webbs were living not far away at Liphook. Feeling most inadequate without Bertie, I received the visitors in the children's dining room, into which one came straight from the front door. Just before tea the children were apt to be at their wildest. They found this tall, bearded visitor most attractive. As Shaw muttered 'Let's get out of here', I hastily led the way into the staff dining room, where I dispensed tea and apologized for Bertie's absence. Shaw remarked on what good wholemeal bread and butter we had. He and Beatrice Webb then began to lecture the staff and myself on the care and education of children. After this, without further ado, they departed. Sidney did make one attempt at fraternization with the young. Stooping, he took Kate by the hand and, gazing at her intently, said: 'Little girl, will you *give* me your eyes?' Kate was speechless with horror. The staff and I could not help reflecting that they were all childless.

In spite of the reverence that they were accorded in the Labour movement, I never could work up any enthusiasm for the Webbs. But they were very appreciative friends of Bertie: we had dined with them in London and met them on rare occasions. In speech and manner Beatrice was so didactic; contemptuous towards those who ventured to disagree. Once in discussion Beatrice was asserting the accepted maxim that science was 'neutral'—a view from which indeed no one dissented at that stage—when, greatly daring, I tried to put forward my hypothesis of the dominant power of science. 'Who is this upstart?' said her withering glance. Naturally, I found it hard to like her.

I did not mind Shaw's arrogance: it became him well and he had a right to wear it. I saw him only rarely. Much later, during the war, he tried to help me save the school financially, and, when I married an Irishman not blessed with this world's goods, congratulated me on one of his famous postcards, adding, 'you should marry money'. I knew he did not mean it. For the essential Shaw was the impecunious rebel Irishman who had sought security for his genius rather than for himself.

I thought then, as I still do, that Shaw, Wells and Russell were the three great emancipators for my generation from Victorian orthodoxies, liberating thought from superstition and prejudice, the individual from the tyranny of the family system, woman from her traditional servitude, the worker from his chains. I felt myself privileged to have been in personal association with all three.

The next events in my life I would for many reasons have preferred not to relate: I have kept silent about them for many years. But in these days every corner of the lives of people in the public eye tends to be researched, discussed and often misrepresented. A great deal has already been written about Bertie Russell, not least by Russell himself. Again, many of the difficulties that later arose between Bertie and myself were the common fate of all thinking men and women in that period of women's emancipation. What should be the right attitude of man to woman, woman to man, parent to child, child to parent? How should women come to terms with, or how alter the rigid patriarchal structure of our society? The solution of these dilemmas is still sought: therefore the tale of our pathetic efforts to resolve them may serve both to warn and to enlighten.

Bertie and I still quite often talked of my having another baby. Kate was now nearly six years old. I felt sure that he really wanted another child: I think that the cryptic remark that I recently noted in his autobiography about his 'failure' as a parent can mean nothing else than the disappointment of his hopes at that time, for I am equally sure that he did not think himself neglectful or inadequate as regards the two he already had. For myself, with my many activities, I was not specially anxious to embark on pregnancy, but above all I would have been glad to fulfil his need. He may, I think, have interpreted my mood at this time as a desire in general for another child, which he seemed unable to give me. Nor could it be denied that my whole life, for as far ahead as one could then see, was occupied with the care of my own and other people's children, not to mention carrying on the battle for the cause of mothers in general. Looking at the matter less subjectively, Bertie would say how much he appreciated me as a mother, both in the bearing of children and their nurture. He would then say that he did think I ought to have more than two children and that he would not object if I were to have one with another father. In one of his cynical moods, which were more frequent than some may know, he would say that no eighteenth-century aristocrat bothered about the paternity of his family once he had obtained his firstborn heir.

Of course this does not mean that I at once set out to avail myself of Bertie's generosity; on the contrary, pregnancy was not what I wanted at that moment, especially when single-handed in the running of the school. But in October I suspected that the worst—or the best— had happened and wrote immediately to Bertie in America to know what he wished me to do. Bertie cabled at once that I should do nothing, and followed the cable by a letter:

Montgomery, Ala.

My Darling Love, 14 Nov. 1929.

I got your letter this morning saying your period was late, and I cabled at once. I should not at all like you to do anything about it— if it is so, much better let nature take its course. Since I cannot do my part, it is better someone else should, as you ought to have more children. But I dare say it was a false alarm. In any case there is no need to worry, you won't find me tiresome about it.

I am glad everything goes well at the school. It is so much better than last time! A month from to-day I sail—I *shall* be glad.

My love, Darling. No time for more.

B.

Later, when it became clear that Griffin Barry and I were certainly having this child, Bertie insisted that he would not agree to my parting with it in any way whatever. He further insisted that he should have full parental rights, which legally would be his in any case, and that it was important that the child should grow up with John and Kate and in Beacon Hill School with us all.

I have reason to believe that this decision cost Bertie much more distress than he was ever willing to reveal, especially to me. This was all a part of that courtly behaviour towards his wife which disdained marital bickering. We never had rows and reconciliations. But how much, if he would have given me a hint of a deep hurt, I would have wished and been able to comfort him with a warmth of love and, indeed, gratitude. For I certainly loved and honoured him more than ever. I hated to hurt him, but I could do nothing to comfort, or try to dispel a hurt which his pride forbade him to let me see. Nor do I think that he realized that I loved him more and not less, for masculine pride seems always to assume that when a loved woman takes an interest in another man, it must inevitably follow that she cares less for him. For my part I had never felt that any 'affairs' Bertie might have could shake the abiding nature of our close relation and trust in one another. At this time I admired and was thankful to him for standing by our agreement that the legal marriage was not relevant to our own moral code. Had I not been legally married, it would have been open to me to have a child by any man that I loved, provided that such children were loved and adequately maintained.

Bertie came back from the States after a lecture tour that was a success, despite the impending economic crisis. For Griffin Barry things were not so good. He had been in Paris making contacts, and then had to watch with horror the slump in the stock market swallowing up the modest income he had hoped to be able to exist on for some time to come. This impending baby suddenly presented him with a responsibility he had not bargained for, though he had known that it might chance to happen and the possibility had been discussed between us. He came to London and met Bertie and they did not dislike one another. I had no intention of imposing any financial burden on either of the two men concerned. But I suppose that Griffin must have brooded and worried. On the eve of New Year Bertie was in bed with a touch of bronchitis, to which he was always liable when tired. Suddenly Francis Meynell rang us from London to say that Griffin was desperately ill and in great pain in the London flat. Francis called in Dr Streatfeild, who had looked after us in London, and there was nothing for it but for me to go up and see what could be done. It was a perforated duodenal ulcer: Griffin was moved to a private nursing home and an immediate operation only just saved his life. Presently I played my part in this drama by developing a lump that definitely was not the baby. I was ordered to bed by the school doctor to avoid a miscarriage, until such time as I could get up to see Mr Richardson, who was able to reassure me that I had not got cancer, but only a fibroid, that would in course of time subside.

In the spring term the school had a measles epidemic. It may appear that this is one long chronicle of illness. In actual fact we had no more illness than is usual in communities of young children; our school Matron was a trained nurse, we had an excellent hard-working staff, I was teaching regularly myself; the work of the school went on day after day and term after term. It was in school holidays that we felt able to pursue our personal aims and lives.

With great relief Bertie and I departed for Cornwall for the Easter holidays. We took with us Kate who, in spite of her attack as a baby, had just recovered from second measles, and John, who seemed to have escaped, as well as Billy Semple, who likewise seemed free of infection, was good company for John, and went home to America only in the summer. Alas, in Cornwall John and Billy went down with measles and Kate with chickenpox. For the 'thing' turned out to be a mixed infection and nearly every measles patient had to endure the chickenpox follow-up. Poor John and Billy, looking forward to their holiday, were almost in tears. I nursed Kate in one room, the two boys in another, and Wittgenstein came to stay. In spite of everything I recall that we were all quite gay.

I was, of course, in spite of all the hard work, very happy to be having another baby. Now that we are all so scared of the population explosion, there is much less enthusiasm for maternity. Some may find it hard to understand my passionate involvement, almost intoxication, in the idea of children as the future of mankind, and the necessity for the main purpose of society to be directed to that end. Bertie and I, for all the individualism of our personal lives, were inspired by an abiding sense of responsibility to humanity. Priggish as this attitude may sound, we could not divest ourselves of it. I really did feel that our life and love had to be worthy to lie ' 'neath Heaven our canopy, the Universe our bed.' A dream evoked for me perhaps by the fairytale mood of the tamarisk tree and my Civil Service father, for Bertie by the tradition of his family's involvement in the history of their country.

Since my child was expected in July, it seemed advisable for me to have leave of absence for the summer term. Kate had had rather a bout of illness, and she stayed in Cornwall with me for the time. Griffin Barry, too, needed to recuperate, so he came down to join us. I had not simply abandoned Griffin after getting him into the nursing home; I managed to get up to see him before school term began again, and when he was convalescent he did not lack friends in London, both English and American. But I was glad to have him down in Cornwall and see that he, as well as Kate, got nourishing food and enjoyed fresh air. Presently I took Kate back to the school, while Griffin and I went to my flat to await the arrival of the baby.

Early in June I was called to Frimley in Surrey where my father was dying. He had bought a small house there, where he and my mother had, more than once, taken care of John and his nurse when Bertie and I had had to go abroad. He had visited the school once, but I had not, of late, been able to see much of him. My dear mother, as is the way of unselfish people, had not wanted to 'worry' us and so sent for me when it was really too late, for my father was barely conscious and I do not know if he was fully aware of the presence of my sister and me. The last words that I heard him say belonged entirely to the person that he was. Offered some kind of stimulant he said: 'No, not that, it comes from a public house.' And, a little later: 'Only one woman, Sarey.' Before morning he was dead: in a chilly, grey dawn I watched the wind stir the bushes of the garden it had been his pleasure to create. I wished that I had had but a few moments really to say goodbye and tell him what he had meant to me in my life. And I was too near the time of birth to be at the funeral.

As is usual, it became tedious waiting in London for that event. Griffin was such a gregarious fellow, and I did not care, just then, to be alone on a top floor, so we were to be found, from time to time, at Kleinfeldt's, the pub which then happened to be the Bloomsbury vogue. There I made the acquaintance of the artist Nina Hamnett, once or twice Augustus John was there and J. B. S. Haldane. There I first met Paul Gillard, a young man who had some job in Plymouth but came to London now and then to escape provincial stagnation. We had him to a meal and put him up once. His beauty and intelligence impressed both of us. Paul was a communist, and—like many who were *not* in the Party—enthusiastic about the Soviet Union, from which the great films *General Line* and *Turk-Sib* were arriving. I was wearing loose Russian blouses with traditional cross-stich embroidery, well suited to my condition. When I knew him better, Paul told me that he associated me, as I appeared then, with the reverence for fertility and creation that seemed to inspire every moment of these films.

My daughter Harriet was safely born on 8 July in the London flat. Bertie had gone down to Cornwall at the end of term with John and Kate and domestic staff. Margery Spence, a student at Oxford, always known as Peter Spence, came to look after John and Kate as a summer holiday job. I intended to look after the new baby myself; John and Kate were past the age for nurses, and, as I would be a bit tied with breastfeeding, I thought that they should have someone young to go about with them. We now had a reliable young man, who had worked for my father, as chauffeur. He drove Griffin and me and the baby down from London, after which Griffin intended to go, via Cherbourg, to Paris, where just then was Henry Luce, who was, I think, about to start his journal *Fortune*. Griffin hoped that he might stand a chance of a job on it.

I was so happy to be coming back to my home, looking forward to the summer and to being with Bertie again; I thought too, that now Griffin was restored to 'health, he would be able to recoup his fortunes. I had not been in the house more than a few hours before Bertie administered the shock of telling me that he had now transferred his affections to Peter Spence. Many years later I learned, what he himself never told me, that Colette (Constance Malleson) had also just been there on a visit. All my happiness at my homecoming collapsed. I could not even speak of it all to Bertie. I wrote, and handed him a letter, saying how, loving him, I had looked forward to our reunion and had so much hoped that nothing more need come between us. Indeed all that he had done about the baby had roused in me a mood almost of exaltation, because he had acted according to what he professed, and proved himself to be all that I had believed of him. I would have given up anything for him at that moment. Of course I did not, had never expected, sexual fidelity and I knew he had been under great emotional strain. All the same I felt that it need not have been just this: to replace me once more with my children in my own home. I felt sick and shrivelled inside. All I could do was to hope that it might end with the summer. But something was gone that I feared might now never return.

Griffin left for Cherbourg on August Bank holiday. As we said good-bye, I remarked in fun that, as he might see Paul Gillard in Plymouth, I hoped they would not get into any mischief. This, however, is precisely what they did, although they were hardly to blame. An urgent telegram arrived from Griffin saying that he had been arrested and was held for £1,000 bail. I knew nothing whatever about how to arrange bail, nor could I imagine why on earth the poor man had been arrested and considered to be worth so much. He had also wired to W. N. Ewer, an old colleague, still with the *Herald*.

Clearly it was impossible to find £1,000 in Plymouth on a Bank holiday. I telegraphed the Plymouth police at once offering bail, and 'Trilby' Ewer, I believe, did likewise. I think that I ought to have gone to a local police station and sworn bail, but I doubt if that would have made any difference. Griffin was remanded in custody in Exeter gaol. Now came a letter from Paul Gillard explaining, as the incoherent telegram had not, that Griffin had failed to register as an alien. Paul feared that the consequences could be serious if he were not defended. Griffin could not be deserted in this plight, however absurd this drastic police action appeared, nor was there much time to spare. I put the three weeks old Harriet, in her travelling basket, and all her paraphernalia, into the car and together we set out for Plymouth to rescue her father. I was very glad of Hines, our quiet and very able young chauffeur. We drove straight to the Grand Hotel where Paul joined me. He fetched a solicitor, Lawrence Spear, and also got hold of the American Consul.

I explained that Griffin had had a very serious operation and this was no doubt why, during his convalescence, he had forgotten that, as an alien, he had to register. I was, even now, worried—since he was as yet hardly very robust—at the effect of this arrest and prison on his health. The American Consul said that he 'had every confidence in British justice'; while I gently suggested that I was not quite so sure, it was evident that no practical help was forthcoming from that quarter.

Paul then told me what had happened at the port. He had gone to see Griffin off, not expecting any trouble. When stopped by the Immigration people Griffin had not been able to understand what was the matter and, with the Irish intransigence with which both Paul and I were familiar, instead of trying to placate them, he became angry and stormed about 'British officialdom'. In his anger he even failed to take the hints which Paul, with a good left-winger's suspicion of the police, made that he should give him his pocket-book and diary. We both thought that it would be inadvisable to put Griffin into the witness box: we could not see him before the case came up and we had no idea what, in his perturbed state, he might say. I was prepared to give evidence.

Next day Paul's mother, who looked quite like my own, came to take charge of Harriet while we went to the Court. I went into an office and found Inspector Hutchings, and saw a notice about bail on the wall. 'Inspector Hutchings,' I said, 'has that notice any meaning, and why was Mr Barry's bail obstructed?' He evaded the question and tried to shake my confidence by saying that this man had been popping to and fro across the Channel and I could not be aware of all that he had been up to. I said that, as this gentleman had been the guest of my husband and myself and had been ill, we might be supposed to know a good deal about him. He then began to make remarks about the writings of my husband and myself, to which I replied as icily as I knew how that all that was entirely irrelevant. But I had caught the smell of politics in the whole affair.

The police case was that, not only had this man failed to register, and 'popped to and fro' across the Channel, but he actually had Soviet visas on his passport and had, into the bargain, come down to the boat with a 'known communist'. At this Mr Spear rose to object to a slur on the reputation of the other man who was not there to defend himself. I doubt if he even knew that Paul was a member of the Party. But now all was revealed: clearly the police thought that they had caught a dangerous Soviet spy, hence the determination to hold on to him and the prohibitive bail.

In the witness box I was able to explain how Griffin had been taken seriously ill in London when other friends and we had come to his help, that he had merely been a courier for a party of American tourists to Russia. The magistrates fined him £5 for the technical offence. When we came out I took some pleasure in asking the detectives to carry the invalid Griffin's bags to the car. The American Consul had been in Court and came up to shake hands with us, but I did not feel very cordial towards him. I received back my Harriet, embraced Paul's lovely mother, and above all, thanked Paul warmly. Then we drove back to Cornwall to meditate on what to do next.

The consequences of this affair, both then and later, were very serious. Press reports had referred to the case, describing Griffin as an 'undesirable alien'. We soon learned that every person whose address or phone number appeared in his diary had been visited by plain-clothes men, asking about his movements, contacts and character. There was a risk that, if he were now to leave the country, he might not be allowed back, which would deprive him of access to his daughter, which neither Bertie nor I wished to happen. When he learned all the details, Bertie was furious at the threat to liberty. In spite of what might have been his personal feelings, Bertie took steps both openly and privately to make sure that Griffin's re-entry would not be prohibited. I was much troubled: the failure to get to Paris had meant the loss of what might have been a job, and above all, it seemed to me that, for his own sake, Griffin should be employed. Paul, at our invitation, came down to Carn Voel to consult with us about the affair. He caused a moment of embarrassment when, looking round the table, he said slyly: 'I wonder what Inspector Hutchings would think of this meeting of the conspirators.' None of us had quite considered how the affair might affect him. Even he had only just realized the extent to which they had kept tabs on him. The affair had, indeed, exposed him. It seems that he quietly sized us all up and went home and told his mother that one day I would be left quite alone.

The uneasy summer came to an end. Griffin went back to London to stay pending the assurance that he would not be an unwelcome visitor to the country, Peter Spence to Oxford for the term, and Bertie, the children and I to the school. From that bad month I remember the affection of the Lancashire woman who became for us all 'our Lil', now one of my oldest friends, then on our domestic staff, who greeted me with a hug when I arrived with the baby, and thereafter did all that she could to help me with her; Bertie's integrity when political persecution was involved; and Paul's willingness, though at risk, to help his friends.

12

Things Fall Apart,
The Centre Cannot Hold

*'Rarely do those whom we love deceive us,
it is we who deceive ourselves in them.'*
Marie d'Agoult

The school was becoming established and being treated with more respect; the children worked in co-operation with one another and began
writing some group poems about which Bertie wrote a controversial
article in the *New Statesman*. In *Marriage and Morals* (1929), as in his
contribution to the Sex Congress, Bertie expressed forthright views
about nudity and sex knowledge, which he considered were beginning
to prove their soundness in the school and could diminish, if not destroy,
interest in pornography. He was totally opposed to censorship. He
immensely enjoyed the children's company, and they his. His mind at
this period was very much occupied with education, on which he began
his second book, which appeared in 1932. More visitors came and the
end-of-term Open Days were crowded. Cyril Joad came to discuss
with us first of all his idea for a Federation of Progressive Societies and
Individuals—the F.P.S.I.—which I mentioned earlier and which
became the Progressive League, the societies being, as usually happens,
unfortunately, too individualistic to federate. I remember John Strachey
coming after he lost his seat in the 1931 election, when he and I paced
the lawn together and I congratulated him on being one of the few
honest candidates in that election.

Marriage and Morals was hailed as the expression by a penetrating
mind of the new outlook on sexual and parental conduct. The partnership between Bertie and me in the school, and in seeking to influence
public opinion by our writings and speeches, began to be recognized
and valued by progressive people. There was every sign, too, that we
were both happy and united in our joint work. There was now in the
school no one to distract either of us from enjoyment of each other's
company: we discussed staff, children, politics, often with joking and
laughter and in full reliance on one another. Although we were all
part of the school community, I now had again a direct relation with
John and Kate and an element of family life, due to the presence of

Harriet. Though a trifle wistful over the new baby, Kate took to her and now and then would hang about us both. Harriet made her own considerable social contribution, for she was a most delightful baby and a source of interest and entertainment to the other children, who liked to watch her being bathed and fed. Breast-fed, she was little trouble.

Domestic staff are a constant problem in a school, but we had good people at this time, of whom Lily Howell and her husband Walter were the mainstay. My association with them was to become life-long. Both were lively north country personalities with social gifts; besides cooking, Walter could delight the children by tap-dancing and the high kick. Lily tidied and cleaned but also mothered, and was, with her warmth and intuition about people, someone whom every small child felt able to trust.

It was all very much a going concern. Had anyone told me that in little over a year Bertie would have left me and the school forever, I would simply not have believed it. The bare sequence of events which led up to our separation can be related. But there still remains the question why? How did it come about that two people who loved one another as Bertie and I certainly did, and who were so much in harmony in their political views and the mode of life and pleasures that both enjoyed, did not succeed in holding on to one another? There were external causes—in the Zeitgeist, the mood of the times, and politics— but at this distance from those years of agony, it may also be possible to disentangle the underlying instinctive and emotional needs that drove us apart.

Politically our mood was despondent, a reflection of the growing crisis. There had been a Labour Government from 1929, with Liberal support, and with right-wing leadership: Ramsay MacDonald was Prime Minister, and Philip Snowden Chancellor of the Exchequer. Arthur Henderson, as Foreign Secretary, was trying to breathe more life into the League of Nations to undo the dire effect of the reparations imposed on defeated Germany, which country had been kept going by American money until the American crash. Now everyone all round seemed to be losing money, unemployment went up by leaps and bounds and presently the Hunger Marches began. No one knew how to cope with these troubles; Ramsay's speeches became ever more rambling and woolly, there came the hackneyed old symptom of such crises—the threat to the pound, with the City and the Bank of England menacing the Labour Government about gold reserves and the need for retrenchment, especially to cut the rate of unemployment pay. The pound was fixed to the gold standard; should it float off? Mac-Donald and Snowden, who did not consult their colleagues, had not the nerve to pin a Labour Government to such a decision; MacDonald formed a National Government and went to the country.

Very naturally, education and freedom of thought, the things that Bertie and I cared about, did not, in these circumstances, receive much attention. We, like other progressives, were still battling to prevent public money, which we thought should be spent on State schools, being used to increase the grants which the Church and Catholic schools already received. We were also always disappointed that the Labour Party was concerned only with providing *more* education, but never seemed to bother about what the content of that education should be.

In the 1931 election, the Labour Party, now leaderless, angry and bitter, fought the MacDonald coalition whose slogan was 'defend the pound', 'we must tighten our belts', with little more policy to oppose this than to curse the financiers and demand that the unemployed be helped and put to work. Against the Conservative and Liberal machines and the press, they had no chance. I spoke in that election and I recall my feeling of contempt for the masochism of the electorate who accepted that it was right to inflict privation on themselves rather than to 'take arms against a sea of troubles, and by opposing, end them'. The victory of the National Government was a foregone conclusion. It came to power and promptly took the pound *off* the gold standard. Labour's defeat was so complete and humiliating that we did not have a Labour Government with a full majority and power until after the war in 1945.

Many old friendships were broken by the MacDonald 'betrayal'. Clifford Allen, with whom our personal and political relations had been close, and whose daughter Polly had been for a time in our school, went with MacDonald and subsequently became Lord Allen of Hurtwood. There was no quarrel, but Bertie and he drifted apart. Labour was in disarray, there was not much room for left-wingers within the Party; the I.L.P. was disgruntled and did not know where to turn. If you went left you now merely bumped into the Communist Party, who, with some truth, though misguided tactics, were still calling Labour leaders the 'lackeys of the bourgeoisie'. Those leaders, equally misguided, believed that their best hope of ultimate victory was to cultivate respectable middle opinion and abuse more vehemently than ever the communists and fellow-travellers. This loss of nerve here and on the Continent, and the resultant disunity, intensified later as Fascism began to appear, and was a contributing cause to the outbreak of war.

Individuals who, like Bertie and myself, had battled on and staked their hopes on helping to achieve some measure of socialist aims and a better life and happiness for our people, were now, in a sense, in a political vacuum. This, for two people who cared greatly and were incurably 'political animals', could not fail to shake our hitherto confident approach to the adventure of living.

It may well be that had Bertie and I severed all connection with Peter Spence and Griffin Barry at that time our partnership would have continued, with perhaps some minor 'affairs', for the rest of our joint lives. Of one thing I am quite certain, I did regard our partnership in work and thought as permanent and I would never willingly have left him. But I did not consider that I had property rights in his body, nor he in mine. In my speech to the Sex Congress I had said: 'No man or woman has any right to invoke legal, moral, or religious sanction to compel another into sex intercourse. No compulsion should here be recognised except the awakening of answering desire.'*

Thus, while I was absorbed in the physical needs and care of my baby, Bertie continued his relation with Peter Spence, but mainly during visits away from the school. Any man whose wife has a young baby tends to feel deprived; more so when that baby is not by him. So far as sex is concerned, I do not think that any man or woman is truly monogamous. I had never pretended that I was, and Bertie, though reared in the strictest Christian principles, had discovered during his first marriage that he was not monogamous either.

The mistake that very many people make is in supposing that the most important emotional element in marital relations is sex. This notion arises out of the patriarchal system, one of whose arch-priests was Freud, whose definitions of sex have misled countless disciples. Owing to his masculine bias, Freud perpetually confused sex with parenthood, whereas the emotions accompanying these instinctive drives are quite distinct. In most animal species, though there are exceptions, the male drive is purely for sexual satisfaction; he could not care less when it comes to feeding and defending the resultant offspring. Parental feeling is, in its origins, female, maternal. In our own species, obviously, a woman distinguishes, even on the physical, biological plane, between the sex act and bearing the child. By a long process of social and cultural evolution parenthood has absorbed also the male, who, linking it all up with property and possession, takes on the dominant parental role. The male will then, as has been too often observed in the struggle for women's liberation, add insult to injury by proclaiming that woman is unfit to take part in the masculine activities of public life, just because she is more closely child-centred and thus, it is alleged, less objective than he.

Since Freud could only imagine sex in male terms, he missed the whole point of the relations between children and their parents: a mother and son who have, as is natural, a tender feeling for one another, are deemed to be sexually in love, similarly a father and daughter. But family ties are infinitely more subtle and complex. Parents feed and protect their young, see in them their own immortality and perhaps the fulfilment of frustrated ambitions; children look for security, for understanding, for persons to serve as models for living, but who will also stand ready to help them achieve their own aims, persons who will not, even in adversity, let them down. I would say that the part of the creative impulse in men and women that is parental is both more powerful and fundamental than sex. For this reason: it does not seek

* *World League for Sex Reform Congress* (Kegan Paul, 1930), p. 27

immediate pleasure, but rather, aiming at survival, subtly pervades a personality, unconsciously guiding both action and thought.

What has all this to do with Bertie and me? In the early days of our love it was clear that, though he was—as I was too—a romantic lover, what drew him to seek a more permanent relation with me was my expressed willingness to have children. Indeed at that point the possibility that I might become pregnant was the determining factor that would clinch our relationship. If this did not happen neither of us was sure that we wanted to be in any way tied or committed. Even so, what drew us to one another was not simply an urgent desire to get into the same bed. Oddly enough, both his generation and mine, who had fed upon the notion of love as some irresistible all-consuming passion, had also been reared in the suppression or concealment of the physical facts of sex. Love to Bertie as a very young man must have been something ethereal, spiritual, unrelated to physical desire. To discover later the strength of those desires which he had been taught to consider sinful must have demanded a difficult, if not painful adjustment. To him love was inseparable from poetry, as indeed it was to me. We had come together in a roseate haze of idealism, and delight in intellectual exchanges, united by our mutual provenance—the cultural revolution issuing from the Cambridge of those days.

In love, too, Bertie was a perfectionist; the 'spiritual' bond must exist, if it were broken then love might come to an end. In this, as in other matters, Bertie was not fully aware of his underlying motives; that spiritual bond might well mean that a wife must agree with him in every detail, so that she might be fully possessed. I was amazed, for instance, when I read in his account of our journey to China that he had thought I did not love him because I argued with him heatedly about Russia! What sort of love is it that does not permit the lovers to disagree? In my mood on returning from Russia, which I have described, the surest proof of how deeply I loved him was that I had agreed to set out for China with him at all. From our very first meeting I had wanted to be with him in order to take care of him, and I believe that this is what he wanted of me too. Deep within Bertie was that rather scared little boy, an orphan, with an imposing, aloof grandmother, a much bigger, more aggressive brother, constantly in the care of servants who gave him exaggerated respect, but not much—at least he gives no hint of this—affection. Once when I was teasing him about his odd feet, he told me that they had remarked in the servants' hall on his high instep. 'Ah, yes,' said one of them, 'that's because of his high birth.' A mother for his son, whose maternal care would spill over to him—perhaps this (under all the trimmings) was his deepest need. The more so after the war years, when, whether hated or admired, he had been virtually alone.

My background had been very different. I was a spoiled child, my father's darling. I had worked hard, and success had come my way; I had much self-confidence, but not when it came to love in terms of a life partnership. In this I was diffident, with all the silly schoolgirl notions of one day meeting 'Mr Right'. So I was looking for a man in whom I might place as much trust as in my father, who, in the whole of my life, though we often disagreed, had never once let me down.

By 1931 I was a very different person from the young woman to whom having a baby had been an inconvenient interruption to intellectual activity, and who had written to Ogden, 'if I have two, I will have done enough'. In addition to my third child, I was mothering the children of other parents; Griffin's illness and other misfortunes had drawn me into some maternal care of him. My mother, instead of my father, had now risen up within me. I was almost, in my faith in the work of the school and my varied political causes, becoming a professional mother-figure. It was very foolish of me, fully occupied as I was, not to have perceived how Bertie must have felt after failing, as he believed, to achieve fatherhood once more, and with a wife virtually overworked in our joint enterprise, as he was in writing to help provide for it financially. But he was equally foolish in not discussing the whole situation with me. We were not only partners in the school; ever since we came back from China, we had been partners in political work. I used to think about him then as a comrade in the socialist cause, marching together side by side, in terms of the first German song I ever learned, *Ich hatt' einen Kameraden*. And had not my love for him, in terms of that sonnet of Shakespeare's that moves me more than any other poem, when he was nearly dying in Peking 'borne it out unto the edge of doom'?

There is indeed nothing more foolish in marriage, or any love partnership, than the failure to open up an honest discussion when a 'dangerous corner' has been reached. A sense of obligation to the two other people concerned was what, I think, inhibited us both. So Bertie went ahead with writing *The Conquest of Happiness*, a book which did well and brought him many new admirers, at the time when our own happiness was on the point of being destroyed.

In 1931 Bertie's brother Frank died suddenly, with the result that Bertie now succeeded to the Earldom. When someone rang me up to congratulate me on becoming a Countess, I remarked that titles were a lot of nonsense, and the name Bertrand Russell was more distinguished than any other he could bear. The press immediately ran a story of the Earl who did not wish to be known by his title. My recollection is that my chance remark set this off, but I may be mistaken. And looking back now over those next few years, I am not sure if this is what Bertie would really have intended. I confess I am still completely bewildered about people's attitude to titles. I can understand a man or woman, who has done good public work, accepting to go to the Lords on a 'life' basis, so long as the Lords exists. There are many debates in the Lords, now that there are many Life Peers, that are far more fruitful in discussion of real issues than the Party-ridden wrangles in the Commons. It is the attitude to hereditary titles that I find hard to understand. It seems to convey a subtle suggestion of mysterious rights, of being a superior person, of the world owing one a living, and certainly owing some respect that the individual concerned would not, in his own right, earn. This sort of thing does happen to people on whom titles descend. Bertie needed no fresh claims to distinction; none the less I am convinced that, with that Earldom, some of the family mantle of dignity and tradition descended on his shoulders and insidiously began to affect his personal attitude, though not at first his public statements of his views.

With the approach of the summer holidays, Bertie suggested to me that, instead of going to Cornwall, we should spend the summer in France, renting a villa in which he and Peter Spence and Griffin and I, with John, Kate and Harriet would stay. This was not my idea of the happiest holiday for me, but it seemed the most in accord with the moral principles by which we had been living, and which I had never expected to be easy. At least this plan would mean the family being together; Bertie and I would not be taking separate holidays to meet other commitments. We decided to investigate Hendaye, which had an attractive 'plage'. We had not been alone together for some time; there was always work and company at the school, and weaning Harriet had been a busier and more complicated process than is normal, for she had shown an intolerance of cow's milk on which I had had to get specialist advice.

Both Bertie and I enjoyed this spurt of freedom from responsibility, with a few days of comfort at the Hotel Eskualduana. As we lunched and chatted undisturbed, 'Why,' said he, 'after all this time you can still laugh at my jokes!' How is it that, while I now recall nothing of our conversation, that remark stands out as the one unforgettable moment of our short stay? I know that, when it was made, I felt more like tears than laughter. I was not tired of him, my feeling was unchanging; it was he himself who had placed a barrier between us, it was not for me, but for him to cross it. I was confident that our loyalty to one another was unbreakable. But, intensely competitive though I was in work at school and college—as the system almost obliged me to be— I was quite unable to fight for my own hand in love, whether by tactics or feminine wiles. Love must be freely given, not obsequiously sought.

We found and rented for the summer the villa Costa Loria, which was admirably suited to our purpose. It faced the estuary rather than the sea; one could open the shutters to the morning sun and a wide view of the River Bidassoa, framed by the mountains, and, just at the edge, by the exquisite spires of Fontarabia, perched on its hill, sounding the rich music of its bells across the water. There was a room for each one of us, simply furnished. With remarkably little fuss we travelled down and settled in, Harriet's cot and playpen and all. A gentle, capable woman, fair-haired and blue-eyed, called Émilie, came to cook and clean for us—she gave us delicious food.

Hendaye was then not much frequented by English people, the clientèle was Spanish and French. The Basque country, both sides of the frontier, was rich in ancient history. Not far away was the pass where Roland and his *preux chevaliers* had not blown the famous horn but died to cover the retreat of Charlemagne's army—a tale which I had always loved. Before long many other *preux chevaliers* would secretly cross those mountain passes and the clear, shallow waters of the Bidassoa to give their lives in another effort to deliver another people from oppression. In 1931, whatever hidden intrigues were hatching on those borders, Hendaye was a beautiful and romantic setting for a holiday. A noisy, boisterous lot of Spaniards, who had an aristocratic air, lived in a villa across the road from us. Harriet, one year old, standing in her cot on the balcony of my room, would be greeted by them with waves and shouts, to which she responded gaily, while we joked about her probably fraternizing with the wrong faction. Harriet was a most vigorous and sociable person. Once, left alone in her playpen while we were all at lunch, she pushed the whole contraption from the lounge through the double doors into the dining-room, beaming with pride at her achievement.

At meals we were often a very gay company, at other times differences of age and taste kept us apart. John and Kate climbed the mountains with their father and Peter Spence, but we could all, including Harriet, enjoy the golden sand and a sea that had tides and Atlantic rollers, just like Cornwall. There were, too, terrific thunderstorms when the tamarisk trees the whole length of the Hendaye front would sway in the strong westerly wind.

The small town of Hendaye stands on a hill some distance from the beach. It had an oblong-shaped 'place' with a bandstand in the middle. Here was staged the fiesta of the Fiery Bull, probably an ancient custom, but then already beginning to be a special show for summer visitors. Everyone dressed up gaily for the occasion, and trekked the mile or more up to the town, where the cafés lining the square were filled with drinkers, and you might be offered a swallow from the neck of a wineskin, a trap for the novice, who would surely receive the wine down his front instead of in his mouth. There was dancing to the band, and the local youths were very free with confetti. Inside the effigy of the bull, which was studded with fireworks, were two men. As the fireworks sparkled and exploded the bull charged about among the crowd who alternately baited him and ran from him. Griffin and John and I were at this fiesta, but I think the others stayed at home. Nine-year-old John became very excited and chased the bull in all directions, until, as he was small for his age, I became alarmed and diving into the excited crowd seized him and stood him on the edge of the bandstand from which he had a good safe view. The final firework on the bull was a rocket from his head, with which his soul—as we liked to say—went up to Heaven. It was 1949 when I went to Hendaye again with a party of friends; we found the fiestas and the Fiery Bull still in vogue, as well as the ancient traditional Basque dances. By then the Spaniards who chose to live that side of the border were the Republican refugees.

One day we found our gentle Émilie in tears: somehow a cat had managed to get her canary. It seemed that there was a 'bird man' in Fontarabia. Unknown to Émilie, Griffin, John, Kate and I hired a boatman to ferry us across. We climbed the steep streets, and there in his kitchen we came upon an elderly man shredding meat to incredible fineness with which to feed his nightingale. In an entire room next to the kitchen, behind wire netting, perched, flew, fluttered, chirped and sang incessantly an endless variety of birds. As we returned with a bird for Émilie, the whole expedition had for us a magic quality. Beauty, magic, and romance will forever be associated for me with the Basque country.

. Unlike many of his compatriots, Griffin had an ability to acclimatize himself, which made it a pleasure to spend time with him abroad. A man with a sense of adventure, a roving man, like my sailor uncles, always had an appeal for me. But such men, by their very nature, are not usually—unlike some sailors when on shore—domesticated. Griffin was immensely proud of his small daughter and delighted to play with her and show her off. But when, as almost invariably happened with him, some friends or acquaintances turned up, he would naturally exercise what he felt was his male prerogative to spend an evening in their company, while if anyone had to mind the baby, it would be me. Although at times I was angry and also lonely, I did not expect anything different. He was not being asked, or even permitted, to establish a family relation with me; what is more I was quite sure that this responsibility was the last thing which he really desired.

A friend of his, Stanley Nott, arrived one day on his own in his car. Griffin thought it would be fun to go with him over the border as far, perhaps, as Pamplona. Émilie found for us a friend of hers, a comfortable woman who would take care of Harriet for a day or two, to enable me to go too. The result was an unexpected and exciting experience. As we drove it seemed to us that a number of people, on foot, some in carts, appearing over the hills and from the side roads, were also on their way to Pamplona. As it was not the time for the famous bull running, we imagined there might be some sort of fiesta. We booked in at an hotel just off the central square, and seated ourselves in a café, watching the crowds milling round the bandstand where the band was playing. Presently what looked like a small disturbance seemed to be taking place among the packed crowd and suddenly people moved out from the arcade under which we were sitting and the waiters began to put up the shutters of the cafés. Wondering why they should start to close so early in the evening, we moved out among the crowd in the square. The band went on playing. An ugly tension began to be felt among the crowd—one sensed that some violent action was imminent. I saw a very military-looking man come to the bandstand and the music ceased. The silence was tense. Some impulse impelled me to get up on a bench in the square to take a look round. What I saw appalled me. The entire square was now surrounded by soldiery, cavalry at the corners. 'Good Lord,' I said, jumping down, 'soldiers! It looks as if they're going to shoot.' At that moment they did—in the air—and the whole crowd stampeded towards the bandstand, we with them, except for Stanley Nott, who, with complete sangfroid, actually *walked* across. As we did not know what all this was about, it did not seem quite the place for foreigners. The door of our hotel was bolted and barred, we had to bang for some time before a scared porter let us in.

So far as we made out, no one got killed, but half the night the soldiers (cavalry and all) and the populace chased each other round the streets. We could see them from our hotel window; men would run round the corner of the narrow streets waving cloaks or scarves and baiting the military like bulls in the ring. Then the soldiers would charge and the demonstrators rapidly retreat. So far as innocent pleasure was concerned, our expedition was a dead loss, but the incipient riot was worth the journey. We learned later that it had been a demonstration in favour of a royalist Pretender. In any case, I remarked that if I were going to be shot in a riot, I would prefer it to be for a cause in which I believed.

How was it possible, some might ask, for the Hendaye household to live together in such harmony? The young people who now live together in communes would probably understand, but this was more than forty years ago in a very different moral climate. The foundation for it all was love for people and especially for children, as Bertie and I then understood it. We were, in the school, running a wider free community, in which the harmony of human relations was a vital element. Creative love, whatever effort might be required, must not indulge in possessive jealousy. But can one love intimately two people at the same time? Men have answered this question for centuries by living with both mistresses and wives, or even by polygamy. Mostly, in Western civilization, they kept their wives in cold storage; the wife who took a lover risked severe penalties, even death. Women who fought against this double standard at first sought to impose their more rigid code upon men; only gradually did they come to demand a less rigid one for themselves. To enjoy the company of two women and sex relations with both is an accepted custom for men: it is no more difficult for a woman with two men, and is, indeed, a marital custom among some peoples. But to act against the current mores of one's own society did require a good deal of nerve and mutual tolerance. In such exchanges as took place between Bertie and myself during the holiday at Hendaye, it was clear that we both felt that our partnership was the stable element. We were embarked on a joint enterprise, were both working to earn for our children. The others, though attracted by our company, were none the less free to live and work as they wished, they were under no obligation to us and thus might at any time depart. At the same time, we did all feel that the quartet in itself had some meaning.

Towards the end of the summer it seemed that for Bertie there came some indication that he might, after all, have another child. This was a possibility that I welcomed; I had always had a fixed idea that no chance of a child for a man of such brilliance must be missed. We all talked about this and there emerged something that I often referred to as the 'pact of Hendaye', in that we all agreed that any child that might be born would not be let down by any of us and could be cared for in the school if desired.

Griffin and I left with Harriet before the others so that I might get things ready for the school term, Griffin remaining in Paris. Since it also seemed possible that Griffin and I might be having another child, I made an appointment to see Mr Richardson soon after I got home. There was no doubt about it, I was pregnant. Mr Richardson would be delighted, he said, to look after me and deliver the baby, as he had done for the other three. But, as a good friend, aware of the situation, he did also imply that there was another way out, though we both knew that it was out of the question for him to undertake an abortion.

This was one of the most difficult decisions of my whole life; nor is it possible even now to make public all the factors which influenced me. I had always supported women's right, for what they thought to be sufficient reason, to the termination of a pregnancy by safe, surgical methods. But I simply could not bring myself to do away with this child. Most mothers who have borne children whom they did not quite intend, usually say that they have no regrets and 'would not be without any one of them'. Nor, in spite of what it was to cost me, have I ever regretted this birth. But my decision was rational as well as instinctive: the child's heredity, as far as we could judge, would give it a good chance, and it was not likely to starve or lack care. Further, in the face of my declared principle that sound motherhood should not be subject to social and legal conventions, I had no right to deny life to this child.

Perhaps this is the moment to say how grateful I am to those two children, when adults, not only for affection, pleasant company, stimulating discussion, practical help and advice, but also for their achievements apart from any relation to me, in which they have fully justified their existence. A parent's testimony could hardly say more.

The autumn term saw me back in sole charge of the school, while Bertie went on another lecture tour to America. The school was becoming less of a financial burden; at the same time Bertie was getting contracts for regular articles which he could dictate in his own time at home. On his return he specially congratulated me on having run the school very well during that term. Peter Spence was with us for the Christmas holidays and returned to Oxford for the term. My relations with Griffin were not easy. I felt that I was unfair to him in that I knew I would not leave Bertie and my work, because they came first in my feelings. At the same time we enjoyed each other's company, except when he would stir a quarrel by his habit of deliberate provocation, often inspired by a masculine anti-female instinct which was very strong in him. He, too, attached importance to what he might achieve in work—this was another bone of contention. Like many journalists, he wanted to write a book which would be something more permanent than the eternal ephemeral articles. The trouble was that, also like journalists when they are not working to a deadline, although there was much in his experience that he might have recorded, he simply did not get on with it. When it came to writing, he was a perfectionist. Mary Vorse, who knew him well, and was herself a very well-known and competent American left-wing journalist, once said to me: 'Griffin wants to be a *writer*; I merely *write*.'

Griffin made it quite plain to me, even at this time, that he did not want to be impeded in his 'chance' in life, which could mean nothing less than a wish not to take on family responsibilities. In the circumstances, he had a right to respect for his liberty; I, too, would have been glad to see him achieve. Some literary friends whom he valued were then in a group at Puerto Pollensa, Majorca. Griffin decided to go there and hoped that I would presently join them for a time. I was to be away from the school in the last months of pregnancy, so in mid-January 1932 I set out for Majorca—a French Customs officer remarked to me: '*Vous partez en Espagne comme ça, Madame?*' so obvious was by then my condition. But it seemed that the alternative would have been lonely boredom somewhere or other.

I have come to believe that this departure was a mistake. It was meant to be tactful towards Bertie, but I cannot say that I really wanted to go or that I took much pleasure in this stay abroad. I have often thought things might have been different had I brought myself to sacrifice that baby. And I now think that, had I remained at home, Bertie and I would have found some way round our difficulties and stayed together. We missed each other terribly: I wrote to him twice from the train en route and telegraphed my safe arrival in Palma; in some ways we had never been closer than at this time. We were in constant touch about the school business and about what was happening in political life. It seems that the staff may have missed me too, to judge by a comical cartoon I received from them headed 'The Pore Staff' showing them seated round a table at a staff meeting, whilst in the foreground I was cycling away towards a signpost marked U.S.A., followed by a toddling child.

Their fears were groundless. There was pleasure for me in the beauty of Majorca, though I thought that part chosen by the small American colony was bare and sombre compared with other parts which I had seen there with Bertie. There were interesting people—Jed Taggard, the poetess, whom I really liked, and whose talented daughter Marcia Wolf later came to the school, and Gilbert Seldes, the well-known American journalist, was there too. Most of such temporary or permanent ex-patriates went abroad in order to lead unconventional lives, to separate from or change husbands or wives. In this respect Griffin and I could not claim to be different. But underlying the parties with long-winded special cookings, drinking and talking which could be fun, there rumbled passionate rivalries and tragic griefs. I was, myself, not happy in this atmosphere, and glad that Griffin and I were able to rent a small whitewashed cottage, with a charcoal stove and a woman called Maria who saved me most of the domestic chores, leaving me free for writing. I did an article on 'Love and Friendship' commissioned by someone, and began to write the book which I had long projected, which was later published as *In Defence of Children*.

From home our splendid secretary, Mrs Harrington, sent me out the weeklies after they had been read: Gerald Barry had started the *Week-End Review* which was enterprising and outspoken. To Bertie's surprise it printed a letter from me which mentioned homosexuality, and which, apparently, the staff and he thought courageous in its frankness. I worked steadily and kept in touch because the money I had came from my earnings from articles, and I had not published a book for some time. Now I had to consider the expense of a second child.

Once we went by bus along the coastal road to Deyá where Griffin said that Robert Graves, the poet, had his home. At Deyá we walked what seemed to me, carrying my burden, a very long way by a narrow path half-way down a ravine that led to the sea, just like such valleys in Cornwall. We *did* find Robert Graves, he came up to the bistro at the top and talked and drank wine with us. Early in 1965 I came across a review of his book *Mammon and The Black Goddess*, in which was quoted that superb remark of Graves—which the reviewer clearly did not take to be seriously meant: 'In my view the political and social confusion of these last three thousand years has been entirely due to man's revolt against woman as a priestess of natural magic, and his defeat of her wisdom by the use of intellect.' I felt impelled to write and thank Robert Graves for his insight. I said that he had possibly forgotten my visit in 1932, and that my 'American friend', who had been with me, was now dead. His reply was witty and, in its brevity, very much to the point:

30 April 1965

Dear Dora,
    Yes: matriarchy and patriarchy were both ugly but necessary experiments—

Mechanarchy is necessary only as a means of bringing about a crash and a return to whatever the original true relation of men and women was in say 300,000 BC: but with a consciousness of its unhappy historic alternatives never to be tried again.

Or words to that effect.

Yours,
Robert Graves

Yes, I remember your visit with Barry, how long ago it seems.

During the month that I was away Bertie wrote to me practically every other day. These letters tell just what was in his mind at that time. He congratulated me again on how well I had run the school when he was away lecturing and said that the one question about its continuance was financial, and that it would be very distasteful to give it up. He was himself actively involved, spending time each day after tea with the children, reading to them, and teaching one small backward boy to read. He wrote to me about prospective pupils and asked my advice about someone who wanted to come on the staff; we agreed that we both thought him unsuitable. He told about the books he was reading. On politics he was furious with the French manipulations of gold in Europe; the world was going to the devil and Russia was the only hope. He went to lunch with the Soviet Ambassador. Labour was feeble and without policy, he wanted to spend more time in London to stir up the Labour Party, and thought he would almost certainly take his seat in the Lords.

After he had left the school and considerably changed his views on education, Bertie did it much harm by speaking and writing disparagingly about it, as he does in the brief mention in his autobiography. But at this time, unless he deliberately misled me, which I find it hard to suppose, he was very much involved with it. I had got some good people on the staff, and that year Bertie found that he did not have to contribute financially to the school funds; we had economized by giving up the extra house for visitors, though this meant that we were really short of accommodation even for children and staff at Telegraph House itself.

Every letter at that time showed his feeling for the children, and there is scarcely one in which he did not say how delicious Harriet had become, he wished she were his own daughter. About Peter and me he said frankly that he was worried, he perceived rightly that I was unhappy in Majorca, but did not know how to avoid hurting both of us. I felt quite unable to pry into their relation to one another, but from Bertie's account of what was happening, it did seem as though they meant, ultimately, to end the affair. I felt concern about both of them, and accepted Bertie's statement that he had some responsibility for her. He suggested that on finishing at Oxford, Peter should come and teach for a time in the school, that we should build another bungalow to make more room. He was sure that Peter, whatever she might feel at the moment, would presently find the call of her own generation irresistible and want to marry a younger man. He proposed to do nothing that would make this less likely. He said in plain words that he did not want our marriage to break up, that his affection for me was deep and indestructible, the more so for no longer being sexual; that he wanted to grow old with me and for John and Kate to have the example of what he called my courage and public spirit. He did not despair. More than once he wrote how much he wished I were at home.

I accepted that all these problems could be considered once I was over the birth of the baby. I believed, as he professed to do, that we were inextricably entangled with one another, as two people are who have shared responsibilities and anxieties over the years, whose minds answered to one another on so many political and intellectual issues. In any union like this each absorbs elements of the other, thus creating a unity, not of the flesh, but such that to separate is to lose a vital part of the inner self.

Early in March I came back to Telegraph House; I remember that Bertie came out to greet me warmly. I was obliged to go almost at once to London, where a friend had lent me, with Griffin, a top floor in Russell Square until I went into the nursing home. On 22 March 1932 I received a letter from Bertie in which he implied that he was now in less doubt about his relation with Peter, and wished to live with her altogether as soon as she left Oxford that summer. I showed Griffin the letter and said something like 'so much for loyalty'. He said, 'I think it is time that I went back to America.' I threw a teacup at him. Although for years afterwards he insisted that I misunderstood his meaning, at that moment any real relation between us came to an end. Suddenly I realized that the baby was starting up prematurely. I rang the doctor and nursing home, packed a suitcase, Griffin got a taxi and in the early hours next day my son Roderick was born.

Even in the hurried departure from the flat, I wrote to Bertie saying that he had shown considerable confidence in my vital strength in sending me such a letter at this critical moment. I was, naturally, a bit confused as to what to do next. Bertie's letter did not even say that the break was meant to be final; he intimated that, though he wanted a domestic life with Peter, how long it would continue might depend on whether or not she had a child. He implied too, that the break was not to come till term at Oxford was over in the summer. Bertie paid a courtesy call at the nursing home and was his usual affectionate self. Gip Wells, who was a good friend, was another visitor; he advised me that I needed a good lawyer at this juncture, something which had simply not occurred to me. However, he sent Mr Maw, of Rowe and Maw, to my bedside to take some preliminary details. My one idea was to get back to the school just as soon as the doctor would permit. I was back on about 8 April, affectionately received by all the staff, only to find that Bertie had departed for our home in Cornwall with Peter Spence. She did not return to Oxford for the final term.

At first I could not believe that Bertie would do such a thing to me, surely this must be some temporary arrangement to avoid his embarrassment when I arrived back with my child. So much had been left over for discussion when I was about again; I had been prepared to consider closing the school, and expected to learn from Bertie what he might have in mind for the future, if we did so, and to let him know my own feelings about our personal lives as well as public affairs. I might 'laugh at his jokes still', but apparently he no longer cared to listen to anything serious I might have to say, or for that houseful of children and staff left in a state of uncertainty. This was entirely out of character. What could have happened to the man I had all but worshipped since I had first met him in 1916? Of course there is nothing unusual about a husband suddenly leaving a wife for a younger woman, but as a rule this happens when there has been estrangement within the marriage, or refusal by the wife to tolerate infidelities. And then Bertie and I had created what is now known as a 'public image' by our unorthodox views on marital conduct. A musical hall song of the day sounded out frequently from the gramophone of the school staff: 'Ain't it grand, to be blooming well dead!' It seemed so appropriate that I forbore to ask them to stop harrowing my feelings by playing it.

Looking at these events coolly, at this distance in time, I can discern Bertie's motives more clearly, as I could not then in my bewilderment; half of me had been torn out by his departure and I was finding it hard to think and take decisions. In point of fact I ought not to have been astonished. He was acting with the recklessness of the gambler and adventurer, the arrogance of an aristocrat—all characteristics which I had known to exist within him, and some of which I admired. He was about to take his seat as a Lord; consorting with the Webbs over procedure, he had become convinced that he could make a greater contribution to public life and politics; like Caesar he was ambitious. The school was in his way; quite rightly he believed that it took too much of his time, energy and finance. An attractive young woman was prepared to join with him in a new life's adventure and—what I think was the strongest impulse—they might have a child. The birth of my son rankled. What was to be done about this wife who seemed to be immersed in the school and wedded to those left-wing views on education, sex and marriage which, it was true, we had been advocating together, but by which, apparently, she actually thought it right to live? He also wished, as became evident later, to dissociate himself from what he thought was my too sympathetic attitude to the Soviet Union, with which he did not agree and which, in part for his own purposes, he greatly exaggerated.

For me in this rupture the main causes of bitterness were that he had not given an opportunity for discussion, had not realized that I, too, was capable of adapting and changing, and, also with a spirit of adventure, would have much to contribute in any work within my competence. Most bitter thought of all, I was positive that had he really greatly desired it, we could have had another child together.

This capacity to up anchor and away, to go off at a tangent, must be seen as the element in Bertie Russell which made possible his several very courageous stands in national and international affairs. Those who have admired him as a brilliant mathematician and philosopher, or those who have seen him as the heroic champion of unpopular causes, almost a Christ figure, perhaps overlook the less admirable motives which sustained him, but without which he would not have been what he was. Pride demanded that he uphold the tradition of a family which had played its part in history, which expected—as he liked to point out in fun—that its men should so live as to have equestrian statues put up to them after death. He was not above intense rivalry, and for himself he needed fame and power over the multitude, though he would 'not follow the multitude to do evil', as instructed on the flyleaf of his Bible by his grandmother.

That such a man would hurt many people on his way was inevitable; the tragic flaw was that he accepted that inevitability with so little regret. Though he loved the multitudes and suffered with their suffering, he still remained aloof from them because the aristocrat in him lacked the common touch.

In the life of his brother Frank, Earl Russell, consistent useful work in public affairs went hand in hand with a certain degree of incompetence in marital life. I have often thought this coolness and detachment in personal relations to be a Russell characteristic; but it may well be that it is not possible, if you spread your love over the human race, to have much left over to dispense within your home. Or, if you are born to a position of responsibility in affairs of State, not to give this precedence over the precarious happiness of individuals, including yourself.

Not that this fully explains Bertie Russell: he was more complex. For a cause in which he believed, or for sheer love of mischief, he would thumb his nose at the Establishment; and he cared a good deal about his personal happiness. He could passionately and romantically 'fall in love', with so deep a devotion that he could not live without the beloved; but he was able, should a new love come his way, so completely to set aside the old one as almost to forget her existence and her very nature.

It may be said that most husbands and wives, when they break their partnership, are well advised to forget in this way; and where, as it now seems, sexual attraction is accepted as the sole motive for the contraction or continuance of a marriage, such capacity to forget may well be easy. It is also very much part of the code that a man of genius, artist or writer, needs a succession of women for inspiration. The code does not as yet hold to quite the same extent for women in regard to their men.

245

That lovers do partake of each other's personality is a sublime truth; what I dislike is the implication that they should so *use* one another, especially as men have been allowed to use women. Such a calculation ought not—though it does often—play a part in love. Those who reviewed Bertie Russell's autobiography at times made great play with the succession of his various wives, as has been done about the mistresses of Picasso and others, as if they were acquired as property for temporary use. I am not sure that this, in the last analysis, was not the view of Bertie himself. However that may be, on behalf of wives so regarded, I resent this. Wives are people, and I so lived with Bertie as to make it clear that this was the case. Which may be why he left me. He expressed much sorrow at hurting me by his departure; the wrench must also have been very painful for him, though, in the circumstances, he could hardly admit it.

Over the next two years there was a good deal of indecision. I missed the easy way we used to consult with one another, the great fun we always had, our frequent laughter. I worried, too, about being deprived of my care of Bertie, in which I had taken some pride. I did not think him a very good judge of people, and had been accustomed to try tactfully to protect him from getting involved with people I thought untrustworthy. Again, it was his habit—as also his effectiveness in propaganda—to exaggerate the cruelty and evil intentions of governments and individuals. In this way he would shake public complacency and stir the public conscience. But at times it meant that he himself was in a fever of rage and distress beyond what the occasion required. I was able then sometimes to soothe him and give him time to avoid a rash statement or action. He would stop pacing the floor in his indignation and say: 'You really think he—or they—is not so bad as all that?' Mostly, of course, his pessimism about human beings in the mass or in power was only too well founded. But a sensitive man should not live at white heat all the time.

In such a sharp rupture one tends to stress—like Shaw's Candida to her husband—how necessary one is to the lost partner, when in truth it is the aching void within oneself for love, understanding, daily habits, long taken for granted, that matters. Bertie, at least, did not divest himself at once of wifely care; he took it for granted that I would send an extra bed or linen and domestic staff down to Cornwall at his request. Maybe he still could not really believe that the separation was permanent. Twice during this time, once on a personal visit, he did suggest calling the whole thing off. Perhaps he realized, as I did, how hard it was, at that time, for us to do without one another, or perhaps he had believed, having never asked me straight out, that I would inevitably leave him for Griffin. He knew that I would never go to live in America. He definitely wanted me to close the school, though with regret, and suggested that, in that event, I should come down with the children to Cornwall, where Peter Spence was. Of course he wanted us both. But after the shock of his repudiation of all he had written to me when I was abroad, I could no longer trust him, and I could not see what my position might be if, in time to come, I should be the one no longer wanted. Without the school, what should I then have left?

Bertie expressed the hope that everything could be settled without ill feeling on both sides. But in a very short time his whole tone changed so much that I could not recognize the person with whom I was dealing; there was no point of contact, no reciprocal feeling left. I suppose this is the common experience of the deserted partner in love or marriage, to come up against a blank wall of indifference so complete as to seem hardly conceivable. Unfortunately it puts the one who cannot help grieving at a disadvantage in negotiations, which require a cool head.

Within just over a week of leaving me Bertie had already intimated that he would like a divorce and would consult his solicitors as to whether this might be possible. This information reached me on 4 April when I was still in the nursing home. After he had so many times told me that it did not matter what we did within our marriage, since we would never want a divorce, this was another bombshell. But before I start on the legal and emotional consequences of this request, I want to make clear in what way Bertie and I differed about the nature of this break and indeed, about our concepts of love.

Bertie has written in his autobiography of how he became less convinced of pacifist principles as he watched the Nazis rise to power, a mood which he carried over into his attitude towards freedom and discipline in the school. Authority, he says, is necessary to prevent the strong from oppressing the weak. Since, however, it was increasing discipline and cruel authority which were the menace within Germany, there is something in this argument that is inconsistent in an educator. But this is not the point I wish to argue. He goes on to relate his changing view of our marriage:

> In my second marriage I had tried to preserve that respect for my wife's liberty which I thought that my creed enjoined. I found, however, that my capacity for forgiveness and what may be called Christian love was not equal to the demands I was making on it and that persistence in a hopeless endeavour would do much harm to me, while not achieving the intended good to others. Anybody else could have told me in advance, but I was blinded by theory . . . To follow scientific intelligence wherever it may lead me had always seemed to me the most imperative of moral precepts for me and I have followed this precept even when it has involved a loss of what I myself had taken for deep spiritual insight.*

* *The Autobiography of Bertrand Russell, 1914–1944* vol. II (Allen and Unwin, 1968), pp. 192–3

When I read this and some of the later passages about how he wanted to get me and the school out of Telegraph House, I thought that either his memory was at fault, or this man had never loved me. How could he forget how we had battled together for his life in Peking, our deep intimacy, our joint efforts for socialism, sex freedom, women's rights? Now I see how he was then, like so many of his and my contemporaries, in close accord with the mood of the times, retreating in alarm from the left-wing cultural revolution, moving back into orthodoxies. It is true that we both, in the enthusiasm at that time for science as a yardstick, had rejected morality that was based on superstition, an attitude that I imbibed largely from him, since I was not much impressed with what science-as-industry was doing in the world. But all this about Christian love and forgiveness had nothing whatever to do with our relations. I had married him at his urgent request to legitimize our son, on the understanding that this marriage was not to be regarded in the orthodox legal sense. I did not lay claim to object to his infidelities, nor to forgive him for them; I did not hold that they required forgiveness. The possessive tone of 'my wife', 'my husband', did not exist in my vocabulary.

Bertie and I had been living outside these proprietory concepts and patriarchal sanctions. He says that his moral attitude to my having children by another man was based upon science; in other words it was a cool, intellectual judgment, not inspired, as I had believed at the time, by a wider, generous altruism, and, in the event, contrary to his natural possessive instincts. But to me the laws enforcing patrilineal descent were contrary to biological common sense, in that a man might legally be the father of a child, with whose conception he had had nothing whatever to do. Hereditary titles, succession and inheritance were all part of the patriarchal, discriminatory process and—to me—antagonistic to children's natural rights, by which each child is born to be a unique individual, irrespective of his origins. In that context I was writing: 'In spite of all our laws for the so-called protection of women and children, the sanctity of the home and the permanence of love, is there yet any guarantee for a man of the paternity of his children, except that a mother should speak the truth? And is truth to be expected from frightened slaves?'* Matrilineal descent was clearly the more logical, none the less I held that a child had the right to know both father and mother.

Perhaps Bertie and I were typical of male and female approaches to love, or what men, for themselves, have made of love in the Christian world. Love to Bertie meant 'spiritual insight', idealizing the loved one, something of the courtly romance of the troubadours; but it also meant the eighteenth-century pleasure in pursuing a desirable young woman. His ideal vision of love did *partake* of the 'creative' impulse extolled by

---

* *In Defence of Children* (Hamish Hamilton, 1932), p. 122

him in his writing, as opposed to the 'possessive'. But to me love was *in itself* the great creative impulse, of the earth, earthy, individual and universal. I could hate people and feel jealousy, but I have never been able really to cease loving and caring about a person once my love has been given. There is nothing Christian either about the universal scope of this love, for it is of the same stuff as the rest of nature: there is no spiritual arrogance, no agonizing dualism, it is not hedged about by laws and regulations. I see this kind of love—the empathy that should be common to all living creatures—rather than religious and intellectual approaches, as the possible reconciling force for peace in the world, and as the basis for the care and education of children. Of course love, so defined, partakes of maternity, which is why I so resented and combated the patriarchal laws in which maternity was imprisoned.

Yet how may any of us define love? We know only that love is something central to our personal, human lives and to our civilization. No matter what came after, or what Bertie wrote with hindsight in his book, he did, at this time, both feel and express this love for the community of children and for his and my children within it; that all-embracing love for which we had both, though by different roads, been striving. We were never closer in love and tenderness than in those last months before the break was made. Now our ideal world, which we had tried to shape with our lives, was shattered. The villa Costa Loria was the last temple for its shrine; the winds that shook the tamarisk trees of Hendaye a mournful omen.

13

According to the Law

The school and my small son required my attention; I worked hard to finish my book in order to get it to the publisher and earn an advance. It was in proof already by the end of the summer holidays. I faced the awkward task of explaining to John and Kate that I would not be with them in Cornwall in the Easter holidays and that their father would not be living with me any more. As we walked about the grounds together, John's first question to me was: 'Then who will look after you?' I said that I should be all right and, in any case, I had my work in the school. Both children found it odd that we could not all be together as we had been so far, but they were not, as yet, troubled, because the familiar life of the school went on day by day.

The Labour Women's Conference came round again, this year in Brighton. At Dorothy Jewson's urgent request I managed to attend by expressing my milk for the baby's midday feed and being driven to and fro. That Conference played its part in the split between the I.L.P. and the Labour Party. We, for the Independent Labour Party, had as usual some amendments down. The platform, quite why I do not recall, refused to let us move them. Consequently our delegation rose with dignity and walked out.

It was a very busy life for me; weekend visitors were numerous. Jack and Mollie Pritchard, who had two boys in the school, and were its strong supporters, often drove down at weekends, as did Gip Wells, whose wife Marjorie was just starting a family. I once asked her to go into partnership with me in the school, but, as secretary to H.G., she could not undertake anything else. Mollie was a doctor, Jack concerned with modern-style architecture and furniture: he was in touch with Walter Gropius of the Bauhaus in Germany. My friends guessed that I needed some distraction, and now and then a party of us would drive out for a meal. Paul Gillard turned up once out of the blue and joined us at dinner. In my unhappiness the only pleasant thing within myself was the realization that I was younger than I had thought. I found myself now on a level with people nearer my own age, whom, when I was with Bertie, I had always thought of as much younger than I.

Our visitors would stay mostly at the Royal Oak, a little pub in a fold between the Downs near Chilgrove, which later became quite famous through the skill and charm of the landlord Alf Ainger, and

Carrie, his wife. Frank Russell once said that he had put it out of bounds for his staff when he lived at Telegraph House. I thought that he was an old spoilsport to do so, for it was the only place within easy walking distance to which one might go of an evening for a pint and some congenial rustic company. For our children it was the 'turkey farm'; they had discovered it, and Mrs Ainger, surrounded by turkeys being fattened for Christmas. Once she had fun with my son John, for, hearing that he had not been baptized, she insisted on performing the ceremony in the pond, whereupon they both fell in.

Since I did not put it out of bounds, the staff would often go down to the Royal Oak for a drink with Mrs Ainger and her customers, as well as with parents who might be there. With its red-brick floor, and a wood fire on a chilly evening, it was homely and welcoming. We soon had friends in Sandy the woodcutter and Joe the former shepherd, who 'minded the day' when the shepherds used to go to church of a Sunday in their smocks and with their crooks, and there would be 'eight hunderd yowes' (ewes) on the Downs. Sandy had saucy, bright blue eyes and would chaff the slower-witted Joe, while Mrs Ainger cooked a meal for the pair on Primus stoves in her Heath Robinson style small kitchen. Alf, the landlord, oddly enough, was a Londoner, with a cockney wit, but he became incensed once when some visitor called him a 'wheel-barrer farmer'.

Early in the summer of 1932 my younger son, baby Roddy, became suddenly ill with an intussusception. Barely arrived for the weekend, Gip Wells unselfishly turned back and drove the baby, Griffin and me to the London Clinic in Harley Street. A prompt operation saved Roddy's life. But the expense wiped out the entire advance on my book.

The horrible business of legal argument and bargaining about the future was now going on. I had said, provisionally, that I would carry on with the school, for I saw it as the best base for my four children and work for myself that I thought worth doing. To Bertie it appeared then as an advantage that the school should continue: he had to pay £400 a year still as alimony to his brother's ex-wife Mollie and, if I occupied Telegraph House, £400 of any allowance that might be paid to me would be deducted as rent for the house. He loved our home in Cornwall and proposed that he should rent it more or less permanently. He says in his book that at this time he 'gave' me Carn Voel. This is not strictly true, the house had been mine from the beginning; thus, on the contrary, he was really trying to take it away. I could not agree to this; I had found the house, created there our family home, and had even to a large extent been financing it. Moreover, Bertie had said to me when we discussed provision for the future, that he would leave Telegraph House to John and I could then leave Carn Voel to Kate. But it was agreed that he might rent it for the summer.

There was no possibility at that date of divorce by consent, or after a few years' separation; the couple were required to adopt punitive attitudes of resentment and revenge. I do not think, however, that there would have been so much bitterness between Bertie and me but for the methods and tactics of his personal friend Crompton Llewelyn Davies. This may not be fair, since the actions taken must have been endorsed or condoned by Bertie himself. Crompton's first act was to accuse me of false registration of Harriet's birth. I had only done what Bertie expressly wished me to do and had said so even before she was born. Inevitably, of course, Harriet got into Debrett, and the row about this, which became very comical, lasted until well after she was grown up. But Bertie himself, at that stage, had not cared about the 'succession'. Now, according to what he has written, 'as anyone could have told me in advance', it had become too much of a strain *not* to act like a patriarch. Perhaps 'anyone should have told me' that, if I were going to tilt against the patriarchal system, I was ill advised to begin by being married to a belted Earl.

As it was, I knew well enough that all the cards were stacked against me. Bertie held title, fame, prestige, money, and most 'right-thinking' people would certainly be on his side. In actual fact, as soon as rumours of a possible divorce got about, people of left views who had begun to value us as a partnership did try to persuade Bertie not to go on with it. Norman Haire was one, to whom Bertie replied that he 'was not going to sacrifice his happiness to a principle', but that he would not 'allow Dora to starve after these years of service to me'. H. G. Wells was against the divorce, he told me personally not to do it, and to others, possibly also to Bertie, he said that the divorce would not be granted, that, on the contrary, the Judge would 'make an example' of us by refusing it.

Most of those who had supported the Sex Reform Congress, if they had any convictions, must have seen that I was standing by principles there enunciated, whereas now Bertie was not. But they also revered Bertie and did not choose to come into the open against him. Miles Malleson, who was fond of both of us, had been a strong advocate of sexual freedom, had written a play on the subject, and had contributed an eloquent plea for a new morality to the Congress; he was, I believe, seriously shaken in his admiration for Bertie. As late as 1967 Miles is reported as having referred to me as a 'good person' who 'stuck to her principles', and to whom he thought Bertie had been unfair.*

The friends who made a point of coming to the school Open Days and inviting me to stay with them in London whenever I needed to do so, were Jack and Ingeborg Flügel, always ready to help during the next few years. James Drawbell, then editor of the *Sunday Chronicle*, though not a personal friend, commissioned regular articles from me for his paper and put me into a book which he brought out called *A Gallery of Fair Women*. I appreciated such help in an unequal contest, the more so as I began to find that, in some circles, my reputation for

* Rupert Crawshay-Williams, *Russell Remembered* (Oxford University Press, 1970), p. 152

intelligence decreased now that I was no longer associated with Bertie. The harsh remarks made by Bertie, as reported to me, may sound unlike him. I can only say that I have heard him being similarly callous on other occasions and about similar topics.

What I want to assert here is that in disregarding the law and defying the patriarchal succession, Bertie and I were then united in an honest and good act of liberation, a principle to which I continued to adhere and still do. I am quite unrepentant: my only regret is that we failed together to bring the whole thing off; it would have been simply glorious if we had succeeded.

Throughout the year the lawyers went on examining the legal position. No final steps had been taken before Christmas, which we celebrated all together at Telegraph House, with George and Mary Slocombe, who came as my guests to help ease what was a difficult social occasion.

When the question of a divorce was raised, I at first said that I thought this was impossible; what is more, I was convinced that the proceedings would lead to estrangement between all of us, from which our relations would never recover. Nor do I say this now from hindsight; I have before me the notes for and against divorce which I gave to Bertie at the time and later to my lawyer. Since there were to be separate households, I wanted to preserve all possible means and occasions for friendly contact, which I knew the intervention of the law in any shape would prevent. In this I was proved entirely right. Since Bertie had said that he would never want a divorce I suggested that if he had now changed his mind, it was for him to start proceedings against me. On 20 April 1932 I wrote to my lawyer Mr Maw:

. . . In all the circumstances I felt some bitterness which however I really will try to control. My husband frequently said to me during the last few years that we were committing ourselves to a course of action which would render our marriage indissoluble by law. We had therefore put that thought from our minds. The change in him is presumably due to the possibility of another child which he wishes to legitimise. A similar change of attitude is natural in Griffin Barry, who had also previously accepted our belief that the legal marriage was indissoluble. It is clear, therefore, that, unless I do my best to secure the legal dissolution of the marriage, I shall incur the resentment of the two men I care deeply about, and of the woman who will have a relation to my older children and an increasingly close influence with my husband. The tacit assumptions on which the arrangement of my life has been built fall to the ground. It seems to me therefore that I must go as far as ever I possibly can towards making the divorce possible—and I hope you may be able to find a road towards that which I can follow.

My belief in a different order of society is very profound, and I feel I have a loyalty to younger men and women, especially women, who have believed my written and spoken words. I think my husband and Mr Barry do realise this, but they think the personal problems involved more important. I have tried to think so, but I am afraid that at bottom I do not . . . If it were possible at law, I think the responsibility for proceedings ought to be my husband's.

The current code of morals at that time among the apostles of freedom was that no one had any right to refuse to set free of a marriage any man or woman desiring that freedom, a principle held alongside the agitation for more humane marriage laws. I felt myself bound by this principle. At the same time, according to the law, I was expected to ask for a divorce on the grounds that I now wished to regularize my position by marrying the father of my two younger children. Not only had I no intention of doing this, but I hated going to the Court to tell a lie utterly at variance with my convictions. But it seemed that, according to the lawyers, Bertie had committed too many matrimonial offences to have a hope of succeeding in an action started by him. The only person able to untie the legal knot was myself.

When we consulted Mr Middleton, K.C., he thought that I had a good chance by making what was called a 'discretion statement'— asking the Court to condone the offences of the petitioner so that he or she could put matters right by being able to remarry. In the draft statement prepared, Harriet and Roderick were referred to as 'two children whose parentage is in dispute'. I said at once that I could not sign such a statement since I was not the kind of woman who did not know who was the father of her children; the name of the father must be put in. Mr Middleton patiently explained to me, poor man, that this was merely a useful legal phrase, and that this was not the first time lawyers had had to deal with ladies who had children that were not by their husbands. We were, in fact, up against the presumption in law, designed, it was said, for the protection of wives and children, that a child could not be made illegitimate if the husband had been there and cohabiting with his wife at the time the child was conceived. Nor was the evidence of husband and wife admissible to bastardize such a child. A long case had recently been fought by the Ampthill family on this very issue; it was known, sadly for us, as the 'Russell baby case', though our connection with that family was entirely remote and certainly unknown to us.

The next plan the barristers thought up was to start with a legal deed of separation, which in itself now seemed advisable. To begin with, the legal custody of John and Kate was still with Bertie; I might find myself with no rights. The very first remark made by the legal gentlemen about my position had been, 'She has put herself in a position where she cannot get money from her husband', obviously quite the silliest thing any wife could do!

Griffin had seen Bertie about the children while I was still in the nursing home, and had told him that I would insist upon equal rights and mutual care of John and Kate. Mr Middleton now tried to give effect to this, but Crompton would red-ink and strike out passages that seemed to diminish Bertie's ultimate control and, though the custody would still rest with him, we could not get agreement for the phrase 'the children shall be in the physical care and control of the wife'. The general agreement was that the children should still be in my school for at least one year, possibly two, and spend the whole of the holidays with Bertie and Peter Spence. Should they go to another school, the holidays would then be divided between us. I found that I had only limited control over the financial trusts which Bertie had made for the children. The Trustees were now, with Bertie and me, Francis Meynell and E. M. Lloyd, the husband of Margaret Russell, a cousin of Bertie's.

It was soon evident that the devastatingly possessive part of the creative impulse was parental emotion. A battle of 'father right' versus 'mother right' raged between Bertie, Griffin and me. The two men had decided that the obvious course was to divide the family in two according to their fathers; they also seemed to assert that 'their needs', of which they spoke frequently, demanded the right to the children and the ministrations of one wife. I replied that, on the contrary, I had a family consisting of four children, and that quantitative values were irrelevant in the sense that 'one is eternally the father or mother of a child, no matter how many one has'. I refused to see John's and Kate's lives chopped up to suit the patriarchal system. I knew that some compromise would have to be reached, but I tried desperately to make Bertie understand what maternal feeling was. I had not, as I pointed out, been a possessive mother, having shared my children with others, and had been at pains to see that they should also have the company of their fathers. Up to the present I was the only woman with whom he, Bertie, had had children. The children were a reason for us not to quarrel. I, who thought that parental relations were something totally different from sex, was surprised to see how easily he could transfer all emotions to the object of sexual and romantic feeling. I was being treated like a woman who had been there only to keep house like any other. Perhaps he had never really known what I was like, since his lawyers seemed to think of me as a criminal likely to grab or steal money. I thought that he and I, who had worked hard together for years and borne the heat and burden of the day, had more right to consideration than the others, who were ready to take all, but contributed very little. On this subject I used very strong language.*

What I have to say about father and mother right is in *In Defence of Children*, published in the autumn of 1932, and which, since it came on

* letter to Bertie, 9 November 1932

the falling tide of the movement for sexual freedom, did not have the success of its predecessors. It was intended, like Mary Wollstonecraft's *Vindication of the Rights of Women*, similarly to defend the rights of children against all comers.

While the legal negotiation went on my peace of mind, whether writing or at work, was constantly disturbed by the arrival of lawyers' letters: at the very sight of one of those long envelopes I would feel sick and unable to open it. Countless wives must have gone through similar experiences. The deed of separation presented other difficulties for me besides money and concern for the emotional security of John and Kate. It was intended as a preparation for my petition for divorce. By this deed we were to make a clean sheet of all the wrongs (legally interpreted) that we had done to one another, and to resolve, though separated, to live in the chastity which we would still owe to our marriage bond. Then, after two years, I would go to the Court, and, pointing out that my husband had, none the less, persisted in his adultery while I was living solitary and deprived, ask the Court now to dissolve our marriage in order that I might be delivered from my chaste prison.

Mr Bayford, K.C. put forward this ingenious plan, which had the advantage, so I was told, that it would deprive the Court of any right to enquire into my previous conduct, thus avoiding the humiliation of the 'discretion statement'. I thought this whole idea abominable. Since it was Bertie who wanted the marriage dissolved, why should I be condemned to live alone for two years or more, whilst he might live as and how he pleased unhampered by any restrictions? I would, it is true, have my four children for most of the two years, but Griffin, of necessity, would be deprived of his.

It seemed to me, I observed, that there was in all this a sacrifice of the substance of real living for the shadow of legality. If Griffin and I were to have any parental relation with our children, we needed to be with one another at this time; I needed not to be left entirely alone in my unhappiness. The long break, the bitterness that would result as the law ground on its way, would mean a rift between the adults, and ultimately between the children and their parents, which would spell disaster and unhappiness for all. All four adults in this affair had been deliberately living outside the law; there was an obligation on us, therefore, to continue to do so. We had no right now to call in the law to regulate our lives.

Needless to say this argument, though logical, was not approved by the other persons concerned: their view, which also had some right on its side, was that so long as the legal marriage continued, I was in a privileged position. For me, the only people who really ought to have any say in the matter were Bertie and myself. Since he definitely desired a divorce, I presently signed the separation deed as a preliminary action.

It followed that Griffin Barry had to leave for America. I made it clear to him that, whatever plans we might make ultimately, there would be no legal marriage between us. Indeed, I vowed then that with regard to our two children and our relations with them, no law would ever be invoked, a promise that was faithfully kept on both sides.

Those who now benefit from the many changes in the divorce laws may find absurd my devotion to principle and my bitter sense of betrayal. But had not my generation felt so strongly and been prepared to fight both by word and deed, marriage, the most intimate association known to men and women, would, even yet, be bound in law—as it still is in countless unenlightened hearts and minds—by the old punitive and revengeful code.

And those who have marched time and again from Aldermaston will know how rich an experience it is to share a passionate devotion to principle and a great cause with such a leader and comrade as Bertie Russell. It is the more revealing that, so strong were prejudice and the tradition of male prerogatives, or 'male chauvinism', that in the end even Bertie Russell could not overcome them. As he said in his auto-biography, to do so would have been a 'hopeless endeavour' which would have done him 'much harm, while not achieving the intended good to others'. In the event, though the 'intended good' may perhaps have accrued to him, in the years that followed, it was 'the others' who suffered irreparable harm. I have often reflected that it might have been better for all concerned, including those who most desired it, if I had refused that divorce. Even now, why, I ask myself, did I continue in a course of action that was manifestly against my own interest and was to end in the greatest tragedy of my whole life? But I, too, was haunted by texts from the Bible implanted in my youth. In what I had always been told was the 'gentleman's psalm', specifying those worthy to serve the Lord, it said: '. . . whoso sweareth unto his neighbour and disappointeth him not, even though it be to his own hindrance.' A maxim which, to this day, I hold worthy of observance.

The savage law required that the parties to a divorce should *not* agree in desiring it. Should they be known to do so, this was 'collusion', and would inevitably mean that the divorce would not be granted. Accordingly Crompton did his best to exacerbate relations between Bertie and myself until one day he notified my solicitor that he thought that 'we' (the legal gentlemen) 'were now sufficiently at arm's length to be able to meet'. There were a number of matters about money and the children which had to be discussed. But, in satisfying the hostilities required by the law, Crompton lost sight of the emotional consequences to two people so deeply involved as Bertie and I. We, who had never known so much as an angry word between us, were made to quarrel with one another. I became angry and distressed and gave vent to my feelings in a letter to Griffin, which, without telling me, he sent to Bertie. In a reply to Griffin, Bertie delivered a vindictive attack on me, denigrating my abilities and actions. In March 1933 I sent to him and to Griffin long identical letters in reply.

I

This was my last attempt to preserve some human relations with Bertie. It was, above all, a plea to him not to distort and destroy the memories of our life together, for the sake of our relation to the children, which would have to continue. I was embittered because I perceived that he saw himself as conferring favours upon me and implied that, left to myself, I would not have achieved anything. He had forgotten that I had sacrificed a promising career and my economic independence to go with him to China, when his own future seemed precarious. I felt that he had never known what it was to have to make one's own way in life, to depend only on one's own brains. Above all he was allowing himself to be influenced by the old codes and had forgotten that once there had been an understanding and even a possibility of love between the parties concerned, and more especially for *all* the children. His defection from what I felt we had stood for had left me choked with a sense of failure in everything by which I had lived.

I was expressing here my deeply held belief, as stated at the Sex Congress, that the marriage laws could be so reframed as *not* to honour and glorify sexual and parental jealousy and possessiveness, but rather to *dishonour* the harbouring of these emotions.

It was of no avail in our personal breach. Bertie would not see me except on one or two rare occasions and then in the presence of lawyers. All kinds of pinpricks began about the movement to and fro of John and Kate. Bertie explained to them that the process of law was necessary since otherwise Roddy might become an Earl; he had, apparently, clean forgotten that he had wanted to assume parentage of Harriet before birth, and she might have been a boy. Roderick had, of course, been registered in such a way as to avoid any ambiguity. I ought to have remembered that the Russells, once in a quarrel, never forgive. Differences had occurred between Bertie and his brother; there was no reconciliation before Frank's death. Similarly, Bertie carried on the dispute and maintained his personal hostility to me right up to and beyond the day of his own death.

These were troubled times and conducive to bad personal relations. While I have no belief in the influence of the stars, I do believe that the trend of national and international events may have profound psychological effects on individuals. Anxiety, fear, and hatred, aroused by what is going on around us in the world, become transferred to the problems in our personal lives. The H-bomb has brooded like an evil genius over the lives of two generations. For us 1932 spelt suspense, 1933 was to prove terrifying.

In the autumn of 1932, none the less, we pursued our activities in education and politics. At a meeting of progressive educationists I met Clifford Allen, whom I had scarcely seen since the Ramsay MacDonald split. Commenting sadly on his old friendship with Bertie, he said:

'With Bertie, when differences arise, it seems as though there is nothing deep enough in him to preserve friendship—one might be dead, so far as he is concerned.' This corresponded so closely with what I was feeling that I have not forgotten it.

In the Chair at this meeting, Allen was trying, as he had always done at the I.L.P., to reconcile opposing points of view. A. S. Neill and I were regarded as so far to the left, educationally speaking, as to be almost beyond the pale. It was said that we might be admitted to the organization, though there were some members who would definitely not wish the names of their schools to be set beside Neill's and mine. I found this very funny and remarked that possibly Neill and I might return the compliment and refuse open association with them. He and I always had to laugh because the general policy of 'progressive' schools was to avoid all discussion of religion, sex or politics. We wondered what there was left to talk about. As I recall, Neill later dropped out of going to 'progressive' conferences and once said to me that we had nothing to do with them because he and I were 'educators'. The lot of the innovator in education was far from easy. Beatrix Tudor Hart, who now had her own school in London, was in some legal suit, for which some of us raised money to help her.

The question of John and Kate's education was so frequently raised that I looked round to see what boarding or day schools might be possible for them, or even for my younger two, if I abandoned my own school. Only Neill, and Curry at Dartington, did not have religious instruction; most schools had corporal punishment, highly nationalist teaching and compulsory cadet corps.

There were still meetings of the Sex Reform League in London. At one I met Miles Malleson, who joked with me about a contribution by Cyril Joad which asserted that women were monogamous. 'Poor Joad,' said Miles, 'perhaps he will learn something from experience before he dies.' There was a fine lecture by Jack Flügel about psychoanalysis and modern morals, in which he explained how guilt about sex made people unhappy, so that they then passed on their unhappiness to others, and hated that anyone should enjoy life. Naomi Mitchison, who had been doing some work in her husband's constituency and had been impressed by the poorer workers there as almost the only people worth anything, said—if I remember right—that we must all feel guilt so long as we allowed the present social system to continue. Flügel rather meant that, once free of the sense of guilt, we would also release our impulse to create happiness: I felt that the whole social system had been built upon guilt about sex treated as a fundamental concept. I spoke at various meetings on education and sex knowledge at which my attempt to reconcile Freud and Marx was not welcome to Marxists, by whom Freud—and I by implication—was denounced as bourgeois.

The Reichstag fire exploded on our well-meaning activities like the bomb on Hiroshima for a later generation. Long before the more insular-minded woke up and took notice, we who had been keeping watch on events knew only too well what this might mean. The first wave of refugees flowed in; the persecution of the Jews had begun. Some of us were aware that socialists and communists were also being rounded up. I remember going to a committee in which Norman Haire was active, in order to help rescue the Jews. I mentioned that perhaps we ought also to concern ourselves with Gentiles who were in danger. There was an embarrassed silence: so great was the growing fear of being associated with left-wing views. I did not go to the committee again.

I was on the London Divisional Council of the I.L.P. and shared their anxieties and dilemmas. At the I.L.P. National Conference in April 1933, at which I was not present, a resolution was passed proposing that they affiliate to the Third International. Like Fenner Brockway, I did not agree with this—which in fact did not happen—and on 23 April 1933 wrote to Griffin:

> I think their position illogical. Why should the Third International accept affiliation of the ILP whose members definitely refuse to become communists? Logically those who want affiliation to the Third International should join the CP. You can't really get a united front with the CP in the long run. If the affiliation goes through, I suppose I must resign for I think it silly to play with communism. Either one joins them and accepts their rather shoddy generalisations —like accepting a religion—or stays out of politics. The ILP was the only party left me—constructive revolutionists—though I wasn't fool enough to suppose they could do more than play a Kerensky role. But preliminary education of people is important . . . one can see what it means and maybe some of us ought to try and survive. They are burning the books of some of the finest left-wing scientists in Germany, colleagues of mine at Sex Congresses, Max Hodann, Magnus Hirschfeld. It is like the Spanish Inquisition—all the brains are pouring over the German frontier. They are destroying nurseries, clubs, kindergartens, schools and community places laboriously built up by the German workers. Just blood and suffering flesh is all that these people want.

With my responsibility for my children I felt that I must be less active in politics, but would still face the risks 'if the hour demanded it and I was ashamed not to'.

So short a time had elapsed since Norman Haire and I had been able to rally the whole of Europe and, in all, twenty-five countries from all over the world, in the cause of sexual enlightenment, which we believed to be the foundation stone of a humane, tolerant, happy and peaceful society. What had been the use of all our striving? Yet my determination that a school like ours ought to survive became all the stronger.

The parallel personal wound of Bertie's defection shook my courage far more. It also had been too sudden, from tender love to nothingness. I have been trying, with some pain, to feel myself back into the person that I was during that year of tragic happenings, because perhaps my personal predicament may illustrate the pressure of law, social consensus and political upheaval on one individual striving to swim against the tide.

I am a person to whom the physical presence of human beings means a great deal. I delight in the revelation of personality in the expression of eyes and voice, gestures, movement of the body. I always took pleasure in watching the children, who revealed so much about their individuality in their unconscious spontaneity—each a unique being compounded of the chance fall of genes, a kaleidoscope pattern never to be repeated again. Not to be able now constantly to experience the presence of Bertie, whose every detail of sight, sound and touch I knew almost as I knew myself, was daily a nagging deprivation. I was, perforce, deprived also of the sight and sound of Griffin Barry. We had never had any period of intimacy like marriage, but we had a strong sexual tie, beyond which we took great pleasure in each other's physical presence. We now had our two children. Just before the autumn term in 1932 I went in our school car to see Griffin off at Southampton, taking with me Harriet, who, though not yet two-and-a-half, was very much a person and already fond of her father. Had I realized how much it would grieve her I would have insisted that she part from him at home. At the last moment she jumped from the car and ran back to hug him, and later almost fought me, crying bitterly until I finally managed to get her to notice the trams in the streets. The letter to her father describing this begins: 'Your lovely face all puckered up with tears, like Harriet's, the last thing I saw, and your resolute attempt at gallantry when you told Hines "drive on" the last thing in my ears.'

I had not wanted this departure. I had wanted Griffin to say that not for all the laws of the Medes and Persians would he part from me and our children, and the others could go whistle for their divorce. I felt sure that, with a more settled life, he would find writing to do in Europe, and perhaps, with me to encourage him, get on with that book he ought to write. But male pride demanded that he shape his family according to conventional law, and further, that he seek his fortune in a man's world, not hang about a woman and *her* school. Once, rebuking him for not 'defending me against the world in everything', I wrote: 'I've seen more clearly just why men are more conventional than women. Because, simply, the conventions suit them and are made for them.'

I lived in a state of anger and near despair. I was angry with the Nazis; with my blind, smug compatriots, who would not see what was going on; with the people who denigrated our school; with Griffin for going away; with Bertie, in part for going away, but more for the ruthless selfishness of his behaviour towards me. I was angry with the law which had been made into a prison for me; angry, above all, at the frustration of action in politics, in defence of the school, and in family affairs.

I was afraid, too. I feared, with good reason, that John and Kate would be taught to disregard their mother and would acquire the snobbish values of class and the intellectual élite; I was desperately lonely, feeling that I had no one on my side. Staunch support came to me from the staff, as loyal to the school, most of them, as I was. But they were also a liability, for I doubted being able, in the short run, to make the school pay, and the divorce, hanging over my head, could ruin it altogether. Money had to be found from my private purse to help Griffin in America until he had got a job.

With Griffin I had no sense of security, no guarantee that his affection for me would survive the separation once he was back in his own milieu and among many friends. Nor did it seem likely that my feeling for him would survive the storm of hatred, anger and grief which overwhelmed me. I had believed him to share with me the values of the new morality; now he looked just like a second Bertie. In any case a burnt child dreads the fire, and I was in no mood to risk putting my life once again into a man's hands. Nor did he understand my anxieties about not abandoning John and Kate. But, knowing how he cared about our two children, chiefly Harriet, I set myself to keep that link between us alive, and wrote to him constantly, telling him all the sort of news a parent likes to get about their doings. I encouraged him about his work, and was overjoyed when he got a good job on *Newsweek*, a journal which was then just starting. Since I kept him posted about the legal situation and had no other confidant about it, poor Griffin received blasts of anger from me about all concerned. In vain did he try to tell me that he was not a patriarch like Bertie. I would not believe it; I was firmly convinced that the two men had struck a bargain about me behind my back.

I have much regretted the injustice of some of my behaviour towards Griffin, but I doubt if, in all the circumstances, we would ever have achieved living together in harmony. Both our lives were dislocated by political events. Griffin's visit in 1920 to the Soviet Union, when he showed considerable courage, dogged his subsequent career. Dos Passos, whom Griffin looked on as a friend, knew him in his heyday as a reporter at the Peace Conference in Paris in 1919, going everywhere, meeting everyone, proud to introduce the eminent to his friends, a 'catalyst' as Dos says,* full of enthusiasm for free love, free speech, stirred by the Russian upheaval.

Of his capacity for making contacts and getting around I was fully aware; I pictured him then back in his own milieu leading a full and active life. For me at home there was the law: it was I alone who now had the raw deal from a law which I despised. There was an official

---

* *The Best Times,* John Dos Passos (André Deutsch, 1968), p. 77

called the King's Proctor, who would, most likely, set his minions to watch me once the divorce suit was filed. Where a Mrs Smith or Jones might get by with a clandestine love affair while suing as an 'innocent' party for a divorce, it was highly improbable, in our case, that I would succeed in such an endeavour. Dear Mrs Ainger had once already come panting up the hill from her pub to let us know that the snoopers were about asking questions about Mr Barry. I noticed cases in the press in which, on the slightest irregularity, the King's Proctor had intervened. Just how unrelenting still was the consensus of opinion on the marriage law is shown by the fate of a Private Member's Bill, brought before the House in 1933 to give divorce after one partner had been insane for five years, as had been recommended by a Commission on Divorce some twenty years previously. Only ninety M.P.s turned up to vote for it and forty-nine voted against. One speaker said that it would destroy the sanctity of the marriage bond. There was not a chance that any measure of reform would come from the Government.

Since little Harriet often talked of going to 'Merika, in those days, I was tempted to go over there myself with the younger two, troubling myself no further about the legal tangle. But this would mean virtually abandoning John and Kate. Nor did I imagine that I could ever settle down and live in a country whose style and values I had, on my earlier visits, always detested. Had not Griffin also, and many of his generation, previously fled from it and lived as much abroad as they could? I knew that I was not made for exile, but fettered to the soil and ingrained culture of my own land, however much I might rail at the follies and shortcomings of my people. But it occurred to me that, since several American children at the school made the trip across the Atlantic in the summer, why should not Harriet and Roderick go also to visit their father? 'Our Lil', their second mother, could go with them; there would have to be someone, in any case, to conduct the other children. John and Kate would be with their father all the summer holidays. I felt that I would not be very happy in Cornwall with only Harriet and Roddy; what is more, I would then let Carn Voel for the holiday season, and, on my own at Telegraph House, I could do some renovating and writing. Betty Cross, who was one of the main props of the school, might stay with me some of the time.

In the Easter holidays, accordingly, we moved all the children who did not go away, in our two cars, down to Cornwall—Bertie having now vacated the house—to see what might need to be done to put it in order. I had dreaded going there without Bertie, but this lively, happy crowd dispelled phantoms. For the first time since Bertie's departure I began to achieve some inner peace: Cornish sea and sky and age-old cliffs once more wrapped their magic about me, as they have done since, whenever I could come to them, all the years of my life. Of course the children and the grown-ups who tended them were having a marvellous time.

I had just lately received from Paul Gillard some articles he had written which I found very interesting: it occurred to me to invite him to stay with us, since Plymouth was not far away. With him I was able to talk about Griffin and all my private affairs, my doubts about the divorce, my indecision as to my whole future. This was what I badly needed, someone who saw eye to eye with me about moral issues and human values and thus could really help with advice. Paul had no more use for the marriage laws than I, 'bughouse' was his word for them. But he had a deep reverence for Bertie and what our partnership meant. He had a romantic idea that we ought to save Bertie from himself and for the world, that perhaps I ought, in fact, to try and get him back. Knowing Bertie, I said sadly that I thought things had gone too far for that. Anyway, Paul thought it quite silly to muck about any further with the law, why not let things be as they were. About him I learned that he was at present out of a job, and was living with his people, trying to write a novel.

When I got back to the school I found that the young dancing teacher, who also acted as my secretary, was not well and needed some treatment for which it was necessary for her to stay in London for the time. Remembering that Paul's parents existed on retirement pensions, which were very small, and that he could have nothing but the dole, I wrote and asked him if he would not come and act as secretary for the term. He could have a room at the cottage and time to do his own work. I also had in mind that I might try and get a publisher to take an interest in his novel. He wrote that he would be a poor secretary. I replied that this was nonsense, and that I really did need some help. So in the end he came.

Paul's presence made a great difference to me and he was soon also a great asset to the atmosphere of the school. I was always up for eight o'clock breakfast and had been working something like sixteen hours a day; I did some teaching, specially in French and German to different age groups, took the smallest ones at certain times, oversaw things in general, tried to keep the peace if the staff did not agree, dealt with letters and accounts, and then, in the evenings, wrote articles. Paul was able to take over much of the routine work, dealing with the money and so on. When I was not teaching I had the pleasure of facing him across the wide dining-room table, discussing the letters, chatting in between on many topics. When my correspondence annoyed me, Paul would note the expression of my face, and putting on a Devonshire accent would say, 'What's the maatter wi' 'ee maaid?' Once when a lawyer's letter came about divorce matters he growled: 'What sort of a man is that, who deals with his wife through *lawyers*?'

Paul was good with the visiting parents and the staff; he had an easy charm and unruffled calm. To the children he was a kind of Pied Piper, once he appeared they would chase him and romp with him. At the same time there was a certain aloofness about him, a self-possession—

he was his own man. I had been told that he was homosexual; he showed no disposition to flirt with either sex, but took a serene friendly path through all. His physical beauty, except to any who might envy it, immediately drew people to him. It was near perfection; he was neither tall nor short, neither plump nor slim; he moved with strength and grace. His head, with his well-cut features and rounded chin, was well posed on his shoulders; he had a bronzed skin, brown eyes and hair of a warm brown tinged with red. It often seemed to me as if he had been fashioned from the red earth of Devon, his native county.

Having someone around who is good to look at is always a pleasure, but in Paul I also had a friend whom I knew I could trust, with whom I could gossip about things unconnected with the school. This also enabled me to keep on even terms with all the rest of the staff and avoid the rivalries that easily develop in small communities. Responsibility weighed on me less, I was less tense. We thought of things to do for fun; this was a socialist school, I said, why did we not fly a red flag? The tower had a flagpole, and before long it carried our colours, visible from as far away as the plain of the weald to the north.

It was Paul's idea to celebrate Midsummer Day in the proper manner. We chose a safe spot for the bonfire, and on Midsummer Eve the children made themselves wreaths of flowers; the school donkey appeared heavily garlanded with wreaths made by Paul. All the children went to bed at their usual time, but were woken about an hour before midnight, dressed and gathered round the bonfire, which Paul, since it was his idea, was allowed to set alight. He crouched beside it, his face lit up by the springing flames, like Pan himself. It was a still summer night there on top of the Down, nothing between us and the luminous sky. We sang and danced, and, on the stroke of midnight, threw the wreaths into the fire. And so away to bed. From then on this became a regular ritual celebration in the school.

I learned from Paul something about his life. Both his parents were retired school teachers, now living on very small pensions. He had an intense hatred of his father, based on what he thought about his treatment of his mother. But his father had also not wanted Paul to try for secondary education, he did not believe in getting out of one's class. Paul had obviously been a thoughtful, sensitive child, possibly not tough and manly enough for his father's taste. He had had a job as a bank clerk in a small town in Devon, but then, doing well, got himself shifted to Paris. The Communist Party had been the natural outlet for an angry young man in his teens. In Paris he had met interesting Party members, among them Paul Vaillant Couturier, famous as one of the *'anciens combattants'* with Barbusse, later to be Mayor of Villejuif, a district in the 'red belt' round Paris. Marie Claude Vaillant Couturier, with whom I worked in the women's movement twenty years later, long after her husband died, was a most remarkable woman, who became a communist member of the French Parliament. Paul got a job with the

Russians in the Moscow Narodny bank in London, but lost this through his delight in mischievous pranks. He and a pal, so he told me, sang the 'Internationale' in the two-minute silence on Armistice Day, with the result that, though his boss had not been able to disguise his amusement, he had been transferred to a job in R.O.P. (Russian Oil Products) in Plymouth, and later in Bristol, until international tension had forced the Russians to withdraw petrol sales. I was once told that their slogan, 'R.O.P., that's the spirit', had been coined by Paul.

From Mrs Ainger came the news that a young gentleman had been there asking questions. I learned that one of Crompton's young men was staying at the Ship Inn in South Harting and had invited two of my teachers to meet him there in order to get information from them about me and the school. I could not understand this and thought it outrageous. The King's Proctor might consider himself to have a legitimate interest, but, from Bertie's point of view, if he wanted a divorce, it was surely not advisable to him to discover anything against me. There was, in fact, nothing. But it was very improbable that, if there had been, he would have learned anything either from the Aingers or the staff.

Politics, as always, bulked large in the thoughts of Paul and myself. He was totally dedicated to left policies, and disturbed at the impending fate of Hitler's opponents. At the same time, he was too intelligent not to perceive the absurdities of much of the communist theory and its adherents. He supported unwaveringly the underdogs— the working class. We differed very little, and it was a relief to our anxieties to talk together. I hated dogma; so, fundamentally, did he. I would say to him that underneath all sectarian party thinking lay something more important—compassion for all human beings. He did not dissent from this, but I knew that he felt this would lead to apathy and inaction. We talked of poetry and writing; he was evasive about his novel, said he had destroyed it and started another.

One day when I was going off to a meeting in the car, I found on the back seat as I entered one of the pads we used for taking notes. On it was written, in Paul's firm, clear hand, the following poem:

> Upon her earth-cored crystal, Scylla broods
> Lean-faced, panting sorceress: sails approach
> Unheeded: Scylla's eyes are fixed
> Where slowly swaying wrack now hides now strips
> Bones—for her lovelier than flesh.
> Soft laughter greets her whirlpool's grip
> Echoing with liquid mischief through stark caves
> Gathering sadness: ships go by
> The helmsman smiles: he has no fear
> Scylla is gone to green infinity.

I put the notepad into my briefcase; I was bewildered, but could do nothing till next day when Paul and I met over the school correspondence.

'Paul,' I said: 'did you yourself write this poem?' though I knew that he must have done.

'Of course,' said he, with a note of indignation, looking straight at me. Those expressive dark eyes unmistakably said that he loved me. But was this an avowal with hope that I might love him? No one knew better than he how entangled and committed I was—a lingering tenderness for Bertie, my misgivings and uncertainties about Griffin, which, since he knew him well, he shared; the problem of the children and the school. Was he saying, 'forget the old bones, youth is at the helm', or warning himself of his own danger? Unbelievable though it may seem, this came to me as a surprise. My generation were so determined to prove that men and women could work together as colleagues without frivolous or sentimental 'nonsense', that I, for one, was often unaware of a man's sexual attraction to me. Now I was dumbfounded: I did not know what to do or say. Intuition told me that Paul was not for fun, not to be treated lightly. Amazed, I realized that I could love him; looking back, I wondered if he had not been there in my mind ever since our first meeting.

At this long distance of time the wonder and beauty of that moment and of the days that followed is still within me, the opening of the gates of Paradise. Here was a man who in his thought and approach to life was like my other self, a man in whom mind and body were in harmony, a whole man, such as I had dreamed and written about and who was, in my knowledge, rare in our world of false masculine values. I could not imagine what we were to make of our relation to one another, but, as the term wore on and we did the work that we shared side by side, there grew between us a new companionship, a certainty that neither of us was any longer alone.

There were many visitors at the end of term Open Day, with the play performed and the children's work on show. Bertie was among them. As hostess I went over the whole place to see if everything was in order. Up in the tower room, Bertie's former study, I found all the pictures of his 'spiritual and temporal' ancestors turned with their faces to the wall. I sought out Paul and challenged him with this prank.

'Why,' said he, 'you should have taken them all down and put up photos of beautiful young men, inscribed to "darling Dora".'

'I thought,' said I severely, 'that you admired and respected the great philosopher.'

'So I do, indeed,' said he and went away laughing. Later I saw him unobtrusively attending to the visitors, grave and official and wearing unneeded spectacles.

Early in July the American children, with my two and Lily, drove away to join their ship. I managed the parting with Harriet without tears on either side, but it required much tact and fortitude. I did not know quite what I would do with the summer; Betty, who had thought to stay on a bit with me, had had chickenpox and needed a change and rest. Paul and I were still there with a skeleton staff, and soon only the outdoor staff would be left. Both of us knew well enough, in view of the spying that had taken place, that this situation could be misconstrued. After doing up the accounts and filing, Paul was making ready to go back to Plymouth.

One morning when he came over from the cottage to breakfast he said there had been a fascist raid on the school. I took this for one of his pranks and was rather angry, thinking this was not the kind of topic for fun and practical joking.

'Come and see,' he said. We went outside: the front door of the house and steps were daubed with legends in tarry black paint: 'Down with Zozo, we have taken your bloody flag and left you ours.' Zozo was a nickname for Stalin. True enough, the rope to the flagpole had been cut, our flag was gone and a Union Jack had been tied to a stanchion on top of the library room which was a one-storey addition. Later we found on a wall by the road from East Marden, in the same black tarry paint, a direction saying 'this way', with a huge black arrow pointing in the direction of our house. We closed both the gates of the grounds, and telephoned down to the friendly postmaster at South Harting to say that, should any visitors or journalists enquire for the school, the term was ended and all staff were away. We thought that possibly there might be some intention to follow up this incident. Presently the phone rang. The voice asked for the Principal. 'What name and business?' I asked. The caller *said* he was the *Daily Express* and 'understood that there had been an outrage at Beacon Hill School'. 'What sort of outrage?' said I incredulously, and 'who could have told you such a thing?' 'We have had,' said the caller, 'a telegram from a Mr Gulliver of Liphook.' 'Then I think you had better get in touch with Mr Gulliver and find out what he means,' I replied and rang off.

A few moments later the phone rang again. This time Paul answered. In a highly cultivated, upper-class voice he said: 'The Principal? No, it is not possible to speak to her, she has now gone away. What? What? School flag? Why, my dear fellow, the school flag is always taken down at the end of term . . . Oh, maybe to the uninitiated eye it might appear to be red.' That night I noted that Paul after putting some broken glass in the back lane, cut himself a strong stick which he took with him to the cottage. In a day or so he left for Plymouth. Later I learned from his mother that, when she expressed surprise at his leaving me alone after the raid, he replied: 'Much safer, for her.' This is exactly what happened. I never found out any more about the perpetrators of the raid. It seemed useless to try. But neither Paul nor I thought it had been just for fun.

I had a letter from Paul shortly from Plymouth, saying that there had been some demonstration there by fascists, and press photographers who tried to take pictures had had their cameras smashed. I had recently been learning to drive the Austin Seven; I was not very proficient, but now I got out the car, left Ben Glue, driver and handyman, in charge, and having sent Paul a letter telling him where to meet me, negotiated the drive, shut the gate behind me and took the road for Plymouth. It was a terrifying journey. I was quite unused to traffic, though it was nothing like what it is now. In Plymouth I told Paul that the driving would be up to him. I found a hotel room; Paul's parents were living at that time in a flat somewhere in the centre of the town. Paul and I met in the daytime and, when his parents went on holiday, more often. We had about three weeks together.

I was so happy to be free, for a time, from responsibility; nor did we need, any more, to play Principal and Secretary, or pretend that there was any doubt about our love. There was such joy in meeting as two individuals, on equal terms, with so much to give to one another. Whatever might be happening in the world, for the time being there were just the two of us, to laugh, to make fun, to tease one another. More than ever I began to realize how much of my own nature in the past few years I had suppressed. Once Paul asked me why I had never cut off my hair, as most modern young women did in those days. Just because it was the fashion, I said, I had preferred to have a coiffure of my own. When loose, my hair was actually waist length. But it occurred to me that, with his taste for masculine companions, Paul might prefer short hair. In any case, it was time for a change. So one day I met Paul with my locks shorn and handed him an envelope containing one of them, with the legend from the fairytale: 'The locks of six Princesses shall be his wedding fee.'

Paul took pleasure in driving me to his favourite places. We went into woods, beside streams, up to Dartmoor, to Yealmpton, Newton Ferrers. We liked to go to the village inn at Meavy, not far from Burrator. Paul was a stickler for sex equality, and would ask in pubs why a 'lady' must always be served with half pints, when, since she could drink two, a full pint could be served at once. Two young workers whom we passed one day in the street smiled at Paul; they were, he said, his 'bodyguard'. Mostly we talked: about the world and its problems, about what faith we lived by, children, the school, our own obligations. Paul felt, as I did, that, though it might not be easy, all children, not only one's own, had a claim on our love. He saw how much the school mattered, yet, though he himself had some need of mothering from me, he thought that the mother in me had been overplayed and overstrained. At times he said it was a great pity that I had ever had children at all. My writing said something to him.

Paul was neither flatterer nor courtier, he was merely probing for the core and quality of me as an individual. I suggested that this would be difficult to assess; I was the woman who had been for many years now

Bertrand Russell's wife. Was it this in me that he valued? How far the imprint of the fathers would presently be imposed upon me by the personalities of my growing children, was something that I had yet to learn. His probing was proof of the depth and genuineness of his love; he wanted to restore my confidence in myself, to help me to live out the person that I was, and not consume myself in service to others. He was convinced that I could never settle down to a partnership with Griffin, he wondered if it would not have been better for Griffin himself if he had died when he was so ill, 'he would have made a good exit, then'. Death was a topic that Paul often thought and spoke about. He expected wars and disturbances in which death would come to many; a fore-boding of disaster was never far from his mind. The fate of comrades in Germany haunted him. Once, on a day when we were in London together, he stood, like a prophet of old, somewhere just behind the British Museum, and said: 'All this is going to be destroyed', a prophecy only too bitterly fulfilled in his native Plymouth.

The cool way in which Paul contemplated death, including his own, often terrified me. I guessed that he did not much want to live to be old and ugly, and, indeed, that he fully expected to die through his involvement in the political struggle. He came of a class that had never known security. I, who knew so little of the loss of it, was, with my 'bourgeois' upbringing, an incurable optimist. My steady nerve, which flowed from this, was one quality in me that he admired. I knew now that his love was given to me in full measure, but I sensed some obliga-tion that he was not willing to divulge. I guessed that he was involved in keeping a watch on fascist activity in Plymouth—they had a centre there in Lockyer Street. I learned later that William Joyce, later reputed to be the notorious Lord Haw-Haw, made it one of his head-quarters. Paul told me once that the fascists had a radio transmitter in Plymouth and that this fact was known to, and connived at, by the local police. Of this, of course, I know nothing, and say only what I was told. But I wondered in what and how deeply Paul was involved, and whether the raid on the school might have been designed by his enemies to winkle him out.

Paul and I had reached a point when we both knew that, so long as we were living, we must come together. How this was to come about was not yet clear: both were torn between love and duty. I had to return to prepare for the autumn term at the school. New staff had had to be engaged, for my science master and the art teacher had gone elsewhere and were shortly married. The children were on their way home; John and Kate would be back, too. I had asked Paul if he would not continue as school secretary, but he had said that he would stay where he was and go on writing. I had brought with my me own small portable typewriter, and I left it with him for his work.

The term began happily enough. Two new pupils for that year were Tibor Szamuely and his sister, whose parents were in charge, either at the Soviet Embassy or the Trade Delegation, I forget which. I thought that they were Russian, but they were, in fact, Hungarian. I was distressed, however, by a furious letter from Griffin, angry at me for having sent the children to him, but still more for writing to say that I thought it must have given him great pleasure to see them. On the contrary, being with them had been for him, he said, a 'painful experience'. It seemed that I could do nothing right. The children's visit had been planned months ahead, nor was it by my choice that their father was the other side of the Atlantic. In fact, it had so happened that Griffin's job came to an end just as they were about to arrive, which I could not have foreseen. He had friends with whom he arranged for them to stay, but no doubt it had caused him anxiety and embarrassment. My own anxiety about their future relation with their father was deepened by the feeling that he was unlikely ever to share responsibility.

About Paul my mind was never at rest. I had an intuition that he must be got away from Plymouth. Having seen the term started, and everything apparently running smoothly, I decided to go down to Plymouth for a few days and persuade him to come up in time for the 5 November bonfire and fireworks, which I knew the children would enjoy with him. Paul met me at the station and we went out to Laira, where he and his parents—who both received me warmly—now lived. None the less, I felt a certain constraint as his father talked with me— Paul's hostility was in the air. The small house was pleasant; in the garden grew a myrtle, of which Paul had put a symbolic spray in a vase in my room. There was a view across the estuary towards Saltram Park, which Paul loved.

We went into town to some of his favourite haunts so that we could talk. The weather was not too good, threatening clouds blew up from the estuary. Paul's mood seemed to match. He was not relaxed as he had been in the summer; I knew something was troubling him, and I could not seem to get near to him. I did not believe that he was the kind of person to retreat from his declared love for me; I inferred that perhaps he was scared of committing himself irrevocably to intimate love with a woman. I told him that I had come to ask him to return to the school, but that it was my intention, if he agreed, to close the school at Christmas, when he and I could go abroad with the two little ones; the divorce would then have to take its chance. I made it clear that I was not suggesting that we should live utterly and completely like a married couple, but maintain some separation. 'That,' was his reply, 'will not be necessary.' So there must be something else. In one small pub as we sat at a round table in the corner, drinking our 'scrumpy', Paul got up suddenly as two men came in, and in so doing, as was very unlike him, upset his glass. 'Come on,' he said, and we hastily left the pub. It might, I thought, be police surveillance that was worrying him. If he did not confide in me, I felt helpless.

The last night that I was with him in Laira we sat in very truth like the lovers of Donne's 'The Extasie', I on a low stool beside him, silently holding hands, speaking only with our eyes. Paul came to the station to see me off. As I was about to get into the London train I urged him to come with me. 'I am getting too old to jump trains,' he said, and waved me off with a smile.

He wrote to me daily and I was expecting him to arrive at the school. Then came a letter from Plymouth, not in his hand. In very formal words his father informed me that I would be sorry to hear that early on the morning of 1 November his son had been found lying dead, presumably by accident. As soon as I could find words at all, I spoke to Betty Cross and others who had known him, and who, I knew, would feel the shock. I felt that I must at once go back to Plymouth.

'Take Ben Glue and the car, Dora,' said Betty, 'then I know that you will come back.'

Ben, ruddy, slow and silent, a true Sussex man, was a comforting companion to travel with. We came to the Gillards' house and, after we had said what we could in sympathy, asked if we might see Paul. To our surprise, they had not brought him back home, he was in the mortuary. I guessed that his mother must have preferred to remember him as he had been alive. I am not sure if, for a moment, I might not have felt the same. But Ben murmured that he supposed we could see him, and in both of us, for I had gathered that Ben had 'thought the world of him', was a need to pay our respects to the dead.

He was proud in death: a gleam of those brown eyes could still be seen under the long lashes, the wide humorous mouth had a scornful twist. But there was a gash about two inches long on one temple, a gash split his nose, and there were gashes round the lips. I remember very clearly what I saw, and pulverized with shock as I was, I could not, from the start, reconcile it with what I was told of the cause of death. He had been found face downwards part-way down the bank of a disused railway cutting, in the shadow where the road bridge crossed it, on the way from the town to Laira. The theory put forward at the inquest was that, perhaps having taken some drink, he had sat down on the coping beside the bridge, and then fallen backwards, somersaulted, and, his head tucked under him and unable to free it, he had died of suffocation. Which, by the medical evidence, was the cause of death. I was quite unable to understand how, on this theory, he had sustained those cuts on his face. His father, who must have identified him, must also have seen them; his mother certainly had not. I was well aware that the one thing Paul's father would wish was to avoid any scandal about his son's death. There were, of course, many things I might, perhaps should, have done then and there. I could have asked for the inquest to be reopened, while the trail was still warm. But Paul was dead, nothing could be of any use now.

I felt entirely alone in the world, I had not even an intimate friend, apart from the Flügels in London. I was utterly numb and stricken down with grief. No one but Paul and I had known what the summer had meant to us, and what had been our hopes of the future. There was nothing left to me but the school and, for the time being, I could hardly bear that. I cut down my classes, for I felt so antagonistic to the children that it seemed unfair to try and teach them. The autumn turned fine, with rich blue skies against the glowing brown of the beech hedges. It seemed to mock me. I knew well that, in such a community, the responsible person at the head sets the mood, and my disturbance would be communicated. On the day I returned from my second visit to Plymouth, Roddy fell out of an upstairs window, but only on to the soil and was not hurt. Next morning I heard the crashing of crockery in the kitchen and found Walter, in a temperamental mood, angry with the kitchen boy and flinging plates about. I tiptoed in my bare feet through the shards to soothe him. So I went to London from time to time when I could no longer endure the lonely agony of the days and nights. Everything within me seemed to come to a stop, I could not even go on with a piece of knitting that I was doing for one of the children. Night after night I lay awake talking with Paul in a kind of delirium, the mournful lament of Scott's 'Coronach' sounding on and on in my head:

> He is gone on the mountain,
> He is lost to the forest,
> Like a summer-dried fountain,
> When our need was the sorest . . .

For the time being, the school was certainly better off without me. On brief trips to London I would find friends in Bloomsbury, who might be throwing a small party; once or twice on my way to the station to go home, I fled from the platform of the Underground back to friends, fearing my impulse to go under the train. For months my rejection of life expressed itself in physical sickness. One or two of the parents, who knew the facts, friends in London, and my school staff, showed me very great kindness and enabled me gradually to pull myself together. I have no recollection at all of that Christmas. I wrote the whole story to Griffin, whose angry letter had made me believe he had become completely estranged. I knew that he had looked on Paul as a friend, and thought that, at least, he would regret his death. The news was that he had now landed another job and might presently come to Europe.

As usual, there were staff problems to cope with. I had to get another cook, and we needed a second chauffeur. I engaged a married couple, who, in the event, did not prove satisfactory. Many decisions would have to be taken the following year, when the time would come to file the divorce petition. Bertie was likely to reopen the question of John and Kate going to another school; I was myself uncertain, assuming that my school could go on, whether it might not be better to move to another house. The water shortage at Telegraph House always caused anxiety, and would limit our expansion, should we ever be able to build.

The coming of Paul had begun to soothe my wounded spirit, to restore my beliefs and trust in people, my confidence in myself. It had offered an undreamed-of personal and mutual fulfilment that had reached down to my very essence and shaken me to the core of my being. This hope of unfolding and flowering would now never come again in my life, such deep personal happiness for me was ended. I had to rouse myself from apathy to live for impersonal ends, first of all for the school, which was now all that I had left.

14

The End of a Chapter

The year 1933–4 was the last that the school was to spend at Telegraph House. I had tentatively approached Bertie about the possibility of my giving up the house at Christmas 1933, when it had been in my mind to close the school. He implied that in agreeing to this he would be doing me a favour, in return for which he wanted my agreement to any plans he might make for John and Kate. This annoyed me, so I dropped the subject.

In spite of everything, that was a good year at the school; the staff who had the care of the children were warm-hearted and competent, things went on much as before. Each term there was, as usual, a play written by the children for the end of term show. A book of these, *Thinking in Front of Yourself*, illustrated with the children's own linocuts, was published in 1934 through the enterprise of a friend of the school, John Sibthorpe, who, with his wife, had at that time started the Janus Press. We were not very kindly reviewed, our children were criticized as being too sophisticated. The prevailing attitude to children was still sentimental; though born in original sin, they were none the less held to be sweet innocents, made of 'sugar and spice'. That young children do concern themselves with adult and life and death questions was not taken into account. Nor did it occur to people that, prior to puberty and thus emotionally undeveloped, the children's approach was cool and critical, almost Shavian.

One of the plays performed that year was about India, in which Gandhi was represented as a holy man called Wata Rau, with a yoyo that went up and down as a symbol of perpetual peace. John and Kate, Richard (son of David Garnett), Jed Taggard's Marcia, all took part in this play, as did Tibor Szamuely, who played the second agitator Horrida Noisa, and who had to let off a pistol in the wings at the end and was heard to exclaim: 'It won't go off!'

Due to another of those periodical Cold War witch-hunts, Tibor and his sister had reluctantly to leave in the summer of 1934. I heard no more of Tibor until 1958, when I was in Budapest with the Women's Caravan of Peace. A young man called at the hotel to see me and said: 'Do you remember? I am Tibor.' He had been through the war in Russia, was teaching at the University now in Budapest, and had, only recently, survived the rising there. He said, with truth, that the women of our Caravan had it somewhat easier. I saw him again in 1963, with his wife, in Budapest, when I was on my way to the Women's Congress in Moscow; then I heard from him in Ghana, and once or twice in London. Finally, to my surprise, he obtained a post at Reading University, even wrote articles for the *Spectator* and was consulted in radio programmes about Soviet affairs. I was able to visit him and his family in London. His early death was a great loss. *The Russian Tradition*, his history of Russia, was published posthumously in 1974.

Tibor told me that it was I who had roused his interest in history, and when he told Cliff Michelmore on television that he had remembered England as a place of blue skies and green fields, I too, remembered that we had made up a school song, based on the tune of '*Au Devant de la Vie*', which went as follows:

> A school on a high hill was founded
> A school for you and for me
> With blue skies and green fields surrounded
> A school in which we are free.
>
> All children shall be welcome here,
> Each girl and boy,
> So let them come from far and near
> To share our joy.

That reunion in London was very happy; and Tibor said: 'I never saw anything wrong with that school.' So, with this tribute, I do what I can to honour his memory.

The political atmosphere was menacing. There had been the drama of Dimitrov's part at the Reichstag fire trial. In May 1934 the Council for Civil Liberties held a packed meeting at the Kingsway Hall, on the platform of which were united the National Liberal Federation, Official Labour, the Independent Labour Party, and the Communist Party in opposition to the Incitement to Disaffection Bill, under which it would be illegal to speak to members of the armed forces in favour of peace. Among those who spoke at this meeting were Harold Laski, Fenner Brockway, Major Attlee, Milner Gray (Liberal), D. N. Pritt, Harry Pollitt, Maude Royden, and myself. Attlee referred to the bill as a 'wretched, mean, class, partisan measure. The question of intent to commit an offence would involve what a man's state of mind was while he had in his possession documents which might cause disaffection. It was a convenient weapon to use against political opponents.'* Maude Royden, famous in those days as a woman preacher, a courageous feminist and pacifist, went further in a remarkable speech. She considered that the armed forces, who in the event of war would pay the

* report in the *Manchester Guardian*, 24 May 1934

first price, should have the means of watching, critizing, and, if necessary, overturning this or any other government. They might also be brought into the class war, and they, more than anybody else, should have the opportunity of knowing what the class war really meant, and what alone would bring it to an end. This united protest clearly indicates the anxiety felt as reaction took an ever firmer hold in Germany.

In July a desperate attempt was made to save the German communists Thaelmann and Torgler from trial and execution. John Strachey and Ellen Wilkinson flew to Berlin; a deputation almost forced its way into the German Embassy in London with a letter urging that the trial be stopped: among those in support, besides myself, were: Norman Angell, Cyril Joad, D. N. Pritt, Professor Flügel, Professor Levy, Dr Somerville Hastings, J. A. Hobson, Professor P. M. Blackett, Henry Nevinson, the Rev. A. B. Belden, George Lansbury, Evelyn Sharp, Lord Listowel, Professor Lascelles Abercrombie, Mrs Haden Guest, Marie Seaton.

The supporters of Ramsay MacDonald and the coalition naturally did not take part in these protests; it is significant also that the name of Bertrand Russell is absent. In May he had written an article in which he said that progressive schools had not as yet solved the problem of discipline, in consequence of which I was informed by well-wishers that it was interesting to know that the school had been obliged to change its policy!

I did have friends and supporters of my educational ideas: Clifford Allen and his wife Joan invited me to visit them, where I met Miss Somerville, then the head of the Education Department at the B.B.C. Allen's opinion was that I was the 'nearest right' (not politically) of the educators whom he knew. The talk was interesting, but in my view skated the surface, and I knew that most of the middle-class progressives would now send their children to Dartington if they could afford it. About this time I met at the Education Fellowship Kurt Hahn, who had only lately come from Germany where he had had a school under upper-class patronage in Bavaria, but had left on account of Hitler. I disliked him on sight and considered him extremely authoritarian and obviously very repressed. When asked questions, he would close his eyes in meditation for a moment, and then reply like a seer. He seemed to me to have no idea of the importance of the early life of children, nor of bringing boys and girls together. He said that he had had 'a few' girls attached to the school, as if this were to let the boys know that such creatures existed. He was challenged by an Austrian woman psychiatrist about punishment, to which she was opposed; he believed, on the contrary, that there existed a sense of guilt that each individual needed to expiate. I was quite furious, because there was I, so much in need of some financial help for our school, and this man was able to appeal on the radio for money and get distinguished patronage to start his school, as he eventually did, at Gordonstoun in Scotland. A parent of one of my pupils wrote to me recently to say that he had considered sending his son on from us to that school, but had fled in a similar mood to mine from an interview, chiefly because he could not stand the religious attitude.

A married couple on my domestic staff gave some trouble. These were the cook and chauffeur who had never fitted in well to the school atmosphere. I had noticed the man sidling along in the evenings to gossip, through the windows, with some of the boys, whose dormitories were on the ground floor. This might be harmless, but something about it made me uneasy. I had decided that I must presently give these people notice. One day the man asked me for a day off, to go, as he said, to Portsmouth to visit his mother who was ill. I did not like the sly and shifty way he looked at me when he asked for permission and after he came back. Somehow I did not believe in that sick mother. I sent for him and told him that they should both leave at once, they would have a month's wages. For the rest of the term we got in some local help for the kitchen and managed somehow.

The petition for my divorce was filed on my birthday, 3 April 1934. In May, as the divorce lists were published, there was a spate of press comment on us both, with the usual nonsense about the 'do as you please school', on which I had to write to some papers in an effort to correct false impressions. In this petition there was only one advantage that I wanted and hoped to get. This was the custody of John and Kate. I had now become completely indifferent to the whole affair, it all became meaningless nonsense after Paul's death. I had no intention of departing from the arrangements we had made about the children in the separation deed, but I no longer trusted anyone and saw no reason why I should not ask for the only thing that I wanted. No sooner was the petition on the file than Bertie countered with a Chancery action designed to evade the jurisdiction of the Divorce Court over the children. I knew nothing whatever about the Chancery Court. Now I learned that it was possible for simply *anyone* to go to the Court and put someone else's minor children in Chancery, and that the parents then have to fight an action to show cause why this should not be done. Bertie had been in southern Spain with Gerald Brenan, and the latter, as 'next friend', acted to put my children in the care of the Chancery Court.

Next came one of those bulky legal envelopes containing affidavits alleging that my school was an unsuitable place for the children, that it was dirty, and that, on an affidavit sworn by my dismissed chauffeur on his 'day off' in Portsmouth, I was frequently drunk, had broken whisky bottles in my room, and had slept there with a male parent and visitor. I was not only flabbergasted at these lies, but distraught, sick and ill. Into the bargain, I learned that the said chauffeur was now in Bertie's service. I think this, having regard to John, worried me even more. I was so desperate that I waylaid Bertie once at Waterloo station and tried to get him to agree to withdraw. I applied to the children's

Trustees. Francis Meynell, as I remember, said that Bertie was only putting up a legal smoke screen. 'Smoke screen!' I said, 'He is breaking my heart.'

Now we had to set about getting affidavits in rebuttal. The only place we ever bought drink for the school was at the Ship Inn in South Harting. Bertie had always had a bottle of wine for the staff at staff meetings, and I think we had continued this. And we occasionally had a small party, over away from the house, in the bungalow classroom, as an entertainment for the staff and their friends. I now had to get information about our bill at the Ship, which, of course, refuted the charge entirely. The whisky drinker was the accuser himself. Parents were at times received in my room for a quiet chat—I had only a bedsitter for any privacy. Mrs Ainger knew that none of us ever got drunk on her premises. I had to invite a Harley Street man down to the Open Day so that he could quietly look over the state of the premises, and I also had to approach some of the parents for support. But it was soon evident that to fight this action would be a costly affair. Into the bargain, it could—and would—be widely reported, because the rules about non-reporting of details in divorce cases would not apply. It took us till the autumn to get the affidavits taken off the file and the case abandoned. It cost my children's settlements £500—at first it was £900, but I made strenuous representations. And the children remained wards in Chancery, unless and until the Divorce Court might act. In the end, of course, I had to abandon the plea for custody. John and Kate did not get out of Chancery until they were of age.

Parallel with the legal battles were negotiations about my tenancy of Telegraph House. On this subject I learned for the first time from Bertie's autobiography what his wishes and motives at that time had been. It did not occur to me that he might sell the house, I believed in his declared intention to leave it to John. I would be sorry to move the school away, yet I knew that the water shortage was a real handicap. I made some enquiries about boring an artesian well through the chalk, and sent particulars to Bertie, suggesting that we might share an experimental trial boring, which would not be ruinously expensive. He was not interested, so I began to look for other premises, possibly nearer to London. I have been told by friends who were recently in that neighbourhood that there is now actually a swimming pool at Telegraph House.

I had supposed that it was a financial advantage to Bertie for me to stay at the house; my allowance had been agreed at £525 a year, less tax, for the duration of our joint lives, and £400 went back as rent. While John and Kate were in the school, their father paid their fees. It was almost certain now that they would go to Dartington in the autumn term, when Bertie would find that he had to pay higher fees, and extras, and would lose the rental of £400 from me. I do not now remember how I found Boyles Court, a lovely Georgian house, in beautiful garden and grounds, not far from Brentwood in Essex. We moved there, taking only the school furniture and equipment and my own furniture, in time to open for the autumn term. I thought that, as I had not wished to give up the Cornish home to him, Bertie wanted to live at Telegraph House. It has hurt me to read his remarks about his wish to get me out.

This whole affair of the house was so stupid. Had we not been kept at 'arm's length', and had Bertie reflected on the kind of person that I was, as he had known me over the years, we might have met to discuss in a sensible fashion our purposes and financial resources, and reached an agreement satisfactory to ourselves and our family. To keep me in ignorance was folly. Had I known that Telegraph House would be sold and lost to John, I would never have vacated it without some agreement being reached.

When it was known that we had decided to leave, our friends at the Royal Oak said that they must give us a farewell party. They really seemed to care about us; Mrs Ainger once told me that I could always come and live with her with my two babes, if driven by necessity. One evening, after closing time, they carried out some crates of beer into the field behind the garden. Each side of this sheltered hollow the grey-green Downs rose up, above was the delicate green of the sky on a clear summer night. This might have been a fourteenth-century celebration: there were mine host and hostess, the shepherd, the woodcutter, and the blacksmith came from the village with his guitar. Healths were drunk, there was music and singing, each contributed a solo if he could. 'Let me give 'ee a drink, me dear, for this once,' said Sandy to me, 'we are losing our Queen of the Earth.' I was in tears. This was, happily, not a final farewell; my family and I have been back there time and again, sure of our welcome.

Under my public 'image', which I seem to have managed somehow to sustain, was still a distraught and desperately unhappy woman. Those who have known intense love or friendship will also know that the person loved is never closer or more apparent than immediately after his or her death. I wrote at this time: 'What does one do about the dead? They live forever.' I felt Paul's presence constantly, it seemed as though he walked close behind me; the mystery of his death was a nightmare. I asked myself time and again if I had not been in some way to blame for it. I had had a pathetic belief in my power to save the lives of those I loved, by nursing them in sickness, helping to shield and shelter them in danger. I cursed myself for having left Plymouth without him, for not having thrown a scene and refused to budge unless he came too. I could not believe in the verdict of accidental death; I did fear that he might have taken his own life, though, knowing him, I believed that he would not have disfigured himself in so doing. I knew that he had winced at every sign of Bertie's shift to the right; surely he had not removed himself in the hope that I would get Bertie back in order to preserve what had been our joint ideals? I determined to find out all that I could about him.

I am recording what I know, not only for the great love I had for him, but also because the unsolved enigma of his death should not be forgotten, nor the remarkable being that he was, the loss of the creative talent which he undoubtedly possessed, and what his circumstances did to him. To this day I remain angry and amazed that no one had perceived the promise of his personality and gifts except for purposes of exploitation. However he died, he was the victim of those many and varied brutal forces of repression, to challenge which was then the central purpose of both our lives.

I had invited his mother to come and stay at Telegraph House soon after his death. From her I learned that after he had met me in London he had loved me. He had always kept in his pocket-book a photo of me cut from a paper. After the affair about Griffin Barry in Plymouth, he had believed, as he told his mother, that I would one day be alone. He was prepared to bide his time. She told him that she did not believe that any woman would leave her children, but would put them before any love affair. He was more troubled about the necessity of earning enough to have something to offer me. He had come to the school on that flying visit in 1932 because he then had a tolerably good job in Bristol. He knew that Bertie had left, but my second child with Griffin was a shock. Then his job came to an end, and he began to write. His mother believed that all this time he had been writing to me, for she found torn fragments of letters. In fact not one had ever been sent. But the manuscript of the novel he had written, and which he had told me was destroyed, was found in his room after he died. His mother gave this to me, as well as his copy of Keats' poems, and a small, grubby, once white edition of 1924 of the poems of the French poet Jules Laforgue. He had evidently been reading this just before his death, for we found, written on a copy of the *Daily Worker*, a phrase from one of the poems:

> *Allez stériles ritournelles*
> *La vie est vraie et criminelle.*

His mother, Maud Gillard, said how the situation in Germany was never far from his thoughts and that he would say to her how terrible it must be for the wives and families of men who inevitably took part in that struggle. Had he then feared what might happen to me if I became involved with him? I thought that he would have given me credit for the necessary courage that it would take. And then, had he meant to die, he would not have had my picture and letters in his pocket-book. Maud and I thought that he had made up his mind to follow me to the school, because, as he went out on his last evening, he had asked her to find out when a friend of his—a lorry driver—was going, as he often did, to Southampton, from where he could, obviously, go on to us at the school. He had the money for the train fare, but it looked as if he had wanted to leave by less noticeable means. No more was known of his movements except his leaving a pub to walk home by the lonely road which he had once said to Maud—as she thought in jest—'would be the death of him'. According to the publican, he was sober when he left; a man who left at the same time did not come forward. When I tried to fathom his mood, Maud told me that just before my visit he had spoken of her 'learning to get on with his wife'.

Paul once quoted to me a poem of Verlaine's which I felt symbolized for him the idealism of his relation to Bertie and me and the children:

Parsifal

Parsifal a vaincu les Filles, leur gentil
Babil et la luxure amusante—et sa pente
Vers la chair de garçon vierge que cela tente
D'aimer les seins légers et ce gentil babil;
Il a vaincu la Femme belle, au coeur subtil.
Étalant ses bras frais et sa gorge excitante;
Il a vaincu l'enfer et rentre sous sa tente
Avec un lourd trophée à son bras puéril,
Avec la lance qui perça le Flanc suprême!
Il a guéri le roi, le voici roi lui-même,
Et prêtre du très saint Trésor essentiel.
En robe d'or il adore, gloire et symbole,
Le vase pur où resplendit le sang réel,
—Et, O ces voix d'enfants chantant dans la coupole!

'But,' said Paul, as he recited this to me, 'il ne rentre pas sous sa tente.'

In Plymouth I had a curious talk with Paul's grandfather. He was deeply distressed. He said, 'He haunts me, I feel I am the one that could have saved him.' He thought Paul had not had enough experience to be able to write well as yet. He then suddenly threw out the remark, 'The men of our family never ought to go out without their mothers.' It was probably Paul's diffidence about sex itself which concerned the old man. As to this, I myself knew well that this was not the trouble. I was told that the grandfather, after being married a fortnight, came home saying he could not 'do it'. But he went back and begot five children and later married two more wives. I had the impression of a family of rich temperament, slow-moving, deep passions, but diffident and unaware of their true worth.

I talked with a comrade in Plymouth, who had known Paul well. He was Greek in origin. He told me that he had often wondered how it was that Paul had not a woman, but that now he had seen me it was all explained. 'You can comfort yourself with one thought,' he said, 'your choice was perfect. No other man had such moral, intellectual and physical beauty.' I saw also one of the men who used to box with Paul at the Young Men's Club, probably one of the two whom he called his bodyguard. He took me into his small backyard and showed me some young cabbages. 'Paul brought them for me to plant,' he told me, 'now I feel I must pull them up, for I shall choke if I eat them.'

The simple direct feeling and expression of those who had loved and appreciated his worth brought me some comfort, though this did not answer the questions which haunted me. His manuscript, *One May Smile*, he had formerly called *Sorrow in Heaven*, meaning, I think, that it described one sinner who did not give Heaven joy by his repentance. It was about his life, partly in Devon, partly his contacts with the Bohemian world of Bloomsbury, something of his relation with the Communist Party, and stopped at the point where the young man of the story was about to leave for Paris. Saltram Park appeared as one of his loves. The style, the insight into character, the feeling for the natural world, the grass roots of his background, showed that here was a writer of very great promise. A second manuscript, a page of which was in the typewriter on the day he died, was to have been about Bristol. Its title was *The Crumbling Steeple*, and evidently would have been about the relation of the complacent middle-class world to that of the Bristol docks. It had a very apt description of the Dean of the Cathedral crossing the quad, his black gown outflung 'like the wing-cases of a beetle'.

Paul had told me he had a friend who was with him in the Party in Plymouth. There was a character in the first manuscript who might well be this man, but I did not know how to find him. I thought of trying to get the novel published, but what would be the use, when the author was no longer there to follow it up. There, for the time being, I had to let the matter rest. I read his novel, I immersed myself in poetry.

All this reinforced my convictions about the class issue: I drew nearer in sympathy to the working people of my own country. In a letter to Griffin, with whom I kept up a correspondence about the fortunes of the school and our children, I wrote:

I have been thinking lately of how people used to come to our house in Chelsea for help when we stood for Parliament, poor people of all kinds in difficulties, and how they were never human beings to us or we to them because of our class and position. And how really I belonged with them like the lady who wanted to run away with the gipsies. When I went lately to the Hunger Marchers Congress in London I felt I was really seeing my own people for the first time— no longer helping them as oppressed inferior people—though of course lots of them are, as lots of the bourgeoisie are—but as my own people, and friends. Their faces were lovely, Devonshire men, Welshmen, Cornishmen, pale mothers from Scotland. I feel like them and I am like them, and like all the people one meets in pubs, or like the real artists and writers, not the fake snobs in Bloomsbury. And so was Paul. If I could only have saved him to write about his people, I would not have wanted anything more of him than his achievement. Ultimately that is what I want of everyone, but I cannot heal when I am choked and tortured myself.

I find another indication of my state of mind in an account of the Rationalist Press dinner, in which I sat next to Gerald Bullett, the novelist, whom, with his wife, I liked very much. He had just written a novel in which a woman was more or less destroyed by the snubbing and ill-wishing of disapproving neighbours. Listening to all the speeches about the power of reason, I was consumed with inward laughter, and kept on talking to Gerald about Magic. He was much entertained, and presently said: 'Do you really think you ought to be here?'

The Chancery action was finally disposed of in September, but not before I had been still more embittered because Bertie had persuaded Kate to write and say she did not like being at my school. I have no record that John did so. One cannot assign any blame for this, the prospect of going to Dartington must have been attractive. Very many years later I learned that Bertie had told the children that the Chancery action was necessary as otherwise I would take them away to live in the Soviet Union. Nothing was further from my intentions. As I have already mentioned, he had said, too, that Roddy might try and claim the Earldom. This was equally absurd; indeed I had told Bertie myself that my second son would never wish to go to the Lords except in the capacity of Guy Fawkes, to blow up the whole nest of pomp and privilege.

Sometime in October or November 1934 the divorce petition came before the Judge. He rejected the separation deed and required full disclosure. He wanted to know about Bertie's conduct prior to the deed, so that he might judge whether I had been guilty of 'conduct conducing' to Bertie's present adultery. As I had already informed him about my relation to Griffin Barry before the deed was signed, he must have had in mind—and this was apparent from 'hypothetical cases' which he put forward—my conduct *after* the deed was signed. He was evidently cognizant of the affidavits in the abandoned Chancery case, presumably from the King's Proctor, whom he had called into the case. The representative of the King's Proctor seemed, according to my account to Griffin, to dislike being in the case and would not have been there had the Judge not invited him in. He proposed to raise no objection based on private enquiry, but—in my words—'disliked the legal quibble [the deed], which would make divorce too easy and spoil his job for him'. My letter to Griffin of 18 November 1934 gives this account of Mr Bayford, K.C.'s argument:

He says: 'By the deed the husband and wife wiped out their past. It is in the interests of sound marriage that husbands and wives should make compacts of mutual forgiveness and be unable to go back on them. Therefore neither of these people can honourably tell you anything about each other prior to the deed. The wife, because of the clause in the deed about Harriet and Roderick (which, my Lord, you are forbidden to look at by the Russell baby decision) has volunteered to tell you she has committed adultery, but the existence of this deed proves that the husband has condoned it, and she does not therefore need to ask your discretion.'

The poor Judge then says pathetically: 'Why on earth did you let your client accuse herself of adultery, and make me take notice of it?'

Mr Bayford says: 'Because of the clause in the deed that you may not look at.'

Judge says: 'But if I may not look at it? . . .'

And so they go on. In other words, they would have loved to give me a divorce on the ground of complete innocence, Harry and Rod being due to the Holy Ghost.

It would seem that in law Bayford is probably right, and would win in the Court of Appeal, which deals not so much with moral and human issues as strict legal correctitude.

The absurdity of the situation was that the Judge really knew the facts about my conduct prior to the deed, and what I had been accused of *after*. These later accusations, if the Judge accepted them as true, might lose me the divorce and Bertie would thus be hoist with his own petard. If the deed of separation were set aside as collusive, then I was not absolved from asking for discretion, but, what was more, my chances of then getting a decree depended on adequate blackening of Bertie's conduct also prior to the deed. Mr Bayford argued further that the Court had no right to say that the deed was dishonest or collusive, unless the King's Proctor could prove by other evidence than any given, or put forward, by Bertie and me, that it was collusive. Though we had agreed not to admit as evidence anything done before the deed, this did not bind the Court, but it did preclude the Court from making us speak against ourselves and each other.

It was possible for me to accept the Judge's refusal of the decree and then go to appeal, which would mean more delay, though the six months' wait for the decree to be made absolute would then probably be shortened, the delay not being my fault. The other course was to approach Bertie to release me of the undertaking in the deed so that I could disclose his infidelities. An approach was made, but, as expected, Bertie declined on account of the reputations of other women, though mine no longer mattered to him. I was not sure, at this stage, if he really wanted his liberty after all. But, if the divorce did not now go

285

through, there would be a hideous muddle about the position of John and Kate. Had it not been for the greater publicity and the possibility of a detailed summing up by the Appeal Court Judge, which could be published, I would have preferred to appeal. In the end, we got by with a discretion statement by me and not by Bertie, with the result that press reports indicated that I was more to blame than he, the children remained in Chancery and at Dartington school. In effect, as I had expected from the start, Bertie got everything that he wanted and I nothing whatever except a modest allowance, which would come to an end on his death. It was March 1935 before I was finally free of my legal marriage. I was in my late thirties. The divorce had taken three years of my life and inflicted tragedies from which I was never fully to recover.

While the case was in progress I used to think that all legal gentlemen—despite the help which no doubt some gave me—were a set of sadistic voyeurs, to whom the law gave every opportunity for indulging their whims at the expense of the poor human beings entangled in the law's meshes. In a case just before mine, as I waited in Court, the Judge complained testily about some delay in producing evidence and said did the applicant really want divorce, for 'no one need come to the Court for a divorce unless he desires it'. For two pins I would have got up and told his lordship that the person who comes to the Court for a divorce is mostly the one who does *not* desire it. It was really, under the old system, a greater advantage to be the defendant than the petitioner. He or she could break away and get free, and not have to put on a hypocritical show of virtue and revenge.

In our complicated situation, if it had not been possible for one of us to set the law in motion, we would perforce have had to come to an agreement based on human values and human exchanges of views. Nor is it possible for honourable people to live and abide by dishonourable laws. Thus, in whatever aspect of life such apply, I have the greatest sympathy with those who feel that they must ignore or defy them.

Not long before the divorce case began I had been to speak at Conway Hall, under the auspices of the Rationalist Press Association. After the meeting, I saw that there was someone waiting to speak to me whom the organizer seemed to think he ought to keep back. This was a man of middling height, very shabbily dressed, with dirty plimsoles on his feet. His face was very pale, almost yellow, and his eyes were so closed up as to give him the look of a Chinese. I saw at a glance that this was someone in trouble. Standing there I said: 'What can I do for you?' 'I think,' he said, 'that you knew a friend of mine, Paul Gillard.' I said: 'I have been looking for you. Why on earth did you not come to me before?' Later he told me that, as I said this, I looked as if he had opened the gates of Paradise.

Boyles Court was not far from London, it had plenty of rooms. I took Pat Grace, as he turned out to be, back with me and put him straight to bed. He was born in Plymouth, had been active in the Communist Party since he was about fifteen, and had marched three times from Plymouth with the Hunger Marchers. His father had been killed on the *Warspite* in the battle of Jutland. He once told me how after the battle the telegraph boys had come along their street with news of a death for nearly every house in the street. His mother had re-married, his life had been hard. Paul had once come upon him crying in the gutter and asked what was the matter. From then he had been with Paul constantly, taking part in his work, learning from him almost all that he knew. He had known Paul for ten years. He was convinced, not only that Paul had been killed, but that, had he not left him, he would still be alive. Consequently he had been living from hand to mouth, unable to sleep, in a state of grief and remorse and anger that I was well able to understand. Paul had spoken to him about me. He had thought that this would mean the end of their relationship. Besides, such was the conviction of both of them, that he could not understand how Paul could become involved with a woman who was not of the working class. Seeing the notice of my meeting, he had decided to come and see what I was like.

That we had both known Paul so well and suffered so from the loss of him drew us together. First of all Pat must have some rest and food. . Then, it seemed to me, since I had now become convinced that they had been involved in some kind of espionage that spelt danger, there should not, if I could prevent it, be another 'accidental death'. For the time being, at any rate, Pat should stay here where he could help with typing letters. At the time, I again needed a secretary and could not afford one. Passionate in politics, Pat was also a warm human being. Presently the life with the children began to mean much to him. His face and bearing changed entirely, his eyes turned out to be a lively brown, he was quick-witted and, as I found later, able to take snap decisions and act upon them. He became a kind of right-hand man to me.

Soon after Pat came to live in the school some of the children told me that they had been approached in the surrounding park by a police-man who asked them questions about the new school secretary. I promptly rang up the local police station, and complained to them of such approaches to pupils in my school. A sergeant called upon me and offered as an explanation that there had been some robberies in the neighbourhood, and they were investigating any newcomers. I said that I did not see why this should indicate suspicion of my school secretary, nor did it excuse approaching young children and questioning them without my presence and permission. Next it appeared to me from some telltale signs that my correspondence was being opened and photo-graphed. My political life had always been an open book, so that I knew that whoever was interested was wasting his time, but that did not lessen the annoyance.

Then came the odd incident about the parcel. Pat went to London to buy some things for the school. While there he called on a young man with whom he had shared rooms, who kindly offered to bring Pat's somewhat bulky parcel to some meeting point before he took the train home. But he did not turn up. Next day, a Sunday, the friend rang up to say that he had been arrested. Pat and I at once went to London, to find the young man charged with unlawful possession of the parcel because he could not give an adequate account of its contents and purpose. No amount of explanation from me, the true owner of the parcel, would induce the police to withdraw the charge. This may have been no more than a coincidence, but that it should have been just this young man and this parcel was a bit strange. Next day, with legal help we had obtained, the case was dismissed, but it was no less unpleasant for a young man in a job.

Like many people of very strong political convictions, Pat was, at that time, excitable. There was good reason for this. There was fighting in the streets with Mosley's fascists, there was a battle royal when the Hunger Marchers tried to take a petition to Parliament and, at one point, the bearers of the petition were besieged by the police in Charing Cross station. Fear of a growing repression similar to that in Germany was quite credible. Some of the things which Pat said to me seemed to me exaggerated, but were later proved to be not far off the mark. He often referred to 'that fellow Joyce', a name which I then heard for the first time.

We decided to try and find out some more about Paul's death. We made several visits to Plymouth, when I wore unusual clothes in order not to be too easily identified. Here again odd things happened. At times we were sure we were followed; once a fight started inexplicably around Pat in a snack bar restaurant where we both were. He ducked out and I followed, to find him held by two men who sheered off when I asked them what they thought they were up to. It was, of course, far from easy to find out anything. When we tried to see the doctor who had examined Paul's body, we found that he had gone away to Ireland. Pat discovered that Paul had, that evening, called at the Young Men's Club to find two men who often walked home with him. But they were not there. It did thus seem as if he had felt in need of his bodyguard that night. Pat found a woman who alleged that she had been the first to find the body, but was not called at the inquest. According to her, the body was not wedged in any way that would have prevented movement. One arm was bent behind his back and his soft felt hat was placed in the crook of that arm. We went and measured the bank by the bridge, the drop was only eleven feet. In the end we both believed that Paul had not died by a fall, but had been killed, perhaps knocked out, held in a half-nelson and suffocated, and his body placed in a spot where it would not immediately be found. As to this conclusion we may both have been wrong. But to do justice to our friend I state this. Somewhere, perhaps in a record or dossier, or the memory of some people, if still living, may be the truth of what did happen on the night of 31 October 1933.

What happened further to the school and to me in life and political activity is beyond the scope of this book. There were very few whose lives were not, in some way, affected by the Second World War. Griffin Barry, who awoke to a belated realization of his need of his children and me, came over from time to time and saw the children as they grew, but did not receive a permanent welcome from me. The war caused a prolonged separation, during which he had various jobs in America. Afterwards he was permanently in England and was able to see much of his grown-up children before he died. There was one occasion when he was in Ireland, and I was arranging for Harriet and Roderick to visit him, that I was met at the passport office with the demand that I produce their father's authority before they could leave the country. I said, loud and plain, and somewhat to the discomfort of the official, that these children were illegitimate (which meant that I had the authority) and were in fact going to visit their father.

Pat Grace and I held on to the school through many vicissitudes, which may presently be related, until a War Office requisition of our premises caused its end. When Pat was about to be called up, and my fortunes, economically speaking, were at their lowest ebb, we got married so that we should have the right to keep in touch with one another, and he would be able to make allotments out of his pay for my two younger children. Pat had undermined his health by his many political activities in his adolescence and had never had the physical care of a better-off family. He had become bronchitic and died, far too early, in 1949.

Reading between the lines, it seemed to me that Bertie felt the break with me more than he cared to admit. Like me, he seems to have had a blank period, when he could not work, and his hope of getting back to philosophy and mathematics did not materialize. It appears, too, as if the divorce, or the prevailing cultural climate, diminished for a time his earning capacity. The best chance of earning seemed the offer of a post in the United States. Presently he also had John and Kate with him. It was again I who had to go to the Court and stand surety with the Chancery Judge for their return if required. But I did tell John when I saw him off in the summer of 1939 that, if he did not want to come back and serve in the war, because of pacifism, I would not mind going to jail in his cause.

It must have been painful for Bertie to be pursued in America for his views on marriage and morals, which I think he might then have been glad to forget. This is in no way to deny him sympathy in what he had to endure at the hands of religious persecutors, nor his courage in opposing them. But it is significant that, much later, when considering

K 289

with Woodrow Wyatt some recordings of his views, he refused to include any statement on sex questions, or what he thought of the Americans. This refusal did have a sound reason: he wanted above all to stress that the need to survive the nuclear threat was what mattered most to the human race.

There came a period when Bertie became recognized and began to receive money and honours of all kinds, which were no more than his due for the brilliance and volume of the work that he had done in so many fields. I have never grudged him this personal success and in the later stages of his political activity I supported him all the way. In fact he had by then about reached the point of view that I tried to put to him in 1920. I happened to be one of the original committee in Hampstead that was the start of the Aldermaston marches, in which Canon Collins, Bertie, J. B. Priestley and many other distinguished figures took part. I sat down and was arrested with the supporters of the Committee of 100. But it was not possible for me, once Bertie had become prominent in the C.N.D. and Committee of 100, to put my name forward publicly or seek special notice about my adherence to the cause. But there were times during those great demonstrations when I did feel that my rightful place was beside him on the plinth in Trafalgar Square. For him and me as comrades in this same battle it was then at least 'forty years on'. From the time that Bertie left me I had resolved not to write or gossip about our personal affairs, because his public work was too important to risk any damage to it from adverse criticism. In effect this also inhibited me from writing a book on topics with which we had formerly been jointly concerned. I would of necessity have had to make clear my individual point of view, which could have led to public comment and controversy. For some time after Paul's death I was, in any case, frozen up and unable to communicate except in letters to friends. I did some accounts of the school and otherwise simply worked in it.

Concerning personal and family relations with Bertie in his later years, it would not at present be proper for me to write. I will only say that, except for practical help to some members of his family, he seemed to me to become remote from understanding of their problems and entirely immersed in his role in world politics. The account which he gives in his autobiography of his differences with his eldest son and heir John, is completely wide of the mark.

About his public image as I see it, perhaps something, for what my opinion is worth, may be said. Estimates of what is valuable in human life and purpose have been changing possibly more rapidly than usual during his last years and since his death. Discussion of such topics as the alternative society, ecology, escape from Newtonian cosmology, contribute to the perspective within which we may view and assess his place. A man who has his origin in the period of Victorian Christian concepts, euphoric industrialization, the dominance of the aristocracy and the upper classes, and spans in his life and mind the changes right through to rational disbelief, Freud, Rutherford, Einstein, women's emancipation and socialism, is a figure of gigantic proportions.

To take the simplest point first: in spite of his championship of women's suffrage, Bertie did not really believe in the equality of women with men. I mean here simply that he believed the male intellect to be superior to that of the female. He once told me that he usually found it necessary to talk down to women. Above all, the male intellect was the object of his admiration and reverence. He delighted in it in his colleagues; and whenever he found outstanding minds in his pupils, he befriended them and furthered their interests.

Thus, to begin with, I place him among the eighteenth-century rationalists of the Enlightenment, as he appeared to me when first I met him. He had their sharp wit, their intolerance of superstition, their reliance on reason, of which was born impartial concern for truth, hence the rise of science with power to alter the world and reshape human destiny. There is no gainsaying the constant emphasis on science, the scientific point of view and the ability of science to find out the nature of matter and the human mind and thus solve many problems, which runs through the greater part of Bertie's writings; nor his annoyance at what he thought to be spurious claims of theories to be scientific. But he adhered to the concept of science as the pursuit of knowledge, science pure and undefiled, part of the Absolute; for him science had nothing to do with politics, and the applied science of industry was of little interest to him. The supreme gift of, and to, the human intellect (especially to the eighteenth century) was mathematics, which has come to be regarded as the secret of the universe.

No one can estimate Bertie Russell without considering those ten years when he was working on *Principia*, and when, as he told me, he often thought of committing suicide, so great was the strain and monotony of being, day after day, 'this man, writing this book'. The soaring flight of minds like those of Leibniz, Newton, Einstein, and Bertie into the region of mathematical calculations and symbols resembles the ecstasy of religious mystics, though it may well be a different faculty of the organism which functions.

We are, as yet, a long way from understanding the complexities of human consciousness, or the varied means by which we reach that strange haven outside time. For the past three centuries we of the so-called advanced civilizations have been living in a world dominated by the intellect, in which mathematics is king, a world in which we are removed, stage by stage, further from and outside our organic body. To take but one very small instance: the decimal system, tool of the mathematician, replaces not only our coinage, but, shortly, the old measures of the foot and the yard, which were directly related to the body. So alien to us is this abstract world that we are incapable of understanding it, we are at the mercy of an élite whose purposes and their results we deeply distrust. There is real danger in this intense, supreme cultivation of the intellect both for the individual and society. For the individual it can involve a schizophrenic split in the mind that spells withdrawal from ordinary life and human relations, for society deep divisions of class and values. The arch-schizophrenic—and magician—is the mathematician.

Freud delved into the world of our dreams and subsconcious in an attempt to understand our aberrations. Bertie, though he intellectually 'took in' Freud, was, I think, too well barricaded within the intellect really to comprehend Freud's meaning. But what Bertie did have, the other wing by which he took his flights into the empyrean, was his spiritual legacy from religion, the 'beatific vision' which was the inspiration of the poets and of William Blake, whom he revered. This, not the intellect or reason, was the faculty that moved in Bertie when he stood alone, defying laws, pleading with governments on behalf of oppressed and suffering humanity. Truth first, then Goodness; the third part of the Absolute—Beauty—to some extent, I feel, eluded him. It is not easy for the devotees of the intellect who have lived for years in the rarefied atmosphere of mathematics to come to terms with the sensuous imagination.

Bertie certainly escaped from the Newtonian universe through his understanding of Einstein and of the 'dissolution' of solid matter by the researches of Rutherford and others. He had a new vision of the universe, but it was still one guided by mathematics and science. He had firmly rejected my contention that human beings try to imitate in their political systems the way things happen in nature, that the devotees of the machine age were emulating the Great Clockmaker.* Yet, when it came to explaining Einstein's universe to me he was obliged to seek for concrete, visual terms, saying that 'dynamic forces hurling lumps of matter about have been replaced by a sort of easy-going system in which things take the easiest path through space-time'.

I was at one with him in the rejection of economic determinism and the materialist conception of history; for both of us human consciousness was the factor guiding man's destiny: the discoveries and ideas of today could be the realities of tomorrow. But should human consciousness apply itself only to the discoveries of science, the theories of philosophy and economics, the ideologies of politics?

I sought my escape from the old cosmology and its technological offspring in a return to the whole human being, to our more simple biological needs, our passions, and those obscure promptings of the heart and imagination which the intellect cannot define and may inhibit or obstruct, but which are the inspiration of family relations and achievement in all the arts. In this perhaps I came nearer to much of the thought that is being expressed today. Though Bertie had rejected

* see Theodore Roszak, *Where the Wasteland Ends* (Faber, 1973), p. 218: 'There has never been a culture whose vision of life and society was not deduced from its vision of nature.'

idealistic philosophy, he remained in the domain of the mind, interpreting in philosophical terms what, over the years, men of science held to be the reality of the world about us. Yet, given his spiritual insight, even at that level there must have been inner conflict.

There was some conflict also in this complex man between his passion for individual freedom and his socialistic and egalitarian beliefs. As he grew older the disillusion he felt at the antics of politicians and the follies of their supporters deepened his cynicism at party politics, but increased his determination that mankind must be saved from itself, must somehow be made to see reason. His public image, in his last years, stirred in me very great admiration, but also much distress. After the manner of old men he became increasingly irascible, dictatorial and power-loving. His courage was as superb and undaunted as ever; magnificent was his demand that the whole world must accept that he was right and agree with him. But there was, in this, just a little of that 'cosmic impiety' for which he himself once coined the telling phrase. He was surrounded by people who flattered him, incessantly blowing up the image of him as a world figure. So he was, but it would have been more becoming in him not to think so. Many of these admirers were quite unworthy of him, and did him, both in his lifetime and posthumously, very great harm. It remains true, as history will one day recognize, that Bertie Russell was a great prophetic figure when he spoke for human survival, and that he spoke for the conscience of the nation and the world. But it was the fallible man, neither prophet nor philosopher, the gay companion of his impudent and less pompous years, that I knew and greatly loved.

It is idle to speculate as to what my life might have been had I never met and married Bertrand Russell. I might have remained in the academic world, or succeeded in my break-out to the theatre, in acting or dramatic criticism. What is often asked about such partnerships is to what extent each was influenced by the other. I think that it was my very different judgment about the Soviet Union in 1920 that prevented Bertie from taking a more old-fashioned liberal line, though it did not affect his fundamentally critical view. It was, in fact, I who first suggested that communism should not be regarded as a political policy, but as a religion. The book on Bolshevism would have been different in tone had we not argued about it. *The Prospects of Industrial Civilisation* would never have been written but for my insistence; it is titled as a joint book. It is of interest that recent attacks on the technological world have caused this book to sell and be reviewed more of late. Our joint crusade against religion reflects the Cambridge mood from which we both sprang. It was all part of the cultural revolution of those years, which included women's emancipation, birth control, sex questions. As to what I meant to Bertie as a wife and the mother of his children, as intimate friend and lover, this must be assessed by those who read this book and what may be written elsewhere.

293

My debt to him began when he was our hero for his opposition to the war of 1914. The impetus which took me on that reckless trip to Russia in 1920 came from what he then told me about politics. But for him I would not have visited China, and both of these journeys were what determined my future thinking. But it is important to note that each of us separately derived something specific and very different from our contact with those two civilizations. It was not as part of Bertie that I saw, felt, and estimated, it was as myself with the background of what knowledge and experience I had acquired. Before I met Bertie I was already, from schoolgirl days, a passionate advocate of women's liberation; I carried this, both in theory and practice, into sexual freedom. Had I not been so, Bertie could not have begun his relation with me at all. What I said to him about mothers' rights at our first tea-party held in it the germ of our future differences.

I had already begun my attack on dualism in my articles in the *Cambridge Magazine*. China, whose way of life I did not merely look at, but which flowed into me, as it were, through my very skin, confirmed me in those views, which I have consistently held. To Bertie I owe the years when he encouraged me to develop my thought, but above all one supreme gift: he taught me to have the courage to speak out and stand alone for an original or unpopular idea. Those were glorious years when our views were identical and we campaigned together—all was for the best in the best of possible worlds. Unfortunately, overshadowed and inhibited by his personality and reputation, I could not help sensing the general view that all my ideas were derived from him. Worse still, where I differed, I was so entangled with him that I could no longer clarify my thought. Thus, though indeed I owed him so much, my development reached a point beyond which I did not pursue my early train of thought, which had possibilities that I failed to realize.

It must not be forgotten that I suffered a traumatic shock at the very height of my powers, and that my course had already been changed by having children. And Bertie was an old-fashioned husband. His first need was for a mother of his child, his pride to support them both; he accepted as normal, and was very dependent upon, his wife's management of his household and domestic affairs. Beyond this he did not much explore the inner workings of the female psyche, but would minister to a mind if it bore resemblance to that of the superior male. This male attitude has made of wives, especially wives of intelligent men, no more than an adjunct to their husbands' lives and not an integral part of them. When Bertie spoke of a spiritual bond, he did mean that he wanted two hearts to beat as one; he sought a wife who would not assert her independence, but would be at one with him in everything that he thought and did. Possibly this miraculous union is what we all seek, but all too rarely find.

For me the term spiritual bond has a somewhat different meaning. Any two people in an intense intimate union partake of one another's essence, give and receive thoughts, emotions, impulses, which nothing can ever take away. No one who is capable of, and passes through, such encounters remains the same person. Within me I have absorbed the essence—I can find no better word—of those whom I have loved or who loved me, the men, our children, some friends and colleagues, some of the children in my school. I hope that I may have contributed something to their psyche.

In one of his most subtle poems, 'The Dissolution', John Donne expresses his obligation to carry on within himself the spirit of someone greatly loved and recently dead.

> And we were mutual elements to us
> And made of one another . . .
> This (which I am amazed that I can speak)
> This death, hath with my store
> My use increased.

In like manner my spiritual bond with Bertie—as with others—stayed in being until death and beyond and will be with me all the days of my life.

Trite as it may seem to repeat this, such communication does not take place without love. Love is the quality most lacking in our harsh and regimented world. There is conflict and self-seeking within nations, between nations suspicion and the threat of war. Religious ideals, theories of economic interdependence, slogans of the international solidarity of the workers, seem unavailing in the search for the reconciliation of men with one another. As I grew up I became aware that there was even a sex war. The voice of woman began to be heard. Thus it is to the cause of women that most of my time and energy has been given. We saw women oppressed, a thousand rights and liberties must be fought for. We lived—as our catchphrase said—in a man's world. We disliked the violence, hate, and war within that world over which, however, we had no control. I wanted women not only to have equality and rights, but also for the very essence of what they represent to count in politics and society.

A deeper study of the problem made me realize that a 'man's world' meant not only the existing state of affairs, but the way things had been in history for so long as we can remember. The social and economic structure, politics, diplomacy, law, philosophy, religion, all have been shaped by man and the vision which he had of the universe. Even the theories as to how man developed from the apes concentrate on the instincts of the male and what happened to him in a changing environment. What happened to the female and her instincts is at least as important, perhaps more so, to the survival of the species. I believe that men have feared the greater biological strength of women and resented their need of it. So they have shaped a system based, literally, on their own sexual image, with its flight from the body and delight in the power of pure thought and invention. In so doing they have made a straitjacket for themselves and all those over whom they have dominion. The prestige of masculine work has led women to despise and denigrate their own special contribution. For women must not merely imitate men. Women have more to give than performing any job in society like neutered robots. Those who talk today of rousing the 'consciousness' of women contribute an idea of real importance. It was such a grievous mistake to leave out women. For whence can come love, compassion and understanding if not out of the relations of men and women and of them to their children? Such love, existing in harmony, should not be exclusive, but extend to the whole community, indeed to all our fellow men and women on the planet. The primal source of creation stems from the union of male and female bodies. There should be, in all things, intertwining of male and female minds. Not, as at present, that women may approximate more to what men call learning, but that men may also discover within their *own* psyche those faculties of intuition and imagination so long neglected as to be near atrophy.

In spite of the violence of our age—perhaps because of it—the hearts of men and women today are moved by a greater need for compassion and tolerance. There are new visions of the world, a new understanding of the place of human beings within it, as of the purposes of human thought and action. I have been glad, in my lifetime, to see the slow emergence of world opinion and a world conscience. My one hope is that these will prove swift enough and strong enough to arrest, before it is too late, the drive of our power-drunk tycoons and statesmen and our materialistic populations to their own destruction.

Index